TALENT MANAGEMENT

IN

EMERGING MARKETS

TALENT MANAGEMENT

IN

EMERGING MARKETS

Edited by

Steve Bluen

KNO RES

PUBLISHING

2013

WHAT EXPERTS SAY ABOUT THE BOOK

"Every organization striving for excellence has to ensure that it has the internal talent to do so both now and in the future. With his extensive background in the executive and academic world, Steve Bluen is ideally placed to contribute to the critical issue of talent management. With his diverse team of contributors, they have produced a volume that will help organizations identify, develop and retain the talented people who will help ensure their current and future success."

Julian Barling, PhD FRSC, Borden Chair of Leadership, Queen's Research Chair, Queen's School of Business

"Albert Einstein once said, 'I have no special talent. I am only passionately curious.' This comment must have resonated with Steve Bluen and his associates, who are keenly aware that human resources are like natural resources; often you have to make a great effort to find them – and dig deeply. In reading their contributions, it is clear that they have made an extraordinary effort to ease this 'digging'. Anyone interested in talent management in the context of emerging markets would do well to read this book."

Manfred FR Kets de Vries, Distinguished Clinical Professor of Leadership and Organizational Change, The Raoul de Vitry d'Avaucourt Chaired Professor of Leadership Development, INSEAD

"Considering the facts that we are living in the knowledge era and that talent is not found in a dam anymore but in a fast-flowing river, talent management has to feature right at the top of every business leader's agenda. This book breaks new ground, as it provides well-researched and useful advice on the challenges pertaining to talent management in emerging markets specifically. It certainly broadened my perspective and deepened my insight into this vital subject."

Brand Pretorius, Director of Companies and GIBS Fellow

"What is both exciting and counterintuitive is the fact that the unique challenges that emerging markets face create the need for powerful innovation that is applicable anywhere – and so great companies will increasingly come from these markets. However, the central challenge to achieving this is identifying and developing talent. Steve Bluen's book provides powerful insights into the 'how' and into what is required, and reflects his huge experience and his powerful grasp of this vexing subject."

Adrian Gore, CEO: Discovery Holdings

"This is one of the most important books of the decade. As economic growth shifts to the developing economies and the availability of new talent in developed economies declines, future talent and skills will need to be sourced and nurtured in developing economies. While basic principles of talent management remain, the context is different. A must-read for all those concerned with growing talent, HR and leaders alike."

Terry Meyer, Leadership SA, Strategy & Leadership Consultant

"Given the plethora of talent management texts from Western countries, this unique, emerging-market talent management book is a major contribution to the emerging science and practice of talent management worldwide. Congratulations to the editors and contributors with this pioneering piece of work; you have proved once again that we have great talent thought leaders in emerging markets, and that the rest of the world should take note of the need to

refocus talent management strategies in these key markets – the economic power engines of the future world economy."

Marius Meyer, CEO: SA Board for People Practices (SABPP)

"This book makes a clear contribution to expand the perspectives on talent management as a multidimensional topic."

Prof Marius Ungerer, University of Stellenbosch Business School

"A most informative and useful reference which elevates the critical importance of appropriately managing this multifaceted challenge. Some great insights and practical tips."

Ari Mervis, Managing Director: SABMiller Asia Pacific
and Chief Executive Officer, Carlton & United Breweries

"In our scarce-skills market, managing talent has become an art. Steve Bluen brings his real, lived experience to this much-needed book, guiding line and HR as they navigate the challenges of building talent for multinational expansion into emerging markets."

Anisha Archary, HR Director: Old Mutual Emerging Markets

"An exceptionally important book for companies competing in emerging markets where the calibre and capability of people are critical to the success of the business. Steve Bluen brings a unique and practical perspective to the subject as a result of his experience as an executive in South African Breweries, complemented with sound research. This is essential reading for all executives – not just HR practitioners – operating in these exciting markets."

Mark Cotterrell , Chairman: Mac Consulting

"Talent management is a complex and contentious issue. This book provides valuable insights and proposes a novel, sound and original approach to the matter of attracting, developing and retaining talent. The research and case studies, practical experiences, solutions applied by various companies, and guidelines (lessons learnt) add to the book's practical value."

Prof Melinde Coetzee, UNISA, Department of Industrial & Organisational Psychology

"This important book could not have been written at a more perfect moment. Emerging markets have become one of the hottest topics in human resource management. The book offers an in-depth treatment of the landscape of talent management in emerging markets, as well as practical examples. It is a must-read for any manager or company hoping to do well in attracting and retaining the right talent."

Prof Stella M Nkomo, University of Pretoria

"A comprehensive, brilliantly written blueprint for companies that are serious about managing talent across borders in rapidly changing markets. An excellent showcase for how a well-articulated talent management strategy can deliver business value. This will be a powerful toolkit for talent management across borders for decades to come."

S'ne Mkhize, HR Director: Sasol

"It is not that the book tackles what's been written very little about; it is that the book leaves you completely empowered. When you have read through the book, you know what your next step is going to be. Undoubtedly.

I can only summarise it like that. My frustration with many books is always that they just reiterate what you know already, and package it in nice terms and models. I thought this was going to be the case here too, but I was pleasantly surprised. Great choice of case studies too."

Lele Mehlomakulu, Head of HR, Allan Gray Ltd

First Published in 2013

ISBN: 978-1-86922-194-2

Published by Knowres Publishing (Pty) Ltd

P O Box 3954

Randburg

2125

Republic of South Africa

Tel: (011) 706-6009

Fax: (011) 706 1127

E-mail: orders@knowres.co.za

Website: www.kr.co.za

Printed and bound: Shumani Printers (Pty) Ltd, Parow Industria, Cape Town

Typesetting, layout and design: Cia Joubert, cia@knowres.co.za

Cover design: Natani van Dyk, natanivd@gmail.com

Editing and proofreading: John Henderson, johnhend@vodamail.co.za

Project management: Cia Joubert, cia@knowres.co.za

Index created with: TExtract, www.Texyz.com

TABLE OF CONTENTS

Acknowledgements iii

Foreword by Prof Nick Binedell iv

About the Editor v

About the Contributors vi

Preface xiii

Chapter 1: Introduction to Talent Management in Emerging Markets
by Steve Bluen 1

Part 1: Key Components of Talent Management in Emerging Markets 13

Chapter 2: The New World of Dynamic Markets
by Lyal White 14

Chapter 3: Talent Management Challenges in Emerging Markets
by Steve Bluen 29

Chapter 4: Inclusive Leadership: the Missing Link in Attracting, Retaining and
Motivating Talent in Emerging Markets
by Steve Bluen 77

Chapter 5: In-Market Action Learning
by Glynnis Rengger 99

Chapter 6: Performance Management and Rewarding Talent in Emerging
Markets
by Mark Bussin 115

Chapter 7: Managing Local Talent in Emerging Markets – from a Global Company
Perspective
by Richard Forbes 163

Chapter 8: People Professionals Fit for Emerging Countries
by Theo H Veldsman 179

Part 2: Managing Talent in Emerging Markets: Case Studies **203**

Chapter 9: The Role of Talent Management in SABMiller's Globalisation
by Steve Bluen, Tony van Kralingen & Lara Hirschowitz 204

Chapter 10: Global Talent Management Case Study: Talent Management in
Anglogold Ashanti
by Italia Boninelli 231

Chapter 11: Case Study: Pick n Pay – the Upside of Exporting Value
by Tamra Veley 259

Chapter 12: Unilever Brazil: a Story of Organisational and Personal Renewal
by Rob Mallick & Marcelo Williams... 273

Chapter 13: Standard Bank – Leading the Way in Africa
by Jennifer Morris & Shirley Zinn.. 299

Chapter 14: Transitioning from a State-owned Factory to a World-class Operation:
British American Tobacco Prilucky Factory (Ukraine)
by Bernd Meyer... 311

Chapter 15: From Fossil to First-in-Class: Transforming Corporate Culture in
British American Tobacco Heidelberg Factory
by Bernd Meyer... 317

Part 3: Emerging-market Talent Management Learnings **329**

Chapter 16: Lessons Learnt from Managing Talent in Emerging Markets
by Steve Bluen... 330

Index... **355**

ACKNOWLEDGEMENTS

This book would not have been possible without the extensive contributions of many dedicated people. My thanks go to the various companies I've worked for, or consulted to, that gave me the exposure to managing talent in emerging markets which has provided the practical base for this book. A huge thank you to all the authors who gave so generously of their time and expertise to share their knowledge and experiences of managing talent in emerging markets. Their colourfulness and creativity have made this book what it is. Special thanks to Linda Human, who has been a great sounding board and support for more years than I can remember. I am grateful to Nick Binedell for his passion for dynamic markets and for challenging me to write the book. To my GIBS (Gordon Institute of Business Science) colleagues, thank you for your support throughout, especially to Lyal White for your insights about dynamic markets and Magdel Naude and Celeste Coughlan of the Information Centre for your invaluable research support. A great thank you to my friend, Karen Grant, who meticulously proofread and edited my chapters and transformed them into readable English. This book would have been a lot longer if it were not for Karen's wise and humorous counsel and red pen! Thanks also to John Henderson, the editor and proofreader, who accommodated the project on short notice and did such a professional job, and to Natani van Dyk for the cover design. I am also grateful to the two academic reviewers for their constructive feedback. Wilhelm Crous, your big-picture vision and empowering style greatly helped shape and shepherd the book. Thanks to you and Cia Joubert, and your team at Knowledge Resources, for coordinating the production and marketing of this book in such an accommodating and professional manner. Finally, this book would have been finished a lot sooner (and, I dare say, would be of a lot poorer quality) if it were not for the feisty debate with, and critical feedback so generously given by, my wife, Vanessa, and my daughter, Kelly-Jo. Thank you for the laughter, your smartness and for saying it like it is.

Steve Bluen
Johannesburg, November 2012

FOREWORD

Globalisation has been driven primarily by energetic businesses seeking to expand their operations beyond their country of origin. The process has been facilitated by a change in the financial and regulatory environments, as well as changes in technology and integrated supply chains. This combination has made deep integration and connectedness of the global economy possible.

Much of this process has been led by multinational corporations from mature and developed economies. However, in the last two decades, a number of companies from the so-called emerging markets have developed their businesses beyond their country of origin. The new major players in the global arena come from countries such as China, India and Brazil, as well as a number of other key emerging economies, including South Korea, Turkey and South Africa, reflecting a changing of the guard economically with growing emerging markets coming to the fore.

As the global economy and the players in it continue to reinvent themselves, the issue of talent management, and how multinational corporations manage that talent to remain competitive in a fast-changing global economy, becomes increasingly important.

This well-researched and theoretically sound overview of talent management in emerging markets gives the perspective of a number of academics and practitioners and will be a useful reference for all human resources and other executives considering the issue of talent management as they continue to drive their businesses forward in a rebalanced global economy.

For multinationals that have come from developed economies, the need to integrate talent from many other environments is firmly established on their global agenda. On the other hand, companies that are increasingly expanding their operations from an emerging-economy base face challenges of understanding different environments, dealing with different cultures and processes, forming appropriate multinational governance structures, and, most importantly, ensuring that they are able to enhance the diversity of talent from many different countries and markets.

Given the Gordon Institute of Business Science's role within South Africa and Africa, we have begun to emphasise the role of general management in dynamic markets in our research and teaching, and it is our intention to contribute to best practice in this area. I commend the authors for their efforts in compiling this important overview, which will help to extend our understanding of global talent management, in particular the challenges facing multinational corporations in emerging markets. This will undoubtedly add to the ability of all of us to manage talent in emerging markets more effectively.

Prof NA Binedell, Dean of the Gordon Institute of Business Science (GIBS)
Johannesburg, November 2012

ABOUT THE EDITOR

STEVE BLUEN   bluens@gibs.co.za

Steve obtained his PhD in Industrial Psychology from the University of the Witwatersrand (Wits). He joined the faculty there in 1982 and, in 1989, was appointed Professor of Industrial Psychology. In 1991, he became Head of the Department of Psychology at Wits. He spent a year at Queen's University, Canada, teaching, researching and consulting in various areas of organisational psychology. In 1993, Steve joined South African Breweries (SAB) as the Consulting Psychologist and subsequently occupied several executive positions within the company. He was appointed HR Director of the Africa and Asia division in 2000 and, in 2002, became HR Director at SAB Ltd, a position he held for over eight years. Throughout his time at SAB, Steve was involved in global talent management as the company moved from a local business to an international corporation. Returning to academia, Steve became a Professor of Human Resources at the Gordon Institute of Business Science (GIBS) at the University of Pretoria in 2011. He also runs a consultancy, which has worked with several multinational corporations on global talent management. Steve is married to Vanessa, who runs the Consultant Powerhouse, a learning and development company. They have a daughter, Kelly-Jo, who is currently completing a master's degree in International Relations at the London School of Economics.

ABOUT THE CONTRIBUTORS

ITALIA BONINELLI   italia.boninelli@gmail.com

Italia Boninelli is Executive Vice President People and Organization Development at AngloGold Ashanti. Prior to that, she held executive positions in the Human Resources functions of Gold Fields (mining) and Netcare (healthcare) and was both HR Director and Marketing Director at Standard Bank (financial services). She is a registered industrial psychologist with a masters in Psychology from Wits University and a postgraduate diploma in labour relations from UNISA. She is a founder member of the National Human Resources Research Initiative of the South African Board for Personnel Practice. She has lectured at various business schools and for national bodies such as the Institute for Personnel Management. She is passionate in her support for women's leadership development programmes and the development of strategic business skills in HR practitioners. In 2008, she received the HR Director of the Year award from the Institute for People Management of South Africa. In 2009, she received South Africa's Most Influential Woman in Business and Government award for the Mining Sector, sponsored by *CEO* magazine together with the University of the Witwatersrand's Business School. She is the author of numerous publications, including three books. Her third book *Human Capital Trends* was published in November 2010.

MARK BUSSIN   drbussin@mweb.co.za; www.drbussin.com

Mark holds a Doctorate in Commerce and is the Chairperson of 21st Century Pay Solutions Group, a specialist reward consultancy employing nearly 50 deep technical specialists. He has remuneration experience across all industry sectors and is viewed as a thought leader in the remuneration arena. He has appeared on television and radio, and in the press for expert views on remuneration. He serves on and advises numerous boards and remuneration committees and has consulted in many countries. He is an Associate Professor at the University of Johannesburg, has been a guest lecturer at various academic institutions and supervises masters' dissertations and doctoral theses. He is a Commissioner in the Presidency as a member of the Independent Commission for the Remuneration of Public Office Bearers.

Mark is the current President of SARA (South African Reward Association) and is a Global Reward Practitioner (GRP) tutor. Mark is the author of a book entitled *The Remuneration Handbook for Africa*, published by Knowledge Resources in 2011.

RICHARD FORBES   www.epapartners.org

Richard is a founding member of EPA Partners, a Performance Improvement and Human Resources consultancy. His last corporate role was that of SVP Human Resources for the Latin American division of SABMiller; a role spanning 7 countries with gross revenues of 7.5 billion USD and circa 23 000 FTE employees. He worked for SABM for 24 years in South Africa, Europe and Latin America. Richard's consulting talents are in the areas of organisational performance improvement and transformation through leadership development and that of human resource strategy. He is also an Executive Coach employing the CTI methodology. Additionally, he is a partner in SkillCentric, a business dedicated to facilitating learning through intuitive online technologies. Richard is a Fellow of the CIPD, UK, and holds postgraduate human resources degrees from the Universities of Natal and Cape Town in South Africa and gained his MBA degree from the University of Wales.

LARA HIRSCHOWITZ   lara.hirschowitz@sabmiller.com

Lara is currently employed by the Corporate Office of SABMiller, based in London, where she heads up the Global Talent Management team. She joined SABMiller plc in 1996. She spent 7 years in the SAB Ltd South Africa business in a variety of HR and Talent roles. At the time of the Miller acquisition, she moved to Milwaukee USA as the Director of Human Capital to support the integration of Miller Brewing Company. In 2005, she was appointed as Group Head of Talent Management in the SABMiller HQ, a new function which Lara has developed. She has been based in the UK since 2005, supporting global initiatives in SABMiller, including the Bavaria acquisition in Latin America, the MillerCoors merger, the global enterprise solution/ business transformation project, and the Fosters Australia integration. She works across their global business in over 60 countries spanning Europe, Latin America, North America, South Africa, Asia and the African continent. Lara is a registered industrial psychologist. She graduated cum laude with an honours and master's degree in Industrial Psychology from the University of the Witwatersrand.

ROB MALLICK   robmallick@mac.com

Rob Mallick is the Principal of Mohan Veena Consulting. At any one time, he works with a handful of CEOs and the leadership teams of prestigious organisations, helping them with their critical organisation development needs. Rob's current clients include: Unilever North America, Bombardier Aerospace and BCX, South Africa's largest listed IT company. Rob combines the analytics and business sense of the McKinsey consultant he once was, the judgement and tools of an experienced OD practitioner, and the sensibility and language of a poet and storyteller. He is able to attend intelligently and sensitively to the 'softer', invisible aspects of organisations where much of the real insight lies and integrate these dimensions into the 'hard', visible domains where most conversations in business occur today. Rob has a first class honours degree in Politics and Economics and was a Rhodes Scholar, graduating from Oxford with an MPhil in Economics. He lives in Boston MA with his wife Camilla Boyce and their children, Lily, Nelson, and Ava. In addition to his family and his work, Rob loves cooking, exercise, reading and the Manchester United soccer team.

BERND MEYER   bernd_meyer@bat.com

Bernd joined British American Tobacco (BAT) 19 years ago as a Production Engineer in the Bayreuth factory before moving into Global Manufacturing. He has held various roles, including Operations Director of the Ukraine from 2004, where he was also a member of the Management Board. In 2007, Bernd joined BAT South Africa as Demand Chain General Manager for the Southern Africa Area. He was also a member of the Southern Africa Area Leadership Team and the Regional Operations Leadership team. In 2011, he was appointed as Global Head of Plan, Logistics and Service and is now based in London. Bernd has a master's degree in Mechanical Engineering from the Technical University in Munich, Germany.

JENNIFER MORRIS   jennifer.morris@standardbank.co.za

Jennifer has extensive experience in organisational design, talent, leadership development, and staffing strategies. She joined the Standard Bank Group in January 2010 as Global Head of Talent, responsible for strategic resourcing, talent management, leadership development and learning. Previously, Jennifer worked with Deloitte Consulting in South Africa and IBM Business Consulting Service in the UK, with responsibility for leading the people change components of large business transformation change programmes, organisational restructuring, and designing and implementing leadership development programmes for senior executives across different industries. Jennifer then moved into Barclays where she worked both in Organisational Effectiveness in the centre and held Head of Organisational Capability for Barclaycard responsible for the culture change agenda, leadership, learning and talent across its business units. In line with her desire to work more in Africa, she joined De Beers as Group Head of Talent, responsible for shaping the talent and performance management strategy, frameworks and development processes across the Family of Companies, together with providing support for the organisation's change journey. Jennifer has a particular interest in emerging markets and providing support for organisations' strategic growth and change initiatives and the challenges and opportunities that provides for leaders.

GLYNNIS RENGGER
glynnis@immersionlab.com

Glynnis Rengger is founder and CEO of The Immersion Lab, a company dedicated to creating high-impact, In-Market Action Learning experiences for high-potential talent in leading organisations. Glynnis has been a leading force behind the refinement of In-Market Action Learning (IMAL) as a key enabler to revitalise and energise corporate thinking. Glynnis's expertise lies in designing and delivering custom-crafted, In-Market programmes running the full gamut of interactive dialogues with thought leaders and senior leaders in successful companies to ethnographic interactions with customers, partners and other stakeholders. The Immersion Lab has set up and run over 180 In-Market programmes in 35 countries for a diverse set of the world's top organisations and brands in Financial Services, Retail, Life Sciences, Beverages, Telecommunications and Government. Born and educated in Johannesburg, Glynnis has lived and worked on three continents. She has a BA (Hons.) and a Masters in Business. She emigrated to Canada in 1989 and is now based in Toronto, Canada.

TONY VAN KRALINGEN
tony.vankralingen@sabmiller.com

Tony van Kralingen was appointed Director: Supply Chain & Human Resources for the SABMiller Group in October 2008. He joined South African Breweries Limited (SAB Ltd) in 1982 and has held a number of senior positions in the Group. These include Operations Director and Marketing Director, SAB Ltd, Chairman & Chief Executive Officer, Plzenský Prazdroj a.s., and, most recently, Chairman and Managing Director: SAB Ltd. In his current role, he is accountable for Group Procurement, Technical and R&D, and Human Resources. He was awarded keys to the city of Plzen, Czech Republic, in 2003 and received the Inaugural *Sunday Times* Chairman Award for Marketing in 2006. Tony is married to Sharon and they have two sons, James and Andrew, both studying at university.

THEO H VELDSMAN
theov@uj.ac.za

Theo has been Professor and Head of the Department of Industrial Psychology and People Management, University of Johannesburg, since 2008. He holds a Doctorate in Industrial and Organisational Psychology, and is a registered psychologist (Industrial and Research Psychology), as well as a registered personnel practitioner. Theo has more than 30 years' extensive research and development, as well as consulting, experience in the fields of strategy formulation and implementation, strategic organisational change, organisational (re)design, team building, leadership/ management development, strategic people/talent management, learning, and development. He has consulted/consults with many leading South African and global companies in the above areas in the roles of Advisor, Expert, and Coach/Mentor.

He is the author of about 180 reports and articles covering the abovementioned areas. He is the author of a book titled *Into the People Effectiveness Arena – Navigating between Chaos and Order* (2002), dealing with pressing people issues. He has also contributed five book chapters on organisational culture, organisational change interventions, strategic talent management (two chapters), and people competence modelling.

TAMRA VELEY (CAPSTICK-DALE)   tamra@corporateimage.co.za

Tamra Veley is the founder and owner of the public affairs and reputation management company Corporate Image, which was founded in 1987. Tamra holds a BA in Communications and Sociology and a postgraduate Masters in Strategy and Innovation from the University of Oxford. The focus of her work is on reputation management, public affairs, crisis management, issues management, and financial PR. She was one of the pioneers of reputation management audits in South African companies, and commissions, manages and oversees a wide range of global market research projects for her clients. She is client service director to a number of South Africa's largest companies as well as three global corporations, which, together, have a combined market capitalisation of over R500 billion. Awards won by her and Corporate Image include the International Award for the Best Campaign in the World in 2004 and the International Award for the Best Research-based PR Campaign in the World, also in 2004. In 2011, an Ipsos-Markinor study conducted amongst editors, news editors, and business journalists rated Corporate Image as the top consultancy in South Africa, and rated Tamra as the most respected professional across a wide range of criteria including integrity, professionalism, and knowledge of industries and clients. She travels widely and sits on the boards of the Cape Town Heritage Trust and the Cape Town Central City Improvement District, among others. Her hobbies include fresh-water fishing, boating, reading military history, horse riding, and travelling. Tamra lives in Cape Town with her one-year-old son, James.

LYAL WHITE   whitel@gibs.co.za

Dr Lyal White is the founding Director of the Centre for Dynamic Markets (CDM) and a Senior Lecturer at the Gordon Institute for Business Science (GIBS), University of Pretoria. As Director for the CDM, he drives research and learning in dynamic markets at GIBS. He also leads monthly executive network meetings to discuss issues of interest and importance in Africa, Asia, Latin America and the Middle East. Lyal researches and speaks on strategic political economy issues in Africa, Asia and Latin America relevant to business and policy makers. He has lived and worked in South Africa, Rwanda, Argentina, Colombia, Morocco and the US, and is associated with a number of institutions across the globe. He has also taught at the University of Cape Town in South Africa, Universidad de Los Andes in Colombia and Al Akhawayn University in Morocco, and was a Visiting Scholar at the Center for Latin American

Studies at UC Berkeley. Lyal is widely published in news media and academic journals. His principal area of interest is in understanding the exciting but complex environment of business in Dynamic Markets, while building linkages between governments and business, harnessing economic potential, and developing firms and individuals for success in new global markets.

MARCELO WILLIAMS   marcelo.williams@unilever.com

Marcelo Williams is HR VP Unilever Latin America and Brazil. He developed his career in Philips and Unilever in Argentina, the UK and Brazil. With 27 years of experience in the HR Function, Marcelo has experienced many different projects in Cultural Transformation. Marcelo combines skills and experience in the HR profession with knowledge in business. He draws on emotional intelligence that allows him to dive into the deepest and most complex organisational transformations in an easy and graceful way. In addition to being accredited by the External Coach Intensive in Columbia University, Marcelo has been recognised with multiple awards:

- Best HR Professional FMCG – *Você RH Magazine* (2011).

- Top 5 of Mind Estadão de Gestão de Pessoas – *Estado de SP Newspaper* (2011).

- HR Professional of the Year – *Magazine Gestão RH* (2011).

Marcelo has an accounting degree from Universidad de Buenos Aires. He lives in São Paulo with his wife Maria Fernanda. He has two children, Sebastian and Tomas, studying in Buenos Aires, Argentina. In addition to his family and his work, Marcelo loves watching soccer (particularly San Lorenzo) and enjoying barbecues and red Argentinean wines with friends.

SHIRLEY ZINN   shirley.zinn@standardbank.co.za

Professor Shirley Zinn is the Human Resources Director of Standard Bank South Africa and Deputy Global Head of Human Resources for the Standard Bank Group. Her previous positions include Group Executive HR at Nedbank, General Manager for Human Resources at the South African Revenue Service, Executive: Employment Equity at Computer Configurations Holdings, Regional Human Resources Director for Middle East and Africa for Reckitt Benckiser, Training Manager at Southern Life, and Director in the Department of Public Service and Administration's South African Management Development Institute. She is also an Extraordinary Professor in the University of Pretoria's Department of Human Resource Management. She started her career as a secondary-school teacher of English, and then moved to the University of the Western Cape where she lectured in Teacher Education. She serves on the Monash South Africa Board, and is the past Chairperson of the Institute of Bankers South Africa, past President of the Institute for People Management, and sits on the Council of BANKSETA. She also served on the HR Committee of the Board at the South African Institute of Chartered Accountants. She is also a patron to the South African Association for Learning and Educational Differences, Past Honorary Patron of the Corporate Governance Framework, and a patron to the Friends Daycare Centre, for children with disabilities. She holds a BA (University of the Western Cape); Higher Diploma in Education (University of the Western Cape); BEd Honours (UNISA); MEd (University of the Western Cape); EdM (Harvard); and a Doctorate in Education (EdD) (Harvard). She was awarded the Top Woman in Business and Government and Top Executive in Corporate South Africa by Topco Media in 2008. She was also recognised by the Black Business Quarterly and received the Award for Top Woman in Business and Government and Most Visionary Woman in 2008. She also received an award in Mumbai in 2007 for Global HR Leadership.

PREFACE

For the past two decades, I have worked for, and consulted to, a variety of multinational companies (MNCs), focusing predominantly on global talent management. This work has taken me to fascinating places and has given me the opportunity to learn about the challenges, experiences and quirks of people working for MNCs. One thing I have noted is that talent management in a single country comprises the exciting challenges associated with handling the dynamic tension between corporate goals and individual career aspirations. The task becomes that much more complex when attempting to manage talent in an MNC operating in emerging countries with their own contexts and cultures. From my experience, most companies have, to some extent, mastered the art of managing talent within a single country. The difficulty that many MNCs are experiencing, however, is managing talent across multiple countries, especially when they have operations in emerging markets.

The talent challenges facing companies operating in emerging markets are immense: attracting, developing and retaining high-potential, home-grown talent to run local MNC operations, especially in the face of an extremely limited talent pool that gives rise to intense poaching attempts by competitors; making expatriate assignments in emerging-market destinations desirable options for home-country employees; working with a younger generation of employees who prioritise family over work; integrating diverse cultures into competitive businesses; and nurturing talent pipelines so that MNCs can capitalise on good business opportunities and staff up operations in emerging markets when they arise represent a few examples of such challenges. The ability to attract, retain, develop and deploy talent in emerging markets has become a major point of competitive differentiation.

Simply stated, there is not enough skilled talent to meet the ever-growing needs of MNCs. This is not a new phenomenon. Ever since McKinsey coined the phrase 'the war for talent'[1] in the late 1990s, the gap between the supply of, and demand for, skilled talent has been increasing. What is a relatively recent phenomenon, however, is that the burgeoning growth of MNCs in emerging markets, most notably China, India and Brazil and, to a lesser extent, South Africa, South Korea and Turkey, has drastically increased the demand for skills, and the war for talent has become truly global. Challenges associated with talent management in emerging markets take on a whole new meaning. It is not surprising, therefore, that talent management has become the number one CEO priority in recent years.[2] This book examines challenges confronting MNCs operating in emerging markets and provides creative ways of dealing with those challenges.

---

1   See Michaels, Handfield-Jones & Axelrod (2001).

2   PwC (2012).

The book is divided into three parts. In part 1, key characteristics of managing talent in emerging markets are covered. Part 2 provides analytical case studies of seven multinationals operating in emerging markets. Each case highlights particular aspects of talent management and provides practical, first-hand experiences of the encounters faced and how the companies successfully address those challenges. The book concludes with part 3, which elucidates and consolidates the key learnings from parts 1 and 2 and provides guidelines for emerging-market talent management for line managers, HR practitioners, consultants, and scholars alike.

There are several areas of this burgeoning field in which this book provides unique insights. First, while a plethora of material has been written on talent management and, to a lesser extent, on global talent management, very little has been written on the increasingly important topic of talent management as it applies in emerging markets. Doing business in emerging markets gives rise to many inimitable talent challenges. Therefore, highlighting specific emerging-market talent challenges and suggesting ways of overcoming them make this book unique. Secondly, combining conceptual features of emerging-market talent management with real-life case studies provides the topic with a unique blend of theory and practice. Thirdly, throughout the book, talent management examples are drawn from diverse emerging markets across Asia (especially India and China), Africa, Central and Eastern Europe, the Middle East, and South America. These diverse examples underline the fact that, while we speak of 'emerging markets' as a single term, managing talent in each emerging country has exclusive features that need to be approached in a specific (rather than generic, one-size-fits-all) manner. Fourthly, in the final section, talent management learnings covered throughout the book are consolidated in a single chapter, designed to provide the reader with a guide to setting up talent management functions in companies operating in emerging markets. This includes some 70 learnings and a set of key performance indicators with indicative targets to achieve when managing talent effectively in emerging markets. Fifthly, many different authors have contributed chapters to the book. They include practitioners, academics, consultants, line executives, HR directors, global heads of talent, and members of multinational executive committees. They are based in South Africa, the United Kingdom, Canada, Brazil, and the United States of America. As such, they bring diverse thinking and perspectives on talent management in emerging markets.

Steve Bluen
Johannesburg, November 2012

References

Michaels, E, Handfield-Jones, H & Axelrod, B. 2001. *The War for Talent.* Boston: Harvard Business School Press.

PwC. 2012. Delivering Results through Talent: the HR Challenge in a Volatile World. 15th Annual Global CEO Survey. www.pwc.com/talentmanagement

1

INTRODUCTION TO TALENT MANAGEMENT IN EMERGING MARKETS

Steve Bluen

Emerging economies have for some time been recognised as the primary engines for future growth, profits, and talent. Forecasts predict that, by the end of 2012, more than half of the world's imports will have been purchased by emerging markets, while mature markets are likely to have faced uneven recoveries, flat growth, and declining talent pools. In response, many leading companies have created global business and operating models that no longer focus predominantly on their home markets. In doing so, they have had, increasingly, to look to global talent pools for high-value skills rather than solely as sources of cheap labour.[1]

In the latest PwC (2012) survey, involving 1 258 chief executive officers (CEOs) in 60 countries, the joint-highest priorities were listed as talent and customers. Furthermore, given the importance placed on talent management, more CEOs claimed to be modifying their talent strategies rather than, for example, changing their approaches to risk, capital investment, capital structure or corporate reputation.[2] The reason for talent being a priority is that the talent shortage is global; there are no hidden pools of talent that companies can access to solve the problem.

Defining Talent Management in Emerging Markets

Talent management in emerging markets can be defined as proactively identifying suitable local and global talent pools and attracting, retaining, developing and effectively managing a disproportionate[3] number of fit-for-purpose, high-calibre, diverse people who can be deployed in the right emerging-market positions to contribute meaningfully to the multinational corporation's (MNC) performance.

Several aspects of this definition need to be teased out. Firstly, the focus of this book is talent management **in emerging markets**. Various terms have been used to describe such economies, including 'emerging markets', 'dynamic markets',

---

1   Deloitte (2012:9).

2   PwC (2012).

3   If a multinational is successful in its talent management, then it will attract and retain a greater proportion of the desired high-potential talent than is typically available in the market. Therefore, MNCs should strive to attract and retain a disproportionate number of high-potential talent.

'developing markets' and 'BRICS'.[4] Regardless of the term adopted, for this book, the critical feature is that the emphasis is on investigating talent management in those markets where the following conditions exist: (a) rapid economic growth and foreign direct investment have absorbed most of the country's skilled and managerial talent base, resulting in a shortage of local talent; (b) local education systems have not produced sufficiently qualified graduates to fill demanding positions required by MNCs, further exacerbating the skills shortage; (c) executives from home (developed) countries are reluctant to undertake assignments in emerging markets because of factors such as a lack of infrastructural support and perceptions of 'strange' cultures, foreign languages, customs and practices, and hostile environments. These dynamics are the source of the talent challenges facing MNCs operating in emerging markets **in addition to** the myriad challenges associated with global talent management. This book is aimed at identifying these challenges and suggesting possible solutions to managing talent in emerging markets.

Secondly, attracting a disproportionate number of talented people contains a competitive element. Ever since the McKinsey researchers identified the systemic gap between supply and demand for talent in the late 1990s and coined the phrase 'war for talent'[5], companies in general, and MNCs in particular, have recognised that talent represents a source of competitive advantage, and that the competition goes beyond market share to include talent share. The war for talent in emerging markets has some specific challenges around the quality and quantity of talent, primarily based on the availability of suitable local talent and the willingness of expatriates to accept emerging-market assignments. Winning the war for talent cannot simply be ordained by the CEO. Instead, it needs to be a strategic objective of the company and, as with any other strategic objective, the necessary time, effort and resources need to be invested in talent management to ensure its success.

A useful tool for attracting and retaining talent in emerging markets is the employment value proposition, which articulates the benefits of working for the organisation versus competitors. To succeed, an employment value proposition should contain three key elements: differentiation, credibility and sustainability.[6] An obvious differentiator emerging-market MNCs can emphasise in their employment value propositions is growth and global career opportunities. If these promises translate into tangible career progressions over time, then credibility and sustainability will also be achieved.[7]

A point worth mentioning is that, instead of attempting to fill **all** positions in the emerging-market organisation with high-flyers, a more focused approach is

---

4   See chapter 2 by Lyal White for a critique of the various terms that abound.

5   See Michaels, Handfield-Jones & Axelrod (2001).

6   See Joyce (2010).

7   See Ready, Hill & Conger (2008).

proposed. Two distinct philosophical talent management options have emerged. One approach focuses on the 'vital many' (the entire workforce) and thereby avoids the risk of alienating the majority of employees by focusing only on high-flyers. The alternative approach assumes that some employees are more valuable than others. Specific positions and people with strategically important competencies,[8] regarded as key to the organisation's competitive advantage, are identified and targeted as the organisation's talent pool(s).[9] Collings, McDonnell and Scullion (2009) borrow the notion of **'the law of the few'** from Malcolm Gladwell's book, *The Tipping Point*, when they argue that MNCs should pinpoint critical strategic positions and identify, develop and retain key people to fill those positions. In so doing, MNCs potentially gain a competitive edge over their competitors. Companies, such as General Electric and Unilever, concentrate their development efforts on a small group (approximately 1% of the workforce) of high-flyers.[10] Huselid, Beatty and Becker (2009) differentiate Type A, B and C players and positions, respectively. The focus of most of their global talent management would be on the **A player–A position** combinations. In emerging markets, a combination of both approaches is appropriate. MNCs need to adopt 'the law of the few' – to identify the **A players** who will be charged with filling strategically important leadership **A positions**. At the same time, MNCs need to focus on the 'vital many' who are employed in the local operations to ensure that the right people are selected, engaged, and developed to perform at the required standards of the global company without creating an alienating 'them and us' culture. Failure to focus on local talent can have dire consequences for the MNC.

Thirdly, to be a **proactive** manager of talent means that MNCs need to move beyond vacancy-led recruitment to recruiting 'ahead of the curve' by attracting people with high potential into global talent pools (irrespective of the existence of vacancies) who can be deployed when the need arises.[11] Attracting a team of talented people available for deployment across the globe as and when required mitigates the risk of uncertainty associated with emerging-market talent management.

Fourthly, employing the right, fit-for-purpose people with the right skills in the right places at the right times underlines the importance of globally integrated, forward-thinking succession planning and ensures that appropriate selection, development, and pipeline management are in place to achieve this. This task is difficult enough when operating in a single country. The challenge is complicated when taking into consideration multiple locations with differing talent pools, different competency requirements, and differing labour turnover and availability rates, to name a few.

---

8   'Competencies' refers to the broad range of relevant skills, knowledge, experience and attributes that a person acquires over time.

9   See: Boudreau & Ramstad (2007); Collings & Mellahi (2009); Schuler, Jackson & Tarique (2011).

10 Collings, McDonnell & Scullion (2009).

11 See Collings & Mellahi (2009).

Talent management is that much more challenging in MNCs than local operations for three reasons: (a) attracting and retaining **internationally competent** managers is a key component of MNC success globally; (b) it is increasingly difficult to attract and retain suitable management talent to run global operations; and (c) because skill sets of international operations are more complex, global talent management is more demanding than domestic talent management, and the costs of failure are far higher in global companies.[12] Also, if MNCs operating in emerging markets are going to be successful at managing talent, they need to ensure that their leadership talent pool, and related development and deployment processes to grow future leaders, is not limited to home-country people but also includes host-country, high-potential talent.

Fifthly, the *raison d'être* of talent management is to enhance company performance. This needs to be demonstrated by establishing clear metrics covering aspects of talent management and linking them to company performance targets and rewards in much the same way that sales, marketing, production or any other function's metrics are linked to company performance targets. Similarly, because talent management is so important, it is imperative to move beyond instinct and gut feel when making talent decisions. Companies that are not using workforce analytics appropriately risk losing their competitive talent edge.[13]

Sixthly, at its core, the focus of any talent management approach is to attract, retain, develop and deploy people. Here, the notion of **effectively managing people** is central to talent management. It is not good enough to ensure that the organisation appoints the right people into the right job; people need to be led in a way that will enhance company performance. Given the diversity of local and expatriated talent, distinctive competencies are required for effective management.[14] This implies that, while the human resource (HR) function is responsible for developing emerging-market talent management tools and processes, accountability lies firmly with line management to manage that talent, especially in emerging markets where managing diversity using an inclusive leadership style is critical.

Overview of the Book

The book is divided into three parts. In part 1, some key characteristics of managing talent in emerging markets are covered. In part 2, diverse challenges experienced by MNCs operating in various emerging countries are presented in seven case studies. Each of the cases highlights particular aspects of talent management and provides practical, first-hand experiences of the challenges faced and how the companies addressed those challenges. The book concludes with part 3, where key learnings, derived from parts 1 and 2, are consolidated and, hopefully, provide guidelines for

12 This point is argued by McDonnell, Lamare, Gunnigle & Lavelle (2010).

13 Deloitte (2011).

14 Farndale, Scullion & Sparrow (2010).

emerging-market talent management for practitioners, line managers and scholars alike.

Part 1: Key Components of Talent Management in Emerging Markets

Chapter 2: The New World of Dynamic Markets

This chapter provides a useful context-setting base upon which talent management in dynamic/emerging markets can be assessed in the rest of the book. In it, Dr Lyal White tackles the topical issue of defining dynamic markets. White argues that existing terms such as developing or emerging markets are dated, limited and do not accurately describe the current global reality. He suggests that the definition of dynamic markets transcends size, demographics and growth trajectories to include measures of governance, leadership, democracy, public policy, development, innovation, diversity and global integration. Defining dynamic markets also goes beyond countries to include companies and leaders. White supports his arguments with empirical evidence of 12 dynamic-market countries across a host of relevant measures. The final part of the chapter describes key features of dynamic-market companies.

Chapter 3: Talent Management Challenges in Emerging Markets

The complexities of managing talent increase as one moves from a single-country operation to a global scenario, and, most markedly, when operating in emerging markets. Steve Bluen suggests that the specific challenges facing MNCs in emerging markets stem from a lack of suitable local and global talent to fill key positions. Differences in all facets of life between home and host countries represent a further set of challenges facing MNCs operating in emerging countries. To address these complexities, he proposes a model of Talent Management in Emerging Markets, linking the broader global business plan to the three main components of the talent strategy (namely the core talent value chain, underpinning processes, and key role players) which, ultimately, impact the MNC's performance. The model also provides a framework in which the remaining chapters of the book have been arranged. Throughout the chapter, Bluen focuses on the challenges experienced by MNCs and how they respond to them.

Chapter 4: Inclusive Leadership: the Missing Link in Attracting, Retaining and Motivating Talent in Emerging Markets

These days, many multinationals provide Inclusive Leadership skills as a component of leadership development. The primary driving force for these interventions is recognition of the need for business leaders and managers to work more effectively with global customers and diverse teams. Inclusive Leadership is the missing link in attracting, retaining and motivating talent in emerging markets. However, what is often not well understood is that Inclusive Leadership is underpinned by an ability to manage a diversity of individual needs, not in terms of what organisations do in relation to underrepresented groups but, rather, in relation to the mind-sets, communication skills and behaviours of those working with diverse customers and leading diverse teams.

In this chapter, Steve Bluen explores the need for leaders and managers to think differently about diversity and its very real benefits, not only to achieve better business results but also to create an inclusive environment in which diverse staff are motivated and engaged. The importance of reconsidering how we think about diversity cannot be overstated; leadership is a key element in the talent process and has a significant impact on the performance, motivation and retention of employees. Bluen argues that an Inclusive Leadership competence, underpinned by a mindfulness of diversity both within, as well as between, particular populations, is critical in the changing world order.

Chapter 5: In-Market Action Learning

Glynnis Rengger outlines the role of In-Market Action Learning as a leadership development approach. In-Market Action Learning places a strong lens on out-of-classroom, real-world learning. From interactive dialogues with thought leaders and senior executives in successful companies to ethnographic-type interactions with customers and partners, In-Market Action Learning is a powerful tool for bringing new ideas and energy into an organisation. This chapter describes how organisations globally as well as in emerging markets have successfully used the methodology.

Chapter 6: Performance Management and Rewarding Talent in Emerging Markets

Dr Mark Bussin discusses two core, interrelated components of the talent value chain, namely performance management and reward and recognition, and outlines the challenges of applying them in emerging markets. Bussin describes how to set up performance management systems in emerging markets and provides practical guidelines to ensure MNCs adopt effective performance management approaches. He discusses the impact of globalisation on remuneration. Bussin outlines the purpose, strategy and elements of reward and remuneration. He also tackles the complex subject of international remuneration, outlining the different types of international employment, components of the international package, approaches to calculate international-assignment remuneration, comparisons between different approaches, and the lessons learnt in international remuneration. Bussin ends by describing latest trends and best practices in global remuneration practices.

Chapter 7: Managing Local Talent in Emerging Markets – from a Global Company Perspective

Richard Forbes discusses the challenges MNCs face when managing local talent in emerging markets, specifically in the areas of attraction and retention, assessment and selection, on-boarding, development and engagement. He also outlines forms of employment that are alternatives to traditional expatriate roles and the vexing issue of replacing expatriates with local talent.

Chapter 8: People Professionals Fit for Emerging Countries

Professor Theo Veldsman argues that People Professionals (ie industrial psychologists, HR practitioners, and organisation development and change practitioners) need specific attributes, competencies and behaviours to manage effectively in emerging countries. At the outset, Veldsman provides an overview of the changing world of work in emerging markets in which People Professionals need to operate. He outlines six critical features that differentiate emerging from developed markets. These cover (a) the nature of the society, (b) infrastructural and systemic imbalances, (c) technological development, (d) the dominance of MNCs, (e) population demographics, and (f) the widening gap between haves and have-nots. With this backdrop, Veldsman presents a framework of the mission-critical competencies required by People Professionals operating in emerging markets.

Part 2: Managing Talent in Emerging Markets: Case Studies

Chapter 9: The Role of Talent Management in SABMiller's Globalisation

SABMiller is the world's second-largest brewer, with more than 200 beer brands and some 70 000 employees in over 75 countries. It is also one of the world's largest bottlers of Coca-Cola products. Its brands include premium international beers such as Pilsner Urquell, Peroni Nastro Azzurro, Miller Genuine Draft and Grolsch, as well as leading local brands such as Aguila, Castle, Hansa Pilsener, Carling Black Label, Miller Lite and Tyskie. The global footprint spans six continents which, in the year ended 31 March 2011, sold 218 million hectolitres of lager, and delivered revenues of US$28 311 million.

Steve Bluen, Tony van Kralingen and Lara Hirschowitz describe the central role that talent management played in SABMiller's globalisation endeavours. They describe contextual factors that supported SAB's global expansion, the company's strong people focus, and the sound people processes that greatly enhanced the establishment of a global footprint across Africa, Europe and the Americas. The authors outline learnings derived from the challenges SABMiller faced in emerging markets. Finally, they argue that, for global companies such as SABMiller, future effectiveness depends on the implementation of a fit-for-purpose global talent management model.

Chapter 10: Global Talent Management Case Study: Talent Management in AngloGold Ashanti

AngloGold Ashanti Limited is a gold-mining company with about 63 000 employees. It has a portfolio of many assets and different ore-body types in key gold-producing regions. The company's 20 operations are located in 10 countries (ie Argentina, Australia, Brazil, Ghana, Guinea, Mali, Namibia, South Africa, Tanzania and the United States of America), and are supported by extensive exploration activities. The operations are run as four distinct regions – Southern Africa, Continental Africa, Australasia and The Americas. AngloGold Ashanti is well positioned for future growth through substantial greenfield and brownfield exploration project pipelines. Its primary listing is on the Johannesburg Stock Exchange. It is also listed on the stock exchanges in New York, London, Paris, Brussels, Australia and Ghana.

Italia Boninelli describes how the company-wide change programme, Project ONE, helped rebuild the company's business processes and enabled AngloGold Ashanti to deal with its many talent challenges. These included current and projected skills shortages, and emerging internal and external talent pools. Boninelli outlines the company's 10 core managerial leadership and engagement practices which shape AngloGold Ashanti's successful approach to talent management across its global footprint.

Chapter 11: Case Study: Pick n Pay – the Upside of Exporting Values

The Pick n Pay Group is one of Africa's largest and most consistently successful retailers of food, general merchandise and clothing. The Group has more than 700 stores, made up of Hypermarkets, Supermarkets and Family Stores (franchise stores). Pick n Pay employs over 42 000 people, and in 2011 generated an annual turnover of R55.3 billion. Pick n Pay remains a family-controlled business. The growth and success of Pick n Pay are attributable to its belief that the customer is sovereign. This principle was put into practice at inception and continues to be the cornerstone of Pick n Pay. The company has expanded into Africa and now has 94 stores outside South Africa.

Tamra Veley describes how its values, culture and guiding principles served as the foundation for Pick n Pay's move into Africa. Those values form the core of Pick n Pay's people-centred culture, which shapes the way the company engages with its people, its customers, and the broader communities in which it operates. Veley describes the talent challenges experienced in its African endeavours and explains how these were addressed.

Chapter 12: Unilever Brazil: a Story of Organisational and Personal Renewal

Unilever Brazil is the Brazilian operation of Unilever Global – a consumer goods business. It is the second-largest company of Unilever worldwide and the number one in emerging countries. It is a €3-billion operation, covering Personal Care – including deodorants and shampoos, Home Care – including powder and liquid detergents, and Ice Cream and Foods – including packet soups and fruit juices. Unilever Brazil employs over 10 000 people, with operations across Brazil.

Rob Mallick and Marcelo Williams demonstrate how a four-year change management project (that included a major corporate restructuring exercise, and focused on gaining greater clarity of strategic direction, enhancing the corporate culture and working closely with the leadership team to unleash their potential) can yield positive talent management consequences. They describe the variety of innovative organisation development techniques that they used to unleash the potential of Unilever Brazil's people and the positive consequences that accrued, not only in terms of business results, but also in the personal growth of their people along the journey.

Chapter 13: Standard Bank – Leading the Way in Africa

Standard Bank Group is the largest African bank by assets and earnings. It operates in 18 countries on the African continent, including South Africa, and 13 countries outside Africa with an emerging-market focus. Standard Bank, which celebrates its 150-year anniversary in 2012, has 52 000 employees who deliver a complete range of services across personal and business banking, corporate and investment banking, and wealth management. Normalised headline earnings for 2011 were R13.6 billion ($1.9 billion) and total assets were over R1 497 billion (approximately $185 billion). Standard Bank's market capitalisation at 31 December 2011 was R157 billion (approximately $19 billion). Standard Bank has a strategic partnership with the Industrial and Commercial Bank of China (ICBC), the world's largest bank, which owns 20.1% of Standard Bank.

Jennifer Morris and Professor Shirley Zinn describe Standard Bank's talent management strategy and how it has supported the bank's drive into Africa. They outline key features of this talent strategy, including leveraging Standard Bank's brand to attract talent; providing the right environment in which talent can thrive; actively growing capability through leadership development and increasing technical depth in key areas; formalising the talent review process to enhance the identification of key talent in the Group; and proactively deploying talent across its African operations, blending the use of expatriates with developing local talent in host countries.

Chapter 14: Transitioning from a State-owned Factory to a World-class Operation: British American Tobacco Prilucky Factory

Operating in 180 countries, British American Tobacco (BAT) is one of the world's most international businesses and the world's second-largest quoted tobacco company. It is a British multinational company headquartered in London. BAT has a listing on the London Stock Exchange and is a constituent of the FTSE 100 Index. Its vision is to lead the tobacco industry through growth, productivity and responsibility by producing high-quality products.

Bernd Meyer describes the implementation of a transformation process undertaken in a country in which linguistic and cultural challenges far outstripped those relating to infrastructure and technology. In 2004, Bernd Meyer was invited to replace the existing administration and production infrastructure of the Prilucky factory, situated in a small town in the Ukraine, with state-of-the-art facilities, whilst continuing existing production until such time as world-class productivity objectives could be achieved. The greater challenges, however, were the social, political and people-management issues emanating from the culture shock of the immediate transfer of 600, mainly local, staff from a communist-regime, state-owned enterprise to the demands of a multinational company. The case highlights how tone at the top, on-boarding the shopfloor, changes in working conditions, challenges associated with attracting and retaining top talent, and empathetic downsizing all contributed to a more productive working environment.

Chapter 15: From Fossil to First-in-Class: Transforming Corporate Culture in British American Tobacco Heidelberg Factory

Bernd Meyer describes the process of transforming a traditional South African workplace into a world-class operation. The stimulus for change was a new business strategy involving the centralisation of manufacturing into a larger, more efficient strategic operation. BAT Heidelberg factory, the largest BAT factory in Southern African at the time, was chosen to become the new strategic hub for this region. The Heidelberg factory now not only supplies the South African market, but also exports to more than 25 countries throughout Africa and the Middle East.

Many of the critical success factors that underpin an effective talent strategy are to be found in this case study. Improving technology and processes was only one component of the business strategy; the human-capital component had to be another. It would have proven impossible with the existing tension and climate in the factory to achieve significant progress on any key performance indicator without first addressing the culture. The success of cultural transformation at the Heidelberg factory can be partially attributed to an effective talent management strategy to increase the levels of engagement, competence and motivation of employees.

Part 3: Emerging-market Talent Management Learnings

Chapter 16: Lessons Learnt from Managing Talent in Emerging Markets

In the final chapter, Steve Bluen synthesises the key learnings, derived from the preceding 15 chapters, and presents them within the Talent Management in Emerging Markets framework.[15] The intent of this final chapter is to provide readers, interested in managing talent in emerging markets, with a condensed set of learnings that should help them in the field.

References

Boudreau, J & Ramstad, P. 2007. *Beyond HR: the New Science of Human Capital.* Boston, MC: Harvard Business School Publishing.

Collings, DG, McDonnell, A & Scullion, H. 2009. Global Talent Management: the Law of the Few. *Poznan University of Economics Review* 9(2):5-18.

Collings, DG & Mellahi, K. 2009. Strategic Talent Management: a Review and Research Agenda. *Human Resource Management Review* 19:304-313.

Deloitte. 2011. Human Capital Trends 2011: Revolution/Evolution. Deloitte.

Deloitte. 2012. Human Capital Trends 2012: Leap Ahead. Deloitte.

Farndale, E, Scullion, H & Sparrow, P. 2010. The Role of the Corporate HR Function in Global Talent Management. *Journal of World Business* 45(2):161-168.

Huselid, M, Beatty, D & Becker, B. 2009. The Differentiated Workforce: Transforming Talent into Strategic Impact. Boston, MA: Harvard Business Press.

Joyce, LW. 2010. Building the Talent Pipeline, in *Strategy-driven Talent Management: a Leadership Imperative,* edited by R Sllzer & BE Dowell. San Francisco: Jossey-Bass.

McDonnell, A, Lamare, R, Gunnigle, P & Lavelle, J. 2010. Developing Tomorrow's Leaders – Evidence of Global Talent Management in Multinational Enterprises. *Journal of World Business* 45(2):150-160.

Michaels, E, Handfield-Jones, H & Axelrod, B. 2001. *The War for Talent.* Boston: Harvard Business School Press.

PwC. 2012. Delivering Results: Growth and Value in a Volatile World. 15th Annual Global CEO Survey 2012. PricewaterhouseCoopers. www.pwc.com/ceosurvey

Ready, DA, Hill, LA & Conger, JA. 2008. Winning the Race for Talent in Emerging Markets. *Harvard Business Review* November:1-10.

Schuler, RS, Jackson, SE & Tarique, I. 2011. Global Talent Management and Global Talent Challenges: Strategic Opportunities for IHRM. *Journal of World Business* 46:506-516.

---

15 See the Talent Management in Emerging Markets framework presented in chapter 3.

Part 1: Key Components of Talent Management in Emerging Markets

Chapter 2: The New World of Dynamic Markets

Chapter 3: Talent Management Challenges in Emerging Markets

Chapter 4: Inclusive Leadership: the Missing Link in Attracting, Retaining and Motivating Talent in Global Markets

Chapter 5: In-Market Action Learning

Chapter 6: Performance Management and Rewarding Talent in Emerging Markets

Chapter 7: Managing Local Talent in Emerging Markets – from a Global Company Perspective

Chapter 8: People Professionals Fit for Emerging Countries

2 THE NEW WORLD OF DYNAMIC MARKETS

Lyal White

There is growing scrutiny around the notion of emerging markets. The world and its leading economies are changing fast. With the rise to prominence of economic powers like China, India and Brazil, while others like Singapore and South Korea have come of age – with per capita incomes outstripping their developed-country counterparts in the West – and as Africa – probably the most exciting 'emerging market' of all – enjoys its best growth decade on record, there is a valid call for a better description for these rapidly growing and progressively changing set of countries.

Lumping fast-growing, less-developed and demographically favourable markets into an amorphous grouping of 'emerging markets' has proven to be narrow, and is increasingly less helpful in market analysis and strategic planning.

'Emerging markets' was a term based purely on economic criteria. It was used to describe fast-growing markets – mostly from Asia – in the late 1970s, and excluded many of the existing growth markets of today. Stronger critics insist it is simply a term "well past its sell-by date".

A more apt description, 'dynamic markets', encompassing a broad range of countries that exhibit exciting economic growth prospects, have undergone significant political, social and cultural change, and show encouraging signs of innovation, better illustrates the factors and actors that make up these economies. These tend to be countries undergoing or pushing for policy and institutional developments to address the general ambiguity and complexities often prevalent in such markets.

Dynamic markets and dynamic-market actors tend to challenge traditional norms or doctrines of business in their markets and beyond.

In the context of business, it is useful to assess these markets from a grounding in general management, basing it on a broad set of principles or factors that make up and influence the general management business environment. This is essentially a measure of economic potential and overall stability. It goes beyond traditional economic criteria to include political, social and cultural issues from institutional effectiveness and governance – crucial in transactions – to levels of inequality and wellbeing, and even degrees of interconnectedness and influence in international relations.

Dynamic markets need ongoing capital for growth and development. They typically have lower levels of savings and therefore compete for foreign investment, which is in short supply under the current constraints of the global economy. It is useful, then, as a measure and categorisation of dynamic markets, to compare competing markets and assess which markets have potential and which are indeed dynamic. This helps distinguish truly dynamic markets from the rest by virtue of their environmental attributes and not simply by growth and size, thus providing a definition useful for comparative market analysis, strategic planning and management practices.

Moving from Emerging Markets and Defining Dynamic Markets

The concept 'emerging markets' is dated and somewhat limited. It does little to describe and explain the essence of fast-growing, rapidly changing and increasingly influential markets that are giving rise to new players and actors that are shaping the global economy. By lumping together everything and anything with a positive growth trajectory or interesting investment prospects, 'emerging markets' fails to truly describe the key attributes and drivers behind the growth and development of this diverse array of countries.

First coined by Antoine van Agtmael in the 1970s, 'emerging markets' was used to distinguish those rapidly growing Asian tigers from the rest of the so-called Third World and developing economies.[1] But most of the original emerging markets like Singapore, South Korea and Taiwan – and even China – have now emerged. China is the second-largest economy in the world (after the United States), and countries like Singapore and South Korea have per capita incomes on a par with the most developed economies in the West. With the prominent role of economies like China and India, it is somewhat understated to refer to them still as emerging.

While these economies may no longer be emerging per se, they certainly are dynamic. The types of companies they are spawning with the characteristics they exude, the high degree of innovation in these markets and their competitive view of the world attest to this.

Investment banks, analysts and even academics have started questioning the notion of emerging markets. While little empirical analysis exists around the concept of emerging markets or the redefining of this amorphous category of countries, those thinkers who scrutinise the popular notion of emerging markets all seem to agree that it is increasingly nondescript and even exclusionary by definition, comprising both established and developing economies while neglecting key virtues of productivity, competitiveness and innovation in the process.[2]

Standard Chartered, for example, has focused on trends like the 'super cycle' in an effort to analyse what these markets are or will be doing, and their contribution to

---

1   Van Agtmael (2007).

2   Even Africa was initially excluded, with regular reference to 'emerging and developing economies' in an effort to include some of the better-performing African economies in the fold of future prospects.

the global economy going forward.[3] Such an approach thus looks at a long-term shift in global growth and production along with the current and foreseeable challenges, instead of focusing on a loose definition of emerging markets.

Goldman Sachs, meanwhile, has long avoided the concept of emerging markets through the coining of BRIC (Brazil, Russia, India and China) and later the Next-11.[4] Jim O'Neill, the economist who dreamed up the acronym, BRIC, and who is now the chairperson of Goldman Sachs Asset Management, based much of his analysis and selection of countries on economic size, growth trajectories and demographics.[5] They have taken this one step further by insisting that "it is time to re-define emerging markets" and have adopted the term 'growth markets' to describe, in their words, "some of the world's most dynamic economies".[6]

Economies that are expected to enjoy rising productivity and growth – and carry greater significance in the global economy – include the four BRIC countries plus Mexico, Korea, Turkey and Indonesia. South Africa, for example, does not feature prominently in Goldman Sachs's outlook.

Finally, Citigroup has come up with arguably one of the more comprehensive reassessments of emerging markets and new drivers of global economic growth. Its analysis of Global Growth Generators – or 3G – encompasses regions, cities, asset classes, activities and products, but does place a particular emphasis on countries themselves.[7] The rationale is based on the need for a different approach to thinking about growth and new markets, and is a conscious and decisive departure from the notion of emerging markets. While Citi claims that "the term 'emerging markets' is used abundantly", it states that "definitions are few and far between". In short, "The expression of 'Emerging Markets' is clearly past its sell-by date." It goes on to say, "Catchy acronyms and labels have spawned unhelpful taxonomies of countries that have become obstacles to clear thinking about future growth and profit opportunities. Developing/Emerging vs developed/advanced/mature, BRIC, the Next-11, the 7% Club… ."[8]

Apart from little advanced thinking and defining of emerging markets over the years, and the absence of clear empirical studies grounded in theory or established literature, a shift toward an alternative description of emerging markets is still sorely needed. This is a space for academics from a cross section of disciplines. The fields of general management, international strategy, economics and political economy, and international relations need to combine their research efforts and thinking to go beyond the loose descriptions and classifications ranging from generic emerging

---

3   Standard Chartered Global Research (2010).

4   Goldman Sachs Global Investment Research (2003).

5   O'Neil (2012).

6   Goldman Sachs Strategy Series (2011).

7   Global Growth Generators (2011).

8   Global Growth Generators (2011).

markets, emerging powers, middle powers and lesser powers to frontier markets, rapidly changing economies and transitional economies.

With this in mind, and couched in the realm of general management and strategy – along with a healthy dose of practical political economy – the notion of dynamic markets seems to be a more useful description of the rich diversity and nature that encompass the actors and factors of the economies in question.

The first point of departure is that these are simply not 'mature markets' and – like other descriptions – they do tend to exhibit high levels of growth. But, with a general management orientation and influenced by various factors in the political economy domain that do shape the business environment, dynamic markets and dynamic-market actors tend to challenge traditional or more established doctrines of business.

The notion of dynamic markets is therefore grounded on the principles of general management or those factors that make up and influence the general management business environment, viewed through a political economy lens. It also has a strong orientation toward the field of institutional economics, which Harvard Business School's Tarun Khanna recently expanded into the study of Institutional Voids and strategic thinking around this core characteristic of economies in Africa, Asia, Latin America and the Middle East.[9]

Compared with other similar terms to describe such categories of countries, the most obvious distinction of 'dynamic markets' is that it is broader than merely comparative size, demographics and growth trajectories. These are important, but fall short of explaining the full story behind such markets. Dynamic markets include measures of governance, leadership and democracy, public policy, human development and institutions, as well as progressive enablers like innovation, cultural diversity and integration in the global economy.

This does cover a broad range of markets, from emerging powers like China and India to second-tier players like Indonesia, Nigeria, Chile, and Turkey, and, finally, 'lesser-knowns' like Ghana, Rwanda, the United Arab Emirates (UAE) and Vietnam.

Another important distinguishing feature behind the understanding of dynamic markets is that it goes beyond evaluating and analysing markets and market criteria, to include companies, entities and leaders emerging from these dynamic markets which exhibit new and innovative business practices and models in their home markets and beyond.

In short, while other terms or acronyms tend to merely categorise these countries, 'dynamic markets' does describe them more comprehensively according to a range of economic, political, institutional and business criteria. These are assessed in a comparative analysis, which – as discussed above – goes beyond economic growth and size to include key environmental attributes like political stability, governance and innovation along with the type of actors or firms emerging from these markets, taking with them the inherent attributes of their home dynamic market.

---

9   Khana & Palepu (2010).

This begs the question: What are some of these dynamic markets and how do they compare with one another?

Measuring and Comparing the Economic Potential of Dynamic Markets

Human nature seems to insist we develop lists and categories of similar countries or like-minded companies. For dynamic markets, there is no fixed set of countries (like BRICS [Brazil, Russia, India, China and South Africa], CIVETS [Columbia, Indonesia, Vietnam, Egypt, Turkey and South Africa] or the Next-11), but there are countries that exude dynamic-market traits and demonstrate key attributes toward harnessing overall competitiveness and economic potential. These include the usual suspects like Brazil, India and China, as well as countries as diverse as Turkey, Vietnam, Chile, Nigeria and South Africa.

We are able to measure these economies and compare them with one another through a composite collection of variables, indices and qualitative anecdotes that combine to form an empirical point of reference with real-world texture. Leading indicators like foreign direct investment (FDI), natural-resource endowments (from oil and gas to metals, minerals and arable land), the workforce and the consumer market are balanced off with a range of social, political, institutional and management measures to provide a picture that is as accurate, realistic and useful as possible.

For example, a country like South Africa – despite its rich array of natural resources – has enjoyed only moderate economic growth over the past 10 years, during one of the largest commodity booms in history, and attracted one-tenth the FDI of Nigeria in 2011. In the areas of socioeconomic development and perceived competitiveness, South Africa is, by and large, below par with comparable dynamic markets, with some lacklustre results.

The United Nations Development Programme's (UNDP) Human Development Index (HDI), which measures the quality of life according to per capita income, education and healthcare, ranked South Africa at 123rd out of 187 countries in 2011 – on a par with far less developed economies like Namibia. More dynamic markets that are still grappling with enormous social challenges like Turkey and Brazil were ranked 92nd and 84th respectively.[10]

South Africa's comparative competitiveness according to the World Economic Forum's (WEF) Global Competitive Index (GCI) of 2011 was a mediocre 50th position out of 142 countries – well below the likes of Poland (in 41st position), Chile (34th) or Singapore (2nd). The country is sorely lacking in basic requirements, including certain macroeconomic and labour efficiencies.[11]

But South Africa does balance the scales with some impressive results measured

---

10 See the UNDP's HDI (www.undp.org).

11 See the WEF's GCI (www.wef.org).

in the GCI. It has a world-class financial market, ranking first in auditing and reporting, and in the regulation of its securities exchange. South Africa's corporate sector is strong, backed by the efficacy of its corporate boards and high-quality business schools, all of which rank among the top in the world. These add to its dynamism.

South Africa's private sector – and especially listed companies – is particularly competitive when compared with other dynamic markets around the world.

South African companies are large relative to the economic size of the country. In fact, it is difficult to think of another country of South Africa's size or level of development that has produced companies of a similar size or of that global reach, which is an important attribute of aspiring dynamic markets seeking to extend their interests and influence in a changing global economy.

This is best illustrated through the market capitalisation of listed companies on South Africa's stock exchange. While economic behemoths like China, Brazil and India have a stock exchange that is roughly 81%, 74% and 93% respectively of their gross domestic product (GDP), the market capitalisation of South Africa's listed companies is over 278% of its GDP. Economies of a similar size, like Argentina, have stock exchanges that are less than 20% of their GDPs, while even Turkey and Indonesia have ratios around 40% and 50% respectively.[12]

This simply means that, while South Africa may be far smaller than the likes of China, Brazil and India in gross economic terms, the collective listing of its companies, and thus the capital it is able to raise, is of a comparable size.

The size of its companies and key economic actors is, in real terms, six or seven times the size of competing dynamic markets like Argentina and Turkey.

These measures above illustrate some of the complexity around dynamic markets and the range of variables that contribute to their dynamic potential. The example of South Africa is useful, as it falls short in certain areas (like HDI or basic areas of competitiveness), but its private-sector actors and the quality of its stock exchange far outstrip those of similar countries. This is a core reason why South Africa is indeed a leading dynamic market.

Related to this, and an important part of the composite measure around the management environment, is South Africa's relatively impressive ranking on the World Bank's Ease of Doing Business survey, where South Africa ranks 35th out of 183 countries. Far more new businesses are registered in countries like Turkey and Indonesia, and these also have a number of better business-related reforms. But South Africa at 35th still ranks higher than both Turkey (71st) and Indonesia (129th) in terms of the ease of doing business. It is also well ahead of any other African country, with Rwanda coming in at 40th position and Morocco, which has a similar level of human development, at an improved 94 in the 2011 ranking.[13]

---

12 These figures were sourced from the World Bank: (http://data.worldbank.org/indicator/NY.GDP. MKTP.KD.ZG).

13 See the World Bank's Ease of Doing Business Report (www.worldbank.org).

Innovation is a key enabler of economic progress and an important point of reference for dynamic markets. Described by the French business school, INSEAD, which compiles the Global Innovation Index annually, as "the essential element of resilience as economies aim to sustain their growth while creating new jobs for their citizens," innovation is growing in scope and relevance as a measure of competitiveness and economic dynamism.[14]

Looking at the performance of certain dynamic markets in the area of innovation: South Africa ranked 59th out of 125 countries in the Global Innovation Index in 2011, lagging behind Chile (38th), Brazil (47th) and Vietnam (51st), but ahead of Turkey (65th) and Kenya (89th). Kenya, an increasingly prominent African dynamic market, is rapidly becoming the recognised poster child of innovation in Africa following new products and processes in a range of sectors such as telecoms, mobile payments and agribusiness.

Kenya is also driving the regional integration agenda in East Africa and positioning itself as a viable gateway between East Africa and Asia (especially India), which ticks another important dynamic-market block of interconnectedness and influence beyond its borders.

Institutional strength and effectiveness, governance, political stability and the regulatory environment are all important facets and measures in the dynamic-market composite, which make up the environment and contribute to the economic potential of these countries.

These indicators represent the intersection of the business management environment and the political economy within which management operates. They indicate levels of efficiency, regulation, political risk and a range of exogenous factors that make up the world of business, especially in these markets.

For example, a comprehensive measure of governance that includes voice and accountability, political stability, government effectiveness, the quality of the regulatory environment and the rule of law provides a very interesting and important perspective of the operating environment in dynamic markets. Those more progressive dynamic markets like Singapore and Chile score well in this area of governance, ranking 17th and 23rd respectively. South Africa (in 51st position) ranks higher than the likes of Argentina (72nd), India (76th) and Colombia (79th). China comes in at 104th position (see table 1).[15]

---

14 See INSEAD's Global Innovation Index and Report (www.globalinnovationindex.org/).

15 These figures were sourced from the World Bank's Worldwide Governance Indicators (www.worldbank.org).

Table 1: Dynamic-market Rankings

Country	GDP, 2010 ($ billions)	GDP Growth (2010)	Workforce 2009 (Total Number in Millions)	Human Development, 2011 (UNDP Ranking)	National Competitiveness, 2011 (WEF GCI)	Market Capitalisation as % of GDP, 2010	Ease of Doing Business (World Bank)	Innovation (INSEAD)	Governance, 2010 (World Bank, Worldwide Governance Indicators)	Interconnectedness, 2011 (DHL's Global Connectedness Index)	Key Companies
1. Singapore	$222	14.5%	2.6	27	3	166.2%	1	3	17	2	Singapore Airlines
2. Chile	$203	5.2%	7.5	44	30	167.9%	39	38	23	41	Concha y Torro Lan
3. China	$5 878	10.4%	786.4	101	27	81%	91	29	104	63	Hauwei Alibaba ICBC
4. India	$1 729	8.8%	459.3	134	51	93.5%	132	62	76	49	Tata Infosys
5. Brazil	$2 087	7.5%	101.2	84	58	74%	126	47	54	68	Vale Petrobras Odebrecht Embraer
6. Vietnam	$103	6.8%	46.9	128	59	19.7%	98	51	97	21	N/A
7. Turkey	$735	9%	24.6	92	61	41.7%	71	65	59	51	Koc

Table 1: Dynamic-market Rankings (continued)

Country	GDP, 2010 ($ billions)	GDP Growth (2010)	Workforce 2009 (Total Number in Millions)	Human Development 2011 (UNDP Ranking)	National Competitiveness, 2011 (WEF GCI)	Market Capitalisation as % of GDP, 2010	Ease of Doing Business (World Bank)	Innovation (INSEAD)	Governance, 2010 (World Bank, Worldwide Governance Indicators)	Interconnectedness, 2011 (DHL's Global Connectedness Index)	Key Companies
8. South Africa	$363	2.8%	18.8	123	54	278.4%	35	59	51	50	SABMiller MTN Anglo American Standard Bank
9. Indonesia	$706	6.1%	118.8	124	44	51%	129	99	91	99	Indo Food
10. Argentina	$368	9.2%	19.49	45	87	17.3%	113	58	72	95	Arcor Los Grobo
11. Nigeria	$193	7.9%	49.6	156	127	26.3%	133	96	142	59	Dangote Cement Zenith Bank Eco Bank
12. Kenya	$31	5.3%	18.6	143	106	46%	109	89	107	N/A	Kenya Airways

Sources: World Bank (www.worldbank.org), UNDP (www.undp.org), WEF (www.wef.org), INSEAD Global Innovation Index (www.globalinnovationindex.org), DHL Global Connectedness Index.

But this measure of governance is particularly useful in distinguishing progressively advancing dynamic markets from others that are merely resource-rich and fast-growing. Countries like Angola and the Democratic Republic of Congo (DRC) are two of the fastest-growing economies in Africa, but they score poorly in areas of governance, political stability, institutional quality and levels of corruption – ranking in this measure of governance at 130th and 154th positions respectively. Ghana ranks at 56th position, exhibiting more dynamic-market attributes than Angola and the DRC as well as many other African counterparts.

Finally, an important feature that distinguishes dynamic markets from other new definitions or acronyms associated with emerging-market terminology is the dynamic-market actors that emerge from them. The companies, individuals and institutions are a core component and shaper of dynamic markets. It is useful to have an idea of who they are and what drives them (or defines them) in an effort to better understand the full complexity of dynamic markets themselves.

Key Management Traits of
Dynamic-market Champions[16]

Dynamic-market companies tend to have a nuanced approach to doing business. This is strongly influenced by culture and an innate set of skills which they take into new markets and draw on when they navigate their way through the unusual challenges they are confronted with. These skills and the alternative approach to doing business help dynamic-market companies not only to overcome institutional voids and adversity in new markets, but also to forge new opportunities by virtue of those voids hampering conventional activities. Such companies fill the voids, creating commercial opportunities for themselves and improving the overall environment in the markets in which they are active. They develop such capabilities from a particular platform created in and by their home markets.

General Management in Dynamic Markets thus comprises a much broader understanding and competency around running a business on a day-to-day basis and with a strategic view of the future. General managers in dynamic markets tend to be broad-based technical experts, with a keen knowledge of the bouquet of business functions together with a cultural awareness and political savvy that allow them to navigate their way through complex but exciting locations. They have an ability to execute effectively in these environments where their business acumen has been attuned for the unexpected and where their role and outcome are well beyond simply the bottom line.

---

16 Much of the information and insights in the section are based on the excellent research conducted by
    Steven Asbury in 2011 on the dynamic-market companies referred to below.

Successful dynamic-market champions from South Africa, Brazil, China, India, Mexico and Turkey all tend to roughly share a common set of traits in their internationalisation strategies and operations. These firms are the new pistons behind the engines of global economic growth. They are employing increasing numbers worldwide. Tata, the diversified conglomerate from India, employs 400 000 people, while Brazilian mining giant, Vale, and telecoms accessory manufacturer, Huawei from China, employ 150 000 and 110 000 people respectively across the globe. These companies are driving productivity and innovation in global markets with fresh approaches to general management and strategic planning.

This starts with a particular style of leadership that is underpinned by long-term stability – perhaps in the form of a family business or through support from the state. The leadership is able to identify opportunities in new markets, see the future and, most importantly, it has the will and energy to pursue them. It is also able to go the distance with continuity and persistence, conscious of strategic, financial and operational imperatives to the business.

These leadership traits are clearly evident from Alibaba, a leading e-commerce group from China, to Vale from Brazil and Tata from India.

Jack Ma, the iconic entrepreneur behind Alibaba, founded the company in 1999 through borrowed funds from friends and family. His obsession with entrepreneurship and the role of small business in 'changing the world' permeates into the values of the company today. He has successfully captured the commitment of local personnel by appealing to a higher ideal with a conscious drive to empower employees and customers, while innovating through various start-ups within the Alibaba group – injecting ongoing energy into the organisation.

Vale, on the other hand, was created as a strategic asset by the Brazilian government in 1942, but underwent radical growth and change following privatisation in 1997 and, more significantly, under the leadership of Roger Agnelli from 2001. Agnelli, an investment banker by training, drove Vale's growth and expansion at an astronomical pace through a series of risky acquisitions and with uncanny vision. This was based on growth in Asia (predominantly China) – for which he sought to develop unique, large ore carriers to overcome the competitive disadvantage of the geographical distance between Brazil and China – and, later, on large-scale projects in unexplored Africa. But Agnelli's visionary ideas – which were more global than Brazilian-focused – led to his ousting from the helm of Vale following political pressures from newly elected Brazilian President Dilma Rouseff in 2011.

Tata, after 140 years, has instilled four generations of ethical business, innovation and philanthropy in its business. It has embraced, or even come to epitomise, what leading academic in strategy from Wharton Business School, Habir Singh, and others call 'The India Way'.[17] This is a set of principles underpinned by the basic premise that the greater good of the nation or simply national development imperatives are just

---

17 Capelli, Singh, Singh & Useem (2010).

as important as the financial bottom line or image of a company. The development and progress of a country are an important prerequisite for the survival and success of a company.

Current chairperson of Tata, Ratan Tata, is the great-grandson of the founder of the company. Tata thrives on social capital – the value created from investing in good community and human relationships – in the same way that it relies on hard assets for sustainable growth. This means basing investments and operating decisions on the needs and interests of all who will be affected: shareholders, employees, customers, and the people of the countries where Tata operates.[18] Under Ratan Tata, and pursuing these values, the Tata group's revenues have grown twelvefold.

Prior to expanding into new markets, dynamic-market champions established a dominant position in their home markets. This is where they honed their skills, built their competencies, identified and focused on what it was they do best, and, ultimately, exported this to other markets. They chose new markets based on what they had to offer and the existing competition – seeking a leading position in those markets. In their expansion, most strived to maintain their corporate culture (and a link to the home-country culture) through a philosophy of 'one company, one system'.

This is most evident in companies like SABMiller, the brewer from South Africa, cement producer CEMEX from Mexico, and diversified conglomerate Koc from Turkey.

Established in 1895, South African Breweries underwent steady expansion over the next 60 years, with operations across South Africa and into Rhodesia and Northern Rhodesia (as they were known at the time). In 1956, in response to new beer taxes and declining volumes, South Africa's three largest brewers, SAB, Ohlssons and United merged their operations under SAB, giving it control of 90% of the market, a position it has defended more or less successfully ever since.

SABMiller prides itself on a standard set of systems and controls which have been honed in its home market of South Africa and, later, Southern Africa more broadly. It has embedded values or ethical guidelines that each entity in the group must sign up to.

Similarly, CEMEX has grown globally competitive through innovative processes and practices developed in its home market of Mexico, where it forged a leading position from humble provincial beginnings in 1906. Like SABMiller, CEMEX has a clear understanding of its business model at strategic, market and operational levels – adding innovation and creativity to the traditionally less colourful practice of cement production.

CEMEX knows where it can add value to a new property, which it acquires at sensible prices, applying its technical skills and operating template to each particular project or scenario, tweaking it for local conditions. It therefore brings its

18 Graham (2010).

management systems to bear to progressively upgrade performance in whichever location it might be active.

The Turkish conglomerate, Koc, also has a long history of market dominance that dates back to the first small grocery store in Ankara in 1917. From there, the company diversified into construction, oil and automotives to become the first incorporated private company in Turkey in 1938. Koc relied on state support for protection in its local market of Turkey, while forging exclusive technology partnerships with leading international players. It also retained control or ownership of its value chain, all of which ensured that it held on to its leading position in the Turkish market and other developing markets it entered.

While ensuring consistency and standards honed in home markets, all leading companies from dynamic markets seem open to learn about and adapt to the specifics of each market and culture. They have a strong affinity for cultural diversity, which is engrained in their strategic thinking and day-to-day operations. Successful companies have a genuine orientation to discover and learn.

In terms of people, management and skills, most of these companies come from dynamic markets where they were fortunate to have a pool of management and technical talent to draw from and which was happy to be deployed abroad. Translating these skills in new and different markets proved challenging, but was imperative. In addition to this, these companies also invested in people and management in the skills-poor environments which they entered. This empowered the locals and signalled a long-term commitment to the country and its people, beyond merely commercial gains, playing an active role in the country's economic development. This built a relationship of trust and confidence with host governments, which is crucial in dynamic markets.

This is evident in most dynamic-market firms expanding abroad, but lessons from SABMiller and Infosys, the leading information technology (IT) services provider from India, are particularly instructive.

SABMiller has been described in some circles as a school of management excellence. Its business hinges on the quality and consistency of management and management systems. SAB has had leading-edge management development programmes and practices in place since the 1970s. This has earned it the reputation as one of the best-managed companies in South Africa. With this has come a deep pool of committed and experienced managers to draw from and deploy around the world.

With over 65 sales offices, and 59 development centres in 33 countries around the world, Infosys employees 130 000 people worldwide. Its talent management and development have helped it earn the ranking as India's most admired company in the popular *Wall Street Journal*. In an effort to win the 'talent war' in India, Infosys invests $5 000 in training cost per new hire, with roughly 25 weeks' training before being assigned to a particular business unit. It also emphasises training and education above immediate pay or earnings, instilling a particular culture or value associated with longer-term goals for the individual and organisation – with a strong mantra of ethical behaviour and practices.

Importantly, besides becoming the employer of choice back home in India, Infosys has focused on hiring and developing local talent in new markets. This has built trust and confidence with governments and their people through the exporting of 'The India Way' into new markets and societies.

Most dynamic-market champions have capital (or access to capital) at their disposal. Resources to expand and to maintain investments abroad, even if the returns on those investments are slow to come, have proven important. This relates back to the market capitalisation of security exchanges. South African companies were well equipped financially to enter new markets post-1994, with sufficient capital support. This is evident in SAB's expansion drive in the mid-1990s, and Vale's International Public Offering (IPO) in 1997, which was soon followed by acquisitions abroad.

Financial constraints and complex markets demand a highly disciplined management structure. Managers in those markets often enjoy a high degree of autonomy, but with greater responsibility and driven toward execution and performance.

Finally, dynamic-market champions are hungry for knowledge and learning. They make a conscious effort to learn from the best practices of others and to constantly evaluate their own track record and performance in an effort to build on their own best practices. They are energetic and willing to try new things in new markets. These are traits they have built off a platform in their home country. Their very existence and the nature of their global activities represent the core of what dynamic markets are all about. Without these companies, dynamic markets would simply not be dynamic.

Concluding Remarks

The world is changing fast and a new breed of countries is driving global economic growth. But these are not simply rapidly expanding juggernauts. They are highly complex political economies, grappling with the prospects of growth and interconnectedness, and mindful of national interests and social development imperatives back home. They are forging progressive structures and institutions, and have increasingly sophisticated actors in the form of companies, agencies, individual leaders and government technocrats to help manage dramatic political, economic and social changes under way, and capitalise on the opportunities emerging by nurturing the restless energy that defines them. These are dynamic markets.

Attempts at redefining the dated concept of emerging markets have tended to neglect some key distinguishing attributes of these new drivers and shapers of the global political economy. The notion of dynamic markets considers a broad array of criteria – beyond linear economic measures – that have come to define these economies. Political, social and cultural factors are not only relevant, but are also key to the operating environment. This includes important enablers like innovation, institutions and governance, which most practitioners would agree form the true essence of dynamic markets and determine the 'terms of business' in those countries.

The old adage that politics and economics are two sides of the same coin should perhaps be updated in this new era of dynamic markets. Politics, in fact, drives economics and shapes our business environment in dynamic markets. It is crucial for business leaders and managers to expand their conventional acumen and have a profound understanding and appreciation of the political and cultural environment in which they operate.

Finally, dynamic markets are defined by their actors. Dynamic-market firms tend to exude similar management traits underpinned by a particular strategic leadership in their growth and international expansion. Many of these are characterised by intergenerational family leadership that informs the organisational values and ambitions of the firm still today. Others have emerged from state control or years of leveraging state support, having built a foundation of capital and skills, which they have now shed as they enter more competitive international markets. This does beg the question around the role of the environment and the various state or public actors in the development of these now globally competitive firms.

But, most of all, it is the nature, approach and ambition of the firms and individuals in dynamic markets that make them truly dynamic!

References

Capelli, P, Singh, H, Singh, J & Useem, M. 2010. *The India Way: How India's Top Business Leaders Are Revolutionizing Management.* Boston, Massachusetts: Harvard Business Press.

Global Growth Generators: Moving beyond 'Emerging Markets' and BRIC. *Citi Global Economics View,* 21 February 2011.

Goldman Sachs Global Investment Research. October 2003. Dreaming with BRICS: the Path to 2050.

Graham, A. 2010. *Strategy + Business.* Booz & Company.

Hawkworth, J & Cookson, G. March 2008. The World in 2050: beyond the BRICS – a Broader Look at Emerging Market Growth Prospects. PricewaterhouseCoopers.

Goldman Sachs Strategy Series. 31 January 2011. It Is Time to Re-define Emerging Markets.

Khana, T & Palepu, K. 2010. *Winning in Emerging Markets: a Road Map for Strategy and Execution.* Boston, Massachusetts: Harvard Business Press.

O'Neil, J. 2012. *The Growth Map: Economic Opportunity in the BRICS and Beyond.* London, England: Portfolio Penguin.

Standard Chartered Global Research. 2010. The Super Cycle.

The World in 2050. HSBC, *Economics Global,* 4 January 2011.

Van Agtmael, A. 2007. *The Emerging Markets Century: How a New Breed of World-class Companies Is Overtaking the World.* New York: Free Press.

3

TALENT MANAGEMENT CHALLENGES IN EMERGING MARKETS

Steve Bluen

Introduction

The projected growth of the BRICS (Brazil, Russia, India, China, and, latterly, South Africa) countries is impressive: Hewlett and Rashid (2011) predict that China will become the world's largest economy by the 2020s, and that India, currently 11th, could leapfrog Japan into 3rd place this year (2012). By 2050, whereas 97% of the 438 million people joining the global workforce will come from developing countries, the workforce in developed countries will have shrunk by 11 million, with emerging economies having grown by 1.7 billion.[1] Multinational companies (MNCs) have been expanding their presence, particularly into emerging markets.

These developments yield important talent implications. For example, in a 3-year period, IBM hired more than 90 000 people in Brazil, China and India.[2] Attracting, retaining, developing and deploying that amount of skilled and managerial talent over such a short period of time create exactly the kinds of challenges facing MNCs operating in emerging markets. Not least of these is the need to develop dynamic, world-class talent management approaches if they are to remain competitive. "While companies are facing significant talent management challenges in several regions of the world … the challenges are most acute … in the emerging markets such as the BRIC economies of Brazil, Russia, India, China and the economies of Central and Eastern Europe."[3]

The focus of this chapter is to describe the challenges inherent in managing talent in emerging markets and the responses MNCs have adopted to address those challenges. Before focusing on emerging markets, some of the dynamics of talent management per se are outlined. The situation becomes increasingly complex when managing talent globally, and the challenge becomes even greater when the MNC's global footprint extends to include emerging markets. To address these challenges, a framework for managing talent in emerging markets is proposed, and issues associated with each element of the model are discussed in turn. Finally, some learnings for managing talent in emerging markets are proposed.

---

1   Accenture (2011).

2   Schuler, Jackson & Tarique (2011).

3   Farndale, Scullion & Sparrow (2010:161).

Increasing Talent Management Complexity: from Local to Global to Emerging Markets

The challenge of managing talent in a single (domestic) business unit is exciting. An indication of the scope of single-country talent management challenges is presented in table 1.

Table 1: Talent Management Challenges Facing an Organisation Operating in a Single Country

Talent Focus Area	Key Questions
Business strategy alignment	What is the five-year business plan, and how does it shape the talent strategy? Do we have a compelling talent management business case? Do we have the right talent mix and bench strength to achieve the business plan?
	Are our desired talent pools aligned to the business strategy?
Succession planning	What are the vacancy and labour turnover rates and the resultant positions needing to be filled?
	Is there suitable talent to fill the vacancies – either from within (internal cover and the multiple knock-on effects that such moves will create) or externally in the market?
	On average, how long do we take to fill each vacancy, especially those that are critical to the business's operations? How can we shorten this time to fill?
	What does the talent mix look like? Do we have enough high-flyers to lead the company in the future?
	Who are the engine room and the negatively plateaued people, respectively? What engagement, advancement and development plans are to be made for each person within these categories?
Attraction and selection	What can we do to ensure that we recruit a disproportionate number of high-calibre talent into the organisation?
	Do we recruit people only to fill vacancies or does the company encourage recruiting people for potential, even if there is no vacant position for them to fill?
	Similarly, do we choose people who have skills required to fill current jobs or do we rather opt for talent with high potential when making selection decisions?
	How do we hone selection and promotion tools and skills to ensure culture fairness and enhance the predictive validity of talent decision making?

Talent Focus Area	Key Questions
Retention and engagement	How do we engage each person individually (rather than adopting a generic engagement plan) so that they are motivated (a) to perform optimally over time, and (b) to remain engaged and committed to the business?
	Who are the restless people – the flight risks (the notoriously difficult task of predicting propensity to leave the business)? Can we accommodate their needs? Who require moves into other jobs? Who are likely to be promoted, and are they ready to take on the additional responsibility? What can be done to speed up this readiness?
Development	Is our career development approach mutually beneficial to employees and the company?
	Does the company have a learning and development plan in place to meet our current and future skills and leadership needs?
	Who needs to be trained, coached or mentored? What is the nature of those learnings and how do we reduce time-to-competence?
	Does everyone have an individual development plan agreed with their manager that is aligned to their competency and performance gaps, management/leadership capability needs and career paths?
	Do we deliberately move high-potential people across functions, regions or geographies as a form of accelerated development?
Managing performance	How do we ensure that the high-calibre people we have attracted, retained and developed perform optimally?
	Are the talent management and performance management approaches dovetailed and mutually supportive?
Reward and recognition	What, how, and at what market level, do we set competitive remuneration levels? What changes are needed to make the benefit structures competitive, yet affordable to the company?
Diversity	How do we maximise transformation to truly embrace diversity?
	How do we ensure that our diversity efforts go beyond headcount targets to transform the culture of the business?
Organisational culture	How do we create a total employment offering and market an employee value proposition that renders the business a true employer of choice – as perceived by existing employees and by aspirant employees in our target market?
	How can we turn this organisation into the most desirable place to work?

Talent Focus Area	Key Questions
Talent information system	How do we run a talent management system that provides all users with real-time, consistent and accurate data upon which to make talent decisions?
Talent review and evaluation	Have we selected the appropriate talent key performance indicators (KPIs) that drive business performance?
	How do we optimise our talent KPIs?
	Does meeting talent KPI targets enhance business performance?
Line management's talent role	How do we enrol the chief executive officer (CEO), the Board and all line managers to fulfil their crucial roles in making talent management effective? How do we make them competent to fulfil these roles effectively?
The human resource (HR) function's role in talent management	How do we substantiate a budget to implement the answers to all these questions and develop an effective talent team to achieve the desired results?
	Does our talent strategy simultaneously meet business needs and conform to best practice?
Talent management's impact on business performance	Ultimately, are we doing all that we can to attract, retain and develop a disproportionate amount of high-calibre talent that will enable the business to achieve its strategic objectives and win in the marketplace?

Given the multiple moving parts, inevitable uncontrollable factors, and unpredictable changes, the dynamism inherent in talent management in a single business unit makes it an extremely exciting and challenging endeavour.

The situation becomes far more complex, though equally strategically important, when managing talent globally. Global talent management is crucially important for three reasons:[4] First, internationally competent business leaders represent a key component of global business success. Secondly, until recently, it has been extremely difficult to attract and retain suitable leaders to run international operations. Thirdly, given the complexities associated with international operations, talent management is more complex in global companies than in domestic firms. Indeed, the consequence of not deploying the right talent in the right places is a leading threat to MNCs. A quarter of the CEOs surveyed in the latest PricewaterhouseCoopers (PwC) CEO Survey[5] said they were unable to capitalise on market opportunities or had to cancel or delay strategic initiatives because of talent constraints, including: talent-related

---

4   According to McDonnell, Lamare, Gunnigle & Lavelle (2010).

5   PwC (2012).

expenses rising more than expected; inability to innovate effectively or pursue market opportunities; cancelling or delaying key strategic initiatives; inability to achieve growth forecasts in overseas markets; and falling production and service-delivery quality standards. Thus, global talent management is a major strategic priority for CEOs. It is not surprising, therefore, that CEOs rated developing talent pipelines (and meeting with customers) as their most important priorities.[6] The reason for talent being so important is that the talent shortage is global and not local. There are no hidden pools of talent that companies can access to solve the problem. The full extent of the strategic importance of global talent management has been articulated by several leading academics in the global talent field.[7] These are summarised in table 2 below.

Table 2: Why Global Talent Management Is an Increasingly Important Strategic Issue for Multinational Corporations[8]

Trend	Implication
The critical importance of global talent management is recognised	The success of MNCs is closely linked to how well they identify, manage and adapt to the many global talent challenges they face. To achieve this, they need to understand the environmental forces shaping talent management.
Competition for talent is now global	Competition for talent has moved from country to regional and global levels: talent resides throughout MNCs' global operations. This requires a global talent management focus if MNCs are to remain competitive. This is becoming increasingly difficult, as MNCs compete in the same, limited talent pools where demand greatly outweighs supply. Consequently, MNCs have to become more attractive and develop compelling employee value propositions to attract and retain talent.
Global talent management is becoming more pervasive	With the rapid growth of both MNCs and the internationalisation of small and medium-sized businesses, global talent management appears increasingly on the strategic agendas of smaller organisations – not just the MNCs.

---

6   15th Annual CEO Survey (PwC 2012).

7   Some of the prominent writers on global talent management include: Collings, McDonnell & Scullion (2009); Collings, Scullion & Morley (2007); Farndale, Scullion & Sparrow (2010); Hewlett & Rashid (2010); McDonnell & Collings (2011); Ready, Hill & Conger (2008); Schuler, Jackson & Tarique (2011); Scullion & Collings (2011); Scullion, Collings & Caligiuri (2010); Tarique & Schuler (2010).

8   Table 2 is adapted from: Schuler, Jackson & Tarique (2011); Scullion & Collings (2011); Scullion, Caligiuri & Collings (2008); Tarique & Schuler (2010).

Trend	Implication
Knowledge-based economies require more highly skilled talent to fulfil more complex roles	The shift from product-based to knowledge-based economies and the dominance of the service sector have shifted the talent challenge to high-value people with higher cognitive abilities, which are typically in short supply. Furthermore, regarding global talent, cross-cultural competencies are required to perform effectively, yet they are relatively scarce.
The critical importance of MNC leaders is recognised	The success of MNCs in increasingly competitive environments depends heavily on the quality of their globally competent leaders.
The shortage of suitable international managers is a key constraint on MNC performance	The talent demand–supply gap is growing. The lack of suitable global managers has become a significant constraint on companies' abilities to implement global strategies. In particular, a shortage of leadership talent has been identified as a major obstacle MNCs face when attempting to operate globally.
Increased cultural and geographical talent mobility	Increased globalisation, lower emigration barriers, and immigration and intercountry disparities in real wage rates have led to greater international talent mobility. This is most apparent amongst professionals and highly skilled workers, giving rise to brain drains in many countries.
Emergence of the truly global elite	Increasingly, people with special talents have no allegiance to country or region and happily cross geographic and cultural boundaries. Owing to their global connections and world-views, they relate better to people with similar skills than to people with the same national or ethnic origins. It requires a different talent management approach to attract and retain them.
Downsizing, due to the global recession, affects trust	Globally mobile talent is increasingly trading security for flexibility, becoming less dependent on a single employer. Lowered trust levels mean that the psychological contract of trading loyalty for job security is being replaced: global employees are increasingly free agents who come and go as they wish and are responsible for their own employability, learning and career development.
Retaining global talent is key	Talent raiding has emerged as an aggressive attempt by some companies to hire employees from competitors. Retention of top-level global talent is a key challenge, particularly when embarking on mergers and acquisitions or joint ventures.

Trend	Implication
Reverse migration has increased	In an attempt to reverse the brain drain, countries are encouraging returnee immigrants, who have very marketable international experience and networks, to come home. This represents a valuable talent pool from which companies can recruit.
However, repatriation is a major cause of labour turnover	Repatriation is a major cause of labour turnover and needs to be addressed, given the valuable experience expatriates possess. Global assignments themselves are used as a means of attracting, retaining and developing talent.
Demographics influence global talent management	Demographic factors that will influence talent availability and recruitment approaches in future include the following: • Declining birth rates and longevity are reshaping age distributions. In certain developed countries, by 2025, the number of people aged 15 to 64 is expected to fall by 7% (Germany), 9% (Italy) and 14% (Japan). Thus the workforce rate is declining in the developed world. At the same time, the populations in emerging markets are increasing and getting younger. • Companies are required to manage two generations (Generation X and Y) of employees with differing needs. • The baby-boomers are ageing and approaching retirement. • With China's one-child policy, gender imbalances (more men than women) are apparent in the Chinese workforce.
Managing diversity is becoming increasingly important	As talent pools globalise, the levels of gender, ethnic, cultural and generational diversity increase, requiring MNCs to manage diversity effectively if they are to succeed.
HR is fulfilling an increasingly important role in MNCs	There is an increased recognition of the role HR fulfils in the success of MNCs. Given the intensification of global competition, HR's role in planning and forecasting talent needs across the firm's multiple locations, ensuring a ready supply of globally competent leaders to run MNCs and facilitating international learning and innovation, is acknowledged.

Leisy and Pyron (2009) highlight the global talent challenges involved when they observe that, to compete globally, MNCs need to adopt certain meta talent management processes, including the following:

- Effectively manage a dynamic and diverse workforce that is dispersed throughout the world,

- Comply with a maze of ever-changing tax, immigration and other laws and regulations,

- Maintain accurate and responsive HR data reporting,

- Address significant business and talent management differences between mature versus emerging markets,

- Deal with rising global labor costs in the face of a diminishing supply of skilled and semiskilled labor in emerging markets,

- Ensure that talent management programs are integrated and consistently applied to allow employees worldwide to be fully utilized, develop their careers and feel a part of one organization,

- Identify, develop and retain future business leaders around the globe,

- Maximize consistency, where appropriate, of worldwide HR policies and employee benefit programs.[9]

The challenges of global talent management are indeed daunting and more complex than those confronting talent managers operating in one (familiar) country. The task at hand becomes even more complicated when managing talent in emerging markets. In addition to the talent challenges discussed thus far, managing talent in emerging markets has unique challenges that need to be addressed. These can be narrowed down to five dynamics:

1. **Sourcing talent in emerging markets: from cheap labour to skilled and managerial talent pools.** Emerging markets have traditionally been viewed as a source of cheap labour. Given the global shortage of skills, emerging markets are being regarded as sources of skilled, professional and managerial talent, which adds to the complexity of the challenge.[10]

2. **Rapid development has absorbed skilled talent in emerging markets.** At the same time, developing countries, such as BRICS (Brazil, Russia, India, China and, to a lesser extent, South Africa), have grown so fast that there are insufficient skilled people to fill all the burgeoning positions opening up, especially in skilled and leadership roles. In fact, emerging-market MNCs are sourcing talent in developed countries. As Ren Jianxin, President of China National Chemical Corporation (ChemChina), observed: "Twenty-five years ago, ChemChina was spun off from China National Bluestar with a staff of just seven. Now we employ 160,000 people. We employ many people from Western countries, including at the management level. ... we work with leading human resource consultancies to recruit more Western professionals."[11]

---

9   Leisy & Pyron (2009:58-59).

10   Deloitte (2012); Manning, Massini & Lewin (2008).

11   PwC (2012:10).

3. **Divergent education levels reduce the number of graduates suited to work in MNCs.** The skills shortage is exacerbated because of the education-technology lag. Also, although tertiary institutions have mushroomed in emerging countries, they do not produce enough of the right calibre of graduates to fill skilled and leadership positions in MNCs.[12]

4. **Problems with employing expatriates in emerging markets.** MNCs have addressed the talent gap by recruiting expatriates to fill senior roles in emerging countries. This, in turn, creates its own challenges. Factors such as political instability, corruption, high crime rates, poor governmental or societal infrastructures, hostile commercial and labour laws, and 'foreign' cultures, customs and practices reduce the attractiveness of emerging-market countries as expatriate destinations.[13] In the 2011 Brookfield GRS Global Relocation Trends Survey, the four countries rated as the most difficult for international assignees were: 1st China, 2nd India, 3rd Russia and 4th Brazil.[14] Furthermore, expatriate cost to company is extremely high – estimated to be between three and four times the person's home salary.[15] Expatriate failure rates are also high (between 10 and 80%), and MNCs are poor at repatriating them post-assignment.[16] Pattie, White and Tansky (2010) report that 27% of repatriates leave their MNC in the first year of returning home, and a further 25% leave the following year. To overcome these problems, MNCs have adopted alternate forms of employment arrangements to meet their talent requirements (eg short-term assignments, commuter assignments, international business travel, and virtual assignments).[17]

5. **Challenges associated with hiring local talent in emerging markets.** MNCs are hiring increasing numbers of high-potential local talent to fill senior positions.[18] Hiring local talent creates its own challenges: to supplement education and competence gaps, MNCs offer extensive training, education and corporate university programmes.[19] Because suitably trained local employees with the MNC-relevant skills are in such short supply, they command excessively high salaries, further increasing the costs of doing business in emerging countries.[20] Also, local professionals and executives working in MNCs are highly marketable

12   Deloitte (2012).

13   Farndale, Scullion & Sparrow (2010).

14   Mercurio (2011).

15   Collings, Scullion & Morley (2007).

16   Sims & Schraeder (2005).

17   Collings et al. (2007).

18   Guthridge, Komm & Lawson (2008).

19   Accenture (2008); Cooke (2011); Ready, Hill & Conger (2008).

20   Farndale et al. (2010).

and therefore easily poached by other MNCs, exacerbating the vicious cycle of salary escalation. A 2010 survey of 2 200 Chinese managers found that, over 18 months, two-thirds had received a compelling job offer and 46% had moved jobs with increases in pay of greater than 30%.[21]

Not only are the talent management challenges different in emerging markets, but fit-for-purpose solutions are also required. Ready, Hill and Conger (2008) identified the following four factors that differentiate successful from the less successful MNCs operating in emerging markets:

1. *Brand*: Employees in emerging countries are beginning to think beyond making a living to making a future. A company with a desirable brand implies personal advancement and the chance of global mobility.

2. *Opportunity*: Besides the regular connotations of opportunity (such as challenging work, development, competitive pay, and challenging assignments), opportunity in the developing world implies accelerated career tracks to senior positions, ensuring that their skills and experience develop in line with the rapid rate of growth in their markets.

3. *Purpose:* Local employees value companies with a game-changing business model – where they can be part of redefining their nation and even the world economy. Given that many have experienced poverty first-hand, they also value MNCs that focus on helping the less fortunate.

4. *Culture*: Four aspects of culture are important to local employees: an authentic brand promise; reward and advancement based on merit – that they were born in the developing world should not limit their global opportunities; receiving individual recognition and being part of a team; and a talent-centric culture.

In this chapter, both the challenges and the solutions associated with managing talent in emerging markets are explored. To help structure the myriad of issues involved, a model of talent management in emerging markets is presented (see table 3), and the challenges and responses associated with each element of the model are discussed. While the components of talent management models are similar across developed and emerging markets, distinctive contextual factors, evident in emerging markets, pose unique challenges for MNCs that require creative responses. These challenges and responses form the content of this chapter.

---

21   PwC (2012).

A Framework for Managing Talent in Emerging Markets

With the exception of three components of the model, namely **localisation**, **expatriates** and **local employees**, the talent management model presented in table 3 could be applied in most settings. However, it is the distinctive contextual factors evident in emerging markets that pose unique challenges for MNCs and that require creative responses.

For a talent management strategy to be effective, it must cater specifically for the talent needs emanating from the broader business strategy. Similarly, the success of the talent strategy is measured by the extent to which the business has the right talent to meet its strategic business plans across its global footprint. The links between the business and talent imperatives are reflected in the model, where the business strategy informs and shapes the talent strategy and the output of the talent strategy impacts business performance. This firmly locates the talent strategy within the broader business context.

The talent strategy is divided into three components, namely the core talent management value chain, underpinning processes, and key role players. The core talent management value chain comprises those sequential elements traditionally associated with the talent management process, namely succession planning, attracting, selecting and on-boarding, engaging and retaining, developing, managing performance, and rewarding and recognising talent. Underpinning the core talent management value chain are several processes, including diversity and localisation, organisational culture, talent reviews and evaluations, and talent information systems. These processes support the talent management value chain.

While the HR function is the custodian of talent management, there are several other key role players in any emerging-market talent management approach, namely business leaders, especially those heading up MNCs in the host developing countries, expatriates and local employees operating in those countries. Set out below are some of the challenges associated with each component of the model and how they can be addressed.

Table 3: Talent Management in Emerging Markets

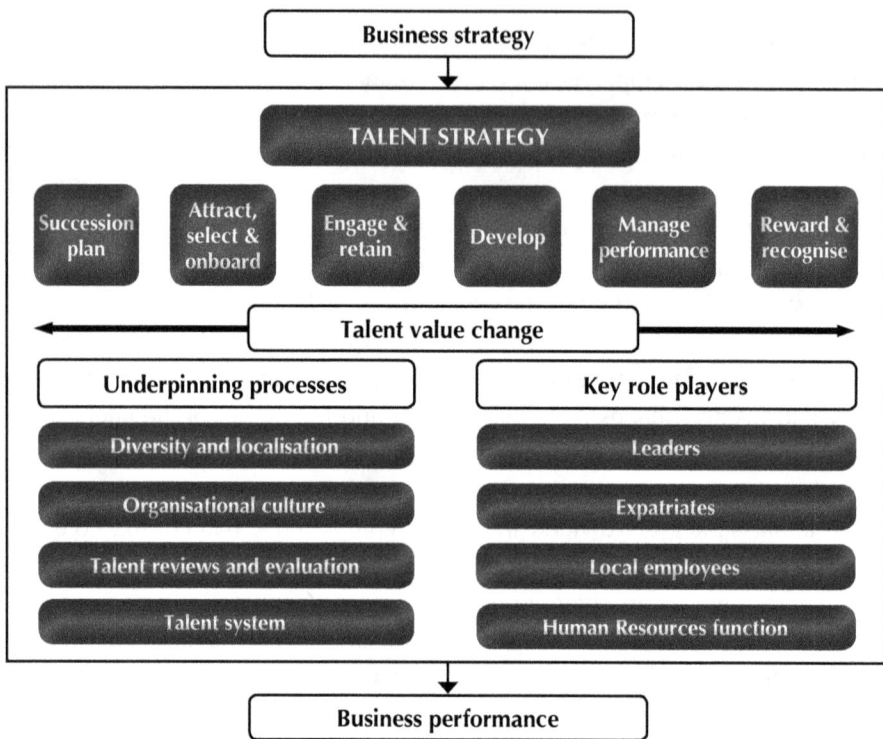

1. Linking the Talent Strategy to the Business Strategy

Challenges. The first, and arguably the most important, rule is that the sole purpose of the talent strategy is to support the business strategy by providing the right quantity and quality of people to implement the business strategies effectively across the global footprint, thereby maximising the MNC's competitive advantage. In their survey of 340 global leaders, Ernst and Young (2010) found that companies whose talent management programmes were aligned with their business strategies delivered a return on investment that was, on average, 20% higher over a 5-year period than companies without such alignment. While talent management should embrace functional excellence and conform to best practice, it has no purpose outside of attracting, retaining and developing people in line with business needs.

> HR Professionals need to know the strategic needs and directions of the firm and the important characteristics of the firm in order to craft a talent strategy, i.e., a strategy that identifies the important global talent challenges and identifies the global talent management initiatives that will effectively manage them.[22]

---

22   Schuler et al. (2011:513-514).

So, the first challenge is to shape the talent strategy in line with business needs and create a compelling business case for talent management. Once the business case has been accepted, the resources necessary to implement a talent strategy can be substantiated and implemented. A clear financial commitment to implementing the talent strategy is important, since the strategy can be costly and time-consuming, especially if it entails recruiting for potential, regardless of available vacancies. Also, during economic downturns, talent-related expenses, such as training, recruiting and, ultimately, retrenchments, are prime cost-cutting targets.[23] Armed with a sound business case, short-term cost-cutting measures might be avoided when the broader, longer-term business implications are considered.

Solutions. Talent pools represent a significant connection point between the business strategy and the talent strategy.[24] Strategically appropriate talent pools are shaped by asking questions such as, "Are our investments aimed at the talent areas that are most critical to the strategic success of the organization?"[25] Once the talent pool has been defined to meet organisational success, the talent strategy to attract, retain, and develop people to fill that talent pool will be aligned with the corporate strategy.

The shortage of suitable and available talent to fill senior positions in emerging markets is well documented.[26] Also, the success of MNCs in competitive environments depends heavily on the quality of their globally competent leaders.[27] Facts such as these represent a strong motivation for a compelling talent business case. Simply stated, without attracting, retaining, developing, deploying and motivating the right number and calibre of people, MNCs will not meet their global aspirations.

South African Breweries (SAB) provides a good example of linking the talent strategy closely to the business plan. In the early 1990s, when SAB started globalising, a component of the business model was to acquire businesses, initially in developing countries, and to send in hand-picked expatriates to run the acquired operation. To do so, the South African operation had to provide talent to fill global positions while continuing to perform optimally, that is, it had to have sufficient bench strength to meet local and international demands. The size of this challenge was impressive: some 200 executives – 40% of the senior management ranks – were expatriated over a 10-year period. To become an effective talent nursery, a strong talent business case was articulated and implemented.[28]

---

23   See Sheehan (2012).

24   Boudreau, Ramstad & Dowling (2002).

25   Boudreau et al. (2002:17).

26   For example: Elegbe (2010); Li & Scullion (2010); McKinsey (2005).

27   Schuler et al. (2011); Scullion & Collings (2011).

28   See chapter 9 outlining the SAB talent case.

2. Emerging-market Talent Strategy: Core Value Chain

Having outlined the importance of linking the talent strategy to the business strategy, the focus turns to the talent strategy itself. In this section, emerging-market talent challenges and solutions pertaining to each of the elements of the talent core value chain are discussed.

(i) Succession Planning

Succession planning in a single business entity is difficult enough, given the number of 'moving parts' involved. The process becomes that much more complex when operating in multiple sites across the world, and, particularly, when some of those operations are located in emerging markets. This succession planning section is divided into internal and external components.

(a) Internal Environment

Challenges. A key planning feature is to achieve the right balance and calibre of people assigned globally across the MNC, especially when faced with a scarcity of talent. There needs to be a match between the strategic importance of the role in question and the candidate being sent to fill the position. This matching needs to be evaluated in relation to all other similar roles and people across the MNC, culminating in the right people being placed in the right jobs across the company and avoiding 'robbing Peter to pay Paul' scenarios. Also, the MNC must include all relevant host-country local employees when making succession plans, rather than focusing solely on home-country talent, which can create an unacceptable, two-tier talent system, deprive local talent of deserving career opportunities, and prevent the MNC from accessing a valuable source of high-potential talent.

To implement a global succession planning system, the MNC needs to calibrate all relevant jobs in terms of size, complexity and strategic importance, and all people within the global talent pool in terms of their experience, capability, potential to take on increasingly complex offshore roles, and emotional and cultural intelligence to operate effectively in emerging markets. This is a huge task if it is to be done accurately. Also, because of the problems associated with employing expatriates, the number of expatriates deployed needs to be kept to a minimum.

Solutions. The traditional approach of succession planning, which assumes stable environments and long-term career plans, is too linear to address the volatile and unpredictable nature of global talent management.[29] Instead, MNCs are increasingly using talent pools, comprising "high-potential and

---

29   McDonnell & Collings (2011).

high-performing incumbents that the organisation can draw on to fill pivotal positions."[30] Central to the talent pool approach is selecting for talent (rather than only recruiting to fill vacancies), and placing people where and when the need arises.[31] This also presupposes people within the talent pool are sufficiently flexible to take on varied roles in diverse locations and still thrive. Another issue is who owns the global talent pool? Traditionally, in decentralised operations, business unit leaders control their talent. This has deleterious consequences for talent management, because local leaders resist 'losing' their high-potential employees. However, given the strategic importance of deploying the best possible talent to take on key global assignments, increasingly MNCs are adopting a centralised approach to talent pool ownership. The solution is to define clearly which positions fall within the global talent pool and agree on guidelines by which people within the pool are attracted, developed, retained and deployed.

(b) External Environment

Challenges. The war for talent has morphed over recent years: talent within the developing world must be taken into consideration when conducting succession planning.[32] With emerging countries clearly representing the growth engine of the world, the demand for top talent has never been greater. The problem has been aggravated because of years of 'corporate imperialism' which ignored the option of fostering local talent and failed to develop local talent pipelines. Now the MNCs have limited local resources to recruit.[33]

Despite recent increased unemployment, a scarcity of high-level knowledge talent exists in emerging markets, and the demand and competition for such talent remains high.[34] McKinsey's (2005) study on China's looming talent shortages predicted that Chinese companies wanting to globalise would need 75 000 leaders who could work in global settings in the next 10 to 15 years, yet the current supply of such leaders is only 3 000 to 5 000. The serious shortage of Chinese professionals and managers is caused mainly by problematic training and education facilities.[35] Although higher education, which was seriously disrupted during the Cultural Revolution (1966-1976), has subsequently mushroomed, it still cannot keep pace with China's rapid economic development.

---

30   Collings & Mellahi (2009:307).

31   McDonnell & Collings (2011).

32   Deloitte (2010).

33   Hewlett & Rashid (2011).

34   Li & Scullion (2010).

35   Ke, Chermack, Lee & Lin (2006).

A curious factor exacerbating talent shortages is spatial immobility of labour. Many African countries would rather hire overseas expatriates than recruit from other African countries, even if they pay up to a 500% premium instead of recruiting comparable and competent Africans.[36]

One of the key challenges is the quality of education in most emerging countries. According to Accenture (2011), there are 33 million university-educated young professionals in the developing world as opposed to only 14 million in the developed world. South Korea produces as many engineering graduates as the United States, despite having one-sixth of the population. China produces more graduates annually than the United States of America, Japan and France combined. But only a small percentage of developing-world graduates are suitable for working in MNCs. For example, India produces 300 000 information technology (IT) engineering graduates annually, and the United States only 50 000. However, in the United States and India combined, only about 35 000 graduates are suitable for employment in the target jobs.

Failure to produce suitable emerging-market graduates to meet MNC needs causes skills shortages.[37] McKinsey (2005) found that less than 10% of Chinese candidates were sufficiently qualified to fill professional positions (eg engineers, accountants, medical staff), reflecting a major problem in the Chinese education system: an overemphasis of theory at the expense of practical application, independent and critical thinking, and teamwork. HR professionals in emerging markets such as China, Hungary, India and Malaysia report huge variations in the skill and suitability levels of their graduates. Poor English skills, dubious qualifications and cultural issues (eg a lack of teamwork experience, and a reluctance to take the initiative or assume leadership roles) were frequently mentioned problems.[38] Similarly, HR professionals said they would consider hiring only 10 to 25% of India's roughly 14 million university graduates, because the majority lacked the necessary training, language skills and cultural awareness to work for MNCs.[39] Also, African and South American companies were falling behind in developing new technology skills that allowed for participation in the global economy.[40]

Solutions. Emerging-market MNCs that cannot find sufficient local talent are recruiting globally. For example, the recruitment programme of

36   Elegbe (2010).

37   Farndale et al. (2010).

38   Guthridge, Komm & Lawson (2008).

39   Holland (2008).

40   Scullion & Collings (2011).

Alghanim Industries, a Kuwaiti-based conglomerate, targets hiring people familiar with the corporate world and comfortable with working in a diverse workforce comprising 49 different nationalities.[41] The booming market of international search firms is further evidence of the trend that MNCs are increasingly engaging in truly global talent searches to recruit top-level leaders.[42]

A neglected source of talent is women. Women are an obvious solution to the dire shortage of top talent in emerging markets.

> Educated women represent the vanguard of talent management. Just as developing markets can bolster a company's bottom line, the lessons learnt in attracting, sustaining and retaining the best and brightest women in those markets can enhance and strengthen an organization's operations worldwide.[43]

(ii) Attraction, Selection and On-boarding

Challenges. Top talent is often not prepared to move to emerging-market locations.[44] Because high-potential employees are in demand, they can choose their assignments and avoid high-risk locations.[45] Different emerging markets pose different risks. For example, political instability has detracted from successful talent management in the Middle East, causing increased employee anxiety, distraction and negative talent flows. This is best illustrated by the instability prevalent in Iraq since 1980, causing mass migration of Iraqi talent to other countries, greatly depleting the Iraqi economy. A survey of 587 Middle East CEOs found that the CEOs perceived domestic political instability and global terrorism as the most serious threats to the business environment and to regional growth.[46]

A selection challenge in emerging markets concerns nepotism in candidate selection.[47] For example, *Waiko-ni-Wako* (a tendency to hire relatives and people from one's own tribe or province) is rife in Zambia, while, in certain cases, getting hired in the Ivory Coast depends more on who you know than what you know. Managers feel morally obliged to help community members who are less fortunate

---

41   Ali (2011).

42   Accenture (2008).

43   Hewlett & Rashid (2011:12).

44   Scullion & Collings (2011).

45   Farndale et al. (2010); Yeung, Warner & Rowley (2008).

46   Ali (2011).

47   While nepotism occurs throughout the world, it poses a selection challenge in emerging markets and, therefore, is mentioned in this chapter.

than themselves. The 'as-man-know-man' practice in Nigeria relies on networks to influence selection decisions.[48]

A key selection consideration is '**horses for courses**'. People who perform well in their home countries do not necessarily excel in developing countries, and vice versa. As Douglas Oberhelman, Chairman and CEO, Caterpillar Inc., says:

> Chinese leadership and needs are so different to those in India, Brazil, Canada and Belgium. Talent has to be regionally directed, and that's what we're working on. Frankly, it's a bigger challenge, because as we're new to some of these places and our growth is strong, we're having trouble teaching what we want our leaders to do and know.[49]

Besides the normal technical and managerial competencies associated with the job, expatriate competencies required in developing countries typically include high levels of resilience, resourcefulness, independence, cultural fluency and sensitivity, political astuteness and statesmanship, being able to interact authentically with people at every stratum of society, and embracing diversity. In addition, given the nature of an expatriate assignment, especially when the destination is in a country that is very different from the home country, the selection choice extends beyond the incumbent to considering the suitability of the partner and family.

Another challenge concerns on-boarding expatriates. A third of new hires leave a firm within their first two years.[50] However, a well-structured on-boarding programme can reduce turnover, increase productivity, and increase a company's attractiveness to potential employees. On-boarding addresses four needs, namely organisational culture mastery, emerging interpersonal networks, early career support, and strategy immersion and direction.[51] Given the differences in all facets of life confronting expatriates in developing countries, the need for familiarisation with both the company and the country is a key requirement for successful adjustment of expatriate families. Similarly, local employees joining a foreign MNC need on-boarding to understand the culture, customs and practices of the company in order to perform effectively.

Solutions. Market mapping, which entails benchmarking talent within a given market outside of one's own company, is a useful means of identifying talent in a host country. It has been used successfully to identify appropriate senior-level skills in new markets or where MNCs are setting up operations in new countries and do not want to alert their competitors to their intentions.[52]

---

48   Elegbe (2010).

49   PwC (2012:26).

50   Stein & Christiansen (2010).

51   Stein & Christiansen (2010).

52   Sparrow & Balain (2008).

To address home-country employees' reluctance to accept emerging-market assignments, an emerging trend in global companies is for the CEO and executive team to 'own' the top talent pool.[53] Top talent pool members receive increased exposure and development and are groomed to take on increasingly senior leadership roles. In return, they are expected to accept assignments in diverse environments. Successful performance in emerging-market roles serves as a stepping stone to advancement in the group. By centralising the top talent pool, companies are able to deploy resources appropriately and fairly across all their global operations, including the traditionally least popular ones, and thereby optimise person–job fit wherever they operate.

Regarding unacceptable labour practices such as nepotism, the MNC needs to ensure that the relevant HR policies and practices are adhered to in host countries. This should eliminate unacceptable practices and ensure that the MNC gains and sustains a global competitive advantage.[54]

As regards on-boarding expatriates, certain companies specifically focus on assisting people embarking on an expatriate assignment into emerging markets. They offer immersion programmes into all aspects of host-country life, including culture, history, geography, politics, eating patterns, and general customs and practices. This greatly helps with expatriate family adjustment to their new environments.

(iii) Engagement and Retention

Challenges. Exacerbating the skills shortage problem, emerging markets are particularly susceptible to losing talent to developed markets. For example, over 75% of graduates in high-tech-related subjects from China's top two universities, Tsinghua University and Beijing University, have gone to the United States since 1985 – a trend that is replicated at other leading Chinese universities.[55] In India, IT and business process outsourcing sectors recorded a 30 to 45% labour turnover even during the 2008 to 2009 economic downturn – businesses need IT professionals to provide software and systems solutions to replace laid-off workers.[56] Nigeria lost 10 694 tertiary-institution academics between 1986 and 1990; in 2007, approximately 36% of tertiary-educated Nigerians emigrated; and, in 2000, 20% of tertiary-educated Ugandans emigrated. The brain drain was also evident in Gambia (65%), Somalia (59%), Eritrea (46%), Mozambique (42%) and Sierra Leone (41%).[57] The continental brain drain from Africa was caused by attractive, developed-market offers for African high-potential employees, as well as political and socioeconomic factors. As local

---

53   SABMiller (2011).

54   Schuler et al. (2011).

55   Cooke (2011).

56   Tymon, Stumpf & Doh (2010).

57   See Elegbe (2010).

conditions worsened due to military rule or civil war, many educated Africans sought refuge abroad.[58]

Poaching is another retention challenge. Schuler et al. (2011) explain one of the causes of poaching in some developing countries: many MNCs have been expanding and relocating to developing countries. For example, in 6 years, Accenture's Indian staff complement increased from 250 to 35 000. By 2008, as a consequence of MNCs moving rapidly to India, its skilled labour supply was almost totally employed. Now MNCs moving to India need to attract workers away from their existing employers.[59] Because there is such a demand for high-level talent, the short-term solution of poaching senior managers with lucrative pay offers is rife in emerging markets. Bohara (2007:31) offers an alternate explanation for high labour turnover rates in India:

> ... for decades, multinationals have hired Indian nationals to run the business 'in country' with no expectation that these managers' own aspirations and skills might take them from a local leadership role to a position of power in the home office. Now in India, talent repays this treatment by moving from company to company and making no promises for long-term commitment.

Once again, this highlights the need for global talent management to incorporate high-potential, host-country talent into the MNC's international succession plans.

Remuneration is the main reason for labour turnover in China.[60] Other reasons include career advancement, unhappy relationships with management, poor culture fit, and seeking better benefits, training and personal development. Similarly, labour turnover is increasing in the Middle East, caused by factors such as diversification of the economy, leading to increased job opportunities, workforce mobility, and a shortage of skilled labour because expatriates are moving elsewhere.[61] Retention of skilled labour has become the most critical talent issue facing MNCs in the region.

Solutions. Greater engagement leads to greater performance and retention.[62] However, in a survey of over 11 000 workers worldwide, only 31% were engaged and only 61% said they planned to remain with their organisations.[63] Regarding scarce skills, because it is a sellers' market, global companies are making longer-term talent investments with increased financial incentives to attract and retain top

---

58 Elegbe (2010).

59 Schuler et al. (2011).

60 According to Cooke (2011).

61 Ali (2011).

62 Corporate Leadership Council (2004).

63 BlessingWhite Research (2011).

talent.[64] Profit-sharing and stock option schemes are an effective means of retaining professional and managerial staff in China, suggesting that the new materialism has overtaken traditional cultural forces promoting egalitarianism and altruism.[65] MNCs operating in China, such as Citigroup, GE and HSBC, compete fiercely with local Chinese businesses for talent. They have tailored their employment value propositions, emphasising opportunities for real decision making, career development, housing, and education and learning. A survey of 113 Russian companies revealed that companies with formalised employer brands reported lower labour turnover rates and invested more in learning and development than companies with no employer brand.[66] Thus, crafting a formal employer brand/employment value proposition helps reduce labour turnover in developing countries. Factors typically associated with retention in the developed world (ie intrinsic and extrinsic rewards, managerial support, professional development practices, and performance management practices) increased satisfaction with, and pride in, the organisation, which, in turn, were inversely associated with propensity to leave the organisation.[67]

One way of retaining emerging-market, high-potential employees is to offer them aspirational jobs with attractive rewards and opportunities for advancement that most local employers overlook. In emerging markets, the war for talent is so fierce that the temptation to overpromise and underdeliver must be avoided.[68] Instead, companies that succeed in retaining talent ensure that they meet their promises. "[M]any of the people we interviewed were seeking a culture that would support the promise of an accelerated career path with growth opportunities for everyone, a commitment to meritocracy, and custom career planning."[69]

(iv) Development

Challenges. A study of 260 MNCs revealed that most MNCs adopted haphazard or ad hoc approaches to succession planning and development.[70] It concluded that MNCs have a long way to go before they fully embrace the need to strategically manage key employees. At least two specific development challenges face MNCs operating in emerging markets. First, expatriates need to develop the competencies

---

64   Deloitte (2010).

65   Cooke (2011).

66   Kucherov & Zavyalova (2011).

67   Tymon et al. (2010) investigated retention and labour turnover in a sample of 4 811 professionals employed in 28 Indian firms.

68   Ready et al. (2008).

69   Ready et al. (2008:6).

70   McDonnell, Lamare, Gunnigle & Lavelle (2010).

necessary to operate effectively in host countries. Secondly, local employees need to develop technical and managerial skills to perform effectively in MNCs.

Although there is a burgeoning tertiary-education industry across the developing world, many tertiary qualifications are not suited to the needs of MNCs.[71] Poaching exacerbates an MNC's appetite to train local people. Chinese organisations are wary of investing in development for fear of losing trained staff. This results in underresourced training efforts, which detract from the availability of suitably competent local talent.[72]

Career development poses unique challenges for MNCs in emerging markets. Compared with employees remaining in their home countries, expatriate career paths are less clear and potentially produce higher levels of insecurity, especially if there are no post-assignment job-placement guarantees. Also, being far away from home base, expatriates may develop a sense of alienation from the company. For local employees, career development is equally important. High-potential employees want to know that they have a future with the company beyond local borders and that they will not be disadvantaged in their career progression because they come from a developing country.[73]

Solutions. One way of preparing managers for overseas assignments is to send them to business schools located in host countries before they commence the assignment, to familiarise them with the local markets. Some Chinese MNCs are sending their top managers to executive development programmes offered by their companies or business schools to give them a broader, global understanding beyond their company-specific knowledge and experience.[74] Chinese employees are also sent abroad to widen their knowledge and to understand the global business better. Some Western companies operating in China (eg P&G and Motorola) have created management development programmes to grow Chinese talent (Cooke 2011). Microsoft offers development programmes (such as rotation to the United States) and recognition programmes such as being selected as a 'Silk Road Scholar'[75], which appeal to Chinese employees.[76]

Action learning has emerged as a popular form of leadership development to familiarise leaders with business practices in emerging markets.[77] Business schools, such as the Gordon Institute of Business Science, have shifted the focus of general

---

71   Accenture (2011).

72   Cooke (2011).

73   Ready et al. (2008).

74   Dietz, Orr & Xing (2008).

75   This is analogous in Western tertiary education to being selected as a Rhodes Scholar.

76   Schuler et al. (2011).

77   See chapter 5 on in-market action learning.

manager development to cater specifically for operating in emerging markets. As such, these programmes cultivate managerial competencies specifically for managing in emerging markets.

Regarding the development of local talent, learning and development opportunities are important talent attractors for local employees keen to climb the corporate ladder. MNCs are attractive to Chinese employees who have strong career aspirations and are seeking development opportunities.[78] Huawei, which has a strong learning and development focus, established the Huawei University in 2005, offering tailored training to employees and customers. New employees receive up to six months' induction training there. Mentoring is used to develop junior professionals. Selected overseas employees are sent to Huawei headquarters to understand its strategies, processes and culture, and disseminate these upon returning home – a further example of leadership development for local talent.[79]

Standard Chartered Bank China developed a 'raw talent superhighway' programme comprising six components. It represents a good example of developing local talent:[80]

1. *Selection*: Once specific skills required are identified, Standard Chartered Bank investigates nonbanking industries with similar expertise and aggressively recruits employees from those industries by offering greater opportunities for career advancement.

2. *Induction and orientation*: Standard Chartered Bank offers intensive induction for new hires to acculturate them and explain the importance of company values and ethics, central in the financial service industry.

3. *Technical training*: The bank includes a five-day 'boot camp' that delegates have to pass before being exposed to the bank's customers.

4. *Professional and management development*: New recruits undergo intensive training in English-language skills, communication and listening skills, and business etiquette. They receive career guidance and are exposed to networking sessions to understand the bank's different career paths. The bank also offers an Asian best-practice management development programme and an extensive suite of e-learning programmes to ensure learning and development are accessible to all. Standard Chartered Bank has also established partnerships with Chinese universities to enhance recruitment and to offer employees ongoing professional development.

5. *Stretch assignments and deployment*: Standard Chartered Bank's talent motto of 'Go places…' tells employees that, if they do well, their careers will progress

---

78   Cooke (2011).

79   Cooke (2011).

80   See Ready et al. (2008) who outline the Standard Chartered Bank China case in detail.

rapidly. It also emphasises that the bank is a global company with international opportunities. Chinese high-potential employees are often moved globally, including to the company headquarters in London.

6. *Personal development and performance management*: The bank's culture is both nurturing and performance-driven. High performance standards are consistently maintained. Katherine Tsang, CEO of Standard Chartered Bank China, says, "We deal with problems openly and honestly, and that has led to the creation of an authentic and trust-based culture."[81]

Standard Chartered Bank's holistic approach to talent attraction, retention and development has created many positive consequences, one of which was to reduce attrition by 3% in a year.

Latin American beverage company, FEMSA, has adopted an innovative development-multiplier plan. FEMSA's Josĕ Antonio Fernăndez Carbajaal says, "We train people by moving those with useful skill sets to train clusters of employees, who in turn train other clusters. Knowledge is disseminated firsthand and spreads fast."[82]

An effective approach to expatriate career development is to appoint a home-executive sponsor for each expatriate, who contacts the expatriate regularly. Once a year, they have a formal career discussion, which forms part of the MNC's career development process. Also, by including expatriates in ongoing key events (eg conferences, leadership forums), the MNC ensures that expatriates remain in touch with the organisational culture and feel part of the larger company. Lenovo, which acquired IBM's personal-computer operations and is strongly rooted in China is a good example of how to approach career development in emerging economies.[83] CEO Bill Amelio describes the company as 'a stage without a ceiling for every employee – worldwide'.[84] Lenovo provides methodical development for its employees, in line with their career aspirations: career maps are created for every member of the high-potential talent pool. Competence gaps are identified and steps are taken to close those gaps. Central to Lenovo's talent-tracking process is that the career maps are linked to key positions across the globe and accountability for the entire process rests with Line Management and not HR.

(v) *Managing Performance*

Challenges. Managing performance is particularly susceptible to cultural interpretation and cross-country differences in custom and practice. Consequently, MNCs need to take care not simply to export their home-developed performance management

---

81   Ready et al. (2008:8).

82   Accenture (2008:27).

83   See Ready et al. (2008) who outline the Lenovo case in detail.

84   Ready et al. (2008:3).

approaches to host countries. For example, when SAB entered Tanzania, it exported its customer-focused goals approach to performance management. This approach experienced initial problems, despite being extremely successful in South Africa. Only once the programme was adapted to meet local needs and the logic in the broader company context was carefully explained did performance management gain traction in Tanzania. In China, performance appraisals display the most enduring influence of Chinese culture, which respects seniority and hierarchy, and values social harmony.[85] Chinese performance appraisal systems are reward-driven, focusing retrospectively on the person's performance. Conversely, Western appraisal systems adopt a developmental approach, focusing prospectively on individual performance and organisational goals. The challenge is to create a blend of the two approaches that achieves the desired performance results whilst maximising employee engagement.

Solutions. If performance management is to be effective in emerging markets, first, it needs to be adapted to local circumstances, and, secondly, it needs a strategic focus. The goals set must be linked to corporate objectives. It also needs to adopt a developmental approach by evaluating employees against their current job competencies and those required in future positions.[86]

One way of managing expatriate performance is to adapt the performance management system to take account of the host context.[87] This entails factoring in the impact of exogenous factors on business performance (eg currency fluctuations), clearly articulating the expatriate's goals, ensuring that performance evaluations measure the same things across countries, and determining the people best placed to evaluate the expatriate's performance.

(vi) Reward and Recognition

Challenges. Salaries of managers and highly skilled employees (locals and expatriates alike) are generally inflated in emerging markets. Because the demand for local, high-potential employees greatly outweighs the supply, salaries are excessively high.[88] Alternatively, expatriates, typically paid according to market conditions in their home countries, plus various expatriate premiums, receive much higher salaries than their local counterparts, who are paid in line with local market forces. This represents a source of injustice and frustration for local employees.[89] However, if companies do not offer expatriates competitive packages, they will decline the

---

85   Cooke (2011).

86   McDonnell & Collings (2011).

87   Collings et al. (2007).

88   Farndale et al. (2010).

89   Leung, Zhu & Ge (2009).

assignments, especially in less attractive destinations. Also, to attract employees to accept international assignments, MNCs often tailor packages to meet individual employee demands.[90] Conversely, to cater for the increased numbers of expatriate assignments, MNCs have begun to standardise their expatriate pay approach. Dynamics such as these pose remuneration challenges for MNCs eager to attract and retain the best available talent without paying too high a premium.

Solutions. The goal of an expatriate package is to keep employees 'whole' – where the expatriate does not experience an overt gain or loss when all elements of the package are combined.[91] To attract suitable talent, MNCs offer expatriates remuneration allowances to keep their sense of wholeness. These include host-country cost of living, healthcare, housing, foreign taxes, children's education, and hardship allowances.[92] These factors account for the unduly high packages earned by expatriates.

Another issue is the choice of a suitable expatriate remuneration approach. Three options have been identified by Sims and Schraeder (2005). The **balance sheet approach** aims at ensuring that the expatriate acquires equivalent purchasing power abroad to maintain home lifestyle. The **host country-based approach** curtails the spiralling costs of expatriate pay. It estimates what competitors are paying and the pay levels of local employees in comparable jobs, sharply restricting traditional allowances mentioned above. This approach also sends a message that doing an expatriate assignment is a prerequisite for upward advancement in the MNC. The **international headquarters approach** assumes all expatriates come from the same home headquarters and are paid on the same balance sheet programme. Gillette used this approach successfully when entering China.[93] Thus the balance sheet approach would address the issue of individual tailoring, the host-country approach deals with local employee resentment, while the international headquarters approach addresses the need for standardisation.

An unduly high salary demand by local, skilled professionals in China has caused some MNCs (eg FedEx, TNT and HSBC) to adopt a 'China plus one strategy' – maintain some presence in China, while moving operations to lower-wage countries such as Vietnam and Bangladesh.[94]

---

90   Warneke & Schneider (2011).

91   According to Sims & Schraeder (2005).

92   Sims & Schraeder (2005).

93   Expatriate pay in emerging markets is a complicated topic that requires much elaboration to cover properly. See Mark Bussin's chapter in this book (chapter 6) for a detailed explanation of how to meet the challenges in this field.

94   Schuler et al. (2011).

3. Emerging-market Talent Strategy: Underpinning Processes

Having outlined some of the challenges and solutions associated with the core talent management value chain, the focus shifts to issues associated with the processes underpinning talent management in emerging markets.

(i) *Diversity and Localisation*

Challenges. MNCs need to manage employees with dissimilar cultures, races, ethnicities, nationalities, religions, genders and generations, and all instances of prejudice need to be eradicated. Hewlett and Rashid (2010) collected data from 4 350 degreed men and women in Brazil, Russia, India, China and the United Arab Emirates and found that women in emerging markets were ahead of the curve regarding education, levels of ambition, and organisational commitment. However, several factors led them to be underleveraged. Problems included social disapproval of women travelling alone, the escalating crime rates which presented a harsh reality for professional women in emerging markets, and the triple whammy of gender, ethnicity and cultural bias. Between 25% and 36% of respondents from Brazil, China and the United Arab Emirates and 45% of the Indian respondents said that women were treated unfairly because of their gender. Another gender problem was work–home role conflicts, interestingly from the older generation, rather than childcare issues. In India and China, filial piety underpins the cultural value system, and daughterly guilt and responsibility are a far greater burden than maternal guilt. As one highly qualified Emirati woman explained, "It is part of the expectation of what children do in the Arab world. We take care of our parents when we grow up."[95]

There is very little evidence of diversity management or the existence of diversity policies in Chinese organisations. Where they are in place, they take the form of conflict avoidance rather than being a value-add to the business. Similarly, in the Middle East, women and foreign labour are still discriminated against, and Westerners and citizens are on a higher pay scale than people from emerging markets.[96]

Regarding localisation, there are many sound reasons why MNCs should employ local talent rather than relying on expatriates. These include the high expatriate costs to company, the reluctance of expatriates to accept assignments, especially in unfamiliar emerging-market destinations, language, custom and practice difficulties, and the expatriate's lack of a deep understanding of local conditions. Also, much goodwill is generated when MNCs appoint local people, especially into leadership positions. However, as outlined previously, it is difficult to find suitable local talent to fill senior MNC positions. Also, once on assignment, many expatriates are reluctant

---

95   Hewlett & Rashid (2010:103).

96   See Ali (2011) and Cooke (2011).

to forego the high salaries they earn, especially when their post-assignment career paths are unclear. Thus the requirement that expatriates find local talent to mentor, develop and ultimately replace them is often unmet, and localisation remains a challenge.

Solutions. Regarding diversity, simply stated, there is no room for unfair discrimination in any organisation. That is especially true in MNCs operating in emerging markets where, typically, local people have endured many forms of hardship and do not need additional adversity in the form of discrimination imposed on them by foreign MNCs. A fundamental (expatriate or local) managerial selection criterion is, therefore, the absence of any discriminatory biases. MNCs must ensure that the policies and practices of their headquarters and all their subsidiaries are free from any form of prejudice. These policies also need to adhere to relevant host-country laws. For example, owing to pressure from civic rights organisations, some Middle Eastern governments have introduced laws to protect and ensure the dignity of all employees, which heralds a new talent-friendly approach to people management in the region.[97]

A host country-specific employment equity strategy, which conforms to local laws, customs, practices and context, needs to be developed in each MNC subsidiary. It must go beyond eliminating unfair discrimination to embrace diversity and ensure that the potential value-add of employing diverse people, each with their own contributions, is realised.[98]

To overcome the gender problems and capitalise on the wealth of female talent, Hewlett and Rashid (2010) propose four solutions. First, MNCs should find talent early by recruiting women directly from universities. For example, the Google India Women in Engineering Award was launched and has been successful in attracting and retaining female engineering talent. Secondly, MNCs need to help top, emerging-market women to build networks and relationships and feel valued. GE is piloting a talent-spotting and mentoring programme in the United Arab Emirates to help women connect with one another across the company. Thirdly, give women international exposure to increase their chances of breaking through the glass ceiling in MNCs. In emerging markets, this works best when companies back it up with flexibility and support to reduce the burden on families and spouses. Fourthly, help professional women to build ties to clients, customers and communities in emerging markets. This helps establish a broad support system dealing with the conflicting work–home demands. It also helps women succeed in business.

Key to adopting a successful diversity strategy is to ensure that it has a sound business case. As Rohana Rozhan, CEO of ASTRO Malaysia Holdings states,

---

97 Ali (2011).

98 This, in turn, poses additional challenges for MNCs operating in countries that have discriminatory laws (eg laws discriminating against women) or where an informal caste system is still in place.

"Diversity is part and parcel of everything we do because to succeed, ASTRO's workforce must directly reflect its market place."[99]

Regarding localisation, targets need to be set and met in much the same way that expatriates are required to deliver on any other performance target. Procter & Gamble, which focuses its growth in emerging markets, provides a useful approach to hiring local talent which ultimately feeds its global leadership pipeline. It has built a global talent supply chain process, which is coordinated globally but executed locally. Regular hiring and promotions are managed locally in the emerging markets, but high-potential prospects and key stretch assignments are identified globally. Hiring local, high-potential employees translates into creating a diverse talent pool for the entire group. At country leader level, there are about 300 executives who come from 36 countries. The leadership (ie top 40) comes from 12 different countries.[100]

Similarly, Hartmann, Feisel and Schober (2010) investigated how seven foreign MNCs operating in China attracted, retained and developed local talent. They found that, in most cases, the MNCs transferred their home-developed talent management practices directly to their Chinese operations. For example, high-potential employees were identified using standard performance appraisals. Round-table discussions were held by executives to determine the high-potential talent pools. Development either consisted of attending internal or external programmes. A common feature was the reliance on overseas assignments to integrate high-potential employees into the broader MNC network and to transfer organisational culture and strategy.

One way in which both diversity and localisation challenges can be addressed is to adopt a far more host-country orientation in selecting, developing, promoting and deploying local talent instead of trying to emulate the MNC's headquarters within the host country. In this way, diversity can be truly embraced, local talent can be engaged, and an organisational culture can be forged that includes the best of both worlds.

(ii) Organisational Culture

Challenges. One of the major challenges facing MNCs in emerging markets is dealing with diverse cultures. Although many MNCs have strong, high-performing cultures, they cannot expect to translate their culture automatically into an emerging-market host operation.[101] Instead, they need to respect the local culture and work within it to move the organisation forward. Cultural differences must be taken into consideration if they are to be successful in their host countries.

---

99   PwC (2012:24).

100   Ready & Conger (2007).

101   As noted by Fealy & Kompare (2003).

Solutions. Presumably, the MNC's culture is one of the features that made it successful in the first place. The challenge, then, is to take the key elements of that culture and infuse them into the host-country operation whilst simultaneously taking account of local cultures, customs and practices. Ultimately, the challenge is to develop a new organisational culture that builds on the best of both cultures and provides a talent-centric environment where high-potential employees thrive knowing that they are critical to the MNC's success.[102] Moreover, culture has an important role to play in effective talent management. If the MNC can create a welcoming culture that embraces all employees, it is likely to succeed in talent management. As Armando Garza Dada, Chairman of the Board of Directors, Alfa SAB de CV, Mexico, commented, "Our capacity to attract, retain and manage executive talent does not depend on the compensation package, but rather on our ability to create a sense of belonging to an organisation that offers a long-term relationship and a professional development opportunity."[103]

(iii) Talent Analytics

Challenges. Because talent management has become such an important issue, it is imperative to move beyond instinct and gut feel when making talent decisions. Companies that are not using workforce analytics appropriately risk losing their competitive talent edge.[104] In the PwC (2012) Survey, two-thirds of the CEOs in their sample consistently implementing new approaches to solve their talent shortages, are seeking relevant data and analysis from talent managers to make informed investment decisions around people. Schweyer (2004) notes:

> If you do proper workforce analytics and planning then you know who to recruit, who to develop, who to redeploy and where to redeploy them, whether you should hire someone externally or promote someone from within, and whether you should look for a contingent worker, contractor, or full-time worker. Workforce planning analytics can help you make the best talent management decisions and align those with your corporate objectives.[105]

The importance of conducting detailed talent analytics in MNCs operating in emerging countries cannot be overstated. The challenge of gathering and analysing the necessary data is immense, especially considering the number of employees involved and the differing geographies, maturities, organisational structures, targeted

---

102　Several authors who discuss features of talent-centric cultures have been cited elsewhere in the chapter. See: Farndale et al. (2010); Hartmann et al. (2010); and Ready et al. (2008).

103　PwC (2011:10).

104　Deloitte (2011).

105　Cited in Lewis & Heckman (2006:147).

jobs, talent pools and performance and potential levels to be considered in such an analysis. However, Lewis and Heckman (2006) caution that, to make informed talent decisions, companies should avoid simply collecting tables of talent data without first adopting a conceptual model to guide the choice of data collected and the manner in which it is interpreted.

Solutions. As MNCs become more global, complex, advanced analytics are being increasingly used to make informed talent-related decisions.[106] Typically, talent reviews, containing all the relevant analyses, are cascaded up the organisation to successively senior levels and appropriate decisions are made at each level in the MNC.

Boudreau and Ramstad (2004) provide a useful framework for ensuring that valid talent conclusions are reached. Their 'LAMP' model describes:

- *Logic:* A rational talent strategy, linking talent pools to the MNC's competitive advantage, to generate meaningful talent questions.

- *Analytics:* Once the logical structure is in place, the right analytics can generate insights into organisational issues. Analytics goes beyond statistics and research design, and requires savvy to ask the right talent questions and answer them intelligently.

- *Measures:* The challenge of measures is to balance precision and usefulness – sufficient data that is timely, reliable and available.

- *Process:* A change management process is needed to implement the talent decisions taken.[107]

Advanced analytic tools and techniques, such as predictive modelling, allow organisations to predict into the future and thereby enhance talent management decisions.[108] Successful MNCs are using modelling to anticipate future talent supply and demand locally and globally. They are measuring recruiting effectiveness not just to forecast who will be hired, but to predict which recruits are likely to rise to leadership over time. Also, because people leave companies for various reasons, by using multivariate predictive modelling, companies can identify key employees who may be flight risks and use the insights to develop tailored plans to retain them.[109]

---

106 Deloitte (2012).

107 See Lewis & Heckman (2006:148).

108 Deloitte (2012).

109 Deloitte (2012).

(iv) Talent Information Systems

Challenges. One way of driving talent analytics is to adopt an enterprise-wide software system. It should provide real-time data that can be mined to gain talent insights upon which informed talent planning and decision making can be based. The logistical challenges associated with designing, implementing and maintaining one standard system across multiple geographies, organisational maturities, languages and bandwidths are immense. Also, not all HR measures are standardised across every business in an MNC, which leads to incomplete or unstandardised data rendering cross-boundary comparisons unreliable. Furthermore, when operating a global IT system, it is extremely cumbersome to effect changes in one business without seriously impacting the entire group.

Solutions. Because of the size and complexity of designing and implementing a global, enterprise-wide talent system, a comprehensive, structured and detailed change management approach should form part of the design, build, implement and anchor phases of the initiative.[110] However, there are alternative solutions to enterprise-wide systems. MNCs can use their existing systems, but with better integration. On the other hand, MNCs can jump-start their IT talent efforts by using cloud technology to host their reporting and analytics infrastructure, which provides analytics support based on industry best practices, thereby saving costs, time, capital expenditure and internal support requirements.[111]

4. Emerging-market Talent Strategy: Key Role Players

Talent challenges and possible solutions regarding the third component of the talent management strategy, namely the key role players, are now discussed.

(i) Leadership

Challenges. Arguably the most important factor determining the success of talent management (and, indeed, the success of MNCs) in emerging markets is the availability of suitable leaders for host-country operations. The shortage of leadership talent is the major obstacle MNCs face.

> ... Demographic shift – notably the impending retirement of baby boomers – along with changing business conditions, such as significant growth in largely unfamiliar markets, like China, have combined to produce something of a perfect storm. Leadership development has become a much more strategic

---

110 For example, see John Kotter's (1995) eight-stage change model that could be applied to, and adapted for, a global talent system implementation project.

111 See Deloitte (2012).

process ...[indeed]... companies have been forced to pass on hundreds of millions of dollars of new business because they didn't have the talent to see their growth strategies through to fruition.[112]

Leaders require distinct qualities and competencies and a desire to manage in culturally and geographically distant countries.[113] Specifically, they need several forms of capital – **cognitive capital:** understanding how knowledge needs to be disseminated across the global footprint; **social capital:** making the necessary connections to perform boundary-spanning roles effectively; **political capital:** the legitimacy to be regarded as a credible leader in foreign countries; and **human capital:** the competency to operate in diverse cultural contexts. However, when selecting leaders, MNCs often focus solely on technical capabilities at the expense of other core capabilities. MNC leaders also need to develop local knowledge in their host countries.[114] This includes information about the local economy, politics, culture and business customs, local demands and tastes, ways to access local labour pools, distribution channels, infrastructure raw materials, and other factors required to conduct business successfully in the host country.[115] Caliguiri (2006) identified 10 tasks that global leaders of MNCs need to perform. These are: work with colleagues from other countries, interact with external clients from other countries, work with internal clients from other countries, speak different languages, manage employees of different nationalities, develop a strategic business plan on a global basis for their business unit, manage a globally linked budget for their business unit, negotiate in other countries or with people from other countries, manage foreign suppliers or vendors, and manage risk on a worldwide basis for their business unit. To do this effectively, global leaders need specific knowledge, skills and abilities, and personality characteristics.

Solutions. Given the capabilities expected of MNC leaders, it is essential that the right criteria are adopted when selecting and developing leaders for global assignments. For example, cultural intelligence is an important selection factor when intercultural effectiveness is required. Intercultural effectiveness is defined as "a set of cross cultural capabilities that describe a person's capacity to function effectively in culturally diverse settings".[116]

Sheehan (2012) found significant positive relationships between management development and perceived subsidiary performance in a sample of 143 Polish, Czech Republic and Hungarian subsidiaries of United Kingdom-based MNCs.

---

112   Ready & Conger (2007:2).

113   Farndale et al. (2010).

114   As argued by Shenxue & Scullion (2010).

115   See Makino & Deklios (1997), cited in Shenxue & Scullion (2010:191).

116   Ng, Van Dyne & Ang (2009a:99).

The most effective means of developing global leaders is by giving them long-term international assignments, sending them on executive development programmes, and selecting them as members of international, cross-functional project teams.[117] Ruddy and Anand (2010) note a 70-20-10 rule for developing global leaders: 70% development via job experience, 20% through coaching and mentoring, and 10% through formal training. The high levels of independence and increased job responsibility inherent in overseas assignments contribute to their growth and career success: executives with overseas experience are more marketable, are promoted more often, perform better, and get paid more than executives with only local experience.[118] However, exposure to cultural diversity and international assignments does not necessarily enhance learnings. Instead, all four components of experiential learning (ie concrete experiences, reflective observation, abstract conceptualisation, and active experimentation) are necessary for learning to take place. It is the **quality** of the travel experience rather than the **quantity** of travel that aids global leadership development."[119]

(ii) Expatriates

Challenges. Three reasons for using expatriates are: (a) to fill positions where suitable local talent is not available; (b) to develop managerial competence; and (c) to ensure knowledge transfer across business units.[120] However, expatriate failure rates have been reported at anywhere between 10% and 80%.[121] The main reason cited is the inability of the expatriates and/or their families to adjust to the host-country culture. It has been estimated that each expatriate failure costs the company over $1 million: taken collectively, expatriate failures cost United States firms about $2 billion per year.[122] A key challenge, then, is to ensure that expatriates succeed, and one way to do this is to closely manage the performance of each expatriate. This depends largely on his or her competencies, which include technical abilities, personal adaptability to foreign cultures, and familiarity with the host country.[123]

Collings et al. (2007) identify several challenges associated with the use of expatriates. First, **limited availability of suitable international managers** to run overseas operations curtails the implementation of global plans. Factors contributing to this challenge include complications arising from dual-career couples – partners

---

117   Ruddy & Anand (2010).

118   Pattie, White & Tansky (2010).

119   As cautioned by Ng, Van Dyne & Ang (2009b).

120   See Edström & Galbraith, as cited in Collings et al. (2007).

121   Okpara & Kabongo (2011).

122   Sims & Schraeder (2005).

123   Shenxue & Scullion (2010).

are often prohibited from working in host countries, thereby retarding their career growth. A further supply-side challenge is the failure of MNCs to implement an effective talent management approach. Expatriates' willingness to move to emerging markets where they may be most needed is becoming increasingly rare. The three countries with the fastest-growing, new expatriate destinations, namely China, India and Russia, are also the three countries with the highest levels of difficulty for project managers and expatriates: 21% of firms reported that China had the highest assignment failure rates.[124] Secondly, **expatriate costs are exorbitant**. Interestingly, although it is estimated that the cost of an expatriate is between three to four times the person's home salary, little is known of the exact benefits of employing expatriates: return-on-investment analyses are scarce. The third challenge is the **mushrooming demand for expatriates**. The growth of foreign direct investment in developing countries has created a demand for global managers with the competencies to operate in these distant markets. Because of the shortage of talent within these markets, particularly shortages of qualified, local senior executives and the strategic roles these managers play, the use of expatriate managers in emerging markets has become inevitable.[125] Fourthly, **expatriate failure** (where expatriates terminate assignments and return home prematurely) is prevalent. The high costs associated with expatriate failure, both direct (eg salary) and indirect (eg loss of market share, reputation damage in host country) suggest that far more attention should be paid to preventing such failures. This leads to the fifth challenge, **expatriate performance**. Factors impacting on performance include technical expertise, self and family adjustment to the host culture, environmental factors (eg politics, stability and cultural distance from one's home culture), support provided by the home country, and peculiarities of the host environment. The final set of challenges identified by Collings et al. (2007) is **the changing nature of careers in the international context**. Increasingly, international assignments are viewed as a means to an end – developing competencies that increase individual employability and marketability, rather than limiting career progress to the MNC in which they work.[126] Also, there is a growing trend for self-initiated foreign work experience rather than being sent on international assignments by the MNC. These self-initiated foreign workers are self-financing and take responsibility for establishing themselves in their host environments.

A further problem is poor retention of repatriates (ie repatriated expatriates). By disseminating useful knowledge and new perspectives gained on assignment, international experience acquired by repatriates is invaluable.[127] However,

---

124   Farndale et al. (2010).

125   Shenxue & Scullion (2010).

126   This is aligned to the notion of a boundaryless career: building market value through transfer across boundaries, rather than pursuing traditional organisational careers.

127   Pattie et al. (2010).

repatriation is typically poorly handled. Over 30% of companies do not discuss repatriation with expatriates at all, and over 40% only discuss their homecoming less than 6 months before the assignment ends. Less than 37% do any form of career planning with repatriates, and only one-third of MNCs have a strategy to address the problems that expatriates encounter when returning home. Many MNCs have no policies or programmes to assist repatriates with their careers. Consequently, it is not surprising that repatriate labour turnover is high. The 2010 Brookfield GRS Global Relocation Trends Survey found that 61% of expatriates left their companies within 2 years of completing their overseas assignment.[128]

Approximately two-thirds of expatriates are accompanied by their partners, children or both, which places the stress of cross-cultural relocation, education and social development of their children on them and their families.[129] Also, over half the expatriate families are dual-career couples, which further adds to the stress of the family – especially when the partner is expected to give up his or her job and be unemployed in the host country.

Given the myriad of challenges associated with the expatriation process, it is surprising that many companies have failed to address the issue of globalisation effectively in their talent management programmes. Ernst and Young (2010) found that 63% of their respondents stated that their organisations lacked standard policies for managing the careers of international assignees, and 47% said their MNCs placed little or no importance on helping repatriates reintegrate into the organisation.

Solutions. To address cultural-adjustment problems, MNCs provide expatriates and their families with cross-culture training, the benefits of which have been widely acknowledged.[130] To overcome difficulties of employees rejecting overseas assignment offers, companies have adopted several alternate approaches. These include (a) hiring **self-initiated movers**; (b) hiring **host-country nationals** – specifically those who have worked for other MNCs and who have global experience and networks; (c) hiring **third-country nationals**, who are particularly valuable when MNCs wish to transfer common standards across diverse countries. This approach has been embraced by Adidas, where over 50% of its internationally mobile talent comprises third-country nationals. Adidas aims to increase that number by 20% as part of a strategy to build its employer brand.[131] Another approach is to hire **already-acculturated talent (inpats)** – expatriates from emerging countries who have worked in developed countries. Inpats are increasingly being used as a source of international management for at least three reasons: first, to create diverse strategic perspectives; secondly, because of the rise of emerging-market assignments, which

---

128 Reif (2011).

129 Cole (2011).

130 Okpara & Kabongo (2011).

131 Farndale et al. (2010).

are unattractive to traditional expatriate pools; and, thirdly, owing to the growing need to provide career opportunities for high-potential employees.[132] Other alternatives to expatriation include short-term assignments, commuter assignments, international business travel and virtual assignments that overcome many of the challenges facing traditional international expatriation.[133]

To address high levels of repatriate labour turnover, Bolino[134] (2007) proposes MNCs adopt three support practices:

- *Career development plans* entail career planning to ensure career progression has been enhanced (rather than sidetracked as many repatriates feel), repatriate agreements and skill utilisation (where repatriates are formally assigned meaningful jobs commensurate with their seniority that use their experience acquired overseas), and formal recognition of the value of international experience.

- *Connectivity mechanisms* include regular home visits and home-office communications. They help keep expatriates abreast of home-country corporate changes. Developing and retaining a meaningful relationship with someone in the home country also assists with repatriate success.

- *Repatriation assistance* includes pre-return repatriate training to familiarise expatriates with the challenges they will face upon homecoming and updating them with any technical or structural changes that have occurred in their absence. Logistical support includes identifying houses, helping select movers and providing family support.[135]

Expatriate success is positively associated with family adjustment in the host country.[136] Employer support for expatriates' spouses increases overall family adjustment, reduces premature assignment withdrawal, and increases the spouse's willingness to accept long-term global assignments. Cole (2011) found that the most valuable form of spousal support was assistance with networking regarding employment opportunities in the host country. Hiring existing expatriate spouses to assist newly arriving spouses also assists with the settling-in adjustment period. Another important form of support is assistance with finding and creating an appropriate social network, which enhances the psychological wellbeing of the expatriate spouse.[137]

---

132 Farndale et al. (2010).

133 Collings et al. (2007).

134 See Pattie et al. (2010) for a full discussion of the career-development practices proposed by Bolino.

135 Pattie et al. (2010).

136 Cole (2011).

137 Cole (2011).

Finally, there are six domains in which immigrants need to acculturate in order to adjust effectively. These include politics and government, work, the economic domain (including consuming goods and services), family relations, social relations, and ideology, which includes ways of thinking, principles and values, as well as customs and religious beliefs. However, most MNCs do not focus on all of these domains in attempting to help expatriates adjust to their host-country environments.[138]

(iii) Local Employees

Challenges. MNCs are increasingly moving away from using expatriates, favouring local talent instead.

> The use of expatriates to turn a business around or to open a new market is declining, mostly because of the cost involved and the limited success of expatriates in these assignments...Allan Church from Pepsi said, "We are having more success with local home-grown talent than with expatriates, as they are better at managing within the local business culture. Expatriates often take three to five years to make an impact on the people they manage and then they move on again."[139]

Similarly, Petr Šulc of the Czech pharmaceutical company, Zentiva, commented, "Strong local management is very important. We cannot do business in a country from outside that country, and it cannot be done by someone who has no experience, contacts or knowledge of the markets."[140] Notwithstanding this recognition of the importance of hiring local talent, in emerging markets, local talent that meets the stringent criteria of MNCs is scarce – either because of poor education or because high growth in those economies has given rise to a shortage of available talent. This poses a major challenge for MNCs.

Solutions. Ways of addressing local talent issues have been discussed under various headings throughout the chapter.[141] These include setting localisation targets to ensure that localisation takes place, sending local employees on accelerated learning and development experiences, sending local, high-potential employees on overseas assignments, deploying them across the MNC's global footprint, and generally providing them with attractive career opportunities.[142] One approach to ensuring

---

138 See Haslberger & Brewster (2008).

139 Ruddy & Anand (2010:587).

140 Accenture (2008:25).

141 See Richard Forbes's chapter (chapter 7), which outlines a variety of approaches to managing local talent in emerging markets effectively.

142 See Ready et al. (2008).

a seamless transition to local leadership is tasking expatriates with identifying, developing and supporting local, high-potential employees to take over from them. As Louis Camillleri, Chairman and CEO, Philip Morris International, Switzerland, said, "Ultimately, you can't rely solely on expatriates to run a local business forever. They certainly have an important role to bring our affiliates in given countries up to certain standards, but they also have the critical role of transferring knowledge and expertise so that those businesses can stand on their own. The goal is that those affiliates are eventually run by country nationals."[143] Similarly,

> ...because the competition for all kinds of talent is truly worldwide, leaders have to solve the global talent problem in their own countries. We cannot outsource our way out of this shortage. Those days are over. Countries like India that in the past have provided resources for outsourcing are now experiencing their own talent shortages. Nor will immigration solve the problem, because countries like China, once sources of skilled talent, are now luring their expatriate workers home to take advantage of higher wages and a growing economy.[144]

Indeed, Jeffrey Joerres (2011), CEO Manpower at McKinsey, states that the era of employing Western expatriates in emerging markets is ending. Instead, he proposes adopting a '**reverse expatriate**' strategy. Reverse expatriates are local managers who are selected to lead the local subsidiary of an MNC. They are sent on a developmental immersion into the MNC's established operations for several months. He cites numerous examples where this growing practice has been tremendously successful and concludes that "any multinational that really wants to grow in emerging markets should think hard about implementing a reverse-expatriate strategy of its own".[145]

There are over 20 million people of Indian origin who live overseas, and the Chinese diaspora is greater than 35 million, which represents a valuable source of local talent.[146] Many MNCs are wooing these people back home by going to overseas recruitment fairs and by maintaining links with overseas-based executives.

Some companies are focusing longer term on increasing the market readiness of talent by providing secondary schooling for local children. Embraer, the Brazilian aircraft manufacturer, runs a school for underprivileged children. It is also creating physics laboratory stations that enable the curriculum's engineering module to be replicated across multiple schools.[147]

---

143   PwC (2011:12).

144   Gordon (2009:viii).

145   Joerres (2011:2).

146   Accenture (2008).

147   Accenture (2008).

(iv) HR Function

Challenges.

> For many HR organizations, emerging markets used to be the last thing they focused on. Now it's becoming the first. ... In fact, a recent Deloitte and Forbes Insight Survey highlighted the competition for talent that is occurring globally and in emerging markets as the most pressing talent concern today.[148]

The complexity of talent management facing MNCs in emerging markets is great. The challenges facing corporate HR functions of MNCs focus on effectively managing two key issues: increased global competition for highly skilled talent, and new forms of international mobility needed in emerging markets.[149] Regarding **talent competition**, Farndale, Scullion and Sparrow (2010) identify three issues: first, to remain competitive, MNCs are demanding increasingly high skills levels and qualities in staff. Secondly, because there is insufficient senior talent to meet these demands in traditional talent pools, MNCs are broadening their search to wider talent pools across the world. Thirdly, to remain competitive, MNCs are extending their pipelines and are increasingly forward planning to recruit ahead of the curve. Marijn Dekkers, Chairman of Bayer AG says, "what is changing is that among Western companies, the ability to hire, develop and retain talent in the emerging economies has become a major point of competitive differentiation".[150]

Regarding the second issue, **international mobility needed in emerging markets**, Farndale et al. (2010) use China and India as examples to demonstrate that local talent in these countries is not meeting the rigorous demands of MNCs. Retention of knowledge workers in emerging markets is a further issue facing MNCs. The need to improve employee engagement and retention in emerging markets is an HR priority. Because of the shortage of local talent and the reluctance of individuals to be mobile, the consequence for HR is to develop alternate methods of sourcing international talent beyond expatriates.[151]

MNCs' changing global business models represent a major challenge for HR. Historically, MNCs adopted an international or federal model, where operations in the rest of the world were subordinate to the MNC's home market. Alternately, the entrepreneurial (or multidomestic) model has been embraced, where multiple geographies are all treated separately.[152] Many MNCs are increasingly moving to a third model, where the businesses are globally integrated and the MNC's home market

---

148   Deloitte (2011:10).

149   Farndale et al. (2010).

150   PwC (2012:20).

151   See the section on expatriates above for a detailed account of this.

152   Deloitte (2012).

is treated as one of many global markets. This shift represents one of the most significant transformations an MNC will ever make, and HR's role in this process (especially regarding the far-reaching talent implications) is central.[153]

Solutions. Common HR outputs in MNCs include focusing on the top talent across the company, developing core management capability by accelerating development of senior leaders, conducting proactive succession planning, and developing a pool of highly competent global managers.[154] Farndale et al. identify four key HR roles:

- *Champions of process* to oversee the global implementation of a talent management strategy that ensures the MNC's talent base is fit for purpose.

- *Guardians of culture* to oversee the implementation of values and systems when developing a talent management culture and employer brand globally. MNCs entering emerging markets may take an expedient approach to implementing global best practice, especially in least-developed countries where labour standards are low and employment regulation enforcement is weak.[155]

- *Network leadership and intelligence* to be in touch with the latest trends in the internal and external labour market and to possess the leadership to act upon those trends.

- *Managers of internal receptivity* to fulfil a role in managing expatriates' careers and ensuring that they are looked after in the process.

To perform these roles, HR needs to shift to a capability-driven perspective, focusing across the MNC to participate in mutual sharing of talent, which, in turn, reflects a move towards a more centralised approach to global talent management.[156]

As globalisation increases, MNCs will need direction and support from HR to develop global talent strategies that provide new skills in new places and to create a leadership pipeline that can be rapidly deployed to capitalise on global opportunities as they arise.[157] Also, MNCs will need HR's help to manage increasingly complex and diverse workforces with vast differences in nationality, culture, socioeconomic background, lifestyle and education, in addition to the traditional diversity factors of gender, race, ethnicity, religion and generation.[158]

---

153 Deloitte (2012).

154 Farndale et al. (2010).

155 It is common for Chinese workers to be asked to work overtime at short notice – paid or unpaid (Cooke 2011).

156 Farndale et al. (2010).

157 Deloitte (2012).

158 Deloitte (2012).

Ultimately, HR is the custodian of the entire talent management strategy. As such, HR needs to design and implement the processes, competencies, and innovative solutions to all the talent management challenges identified throughout this chapter. The measure of HR's success is the extent to which it is able to shift the notion of talent being an inhibitor of global expansion to a competitive advantage that is widely regarded as a cornerstone of the company's success across the world.

5. Business Performance

This leads directly into the last stage of the model, the impact of the talent management strategy on business performance. If the MNC meets all the challenges associated with talent management in emerging markets, then the company will have become successful in attracting, retaining and developing a disproportionate number of high-calibre, diverse people with the right skills and motivation that can be deployed in the right place at the right time and right price to enhance the corporate culture and contribute meaningfully to the MNC's performance.

Conclusions

Managing talent in emerging markets poses certain challenges. However, with the right creativity and compassion, these can be addressed in a way that enhances the MNC's competitive advantage. From the preceding analysis, several learnings accrue for MNCs on how to manage talent in emerging markets:

1. The sole purpose of a talent strategy is to support the MNC in achieving its strategic goals. Therefore, it needs to be derived from the corporate business plan and must be measured in terms of its contribution to the achievement of company goals.

2. Because there are so many moving parts involved in global talent management, it is important to adopt a systemic, holistic approach that includes the overarching corporate strategy, all the components of the talent value chain, the underpinning processes, and the key role players.

3. Critical to this is the need to attain relevant, accurate and current information on all people in the defined talent pools upon which informed, talent-related decisions can be made. The existence of an enterprise-wide IT system that provides real-time talent data helps streamline talent management across multiple geographies.

4. The adoption of a global talent pool of senior executives, managed centrally in the MNC's headquarters, provides the best approach to dealing with the selection, retention, development and deployment of people to lead the various businesses across the globe.

5. Because the challenges facing MNCs in emerging markets are so different from home-country jobs, the criteria for success and subsequent selection, on-boarding, retention, development and promotion of both expatriates and local talent need to be tailored to meet each host country's explicit needs.

6. Because the circumstances of each of the talent pool members operating in an emerging-market MNC is unique, a 'one size fits all' approach needs to be replaced with an individually tailored talent management approach that caters to their specific needs and family circumstances.

7. Because of the dramatic changes in global talent dynamics, MNCs need new and innovative approaches to resourcing their operations. These include finding appropriate ways of sourcing and developing talent across the world (in particular local, high-potential talent in host countries), adopting alternative approaches to the traditional expatriation process, and optimising the skills and experiences of repatriates as well as local, high-potential employees when they move from host to home countries.

8. Besides the regular leadership criteria, specific characteristics of successful MNC leaders in developing countries include high levels of emotional and cultural intelligence, resilience, political astuteness, ethics, the common touch, an absence of any prejudice, and a strong and supportive family structure.

9. The MNC operating in emerging markets has an opportunity to be a good corporate citizen that goes way beyond making financial gains. By imparting lessons learnt from the home country and being receptive to the culture, customs and practices of the host country, the MNC can benefit from the best of both worlds. Local talent and the broader community thrive as a result of the employment, development, advancement and global opportunities that the MNC brings. At the same time, the MNC benefits from the unique skills, culture, diversity and creativity that local talent brings to the workplace, not only in the local environment, but also globally.

10. At the heart of any talent management approach is the key relationship between an individual employee and his or her manager. If that relationship is poor, then talent management will suffer, no matter how good the systems and processes. As well-known authors Buckingham and Coffman[159] observed – people join companies, but they leave their managers. "The manager creates the connection between the employee and the organization, and as a result, the manager-employee relationship is often the 'deal breaker' in relation to retention."[160]

---

159 Marcus Buckingham and Curt Coffman of the Gallup Organization, coined the phrase in their in-depth study of great managers across a wide variety of situations in the best-seller 'First, break all the rules: What the world's greatest managers do differently'.

160 Lockwood (2007:5).

11. Finally, there is no single silver bullet for success in talent management. Instead, if an MNC wants to be competitive in attracting, retaining, developing and deploying high-calibre talent, it needs to create the right environment and to adopt a total employment offering that will be attractive to its target talent pools. This is as applicable to a small business operating in a single town as it is to a global MNC.

References

Accenture. 2008. Multi-polar World 2: the Rise of the Emerging-market Multinational. www.accenture.com/forwardthinking

Accenture. 2011. War for Talent. http://www.Accenture.com/.../WarForTalent.aspx

Ali, AJ. 2011. Talent Management in the Middle East, in *Global Talent Management*, edited by H Scullion & DG Collings. New York: Routledge.

Andors, A. 2012. Hidden in Plain Sight: in the War for Talent in Fast-growing Markets, Local Women Are the Not-so-secret Weapon. *HR Magazine* January:34-35.

Bhatnagar, J. 2007. Talent Management Strategy of Employee Engagement in Indian ITES Employees: Key to Retention. *Employee Relations* 29:640-663.

BlessingWhite Research. 2011. Employee Engagement Report 2011. Princeton, New Jersey: BlessingWhite, Inc.

Bohara, A. 2007. Managing Talent in a Global Work Environment. *Employment Relations Today* Fall:27-35. www.interscience.wiley.com

Boudreau, JW & Ramstad, PM. 2004. Talentship and Human Resource Management Measurement and Analysis: from ROI to Strategic Organizational Change. Working Paper G 04-17 (469). Los Angeles: Center for Effective Organizations, University of Southern California.

Boudreau, JW, Ramstad, PM & Dowling, PJ. 2002. Global Talentship: toward a Decision Science Connecting Talent to Global Strategic Success. Working Paper. Ithaca, NY: Center for Advanced Human Resources Studies, Cornell University.

Buckingham, M & Coffman, C. 1999. *First, break all the rules: What the world's greatest managers do differently*. Simon & Schuster: USA.

Caliguiri, P. 2006. Developing Global Leaders. *Human Resource Management Review* 16:219-228.

Cole, ND. 2011. Managing Global Talent: Solving the Spousal Adjustment Problem. *The International Journal of Human Resources Management* 22(7):1504-1530.

Collings, DG, McDonnell, A & Scullion, H. 2009. Global Talent Management: the Law of the Few. *Poznan University of Economics Review* 9(2):5-18.

Collings, DG & Mellahi, K. 2009. Strategic Talent Management: a Review and Research Agenda. *Human Resource Management Review* 19:304-313.

Collings, DG, Scullion, H & Morley, MJ. 2007. Changing Patterns of Global Staffing in the Multinational Enterprise: Challenges to the Conventional Expatriate Assignment and Emerging Alternatives. *Journal of World Business* 42:198-213.

Cooke, FL. 2011. Talent Management in China, in *Global Talent Management*, edited by H Scullion & DG Collings. New York: Routledge.

Corporate Leadership Council. 2004. Employee Engagement: Framework and Survey. Corporate Leadership Council. Washington DC: Corporate Leadership Board. ww.corporateleadershipcouncil.com

Deloitte. 2010. Talent Edge 2020: Blueprints for the New Normal. www.Deloitte.co/us/talent

Deloitte. 2011. Human Capital Trends 2011: Revolution/Evolution. Deloitte.

Deloitte. 2012. Human Capital Trends 2012: Leap Ahead. Deloitte.

Dietz, MC, Orr, G & Xing, J. 2008. How Chinese Companies Can Succeed Abroad. *McKinsey Quarterly* May.

Edström, A & Galbraith, JR. 1977. Transfer of Managers as a Coordination and Control Strategy in Multinational Organizations. *Administrative Science Quarterly* 22:248-263.

Elegbe, JA. 2010. *Talent Management in the Developing World: Adopting a Global Perspective.* United Kingdom: Gower.

Ernst & Young. 2010. Managing Today's Global Workforce: Elevating Talent Management to Improve Business. United Kingdom: Ernst & Young Global Limited.

Farndale, E, Scullion, H & Sparrow, P. 2010. The Role of the Corporate HR Function in Global Talent Management. *Journal of World Business* 45(2):161-168.

Fealy, L & Kompare, D. 2003. When Worlds Collide: Culture Clash. *Journal of Business Strategy* 24(4):9-13.

Gordon, EE. 2009. *Winning the Global Talent Showdown: How Businesses and Communities Can Partner to Rebuild the Jobs Pipeline.* San Francisco, CA: Berrett-Koehler Publishers.

Guthridge, M, Komm, AB & Lawson, E. 2008. Making Talent Management a Strategic Priority. *McKinsey Quarterly* January:49-59.

Hartmann, E, Feisel, E & Schober, H. 2010.Talent Management of Western MNCs in China: Balancing Global Integration and Local Responsiveness. *Journal of World Business* 45:169-178.

Haslberger, A & Brewster, C. 2008. The Expatriate Family: an International Perspective. *Journal of Managerial Psychology* 23(3):324-346.

Hewlett, SA & Rashid, R. 2010. The Battle for Female Talent in Emerging Markets. *Harvard Business Review* May:101-106.

Hewlett, SA & Rashid, R. 2011. *Winning the War for Talent in Emerging Markets: Why Women Are the Solution.* Boston, MA: Harvard Business Review Press.

Holland, K. 24 February 2008. Working All Corners in a Global Talent HUNT. *The New York Times.* http://nytimes.com/2008/02/24/jobs/24mgmt.html

Joerres, J. 2011. Beyond Expatriates: Better Managers for Emerging Markets. *McKinsey Quarterly* May:1-4.

Ke, J, Chermack, TJ, Lee, YH & Lin, J. 2006. National Human Resource Development in Transitioning Societies in the Developing World: the People's Republic of China. *Advances in Developing Human Resources* 8(1):28-45.

Kotter, J. 1995. Leading Change: Why Transformational Efforts Fail. *Harvard Business Review* March-April:59-67.

Kucherov, D & Zavyalova, E. 2011. HRD Practices and Talent Management in the Companies with the Employer Brand. *European Journal of Training and Development* 36(1):86-104.

Leisy, B & Pyron, D. 2009. Talent Management Takes on New Urgency. *Compensation and Benefits Review* 41:58-63.

Leung, K, Zhu, Y & Ge, C. 2009. Compensation Disparity between Locals and Expatriates: Moderating the Effects of Perceived Injustice in Foreign Multinationals in China. *Journal of World Business* 44:85-93.

Li, S & Scullion, H. 2010. Developing the Local Competence of Expatriate Managers for Emerging Markets: a Knowledge-based Approach. *Journal of World Business* 45:190-196.

Lewis, RE & Heckman, RJ. 2006. Talent Management: a Critical Review. *Human Resource Management Review* 16:139-154.

Lockwood, NR. 2007. Leveraging Employee Engagement for Competitive Advantage: HR's Strategic Role. *SHRM Research Quarterly* 1-11.

Makino, S & Deklios, A. 1997. Local Knowledge Transfer and Performance: Implications for Alliance Formation in Asia. *Journal of International Business Studies* 27:905-928.

Manning, S, Massini, S & Lewin, AY. 2008. A Dynamic Perspective on Next-generation Offshoring: the Global Sourcing of Science and Engineering Talent. *Academy of Management Perspectives* August: 35-54.

McDonnell, A & Collings, DG. 2011. The Identification and Evaluation of Talent in MNEs, in *Global Talent Management,* edited by H Scullion & DG Collings. New York: Routledge.

McDonnell, A, Lamare, R, Gunnigle, P & Lavelle, J. 2010. Developing Tomorrow's Leaders – Evidence of Global Talent Management in Multinational Enterprises. *Journal of World Business* 45(2):150-160.

McKinsey. 2005. *Assessing China's Looming Talent Shortages.* Boston: McKinsey Consultants.

Mercurio, V. 2011. Brazil: a Mobility Road Map for an Emerging Market. *Strategic Advisor* 7(64) June:1-4.

Ng, K, Van Dyne, L & Ang, S. 2009a. Beyond International Experience: the Strategic Role of Cultural Intelligence for Executive Selection in IHRM, in *Handbook of International Human Resources Management: Integrating People, Process and Content,* edited by PR Sparrow. Sussex, United Kingdom: Wiley.

Ng, K, Van Dyne, L & Ang, S. 2009b. Developing Global Leaders: the Role of International Experience and Cultural Intelligence. *Advances in Global Leadership* 5:225-250.

Okpara, JO & Kabongo, JD. 2011. Cross-culture Training and Expatriate Adjustment: a Study of Western Expatriates in Nigeria. *Journal of World Business* 46:22-30.

Pattie, M, White, MM & Tansky, J. 2010. The homecoming: a Review of Support for Repatriates. *Career Development International* 15(4):359-377.

PwC. 2011. Growth Reimagined. The Talent Race is Back On. 14th Annual Global CEO Survey 2011. PwC. www.pwc.com/ceosurvey

PwC. 2012. Delivering Results: Growth and Value in a Volatile World. 15th Annual Global CEO Survey 2012. PwC. www.pwc.com/ceosurvey

Ready, DA & Conger, JA. 2007. Make Your Company a Talent Factory. *Harvard Business Review* June:1-10.

Ready, DA, Hill, LA & Conger, JA. 2008. Winning the Race for Talent in Emerging Markets. *Harvard Business Review* November:1-10.

Reif, C. 2011. Repatriation the Right Way. *Strategic Advisor* 7(60):1-4.

Ruddy, T & Anand, P. 2010. Managing Talent in Global Organizations: a Leadership Imperative, in *Strategy-driven Talent Management,* edited by R Silzer & BE Dowell. San Francisco: Jossey-Bass.

SABMiller. 2011. Global Model for Talent Management (TM) 2011. Internal company document.

Schuler, RS, Jackson, SE & Tarique, I. 2011. Global Talent Management and Global Talent Challenges: Strategic Opportunities for IHRM. *Journal of World Business* 46:506-516.

Scullion, H & Collings, DG. 2011. Global Talent Management: Introduction, in *Global Talent Management,* edited by H Scullion & DG Collings. New York: Routledge.

Sheehan, M. 2012. Developing Managerial Talent: Exploring the Link between Management Talent and Perceived Performance in Multinational Corporations (MNCs). *European Journal of Training and Development* 36(1):66-85.

Shenxue, L & Scullion, H. 2010. Developing the Local Competence of Expatriate Managers for Emerging Markets: a Knowledge-based Approach. *Journal of World Business* 45:190-196.

Sims, RH & Schraeder, M. 2005. Expatriate Compensation: an Exploratory Review of Salient Contextual Factors and Common Practices. *Career Development International* 10(2):98-108.

Sparrow, JP & Balain, S. 2008. Talent Proofing the Organization, in *The Peak Performing Organization*, edited by CL Cooper & R Burke. London: Routledge [108-128].

Stein, MA & Christiansen, L. 2010. *Successful Onboarding: a Strategy to Unlock Hidden Value within Your Organization.* New York: McGraw Hill.

Tarique, I & Schuler, RS. 2010. Global Talent Management: Literature Review, Integrative Framework, and Suggestions for Further Research. *Journal of World Business* 45:122-133.

Tymon, WG, Stumpf, SA & Doh, JP. 2010. Exploring Talent Management in India: the Neglected Role of Intrinsic Rewards. *Journal of World Business* 45:109-121.

Warneke, D & Schneider, M. 2011. Expatriate Compensation Packages: What Do Employees Prefer? *Cross Cultural Management: an International Journal* 18(2):236-256.

Yeung, AK, Warner, M & Rowley, C. 2008. Growth and Globalization: Evolution of Human Resource Practices in Asia. *Human Resource Management* 47:1-13.

4

INCLUSIVE LEADERSHIP: THE MISSING LINK IN ATTRACTING, RETAINING AND MOTIVATING TALENT IN EMERGING MARKETS[1]

Steve Bluen

Introduction

The central role that leadership plays in talent management is evident from the familiar observation that people join companies, but leave their managers.[2] It is not surprising, then, that many multinational companies (MNCs) are providing inclusive leadership[3] skills as a component of leadership development to enhance effective talent management. The primary driving force for these interventions appears to be recognition of the need for leaders to work more effectively to attract, engage, develop and motivate diverse talent in a dynamic, varied and complex global environment.[4]

As a starting point for this chapter, an inclusive leader[5] is defined as someone who:

- Appreciates difference but still makes effective business decisions.

- Identifies and eradicates bias and exclusive behaviours in his or her team.

- Embeds inclusiveness into relationships with all stakeholders.

- Understands diversity and can express his or her ideas about it.

- Is a business relationship builder in the organisation, in his or her team, and with diverse stakeholders.

---

1   I am indebted to Linda Human whose knowledge of inclusive leadership, expatriates and diversity in emerging markets contributed greatly to the contents of this chapter.

2   Buckingham & Coffman (1999).

3   The term 'inclusive leadership' is most closely associated with Ed Hollander (2009) who has spent over 50 years researching and writing about inclusive leadership.

4   See, for example, Caligiuri (2006).

5   See, for example, Business in the Community (2011); Conference Board European Council for Diversity in Business (2010); Schmitz & Curl (2006).

This, in turn, requires abilities such as:

- An acceptance of complexity and a willingness to manage it.

- A commitment to making good business decisions in the interests of his or her employer.

- Self-awareness, flexibility, curiosity and a willingness to learn.

- An openness to new ideas and an ability to listen and understand.

- Consistency, fairness, honesty and assertiveness.

In this chapter, it is argued that inclusive leadership is the missing link in attracting, retaining and motivating talent in emerging markets. What is often not well understood is that inclusive leadership is underpinned by an ability to manage diversity effectively, not in terms of how organisations deal with underrepresented groups, but, rather, in terms of the mind-sets, communication skills and behaviours of those people working with diverse employees.

MNC leaders need to think differently about diversity and its benefits to achieve better business results and to provide an inclusive environment in which diverse employees are motivated and engaged.[6] The importance of reconsidering how we think about diversity cannot be overstated; leadership is a key element in the talent process and has a disproportionately large impact on the performance, motivation, engagement and retention of employees.[7] If leaders are either making assumptions about, or misreading the needs of, critical talent, the chances are that performance and retention rates will be suboptimal. This is particularly the case in emerging markets where the war for skilled talent is intense and where stereotypes and assumptions about local talent abound.

In order to illustrate the competencies required by leaders in a changing world order, two examples of less than optimal talent management are discussed, namely the employment of expatriates and women by MNCs in emerging markets.

Expatriates and Their Hosts

It has been estimated that there are between 650 000 and 850 000 subsidiaries of MNCs operating across the world.[8] Thus MNCs that have historically deployed expatriate managers to bolster skills and experience in their operations in emerging markets will continue with this practice into the future. In recent years, however, questions have been asked about the costs and benefits of expatriate use. Not only is expatriate deployment expensive, but it can also lead to challenges in terms of

---

6   Human (2005).

7   See, for example, Caligiuri & Tarique (2009); Farndale, Scullion & Sparrow (2010).

8   Colakoglu & Caligiuri (2008).

motivating, engaging and developing local talent.[9] Furthermore, some overseas governments have begun to question the value of expatriates to the development of local skills and have either instituted localisation initiatives and/or restricted the granting of work permits, based on their assessment of the extent to which such developments would assist local talent development.

This section explores some of the pros and cons of expatriate deployment and its impact on the attraction and retention of expatriates and local employees, and suggests ways in which some of the challenges experienced by both expatriates and hosts can be overcome. It highlights the critical role played by leadership in MNCs in terms of optimising the attraction and retention of both local and expatriate talent.

Challenges Confronting Expatriates and Their Hosts

According to the Economist Intelligence Unit (2010), the challenges confronting expatriate managers, in order of mention, are as follows:

- Cultural conflict between employees 50%.

- Problems understanding the local culture 47%.

- Variations in working styles and norms of behaviour in the office 42%.

- Lack of local language proficiency 33%.

- Resentment of what expatriate managers earn compared with local managers 28%.

- Perceptions of superiority or arrogance on the part of foreign managers 25%.

- Lack of company training for expatriates 16%.

- Poor quality of life 10%.

- Lack of respect for new expatriate managers 9%.

Based on diagnostic studies, experiences and global research,[10] challenges in expatriate/local employee relationships also include the following:

- Housing and environment. The facilities and accommodation provided by MNCs for their expatriate workforce are often superior to those found in local communities.

- Access to facilities. In some instances, members of the local labour force are either restricted in terms of access to, or perceive themselves as unwelcome in, areas occupied by expatriates.

---

9   See chapter 9; Collings, Scullion & Morley (2007).

10 See Deloitte South Africa 2009-2011; Human (1996b); Jassawalla, Truglia & Garvey (2004); Oltra, Bonache & Brewster (2012).

- Expatriate allowances are often seen as unfair, especially when part of the local labour force is drawn from distant towns. The research of Leung, Zhu and Ge (2009) suggests dissatisfaction amongst local employees with expatriate compensation. However, where expatriates proved themselves to be trustworthy, the perceived levels of unfairness tended to decline.

- Leave allocations. Members of the local labour force living far from home feel they too should enjoy the terms and conditions in respect of leave allocation that expatriates do.

- Expatriates working on, for example, a 28 days on and 28 days off basis often choose to work long hours and weekends. Some of the local labour force may feel that this level of perceived commitment prejudices perceptions of the work ethic of local employees with family responsibilities. Whilst such practices may benefit the individual in some respects, they may also create challenges for the expatriate manager on a personal level, particularly in relation to family dynamics and work–life balance.[11]

- High involvement in work positively correlates with expatriate job satisfaction and performance.[12] However, such involvement also correlates positively with work–family conflict. This research points to the difficulty experienced by the partners of expatriates, who often feel more marginal than their employed spouses. MNCs can underestimate the influence of unhappy spouses; and a great deal more can be done to support those accompanying expatriates overseas.[13] Similarly, Van der Zee, Ali and Haaksma (2007) found that the job satisfaction of expatriates was significantly related to their children's adjustment. Ultimately, spouses play a fundamental role in the successful expatriate's adjustment to, and completion of, a global assignment.[14]

- Some MNCs facilitate the paying of accounts and other administrative arrangements for expatriates by providing dedicated support for them. Members of the local labour force can perceive this as unfair when, in countries such as Angola, this can take considerable time (often during working hours).

- Certain members of local workforces perceive themselves as more experienced in their jobs than those brought in to supervise them.

- Some organisations feel that 'a smart employee can be successful anywhere' and more successful than a local incumbent. However, it is a myth that people who

---

11 See, for example, Haslberger & Brewster (2008) for the array of challenges faced by expatriate families on assignment.

12 Shih, Chiang & Hsu (2010).

13 Cathro & Kupka (2007); Kupka, Everett & Cathro (2008).

14 See Lin, Lu & Lin (2012) for a review of the literature.

are successful in their home context can be successful anywhere. Working in an international context is far more complex and requires skills not necessarily required to be successful in the home environment.[15]

It is becoming increasingly clear that an individual's emotional intelligence is far more important than his or her intelligence quotient.[16] Goleman (1995) argues that emotional intelligence involves abilities such as the effective management of social relationships through social skills, empathy, motivation, self-regulation and self-awareness. In other words, it requires flexibility, the ability to accommodate and compromise, risk-taking and an excitement about new experiences. All of these are core inclusive leadership competencies, as discussed below.

The proliferation of corporate villages for expatriates, whilst understandable, is often felt to reduce social mixing and to increase the formation of cliques. Some local employees also feel that this arrangement gives expatriates access to managers, which they do not have. This challenge is exacerbated by the use of a 'foreign' language, often perceived as exclusionary by local employees. Conversely, the use of indigenous languages by local employees is also felt by some expatriates to have exclusionary consequences.

There are certain assumptions by expatriates that can impact their success in the host country. These include the fact that expatriate assignments are glamorous and that superficial appearances determine how people feel. Similarly, we cannot assume that our successes are transportable across international or even regional boundaries or that, because the business language is English, there is no need to learn other languages.

Sensitivity to local feelings is crucial and, although it has often been assumed that men will 'cope' better than women in a new environment, research suggests that this is not necessarily the case. Studies of female expatriates (largely from the USA) highlight a lack of women in such positions,[17] often because it is felt that women are not internationally mobile because of dual-career relationships. In fact, half of the human resource (HR) executives interviewed by Moore (2001) attributed the paucity of women on international assignments to their spouses' careers and family issues.

However, it could be argued that dual-career issues are those of both parties and not just those of women. The number of women staying at home declined from 63% to 16% from 1950 to 1999. Moore (2001) found that few differences exist in adjusting to expatriate situations between men and women and that 52% of married expatriates found adjustment easy compared with 55% of single expatriates. It would thus appear that employers can better support dual-career couples by addressing

---

15 PwC (2012).

16 Beaman (2004); Gabel, Dolan & Cerdin (2005).

17 Harris (2002).

issues of assimilation for both parties, providing career support and career path flexibility and facilitating relocation as a family unit.[18]

Many local employees feel that expatriates are 'stealing' their jobs and doing little to transfer skills and knowledge to the local population. Some local employees feel that, by not developing local people, expatriates are afforded the opportunity to gain access to jobs for friends, family members and other members of their group, thereby bolstering a critical mass and increasing their own comfort levels.

Apart from an introduction to the society in which expatriates are due to operate, there is also a need to think clearly about the reason for expatriation and how it is to be achieved. For example, localisation or legislation often has the purpose of facilitating the transfer of skills from expatriates to the local population. However, many MNCs do not specify in the employment contracts of expatriates that they are there to perform a skills-transfer role. Neither are they assessed in terms of competence or performance-managed on objectives relevant to this role. It is small wonder, therefore, that many expatriates fail to fulfil the coaching role and have a vested interest in extending their performance contracts for as long as possible.

Many local employees also feel that they are not provided with enough information about:

• The MNC, its history and current functioning.

• The strategic plan and company performance.

• Why and how particular policies, procedures and practices came into being.[19] [20]

It would be a mistake, however, to assume that all of the challenges in host-expatriate relationships are caused by expatriates. Toh and DeNisi (2005:132) point to the potential for a negative, vicious cycle that can be created in the expatriate-local employee relationship:

> Many expatriate human resource (HR) policies, particularly in the area of compensation, remain rooted in the past because they continue to favor the expatriate over local staff and do not take into account the increasing qualifications and aspirations of these local employees. Inequitable treatment leads to low commitment and poor work performance among local staff. More importantly, inequitable treatment creates tension between local and expatriate employees and causes the local staff to be less willing to be cooperative or supportive of the expatriates with whom they have to work. Without local

---

18 Moore (2001).

19 Ready, Hill & Conger (2008).

20 These are often 'taken for granted' by those who have worked in large corporations for a long time and who fail to realise that the implicit assumptions on which production and performance are based may be foreign to those from different backgrounds.

support, expatriates may experience greater difficulty adjusting to their new jobs and the new environment, which is a contributing factor in the failure of expatriates.

Host employees, then, can also foster challenges in relationships through their own attitudes and behaviours. It would appear that, in addition to language proficiency, local employees require training in aspects such as:

- The reasons for employing expatriates and their likely impact on the host operation.

- The communication channels that have been formalised to handle diversity challenges which could arise.

- How host employees will be partially responsible for the induction and socialisation of expatriates.

- How diversity competences will be performance-managed and incentivised.

- Diversity training.[21]

Ultimately, if expatriates are to adjust to local emerging-market conditions, MNCs need to focus on both parties of the often-overlooked partnership between expatriates and local employees in the expatriate adjustment process.[22]

MNCs tend to assume that overseas assignments are effectively managed. The management of these assignments, however, usually concentrates on administrative issues such as relocation, remuneration and taxation. Often, such assignments are decided by someone volunteering rather than the individual's intercultural competence.[23] The success of expatriates, however, has much more to do with the effective selection of people for international assignments as well as continuous support before, during and after the assignment.[24] MNCs have often been remiss in ensuring that expatriates have jobs to return to on completion of an overseas assignment.[25] This can result in expatriates hanging onto their jobs and failing to develop local talent, as well as feeling 'forgotten' by their employers.

The attributes considered most important in a successful expatriate are listed by the Economist Intelligence Unit (2010) as the following:

---

21 See chapter 7 for a detailed account of the management and development of local talent in MNCs.

22 Toh & DeNisi (2007).

23 See, for example, research on self-initiated expatriates: Altman & Baruch (2012); Doherty, Dickmann & Mills (2011); Lee (2005); Richardson (2006).

24 Beaman (2004).

25 Pattie, White & Tansky (2010); Reiff (2011).

- Cultural sensitivity (73%).

- Overseas work experience and experience of living abroad (39%).

- Ability to role-model behaviours (38%).

- Ability to speak foreign languages (32%).

- Good networker (27%).

- Experience in operating in difficult and fast-moving markets (22%).

- An in-depth knowledge of the company products (16%).

- Company loyalty and an upholder of company values (12%).

- A champion of the company brand (12%).

- Being born in the country (6%).

The Economist Intelligence Unit (2010) goes on to provide a list of interpersonal skills that may be more important in the host country than 'at home'. Apart from a series of competences that the expatriate would probably need to operate in the relatively unstructured context of emerging markets, it[26] also suggests that the expatriate should:

- Be able to listen and learn.

- Be flexible and adaptable.

- Be an experienced negotiator with experiences in other emerging markets.

- Be able to make quick, practical decisions in a collaborative way.

- Have superior interpersonal skills.

- Be skilled at conflict resolution.

- Be a strong advocate of all the company stands for, including its values.

- Have an ability to create trust and loyalty.

- Have a broader vision of what the company is trying to achieve and be motivated by this.

- See the opportunity of being an expatriate as an adventure.

But how do we explain and situate these skills within a broader leadership framework? This point is covered later when inclusive leadership is addressed.

---

26 The Economist Intelligence Unit (2010).

The Gender Challenge

Introduction

The global competition for talent, an ageing population in the developed world, the rise in the population of knowledge workers and the questions being asked about the skills generated in emerging markets have created a context in which the attraction and retention of skilled talent have become a critical strategic issue. It seems strange, therefore, that lip service has not produced real progress in the advancement and retention of women. In the USA, for example, research on the progress of women in the workforce between 2000 and 2007 found that the percentage of female managers had only increased by 1% (to 40%) and that the percentage of nonmanagerial female staff had not increased at all.[27] Neither has the percentage of female corporate officers and board members of Fortune 500® companies. The situation is similar in Japan and in Europe where women make up the numerical majority of college graduates and nearly half the workforce, yet they comprise only 11% of corporate executives.[28]

In the United Kingdom, only 12.5% of FTSE 100 directorships are held by women, and public administration, education and the health service account for nearly four out of every five ethnic minority members in management positions.[29] Women are also less likely than men to be selected as expatriates. Less than 15% of MNC-assigned expatriates are female[30] and they occupy fewer of the top international assignment positions than their male counterparts even when they have higher education and qualification levels.[31] According to the World Economic Forum's Global Gender Gap 2010 study, female representation in business is lowest in emerging markets; for example Brazil (35%), Turkey (26%) and India (23%).[32]

However, these arguments should be qualified by the fact that the concept 'women' is itself diverse. The need for 'situational adaptability' is as much a requirement for the reasonable accommodation of women as it is for diversity generally; to stereotype, or generalise, about women would be as counterproductive as doing nothing at all.

---

27 Pellegrino, D'Amato & Weisberg (2011).

28 Pellegrino et al. (2011).

29 Business in the Community (2011).

30 This figure represents an increase from 3% in the 1980s (Berry & Bell 2012).

31 Berry & Bell (2012).

32 Borchers & Kasebekar (2011).

Female Talent in Emerging Markets

In their research on winning the war for talent in emerging markets, Hewlett and her associates[33] argue that women are an important solution to talent shortages. Rather than being victims, in some respects, women can be regarded as role models for women in developed countries, although what they are looking for from their employers is often different from what men look for. Some of the myths relating to female professionals in emerging markets can be gleaned from Hewlett's research:[34]

- **Myth # 1** Women in emerging markets do not get access to educational opportunities.

  Sixty per cent of women in Brazil, 57% of women in Russia and 65% in the United Arab Emirates (UAE) are in tertiary education compared with 58% in the USA and the UK.

- **Myth # 2** Women in emerging markets do not aspire to top jobs.

  Ninety per cent of women in the UAE, 86% in India, 80% in Brazil, 76% in China and 60% in Russia aspire to holding a top job, compared with 36% in the USA. In India, 11% of chief executive officers (CEOs) are female compared with 3% in Fortune 500® companies.

- **Myth # 3** Women in emerging markets are limited by domestic responsibilities.

  The average work week for women in Russia and China is more than 60 hours and the average in MNCs is generally longer than in local companies. Although the vast majority of women in BRIC nations and the UAE have responsibilities towards elders, the majority would prefer to use hired help (than place family members in care) and live in an extended family environment. It is also common throughout BRIC countries for young couples to live with parents. This also provides support with childcare responsibilities.

- **Myth # 4** Women in emerging markets cannot travel internationally.

  Although the majority of female respondents in India, China and the UAE felt that they would face family disapproval if they were to accept an international assignment, they nevertheless felt that mobility was crucial if they hoped to advance in their jobs.

---

33 Hewlett & Rashid (2010; 2011); Hewlett & Leader-Chivèe (2012).

34 Hewlett & Rashid (2011) and Hewlett & Leader-Chivèe (2012) surveyed 4 350 respondents in Brazil, Russia, India, China and the UAE, and 2 952 respondents in the USA. Respondents were college-educated men and women who participated in focus-group discussions, virtual strategy sessions and one-on-one interviews.

- **Myth # 5** Gender stereotypes prevail in emerging markets.

  When asked whether they believed women were treated unfairly in the workplace because of their gender, women and men from the BRIC nations and the UAE had similar perceptions of stereotyping and bias. For example, 45% of both men and women in India, and 36% of men and women in China, felt that women were treated unfairly because of their gender. The figures for Brazil were 25% of women and 23% of men; for Russia 19% and 13% respectively, and the UAE 32% and 36% respectively.

Finally, the key question is – do women expatriates operating in emerging markets perform as well as their male counterparts? Sinangil and Ones (2003) investigated this question in a sample of 193 expatriates from 36 countries working in Turkey. They found that, on average, men and women expatriates were rated similarly on job performance, supporting the call for greater gender diversity in the selection of expatriates for assignments in emerging markets.

Inclusive Leadership: the Missing Link

Challenges in host-nation expatriate utilisation and the optimal deployment of women highlight the need for leadership commitment to ensuring an inclusive workplace and an up-to-date understanding of the dynamics, aspirations and needs in a diverse context. In terms of relationships with diverse employees, MNC leaders need to become increasingly adept at managing the complexity of individual needs with which they are confronted. But what is inclusive leadership and how will it assist? First, effective diversity management as the foundation on which inclusive leadership rests is examined, before extending an understanding of this competence to related aspects.

Inclusive Leadership for Effective Diversity Management

Most managers have expectations of their direct reports; some positive, some negative. These are often conveyed by managers to employees in their communications. Expectancy communications (the belief that someone has or has not 'got what it takes')[35] are verbal and nonverbal expressions of what one person expects of another. They have a powerful impact on performance because of their influence on behaviour and cognition. With regard to behaviour, expectations affect self-confidence and hence intensity of effort and willingness to take reasonable risks. Cognitively, expectancies influence the way people explain good and poor performance, either in terms of a lack of effort (in which case they will probably put more effort into

---

35 Human (1996b).

getting it right) or a lack of ability (in which case they will probably give up).[36]

Negative expectations from a manager will have serious consequences for individuals who lack self-confidence. The negative expectancy will initially impact behaviour in the form of underperformance. Individuals will then probably tend to blame their underperformance on a lack of ability rather than the actual (and correctable) problem of inadequate effort. This tendency to attribute failure to the wrong cause in turn becomes the basis of a new negative expectancy with individuals and their managers becoming increasingly convinced that the staff members lack ability. To equate performance simply with ability is misleading; performance depends on ability and, crucially, on the expectations the individuals have of themselves and the managers have of them (in other words, people need to feel able, willing and allowed). Leaders thus have a duty to consciously control the effects of negative expectancy communications in the way they interact with staff.[37]

Thus, the way we think about, and communicate with, ourselves and others will have a significant impact on our and their performance. The problem is that some of our judgements of people may not even be conscious. This is problematic where such judgements are not of individuals but rather of groups.

In 2009, the National Centre for Social Research in the UK published the results of nearly 3 000 job applications that were sent under falsified identities to find out whether job applicants with foreign names were discriminated against. Nine occupations were chosen for the study and all of the candidates had the same educational qualifications and work histories. Candidates who were assumed to be 'white' received one positive response for every nine applications. For the remaining applicants, the ratio was 1 to 16.[38]

People generalise and classify people and objects into groups based on direct or indirect experience; this is because the world would be an impossible place to understand without doing so. (Un)conscious bias or stereotypes are a form of generalisation, but with one simple and problematic rider: they normally have a positive or negative judgement attached to them. Thus, stereotypes tend to convey not only situational information but also evaluative information. In the work environment, such information usually manifests as an expectancy communication about what type of performance is expected. In other words, unconscious bias can interfere with our ability to make objective decisions.[39]

The problem is that unconscious bias tends to compound perceptions of unfair discrimination and feelings of exclusion. It can also result in reduced levels of performance, retention and motivation. There is, thus, little point in

---

36 Howard & Hammond (1985).

37 Human (1996b).

38 National Centre for Social Research (2009).

39 Human (1996b).

proactively increasing recruitment, on-boarding and development opportunities for underrepresented groups unless such employees are not only willing and able, but also allowed to do the jobs for which they have been recruited.

Effective diversity management is not only about 'them, out there'; it is also about 'me, in here'. It is about consciously managing bias through self-questioning and humility as a forerunner to developing a global diversity competence.

The world is dynamic and complex and so are the individuals who populate it. Individuals have many facets to their identities; gender, age, ethnicity, ways of thinking and qualifications are just some. This is why situational adaptability underpins an inclusive leadership competence. Situational adaptability, in turn, requires the following:

- To be comfortable with complexity and ambiguity.

- To recognise unconscious bias and to have positive expectations of what people might be able and willing to deliver, given the chance.

- To accept the fact that we don't know about these individuals and what they are capable of, until we gather the relevant facts.

- To make decisions based on relevant information (to the situation).

- To accommodate diverse needs and expectations but to redress poor performance (fair discrimination in the work context).

- To learn to discuss challenges and find workable solutions.

- To practise fair discrimination in every aspect of our working lives.[40]

Various authors[41] support this understanding of inclusive leadership and define the concept in terms of what an inclusive leader looks like:

- Understands, is committed to, and communicates the business case for, diversity in the company and his/her own function.

- Integrates diversity into business planning.

- Listens and is open to new or different ideas.

- Is self-aware.

- Is flexible.

- Practises what he or she preaches.

- Is curious and willing to learn.

---

40 For a detailed explanation of situational adaptability, see Human (1996a); Marsh (1993a; 1993b).

41 See, for example, the Conference Board European Council for Diversity in Business (2010).

- Is accessible, mentors and provides open, honest and constructive feedback on performance.

- Is able to understand and motivate individuals.

- Is a relationship-builder, both inside the organisation and externally.

- Understands diversity and is able to express his or her ideas about it.

- Has the courage to comment on, or to constructively correct, exclusive behaviours and a lack of commitment to diversity.

- Applies policies and procedures consistently, openly and fairly.

- Is able to find solutions through engaging in constructive conversations about issues, needs and concerns.

The research of Business in the Community in the UK (2011) also indicates that inclusive leaders make a great difference in terms of levels of performance and employee engagement.

Of their respondents:

- 84% felt that inclusive leaders made them feel more motivated.

- 83% that inclusive leadership increased their loyalty.

- 81% that he or she improved performance and productivity.

- 81% that he or she motivated them to go 'the extra mile'.

According to Schmitz and Curl (2006), inclusive leadership is built on the following world-view:

- To sustain a competitive edge, businesses need to recognise the importance of future-orientated strategic planning.

- If they are to thrive, organisations are required to prove that they are ethical and responsible corporate citizens.

- Freedom from discrimination is a human right.

- The only permissible standard in an organisation is individual performance.

- Diversity of thought, experiences and perspectives are essential for innovation and growth.

A recent PhD thesis[42] has confirmed the proposition that an inclusive or engaging leadership style[43] correlates positively with a positive diversity management experience.

---

42 Gildenhuys (2008).

43 Mintzberg (2004).

Inclusive leadership is developed by employing the following three stages[44]:

1. Appreciate difference.

2. Identify and eradicate exclusive behaviours.

3. Embed inclusiveness into organisational culture.

Part of the process of reaching stage 3 is to work with mind-sets to create an appreciation of others and to identify, and find solutions for, actual or perceived exclusion. It is also useful to instil a process of engagement in constructive conversations supported by institutionalised practices and processes that are underpinned not only by the continual reinforcement of the business case for diversity but also by how rewards and recognition are allocated.

If a diversity strategy is to be implemented effectively, it needs to be embedded in the business in many different ways and on many different levels.[45] Diversity management is not simply 'tacked on' to the HR function, but rather is embedded in the strategic core of the business. From research and experience, it is clear that four dimensions of critical success need to be addressed, and institutionalised, if the diversity strategy is to succeed.[46] These four dimensions are:

1. **Strategic alignment,** which includes, for example, making diversity a strategic objective and formulating and communicating the business case; top-management commitment; the development and appraisal of diversity key performance indicators (KPIs); and diversity as an item on management meeting agendas.

2. **Sourcing and managing a diverse workforce** that involves the application of inclusive leadership skills.

3. **Creating an inclusive culture** comprises a proactive, ongoing, solution-oriented extension of inclusive leadership skills to ensure that diverse individuals feel that they belong and are appreciated for their contribution.

4. **External stakeholder diversity activities** that extend the diversity strategy to constructively employing the internal diversity competence to build external partnerships; to promote the corporate brand; to meet the needs and expectations of diverse clients and customers; and to ensure innovation and product differentiation.

---

44 According to Schmitz & Curl (2006).

45 See, for example, Human, Bluen & Davies (1999).

46 Human (2005); Human et al. (1999).

Inclusion: Best Practice

Identify the Business Case

Investment in women will be the next source of economic growth in terms of increase in national gross domestic products.[47] Deloitte (2011) found a positive, double-digit difference in productivity between those organisations with a greater percentage of female leaders compared with less. It makes little sense to exclude half of the population from the labour force, especially when it can provide a diversity of perspectives, often make more balanced investment decisions and assist with the understanding of women as consumers.

Investment decisions made with a brokerage firm by 35 000 households in the USA were researched in 2011. The study found that, although men were confident to make many changes to investments, their annual returns were an average of one percentage point below those of married women and nearly two percentage points below those of single women. Similarly, a study undertaken during the financial crisis of 2008 and 2009 found that men were more likely than women to sell their shares at stock market lows. Men appeared to be overconfident about their ability to make sense of short-term financial news. Women were more likely to confess ignorance and obtain advice. This led them to shift their positions on a more infrequent basis than men and to earn more money as a result.[48]

In both India and South America, female-established businesses are starting to be successful, not least because microloans are now granted to women. In the USA, women are no longer a minority; they wield purchasing power of more than $5 trillion and are nearly a half of all shareholders.[49] These are just some of the reasons for tapping into the female labour pool. There is a need for all companies to develop their own business case and to communicate it to all relevant parties.

The business case for the development of local talent through the use of expatriates is also clear:

- Significant reduction in costs.

- Compliance with localisation laws (where they exist).

- Building of corporate brand, image and goodwill.

- Utilisation of all available skills.

- Local knowledge and contacts.

---

47 Deloitte (2011).

48 Adams (2011).

49 Deloitte (2011).

- Much quicker at making an impact in the business.

- Higher levels of engagement from a significant portion of the workforce.[50]

Set Targets

Fagerland (2011), an adviser to the Norwegian government, describes a law passed in Norway for 40% of all boardroom members to be female. The panic this quota created has now been replaced by relief at the achievement of the intended result. She argues that, for all the talk in the UK, very little positive has happened and the quota she suggested was a means of accelerating a process.[51]

Rather than setting a quota, antidiscrimination, localisation and employment equity laws in many countries require companies to set targets for the advancement of members of formerly excluded or underrepresented groups, such as women and local employees. The argument behind such targets is that, without them, little is likely to change. This is not only because 'what gets measured gets done', but also because unconscious bias and economic patterns of privilege, power and economic advantage have become entrenched.

Move beyond Compliance to Inclusion

Creating the optimal workplace for a diversity of staff requires more than simply meeting headcount targets. MNCs need to create an inclusive and supportive environment by instituting behaviours, policies, practices and a culture that allow a diversity of employees at all levels to achieve their potential. An inclusive culture values diverse perspectives for the benefit of the business, its employees, customers, suppliers and the communities in which it operates. This requires ongoing, top-management commitment; open and transparent two-way communication; clear accountability and performance management; and diversity-focused metrics and measures.

A good example of how an appropriate, inclusive leadership style, coupled with the local practice, personal *guanxi*[52], leads to effective work-related outcomes was demonstrated by Chen and Tjosvold (2007).They studied the relationships between the Chinese and American managers of 163 Chinese employees from various

---

50 See, for example, PwC (2012); Ready et al. (2008); Ruddy & Anand (2010).

51 Fagerland (2011).

52 *Guanxi*, which literally means 'relationship' in Chinese, is typically developed through social occasions and gift-giving. In the Chinese business world, it refers to the network of relationships amongst people that cooperate and support each other. Personal *guanxi* is used to exchange promises for doing favours for each other, such as finding a job (Chen & Tjosvold 2007).

industries in China. They found that quality leader member exchange and personal *guanxi* promoted open-minded dialogue with employees, which, in turn, led to challenging jobs and promotions for employees. The positive consequences of this style of leadership are not only for employees; open relationships with employees can increase expatriate managers' chances of success, as they can confidently rely on their employees for local knowledge, custom and practice – vital for success in any host country.

Conclusion

MNCs that invest in inclusive leadership can leverage this competence to improve attraction, engagement and retention, to lower attrition levels and to create a robust pipeline of critical talent. The business case for inclusive leadership is indisputable. Hence, its inclusion in a talent management strategy is non-negotiable for organisations committed to using the full range of talent available in developed and emerging markets.

References

Adams, T. 2011. So Why Not Bring on the Women? *The Observer, The New Review,* June 19:12.

Altman, Y & Baruch, Y. 2012. Global Self-initiated Corporate Expatriate Careers: a New Era in International Assignments? *Personnel Review* 41(2):233-255.

Beaman, K. 2004. Myths, Mystiques and Mistakes in Overseas Assignments: the Role of Global Mindset in International Work. *IHRIM Journal* 40-53.

Berry, DP & Bell, MP. 2012. 'Expatriates': Gender, Race and Class Distinctions in International Management. *Gender, Work and Organization* 19(1):10-28.

Borchers, V & Kasbekar, A. 2011. *Emerging Women in an Emerging Market.* India: Deloitte.

Buckingham, M & Coffman, C. 1999. *First, Break All the Rules: What the World's Greatest Managers Do Differently.* USA: Simon & Schuster.

Business in the Community. 2011. *Inclusive Leadership from Pioneer to Mainstream.* London.

Caligiuri, P. 2006. Developing Global Leaders. *Human Resources Management Review* 16:219-228.

Caligiuri, P & Tarique, I. 2009. Predicting Effectiveness in Global Leadership Activities. *Journal of World Business* 44:336-346.

Cathro, V & Kupka, B. 2007. Desperate Housewives – Social and Professional Isolation of German Expatriated Spouses. *Human Resources Management* 18:951-968.

Chen, NY & Tjosvold, D. 2007. Guanxi and Leader Member Relationships between American Managers and Chinese Employees: Open-minded Dialogue as Mediator. *Asia Pacific Journal of Management* 24:171-189.

Colakoglu, S & Caligiuri, P. 2008. Cultural Distance, Expatriate Staffing and Subsidiary Performance: the Case of US Subsidiaries of Multinational Corporations. *International Journal of Human Resource Management* 19(2):223-239.

Collings, DG, Scullion, H & Morley, MJ. 2007. Changing Patterns of Global Staffing in the Multinational Enterprise: Challenges to the Conventional Expatriate Assignment and Emerging Alternatives. *Journal of World Business* 42:198-213.

Conference Board European Council for Diversity in Business. 2010. *Mind the Gap: Overcoming Organisational Barriers to Develop Inclusive Leaders.* New York.

Deloitte. 2011. Women As the Next Smart Business Strategy: Tapping Female Talent Increases the Bottom Line. Johannesburg: Deloitte Consulting.

Deloitte South Africa. 2009-2011. Confidential Organisational Diagnostics for Multinationals Operating in Africa.

Doherty, N, Dickmann, M & Mills, T. 2011. Exploring the motives of Company-backed and Self-initiated Expatriates. *The International Journal of Human Resource Management* 22(3):595-611.

Economist Intelligence Unit. 2010. Up or Out: Next Moves for Modern Expatriates. *The Economist.*

Fagerland, BS. 2011. It Makes No Sense to Exclude Half the Population from Leadership. *The Observer, The New Review* June 19:15.

Farndale, E, Scullion, H & Sparrow, P. 2010. The Role of the Corporate HR Function in Global Talent Management. *Journal of World Business* 45(2):161-168.

Gabel, RS, Dolan, SL & Cerdin, JL. 2005. Emotional Intelligence as Predictor of Cultural Adjustment for Success in Global Assignments. *EQ* 375.

Gildenhuys, A. 2008. Leadership Style as a Component of Diversity Management Experience. Potchefstroom, University of North West, (unpublished) PhD thesis.

Goleman, D. 1995. *Emotional Intelligence.* New York: Bantam.

Harris, H. 2002. Think International Manager, Think Male: Why Are Women Not Selected for International Management Assignments? *Thunderbird International Business Review* 44(2):175-203.

Haslberger, A & Brewster, C. 2008. The Expatriate Family: an International Perspective. *Journal of Managerial Psychology* 23(3):324-346.

Hewlett, S & Leader-Chivèe, L. 2012. Winning the War for Talent in Emerging Markets, New York, ICDER Leadership Seminar: Breaking through the Last Glass Ceiling: Are Women in the BRIC Countries Doing Better Than Their Counterparts in Mature Markets? 12 April.

Hewlett, SA & Rashid, R. 2010. The Battle for Female Talent in Emerging Markets. *Harvard Business Review* May:101-106.

Hewlett, S & Rashid, R. 2011. *Winning the War for Talent in Emerging Markets. Why Women Are the Solution.* Massachusetts: Boston Harvard Business Review Press.

Hollander, EP. 2009. Inclusive Leadership: the Essential Leader-Follower Relationship. New York: Routledge.

Howard, J & Hammond, R. 1985. Rumours of Inferiority: the Hidden Obstacles to Black Success. *The New Republic* (9):17-21.

Human, L. 1996a. *Contemporary Conversations: Understanding and Managing Diversity in the Modern World.* Senegal: Gorée Institute.

Human, L. 1996b. Managing Workforce Diversity: a Critique and Example from South Africa. *International Journal of Manpower* 17(4/5):46-64.

Human, L. 2005. *Diversity Management for Business Success.* Pretoria: Van Schaik.

Human, L, Bluen, S & Davies, R. 1999. *Baking a New Cake: How to Succeed at Employment Equity.* Johannesburg: Knowledge Resources.

Jassawalla, A, Truglia, C & Garvey, J. 2004. *Management Decision* 42(7):837-849.

Kupka, B, Everett, A & Cathro, V. 2008. Home Alone and Often Unprepared – Intercultural Communication Training for Expatriated Partners in German MNC's. *The International Journal of Human Resource Management* 19(10):1765-1791.

Lee, CH. 2005. A Study of Under-employed among Self-initiated Expatriates. *Journal of World Business* 40(2)172-187.

Leung, K, Zhu, Y & Ge, C. 2009. Compensation Disparity between Local and Expatriates: Moderating the Effect of Perceived Injustice in Foreign Multinationals in China. *Journal of World Business* 44:85-93.

Lin, CYY, Lu, TC & Lin, HW. 2012. A Different Perspective of Expatriate Management. *Human Resources Management Review* 22:189-207.

Marsh, D. 1993a. *Self-perception of Intercultural Communication Behaviour.* Jyväskylä: University of Jyväskylä.

Marsh, D. 1993b. The World's in Collision Conspiracy: Intercultural Situational Adaptability as a Success Factor. Fifth International Seminar of ENCODE: Languages and Culture: Bridges to International Trade. Preston: Lancashire Business School.

Mintzberg, H. 2004. *Managers Not MBAs.* London: Prentice-Hall.

Moore, J. 2001. Same Ticket, Different Trip: Supporting Dual-career Couples on Global Assignments. *Women in Management Review* 17(2):61 -67.

National Centre for Social Research. 2009. *Racist Recruitment Policies in the UK*. London.

Oltra, V, Bonache, J & Brewster, C. A New Framework for Understanding Inequalities between Expatriates and Host Country Nationals. *Journal of Business Ethics,* Online First, 13 July 2012, DOI: 10.1007/s10551-012-1397-0.

Pattie, M, White, MM & Tansky, J. 2010. The Homecoming: a Review of Support for Repatriates. *Career Development International* 15(4):359-377.

Pellegrino, G, D'Amato, S & Weisberg, A. 2011. *The Gender Dividend*. USA: Deloitte.

PwC. 2012. Delivering Results: Growth and Value in a Volatile World. 15th Annual Global CEO Survey 2012. PwC. www.pwc.com/ceosurvey

Ready, D, Hill, L & Conger, J. 2008. Winning the Race for Talent in Emerging Markets. *Harvard Business Review* Nov:63-70.

Reif, C. 2011. Repatriation the Right Way. *Strategic Advisor* 7(60):1-4.

Richardson, J. 2006. Self-directed Expatriation: Family Matters. *Personnel Review* 35(4):469-486.

Ruddy, T & Anand, P. 2010. Managing Talent in Global Organizations: a Leadership Imperative, in *Strategy-driven Talent Management*, edited by R Silzer & BE Dowell. San Francisco: Jossey-Bass.

Schmitz, J & Curl, N. 2006. *The Guide for Inclusive Leaders*. Princeton: TMC.

Shih, H, Chiang, Y & Hsu, C. 2010. High Involvement Work System, Work-Family, Conflict, and Expatriate Performance – Examining Taiwanese Expatriates in China. *The International Journal of Human Resources* 21(11) September.

Sinangil, HK & Ones, DS. 2003. Gender Differences in Expatriate Job Performance. *Applied Psychology: An International Review* 52(3):461-475.

Toh, SM & DeNisi, AS. 2005. A Local Perspective to Expatriate Success. *Academy of Management Executive* 19(1):132-146.

Toh, SM & DeNisi, AS. 2007. Host Country Nationals as Socializing Agents: a Social Identity Approach. *Journal of Organizational Behavior* 28:281-301.

Van der Zee, K, Ali, AJ & Haaksma, I. 2007. Determinants of Effective Coping with Cultural Transition among Expatriate Children and Adolescents. *Anxiety, Stress and Coping* 20(1) March:25-45.

5 IN-MARKET ACTION LEARNING

Glynnis Rengger

Context

> The real voyage of discovery consists not in seeking new lands,
> but in seeing with new eyes. – Marcel Proust[1]

Action learning in its many forms has long been an effective platform for developing leaders. Its bias towards experiential learning, solving real-world problems in cross-functional teams, and a rigorous focus on reflection has created a powerful platform embraced by many of the world's top organisations in their efforts to create learning organisations.

In-Market **Action Learning** builds on classic action learning, applying the same concepts of teams working on real business challenges in an experiential and reflective process. However, it differs in the focus it places on 'outside-in' thinking and on teaching leaders the value of actively looking externally for insight from diverse businesses and industries, customers and partners. It could be said that In-Market Action Learning emphasises the 'Q' in Reg Revans's[2] original Action Learning Formula of $L = P + Q$ (learning equals programming plus questioning). His view that "people had to be aware of their lack of relevant knowledge and be prepared to explore the area of their ignorance with suitable questions and help from other people in similar positions" launched the idea that going outside the boundaries of

---

1   Marcel Proust (1871-1922) was a French novelist, critic, and essayist, best known for his monumental *À la recherche du temps perdu* (*In Search of Lost Time*).

2   Reg Revans is attributed with originally coining the term 'action learning'. An excerpt follows which was taken from the International Institute of Management Education at http://www.iim-edu.org/managementgurus/Reg_Revans.htm:

> Action learning is an educational process whereby the participant studies their own actions and experience in order to improve performance. This is done in conjunction with others, in small groups called action learning sets. It is proposed as particularly suitable for adults, as it enables each person to reflect on and review the action they have taken and the learning points arising. This should then guide future action and improve performance. The action learning method differs with the traditional teaching methods that focus on the memorization and presentation of knowledge and skills, by focusing on experiential reflection as a major learning tool. Revans argued against the over value of the traditional 'chalk and talk' management education and he believes that people learn most effectively not from books or lectures but from sharing real problems/projects. He called it 'action learning'. The contribution of Revans is being seen today through initiatives in leadership development working towards organization development.

one's own narrow view of the world to supplement knowledge is an effective way to embed learning and positively impact business results.

It has always been true that effective chief executive officers (CEOs) and senior leaders recognise the importance of timely insights. They actively seek early signs of future disruptions, as well as scan for lessons that can be gleaned from competitors, innovators and other thought leaders. Successful leaders routinely seek market intelligence, external opinions and support to help shape their judgement and thinking on how events might affect their business. They understand that getting an external perspective offers a key means of stimulating breakthrough thinking and creating a culture of innovation. This acknowledgement has led to an impressive array of consultants who are routinely hired to provide an expert point of view on a specific subject, as well as fresh perspectives on how to tackle knotty business challenges.

Having an external perspective has never been more critical. Business today takes place against perhaps one of the most turbulent and volatile landscapes we have ever known. The speed of change and the interconnectedness of ecosystems show up every day with faster and shorter business cycles, disruptive innovation surfacing in unpredictable places, and consumers across the globe behaving in completely new and different ways. In this highly connected world, organisations are flatter, acting more like 'neural networks' where information flows in all directions through the enterprise and its value chain. Ad hoc relationships and informal arrangements coexist with the more formal vertical and hierarchical systems, and leaders recognise that there are new ways to include external stakeholders in novel ways for business goal achievement. Ideas and innovation are being championed everywhere and diversity embraced as a means to enriching the organisation's culture, thinking and strategy.

In the past year and a half, we have seen these developments significantly accelerate, with traditional notions of the organisation and its boundaries being seriously challenged. Microsoft has referenced 'the untethered organisation'[3] for a few years now as mobility of the workforce keeps growing and cloud computing enables flexible organisational arrangements previously not possible. Today, this notion of untethering has gone beyond anyone's ability to predict the shape of the emerging enterprise, with social networking and collaborative communities enabling entirely new operating models. Virtual workforces, crowd sourcing and social Customer Relationship Management (CRM) provide new ways of building engagement with staff, customers, partners and other stakeholders. These new platforms allow unprecedented collaboration, enabling companies to leverage great ideas from a broad base of stakeholders. Novel opportunities are being created as ad hoc communities assemble in an enterprising array of ideas and activities.

In-Market Action Learning has also proved to be one of the most effective ways to

---

3   Building the Untethered Organization – Microsoft White Paper; can be downloaded at http://ebookbrowse.com/building-the-untethered-organization-pdf-d107720968.

accelerate executives' appreciation of the challenges and realities of doing business in an emerging market. A well-designed in-market immersion will significantly shift senior leaders' perceptions and knowledge, enabling insights into sociocultural norms, market context, and the opportunities and challenges leaders face in these emerging markets. Building brand, innovation, talent management, and the broader roles of a leader in emerging markets come to life in a way that no other experience can provide. In these markets, characterised by high growth and high complexity, the opportunity to engage in dialogue with external stakeholders on these key business topics is critical.

So why is it in this fast-paced world where staying connected and being externally focused is critical, do companies continue to be too inward-looking – missing market signals that could spell a win or a disaster, losing line-of-sight to customers' changing preferences, and overlooking opportunities to collaborate with external partners?

Why don't organisations mobilise their own talent more extensively to solicit these insights? How could an organisation build this external perspective so that its leaders habituate behaviours associated with constantly seeking ideas and insights in less-typical places? How do we unleash the creative and intellectual horsepower of our own people to become the organisation's key consultants with fresh opinions, ideas and initiatives?

The reality is twofold. 'Outside-in' thinking is not intuitive to most business leaders. We tend to rely on our chosen few for input and advice. And even when executives embrace the outside-in perspective, time pressures make it challenging to take action and include these kinds of exchanges in a structured and regular way.

The benefits of supplementing one's own knowledge with external perspectives are well known. It enables organisations to break the habit of focusing inwardly. It accelerates understanding of how different businesses work and consumers think, enabling leaders to find fresh perspectives and novel ways of combining ideas to produce innovative solutions.

Steve Jobs[4] said, "creativity is just connecting things". And therein lies the simple power of In-Market Action Learning. It is the platform for connecting people and ideas and, as a result, is one of the fastest ways to invigorate executive thinking, and replenish an organisation's pool of ideas.

---

4   Steve Jobs on Creativity appeared in *Wired*, February 1995. The full quote was:

> Creativity is just connecting things. When you ask creative people how they did something, they feel a little guilty because they didn't really do it, they just saw something. It seemed obvious to them after a while. That's because they were able to connect experiences they've had and synthesize new things. And the reason they were able to do that was that they've had more experiences or they have thought more about their experiences than other people. Unfortunately, that's too rare a commodity. A lot of people in our industry haven't had very diverse experiences. So they don't have enough dots to connect, and they end up with very linear solutions without a broad perspective on the problem. The broader one's understanding of the human experience, the better design we will have.

Organisations in developed markets regularly use In-Market Action Learning to enable their leaders to:

- Develop a global mind-set and appreciation for the realities of doing business around the world (often in developing economies like China, India and Brazil).

- Better understand the market realities of emerging economies in which they are doing business.

- Understand the leadership challenges and opportunities in leading business in these countries.

- Gain fresh perspectives on, and new insights into, a particular business challenge

- Practise the skill of 'outside-in'.

For developing economies, In-Market Action Learning can be used very effectively for:

- Real-world, applied best-practice benchmarking.

- Strategic think tanks to solve immediate business challenges.

- Leadership development.

But let's breathe some life into this. The following section provides an example of an entire sector in a emerging market collaborating to solve a critical industry problem using In-Market Action Learning.

Using In-Market Action Learning to Accelerate the Leadership Pipeline for the Retail Sector in South Africa

Around 2002, an upcoming, young South African executive started to tackle the challenge of building the pipeline of leaders for the banking sector in South Africa. Frank Groenewald was, at that time, CEO of the Banking Sector Education and Training Authority (BANKSETA), a parastatal established to oversee skills development for the banking sector. Twenty-three SETAs (Sector Education and Training Authorities) had been established in 2000 through an Act of Parliament to focus attention on the imperative for skills development in South Africa. The real stimulus for Frank's vision, however, was the rapidly evolving Financial Services Charter, a sector-led initiative that included a set of far-reaching and ambitious initiatives intended to correct economic inequalities that existed in the country at that time.

The initial idea proposed by BANKSETA was a workplace exchange programme where high-potential South African bankers could spend three to six months in a leading Canadian bank shadowing key executives. Canada seemed like an excellent choice. The two countries have always enjoyed a good relationship, and Canada has been a proactive supporter of South Africa's transformation both prior to and after the transition to democracy. There are marked similarities between the Canadian and South African banking models, and Canada is a world-leading example of a society that embraces diversity and inclusiveness as a key to prosperity.

The Canadian financial services sector applauded the idea and an impressive array of partners (which included the City of Toronto, the Toronto Financial Services Alliance, the South African High Commission in Ottawa and the South African Consul General in Toronto, the major banks, the Rotman School of Management, the Schulich School of Business, the Institute of Canadian Bankers, the Canadian Bankers Association, and a host of other leading Canadian organisations) signed up to support the initiative. The International Leadership Development Programme (ILDP) was launched with two local residential modules in South Africa and six weeks of In-Market in Toronto, Canada. Thirty-eight high-potential leaders in the banking sector over a three-year period learnt about and tackled common industry projects together with input from a wide and diverse group of external partners.

However, the real refinement of the ILDP came about when Joel Dikgole, another visionary SETA CEO, and his board introduced the programme to their retail and wholesale stakeholders. In 2009 and 2010, the Wholesale and Retail SETA (W&R SETA) delivered 37 ILDP alumni to the sector, and, in 2011, another 40 successful candidates went through the programme, this time with the addition of accreditation from the Gordon Institute of Business Science (GIBS). In its first three years, a hallmark of the W&R SETA ILDP was the high degree of in-market experiences where participants had an opportunity to directly learn about business and retail leadership both within and outside the retail sector in South Africa, the United States of America, Canada and the United Kingdom.

Key success criteria for the ILDP included the following:

1. **The focus on In-Market experiences:** Core to the design of the ILDP was the focus on providing extensive In-Market experiences – practical, out-of-the classroom, direct interactions with a diverse group of thought leaders, senior business executives in and outside retail, customers, government officials, and other stakeholders around the world. In-Market experiences were aligned with the formal leadership curriculum as well as the industry challenges on which ILDP participants were working.

2. **Selection of participants:** Selecting candidates from across an industry sector poses particular challenges. Titles have different meanings, job descriptions vary widely, and 'high potential' means different things in different organisations. The assessment and selection process is key to the success of the programme. The danger in having excessive variation in the competencies of participants plays out in various ways, much of which can compromise and derail the learning experience for the broader group. This risk was mitigated by working with an organisation like Pure, based in Cape Town, with its sophisticated talent-mining tools, which proved to be invaluable in assessing and selecting candidates.

3. **Industry challenges/projects:** Collaboration with the sector was essential in determining industry-appropriate projects for the ILDP participants to tackle. A SETA-like structure, with its deep reaches into the sector, facilitates this process. In addition to the more typical criteria for action learning projects, the following principles are important in the selection of industry challenges:

- Applicability to the sector as a whole; solutions and recommendations must provide value for a wide group of industry stakeholders.

- It must not encroach on the 'Chinese walls' that need to be clearly defined in a cross-sector developmental initiative. Participants need to understand early on in the process how to differentiate between information that is strategic and competitive to their own organisations, and that which is in the general industry's domain and interest.

4. **Action coaching:** Outcomes are stronger when participants and syndicates are supported with action coaching. This typically comprised two to three one-on-one coaching sessions with each participant, and regular coaching and reflection sessions with the team throughout the programme. Information available from the selection process as well as additional assessment such as the Meyers-Briggs Type Indicator proved invaluable.

Table 1 describes the types of experiences typically included in each ILDP, and the value each of these experiences offers.

Table 1: Examples of International Leadership Development Programme Experiences

Activity	Value
Retail safari/scavenger hunt: A two- to three-hour ethnographic excursion to a diverse set of retailers. Participants are set up in competing teams and given a set of tasks they need to complete. Extra points are earned for novel interactions with customers and retail staff, as well as any special memorabilia the team collects en route.	• Best practices observed and, more importantly, directly experienced. • Provides benchmarks for their own organisation's performance as well as the overall industry. • Direct interaction with consumers results in new insights. • New ideas that can be adapted and applied back in their own organisation. • Team building. • Affirmational – participants become aware of how well their own organisations and the country are performing.

Activity	Value
Diplomatic and trade personnel: Interactive exchanges with senior South African diplomatic and trade personnel at formal receptions, networking events and informal meetings.	• Increased appreciation for the realities of promoting the country internationally. • Exposure to South African leaders in high-profile, global positions. • Increased awareness of international trade opportunities for the country's retail sector.
Industry associations: Meetings with key industry associations.	• Greater appreciation for the contribution that effective industry bodies make to the prosperity and sustainability of a sector. • Understanding of the value of collaboration in the industry. • Increasing awareness of the more 'externally facing' role executives have to assume as they move up in seniority in their organisations.
Thought leaders: Briefings from thought leaders with expertise in, and perspectives on, both retail and other critical business such as talent, innovation, enabling technology, and others.	• Insight into major global and regional trends impacting business today and in the future. • Appreciation for the external landscape and how this impacts the participant's own business. • New ideas and best practices that can be applied to action learning projects.
Leader-to-leader dialogues: Interactive exchanges with senior leaders from organisations, both within the retail sector and from other industries.	• Better understanding of how senior executives manage their business realities. • Gain new insights across a broad spectrum of topics that can be applied to participants' own businesses. • Directly experience leadership in action. • Energise and revitalises participants' thinking and ideas.
Industry challenge exchanges: Meetings with executives in organisations that are able to provide insight into the specific topic area of the industry challenge.	• Provides practice and usable new insights and breakthrough thinking on the industry challenges. • Heightens awareness of being more externally focused.

Activity	Value
NGO (nongovernmental organisation) experiences: Meeting with leading NGOs in the region to understand the broader needs of the community and how these are being addressed.	• Heightens awareness for the broader role of a leader in their community. • Provides a different lens on leadership from successful and inspiring NGO leaders.

The ILDP has proven to be a highly successful and pragmatic way to build the leadership pipeline in the retail and wholesale sector in South Africa. It has:

1. Increased the talent pipeline of highly promotable, future leaders.

2. Created 'stickiness' to the sector. (The ILDP has become fairly high profile in the sector and is creating an effective talent retention and acquisition tool.)

3. Created 'champions' for the sector: highly visible, successful young leaders who are able to influence other young leaders.

4. Progressed thinking on key industry topics and brought best practices, new ideas and revitalised thinking back to the sector.

5. Created awareness of the South African wholesale and retail sector internationally and potentially created new business opportunities.

In addition, the South African retail and wholesale sector has benefited from having some of its brightest emerging talent provide their insights into, and recommendations on, strategic and relevant business issues from best practices on loss prevention, to multichannel retailing, and sustainability practices for small, medium and micro enterprise (SMME) retailers, to customer centricity and serving the connected social shopper, amongst others. Reporting out to an impressive guest list of senior executives in the sector in a formal setting provides the ideal platform for these young leaders to showcase their learning and growth. Always well received, the quote below captures the feeling of one of the key sponsors of the programme.

> I felt it necessary to write this note to you regarding your International Leadership Development Programme (ILDP) and the impact it has had on our candidate. I have just listened to our candidate's group presentation at Emperors Palace and I have been 'blown away' by his obvious growth. To see him stand up in front of a room full of strangers and confidently introduce his team and his team's presentation is testament to this. The ILDP has transformed this young man, possibly more than any other candidate over its two-year existence, and, for this, we salute you all. This, after all, is surely what the ILDP is all about. Once again, our sincere thanks and we hope to be associated with the ILDP for as

long as the programme exists. – Human Resources (HR) Executive from one of the sponsoring retailers.

Other In-Market Action Learning Examples

The following thumbnail points describe how some of our clients have applied In-Market Action Learning. These illustrations are provided to demonstrate how both organisations in developing markets as well as global enterprises are using In-Market Action Learning to achieve their learning objectives.

- **Changing culture:** In 2004, like many banks at the time, a leading African retail bank was heavily focused on shifting its auditing-oriented culture to a more dynamic, customer-focused sales culture. A business challenge, crafted around this theme, was incorporated into one of its leadership development initiatives targeting mid-level management. One of the three residential sessions was spent in-market in New York, an overwhelmingly rich environment in which to understand effective selling and the demands being made on consumers' attention. Participants spent the week meeting with executives from within and outside the banking industry to get new ideas on how to shift culture and better understand the realities of creating and leading sales teams. Particularly powerful was a field experience where each of the participants was asked to go onto the streets of New York and 'sell' small bracelets made by local African women – a fundraising initiative the bank had been using in its home market. Participants were divided into small teams and tasked with having to sell the bracelets on a busy, hot afternoon in Manhattan. The winning team raised over $1 000, but the real win of the day was the tangible shift in consciousness and awareness of the challenges associated with the act of selling. The debrief and reflection session at the end of the day was particularly powerful, with participants sharing both the difficulties and the fun they had with the assignment. There was a newfound appreciation for the challenges their salespeople face every day in the branches and a renewed energy for making the transition less painful for their staff. A note in closing – as long as you don't set up a permanent structure (a blanket on the ground in Manhattan is considered such a structure), you aren't considered to be transgressing the law in any major way. Fortunately, our friends at the New York Police Department promised to turn a blind eye that day, and they did.

- **Entering new markets or developing new offerings:** Immersion, in the form of In-Market Action Learning, can accelerate understanding of the opportunities and challenges in a specific market. The year 2011 was a pivotal point for a European multinational's senior leaders when the company ran a residential session in India aimed at increasing their understanding and appreciation of the business realities in which they have growing business interests. For many of their executives, this was a first visit to Mumbai and the programme was designed to optimise out-of-class, direct experiences to ensure the impact was memorable and sustainable. Creating an understanding of Indian consumers was achieved through an afternoon of ethnographic experiences. In smaller teams, participants visited consumers' homes in slums and middle-class areas, as well as observing and interacting with a diverse set of retailers from bottom-of-the-pyramid to emerging middle-class and wealthier neighbourhoods. We tapped into one of our all-time favourite companies and spent an afternoon with HCL Technologies, learning about building high-engagement cultures and best practices in talent management in India so well captured in its best seller, *Employees First; Customers Second*[5]. Smaller teams spent one day meeting with senior executives from the Indian greats – TATA and Reliance – and with other leaders from a diverse set of industries and organisations. It was a mind-shifting experience, with participants deepening their insights as well as clearly understanding the opportunities for their business and the leadership challenges associated with doing business in a fast-growing country like India. More importantly, they witnessed and experienced Indian leadership with its wisdom, patience and long-term view of success and came away inspired by the sophisticated business practices they found in India.

- **Shifting mind-sets through applied best-practice benchmarking:** A leading, global pharmaceutical client has successfully incorporated one-day, in-market experiences into many of its enterprise-level leadership development initiatives. Building on this idea, it took the concept to its local Chinese team, which dedicated one day of a four-day residential session to learning from successful local and multinational businesses in and around Shanghai. Teams were tasked with bringing back insights and best practices on innovation, talent engagement and customer centricity from some of the world's top organisations. They were asked to answer the all-important question, "So what?", and to develop some initiatives based on the implications they identified. A very robust debrief at the end of the day provided some excellent recommendations for the way forward, again proving the usefulness of connecting people and ideas in a value-driven discussion.

- **Solving a strategic business challenge:** A senior executive, who had been newly appointed by a leading emerging-market bank, approached us some years ago

---

5   'Employee First; Customer Second' is a management philosophy espoused by HCL Technologies, the India-based global information technology services company. It was the brainchild of Vineet Nayar, CEO of HCL Technologies, who also authored the book by the same name – *Employees First, Customers Second: Turning Conventional Management Upside Down* (Harvard Business Press, June 2010). He hosts two blogs, one at *Harvard Business Review*, and the other at http://www.vineetnayar.com.

with a challenge. He had been chartered to build the bank's capability around strategic partnering and alliances, an area of expertise lacking in the organisation, which was more accustomed to handling mergers and acquisitions. This was considered to be an essential skill set to acquire as the bank launched itself on a highly ambitious growth trajectory. Our client had a strong preference for tackling the job of discovering best practice and figuring out how to apply it to the bank, on his own. He wanted to talk to real leaders about their experiences in this area and learn more about what worked and what didn't. The road trip he embarked upon was arduous – two weeks, starting in London, for discussions with a minimum of three organisations a day, to New York and then on to Silicon Valley, the heartbeat of collaboration and partnering. He met with a diverse array of strategic alliance professionals in retail, information and communications technology (ICT), banking and pharmaceuticals. Ten days later, the business plan was wrapped and he and his sparring partner, a direct report, flew home. The business plan was presented to the bank's CEO two days after their return, and, five years later, it has been only marginally tweaked. One of the initiatives that was launched as a result of the bank's new strategic alliance capability is today the market-leading mortgage company in the country.

- **Doing business in an emerging market – some examples of First World firms appreciating emerging-market realities:**

  - A visit to one of India's leading, fast-moving consumer goods (FMCG) firms reveals an unmatched capability to sell and distribute over-the-counter products to the 'bottom of the pyramid' in urban and rural India. Our client is shaken to learn this capability is being deployed in other emerging markets in which it is active. The big realisation is that successful emerging-market players are better equipped to win in markets our client is targeting – along with the awareness that this is competition that it isn't even tracking.

  - Frugal innovation[6] (TATA with Ginger Hotels and NANO; microfinance across the world) again reveals unique capabilities to create value at the bottom of the pyramid. The focus most Western companies have doing business in these markets is on premier and emerging middle-class segments; winning in other segments is going to prove challenging without a significant revamping of strategy, investment, and organisational design and capability.

---

6   "*Jugaad* is a Hindi colloquialism that refers to constraint-based innovation. While it may also be a way of life in India, where 'inventing what you need by using only what you have' is an imperative, it also has been the source of breakthroughs that have improved the lives of millions beyond India in the developing world." – Mitali Sharma, Accenture, India – *Innovation Management*'s issue dated 3 May 2012. Frugal innovation, or *Jugaad* as it is called in India, is best exemplified in TATA's innovation in hospitality with Ginger Hotels and in Automotive with the TATA NANO – a $2 100 car.

- Sociocultural differences are highlighted, particularly with regard to communication, where our Western colleagues begin to appreciate the many nuances of effective communication in cultures where nonverbal and other clues are more important to understanding the message being conveyed than the words being said. Relationship supersedes business deals. The perception of time and its impact on business decisions becomes a vigorous discussion, particularly in cultures embracing a more polychromic view of time. Unlike the North American approach, where time is systematically scheduled, organised and managed, there are cultures that are more fluid in their scheduling. This has immediate implications for their leaders, who hold a longer-term view of the organisation, its results and talent, resulting in a very different culture and climate in the organisation.

- For our Life Science clients, an immersion into a variety of healthcare settings in Africa, Asia and South America has proved vital in truly understanding the disparity of patient care and the challenges government, private sector and NGOs face in advocating for and delivering high-quality and effective patient care. From government to private sector, ambulatory clinics and traditional medicines, these experiences provide unique insights into the unmet needs in a country and the opportunities for innovative companies to create value.

- Unlocking and truly understanding the paradoxes of these countries is made possible with in-market immersions. Shifts in mind-set can be profound, especially when creating experiences that challenge participants' prevailing norms and beliefs. For example, a visit to a major slum such as Dharavi in Mumbai – a hive of economic activity, both formal and informal – creates the perfect platform for discussions about happiness, prosperity and aspiration, challenging the belief system of many of our Western colleagues. Inadequate infrastructure coexists with enormous wealth and success. Bureaucratic and unwieldy processes work side by side with agile, super-convenient service and systems. People living in poverty appear happy. Parents want the same things for their children – a good future, health and education. Basic infrastructure (roads, water and electricity) is unpredictable, but mobile phones are everywhere and the networks work faster and better than in many Western countries.

- Nothing beats a Beijing, Mumbai, São Paulo, Nairobi immersion for truly understanding the day-to-day challenges of going about your business in these cities. Congestion is extreme, traffic is unpredictable, roads are poor, and there is construction everywhere – again coexisting with some of the world's most impressive skyscrapers and expensive real estate.

In-Market Action Learning Essentials

Whether you plan to use In-Market Action Learning to develop new business strategies, transfer best practices or develop your talent, there are a few key considerations to keep in mind:

1. Selection of In-Market business challenges or themes: This process clearly varies, dependent on the overall programme objective and structure. For larger executive development programmes, business challenges will likely already be a key part of the programme design. For one-day programmes, in-market themes should be broad and address issues the organisation is currently prioritising. The list below reflects common themes that were top-of-mind for organisations in 2011:

    *   Building high-engagement cultures.
    *   Talent innovation.
    *   Creating a culture of innovation.
    *   Growth through collaboration and strategic alliances.
    *   Leading in high-growth markets.
    *   Brand building in high-growth markets.
    *   Customer centricity.
    *   Managing the external environment.

2. Designing the immersion: The intent in designing an in-market immersion is to optimise the diversity of perspectives the group is able to obtain. To illustrate: if one of the themes is Brand Building in high-growth markets, it is very effective to expose participants to both successful domestic brands as well as multinational brands being tailored to suit local consumers' taste and reverse engineered into the corporate portfolio. In the talent sphere, it is always effective to meet emerging talent to hear their views on employers of choice and their career aspirations. To the extent that it is possible, include 'ethnographic' experiences where teams are able to directly observe and interact with key consumers, customers and other key stakeholders in their value chain.

3. In-Market team composition: Teams are optimised for diversity (functional, gender, experience, and function). Avoid having subject-matter experts on the team.

4. Preparing participants for In-Market immersions: The key to a successful In-Market is ensuring that participants appreciate that they are embarking on an insight-discovery process; the success of which is directly correlated to their own behaviour. Staying intellectually curious, being open to new ideas, reflecting on these, and being prepared to consider the implications of these insights for their own businesses, positively impacts the richness of the experience.

5. The role of the coach: The role of the coach in In-Market Action Learning can be somewhat more interventionist than in classic action learning. Whether in large multiday or one-day immersions, the coach has to rapidly use his or her observations of the participants and team to feed back into the learning process. Coaches may also have to play a 'business' coaching role, supporting participants as they think through the implications of what they have learnt in-market. This dictates the need for a new breed of coaches who are more business-savvy and can be more relevant in strategic conversations.

The DNA of Externally-facing Organisations

In-Market immersions only happen because of the willingness of outside organisations to meet with others. So what are the attributes that exist in companies that are willing, completely on a goodwill basis, to meet with relative strangers and share their insights and experiences? These organisations are also time-pressured, so how come they appreciate the value of dialogue with less-typical partners and agree to host meetings regularly? What is the culture that exists in these companies that routinely externalise their perspective, both sharing and soliciting insights and market intelligence in these immersive exchanges?

Our team tried to find some common attributes in the organisations that appeared, at least at first blush, to be very externally focused. Five common attributes started to emerge:

•   **Open and accessible:** Leaders in these organisations can be easily contacted; their public profiles are updated and available, and support staff facilitate access to them. In fact, one of the most remarkable impressions we have of India is the accessibility of their senior executives, especially C-Suite, and their generous willingness to give of their time.

•   **Content:** These organisations have areas of expertise that are recognised over and above their core business. They have a strong point of view on these skill sets and a systemic approach to honing these capabilities in their organisation (think 3M on Innovation; Cisco on Collaboration and Strategic Partnering; HCL Technologies on Employee Engagement).

•   **Innovative:** More often than not, these companies are innovators. Each of them has examples in their own business of a new business model, disrupting current mainstream players, new delivery models, and product innovation, amongst others. Interestingly, many of them, particularly the younger firms, did not even think about innovation as a unique capability. It's embedded.

•   **Entrepreneurial:** Large or small, our top In-Market partners maintain an entrepreneurial spirit. The tension of risk and initiative is effortlessly balanced with organisation and structure. Ideas flourish in an empowered and engaged culture.

- **Inspiring leaders:** No surprises here. Participants return from meetings with our favourite In-Market partners, energised and inspired. Leaders from these organisations walk-the-walk and demonstrate a high alignment with their organisation's values and their own behaviour.

We ranked our top five 2011 'outside-in' organisations against this list of criteria as being:

1. Cisco.

2. HCL Technologies.

3. 3M.

4. Impact India.

5. Mandarin Oriental.

Concluding Comments

In describing those returning from In-Market immersions, participants use words like 'energised, revitalised, transformed, enriched'. The business results range from the very concrete (such as an action plan to tackle a strategic challenge) to less measurable, but equally important, transformations in the organisation's culture and its leadership – more innovation, creativity unleashed, greater customer focus, more attuned to the market and prepared to seize opportunities.

As Jack Welch said, "the hero is the person with a new idea"[7]. In-Market Action Learning will invigorate your team's thinking, breathe new energy into your business, and refresh creativity and ideas.

---

7   Jack Welch, speech, General Electric Annual Meeting, Charlotte, North Carolina, 23 April 1997.

References

Building the Untethered Organization – Microsoft White Paper. http://ebookbrowse.com/building-the-untethered-organization-pdf-d107720968.

Innovation Management. 3 May 2012.

International Institute of Management Education: http://www.iim-edu.org/managementgurus/Reg_Revans.htm.

Jobs, S. February 1995. Creativity. *Wired.*

Nayar, V. 2010. *Employees First, Customers Second: Turning Conventional Management Upside Down.* Harvard Business Press.

Welch, J. 23 April 1997. Speech delivered to General Electric Annual Meeting. Charlotte, North Carolina.

6

PERFORMANCE MANAGEMENT AND REWARDING TALENT IN EMERGING MARKETS

Dr Mark Bussin

1. Introduction

A particularly crucial part of successful talent management in emerging markets involves setting up appropriate performance management, remuneration and benefit structures. Employees are hired by organisations for the purpose of performance. The nature of the performance varies, but the expectation of compensation in exchange for performance does not. Just as employees have a right to expect to be paid for the work they perform, so organisations have a right to measure performance and reward employees commensurately with this measurement. The apparent simplicity of this quid pro quo relationship is dispelled when one delves a little deeper and starts to question how performance is measured, and what qualifies as fair/appropriate remuneration. The complexities become even more pronounced when considering the differing local-versus-expatriate pay universes and cross-cultural differences in seeking to understand what constitutes both performance and value for organisations and employees. This chapter examines the importance of performance management and describes how to set up a balanced, equitable – yet competitive – reward and remuneration system in an emerging-market context.

2. Global Practices *or* the Need to Contextualise/Localise

Some experts argue that globalisation has been a contributor to convergence of managerial mind-set and practice. Others suggest that there is a need to contextualise human resource management practices for the country and company. In this case, the following factors need to be considered:

- National culture across countries and differences in values across societies. This has a bearing on whether to lean towards, for example, 360-degree feedback or traditional performance feedback by the manager – or whether to focus on individual or team incentives.

- Employee attitude to performance management, and collective versus individual outlook.

- Industry type and job family category have a bearing, because certain processes lend themselves better to certain industries and job families. For example, consulting companies are more likely to measure contribution, outputs and billing.

- The extent to which the chief executive officer (CEO) owns the performance management process. In high-performing organisations, CEOs own the performance management system and use it to drive organisation strategy.

The suggested approach, especially for multinational companies (MNCs), is to use a hybrid approach of providing the international or corporate framework, but guiding organisations on how to adapt it for local circumstances. In my experience of having worked in 23 countries across all continents, there is one golden rule – keep the performance management and reward system simple and easy to explain and understand. Do not overcomplicate the process or the system.

The text that follows is intended to provide practical building blocks, much like Lego where you can build your own system, but based on good practice and best fit.

In emerging markets, there is the opportunity to take the best practices and lessons learnt from developed economies and improve on them. Similarly, one has the opportunity not to adopt the strategies and systems that did not work. Set out below is a description of some of the global practices that have been adopted in many emerging markets because they work there, plus strategies and practices that may be unique to emerging markets. There are many emerging-market practices that could be exported to developed economies, but that is a subject for another place. Recommendations are made along the way.

3. Performance Management

Organisations have traditionally focused on the process of **performance evaluation**, which is effectively the measurement or appraisal of performance. In the last two decades, the concept of **performance management** has emerged, which adopts a future-oriented strategic focus aimed at maximising current performance and future potential. Performance management extends beyond the concept of performance appraisal and refers to the system or framework through which organisations set work goals, determine performance standards, assign and evaluate work, provide performance feedback by means of performance appraisals or formal reviews, determine training and development needs, and distribute rewards.[1]

The conceptual foundation of performance management relies on a view that performance is more than ability and motivation. Clarity of goals is seen as key in motivating and helping employees understand what is expected of them. The objectives of performance management often include: motivating performance, helping individuals develop their skills, building a performance culture, determining who should be promoted, exiting individuals who are poor performers, and helping implement business strategies.[2] Performance management supports the overall business goals by linking the work of every individual employee and the manager to

---

1   Briscoe & Claus (2008).

2   Lawler (2000).

the overall mission of his or her work unit. When employees are clear about what is expected of them and have the necessary support, their sense of purpose, self-worth and motivation increase.[3]

Performance management establishes an organisational culture in which all employees take responsibility for the continuous improvement of their performance. The main purpose of appraising and coaching employees is thus to instil in them the desire for continuous improvement.[4]

3.1 Performance Appraisal

To be effective, performance appraisal and measurement should form an integral part of the overall performance management system of the company. Organisations use performance appraisals to formally assess and evaluate employees' job performance. They provide the opportunity for employees and managers to sit down and have a dialogue about performance and development at least twice a year. Appraisals look back over the past year to review performance and objectives, then look forward to set objectives and targets for the next year and to identify learning and development needs to improve performance.[5]

Within a performance appraisal, performance should be assessed on the basis of predetermined organisational standards. This allows for a comparative and normative assessment of individuals and productivity. The assessment, in turn, functions as the foundation for pay increases and promotions, provides feedback to help improve performance and recognise weaknesses, and offers information about the attainment of work goals.

The nature of performance appraisal causes it to be a management activity fraught with difficulties. There is a personal nature to assessing or rating the work efforts of another human being that is difficult to overcome, and, in a sense, performance appraisal should be a personal as opposed to an impersonal experience for employees. Most employees want to feel that their efforts are noticed and appreciated by their organisations. The manager must therefore maintain a fine balance between being a counsellor or coach and a fair judge of employee performance.

3.2 Performance Management Challenges in Emerging Markets

Multinational enterprises in emerging markets are increasingly using cross-cultural virtual and situational teams to increase speed in launching products to market and in bringing together employees from different locations, functional areas, and cultural perspectives. While the diversity of this type of workforce is a significant source

---

3   Costello (1994).

4   Latham, Almost, Mann & Moore (2005).

5   Porter, Bingham & Simmonds (2008).

of competitive advantage, the impact of geographic spread and cultural diversity also presents many challenges to conventional management practices. For example, there can be significant differences in how individuals in different cultures provide and seek performance feedback.[6] The definition of what constitutes performance and the consequences of poor performance are also varied.[7]

The Western concept of performance management may not always suit other cultures. The manager–subordinate relationship is often a point of contention owing to power distance or discomfort with critical feedback. For example, Chinese culture sometimes shows a preference for group-oriented appraisals rather than individual assessment; and, in India, it may be inappropriate and disrespectful to disagree with one's supervisor.[8]

One of the purposes of global performance management is to build and maintain a strong, overarching, integrative corporate culture.[9] To achieve this corporate culture, a thorough acknowledgement and understanding of the diversity of local cultures are essential. Training for managers about how to utilise global performance management systems, including diversity and cultural competency, is vital; otherwise, implementation could well be a waste of time and money.[10] Adequate training must be provided for both the appraiser and the appraisee in order to avoid the many rating errors that are common in performance appraisal. Training should include cultural, legal and customer differences by country, providing managers with the tools to improve on the process. Managers must also be given the opportunity to build the required relationship with their employees.[11]

3.3 Characteristics of Performance Management

Performance management is not an appraisal event, but an ongoing process involving performance planning, feedback, evaluation and development. The emphasis is on providing employees with feedback on their success in achieving specific performance goals and expectations, as well as on their ability to develop core competencies and skills.[12] The three core phases of the performance management cycle are illustrated in figure 1.

3.3.1 Performance Planning Phase

The performance planning phase refers to the confirmation of business performance

---

6 Milliman, Taylor & Czaplewski (2002).

7 Evans et al. (2002).

8 Evans, Pucik & Barsoux 2002; Cascio (2006).

9 Hellqvist (2011).

10 Cascio (2006).

11 Appelbaum, Roy & Gilliland (2011:570).

12 Chingos & Marwick (1997).

goals, technical/functional knowledge areas and behavioural competencies used to measure job performance. The planning phase starts before the period over which performance is measured. It involves identifying applicable performance criteria that link to the organisation's business plan, and defining success at varying levels of the organisation.

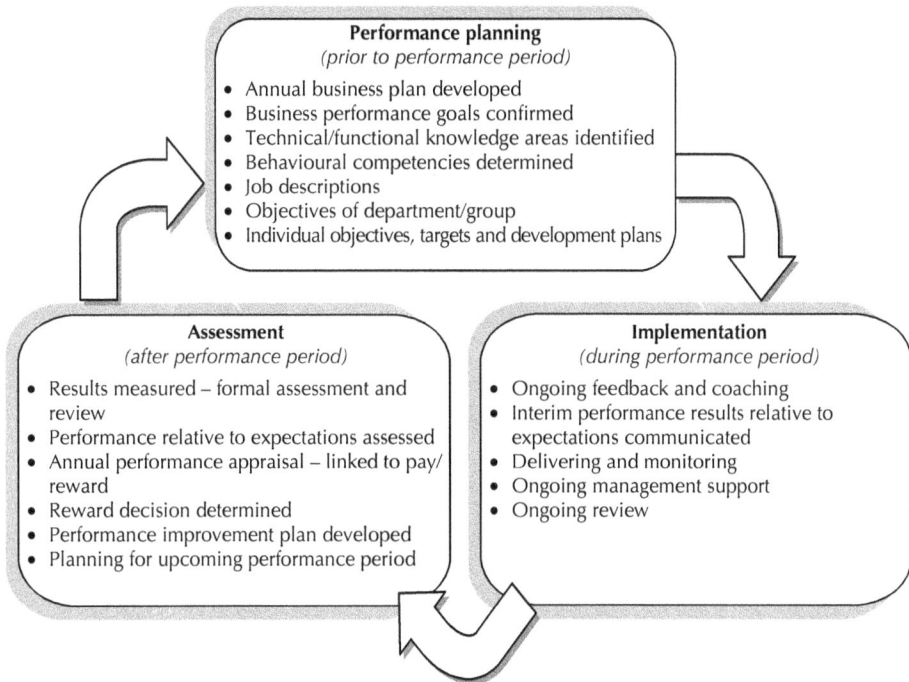

Performance planning
(prior to performance period)

- Annual business plan developed
- Business performance goals confirmed
- Technical/functional knowledge areas identified
- Behavioural competencies determined
- Job descriptions
- Objectives of department/group
- Individual objectives, targets and development plans

Assessment
(after performance period)

- Results measured – formal assessment and review
- Performance relative to expectations assessed
- Annual performance appraisal – linked to pay/reward
- Reward decision determined
- Performance improvement plan developed
- Planning for upcoming performance period

Implementation
(during performance period)

- Ongoing feedback and coaching
- Interim performance results relative to expectations communicated
- Delivering and monitoring
- Ongoing management support
- Ongoing review

Figure 1: The Performance Management Cycle[13]

This process of performance planning is most effective when there is broad employee participation. It requires the manager and the employee to get together for a performance planning meeting where they discuss what the person will achieve over the next 12 months (the key responsibilities of the person's job and the goals and projects the person will work on) and how the person will do the job (the behaviours and competencies the organisation expects of its members).[14]

Translating organisational objectives into individual performance targets and responsibilities begins with accountability. In the context of performance management, a key accountability is simply an area of responsibility for which the employee is expected to produce results. Each job holder, regardless of current levels of performance, can achieve better results if behavioural objectives based on personal development are built into the planning process.

---

13 Costello (1994).

14 Chingos & Marwick (1997); Grote (2002).

3.3.2 *Implementation Phase*

The implementation phase is ongoing throughout the performance period. It emphasises opportunities for informal feedback and coaching by managers to improve and develop employees' job performance. In this regard, feedback is important, because employees want to know how they are doing relative to performance expectations. The most significant aspect of this phase is the opportunity for enhancing communication and interaction between managers and employees throughout the performance period.

3.3.3 *Results Assessment Phase*

The results assessment phase typically occurs at the end of the performance period. At this time, results on all dimensions are evaluated relative to expectations, and a performance improvement plan is developed. This phase serves two main purposes. The first is to determine the appropriate employee reward system linkages such as annual cash incentive payouts, base salary increases, and general development and training needs. Secondly, it contributes to planning for the upcoming performance period by highlighting necessary adjustments to business performance goals, functional knowledge areas and behavioural competencies that may be necessary in response to changing job and organisational requirements.[15]

3.4 Developing a Performance Appraisal System

The performance appraisal system forms an integral part of the overall performance management framework of the organisation. The development of a formal performance appraisal system can be divided into 10 interrelated phases (see figure 2) similar to the performance management process, the development of a performance appraisal process is an **ongoing process** – every time there are changes in the organisation's focus that influence personnel practices, the performance appraisal process should be reviewed and the necessary changes should be implemented.

---

15 Chingos & Marwick (1997).

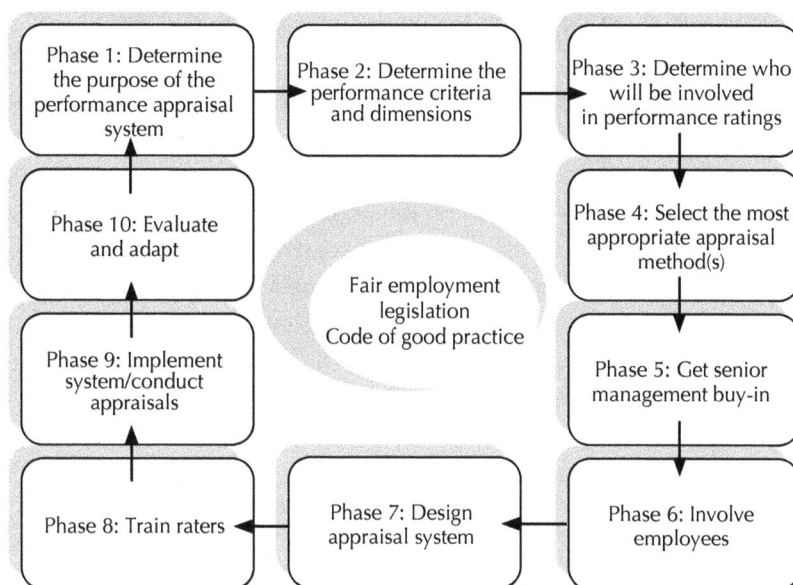

Figure 2: Phases in Developing a Performance Appraisal System[16]

Performance appraisal information can be used for **three broad purposes** in the organisation.[17] **Firstly**, it can be used to make personnel decisions regarding matters such as salary increases, incentive payments, promotion and demotion, and even dismissal. When performance appraisal information is used to make personnel decisions, employees are often compared with one another. Someone may be promoted to the managerial position because he or she had a higher performance rating.

Secondly, performance appraisal information can be used to identify employee strengths and weaknesses. This can assist the manager or employee to identify performance problems and produce personal development plans to address these performance problems. The purpose is to change or reinforce behaviour, not to compare employees' work behaviour.[18] Information on an employee's job-related strengths and weaknesses can be utilised in the **third** broad category of performance appraisal information uses, which is employee career planning and development, including further training and development. If managers/supervisors know what their employees' strengths and weaknesses are, and employees know how they want their careers to progress, the performance appraisal information can provide valuable information on what employees need to do in terms of further training and development to move on to the next step in the career plan.

---

16 Bussin & Botha (2010).

17 Bussin & Botha (2010).

18 Mathis & Jackson (2004).

3.5 Performance Appraisal Methods

There are many different performance appraisal methods in use today. As shown in table 1, the different methods can be grouped into six broad categories: performance can be assessed by using objective methods, subjective methods, comparative methods, rating methods, goal-based methods, and methods of computerised performance monitoring. Each set of methods uses different performance dimensions and/or different ways to collect and interpret the performance information in order to produce a performance rating for every employee. It is essential to ensure that employee job performance is measured using valid and culturally relevant performance criteria and standards for each performance dimension.

Table 1: Categories of Performance Appraisal Methods[19]

Common Categories	Typical Methods
Objective methods	• Quantity of work • Quality of work • Attendance • Safety • Critical incidents
Subjective (judgemental) methods	• Essays • Narratives
Comparative methods	• Ranking • Paired comparisons • Forced-distribution
Rating methods	• Graphic rating scales • Behavioural check lists • Frequency of desired behaviours • Behaviourally anchored rating scales (BARS) • Behavioural observation scales (BOS)
Goal-based methods	• Management by objectives (MBO) • Balanced scorecard • Outputs
Computerised performance monitoring	• Electronic performance monitoring and evaluation

It is important to note that no single performance appraisal method is suitable for all jobs and situations. Therefore it may be more appropriate to use a combination

---

19 Bussin & Botha (2010).

of methods. The most successful implementations have involved the concept of setting objectives or preferably outputs, within key result areas (KRAs) and key result indicators (KRIs). A five-point rating scale is most commonly used with the following descriptors, with approximate, desired distribution of scores in brackets:

1. Far exceeds expectations (15%).

2. Exceeds expectations (25%).

3. Meets expectations (40%).

4. Meets some expectations (15%).

5. Does not meet expectations (5%).

3.6 Raters of Performance

The most common method of rating performance is still the manager rating the subordinate.

The use of **multisource (360-degree)** feedback is becoming more popular. With this approach, performance information is collected from managers, supervisors, peers, customers and subordinates. The information from all these sources is collated, provided for the employee and discussed with the manager. The employee and manager collaborate to compile a personal development plan to address any weaknesses that are identified. Multisource feedback is more effective when all the participants know that the information will be used for development purposes and not for making promotion or salary increase decisions. In some organisations, it may be essential to guarantee that raters will remain anonymous, although this may have a negative influence on the ability of multisource feedback to improve organisational communication.

Not only can the appraisal instrument assess the wrong performance dimensions, it can also unintentionally drive the wrong behaviours. A good example of this is the parable of the beekeepers described below.

Show Me the Honey!

Once upon a time in Yemen, there were two beekeepers, each of whom had a beehive. The beekeepers worked for a company called YemBees Ltd. The company's customers loved its honey and the business aimed to produce more honey than it had the previous year. As a result, each beekeeper was told to produce more honey of the same quality. With different ideas about how to do this, the beekeepers designed different approaches to improve the performance of their hives.

YemBees – Beekeeper One

The first beekeeper established a bee performance management approach that measured how many flowers each bee visited. At considerable cost to the beekeeper, an extensive measurement system was created to count the flowers each bee visited. The beekeeper provided feedback for each bee at midseason on his individual performance, but the bees were never told about the hive's goal to produce more honey so that YemBees Ltd could increase honey sales. The beekeeper created incentives in the form of special awards for the bees who visited the most flowers.

YemBees – Beekeeper Two

The second beekeeper also established a bee performance management system, but this approach communicated to each bee the goals of the hive – to produce more honey. This beekeeper and his bees measured two aspects of their performance: the amount of nectar each bee brought back to the hive and the amount of honey the hive produced. The performance of each bee and the hive's overall performance were charted and posted on the hive's bulletin board for all bees to see. The beekeeper created a few awards for the bees that gathered the most nectar, but he also established a hive incentive programme that rewarded each bee in the hive based on the hive's production of honey – the more honey produced, the more recognition each bee would receive.

YemBees – Performance Prediction

What do you think might have happened to each hive at the end of the season when the Queen Bee would report back to each beekeeper?

YemBees Beekeeper One at the End of the Season

The first beekeeper found that his hive had indeed increased the number of flowers visited, but the amount of honey produced by the hive had dropped. The Queen Bee reported that, because the bees were so busy trying to visit as many flowers as possible, they limited the amount of nectar they would carry so they could fly faster. Also, because the bees felt they were competing against one another for awards (because only the top performers were recognised), they would not share valuable information with one another, like the location of the flower-filled fields they'd spotted on the way back to the hive that could have helped improve the performance of all the bees. After all was said and done, one of the high-performing bees told the beekeeper that if he'd been told that the real goal was to make more honey rather than to visit more flowers, he would have done his work completely differently.

As the beekeeper handed out the awards to individual bees, unhappy buzzing was heard in the background.

YemBees Beekeeper Two at the End of the Season

The second beekeeper, however, had very different results. Because each bee in his hive was focused on the hive's goal of producing more honey, the bees had concentrated their efforts on gathering more nectar to produce more honey than ever before. The bees worked together to determine the highest nectar-yielding flowers and to create quicker processes for depositing the nectar they'd gathered. They also worked together to help increase the amount of nectar gathered by the poor performers. The Queen Bee of this hive reported that the poor performers either improved their performance or transferred to another hive.

Because the hive had reached its goal, the beekeeper awarded each bee his portion of the hive incentive payment. The beekeeper was also surprised to hear a loud, happy buzz and a jubilant flapping of wings as he rewarded the individual high-performing bees with special recognition.

The Moral of This Story Is:

Design your systems carefully, because they will affect the behaviour of your staff. Measuring and recognising accomplishments rather than activities – and providing feedback for your **'worker bees'** – can often improve the results of the hive.[20]

3.7 Performance Appraisal Interviews

The performance appraisal interview is essentially an interactive conversation between a manager and his or her employee. At this interview, the manager communicates his or her perception of the level of job performance to the employee – whether the job performance exceeds expectations, or not, and to produce action plans that will lead to improved job performance, where necessary. A proposed structure for a performance interview is included in table 2.

---

20 Nixon (2011).

Table 2: A Proposed Structure for a Performance Appraisal Interview[21]

Purpose	Discuss the purpose of the performance appraisal system and the interview with the employee. Provide the employee with the opportunity to indicate what he or she wants to achieve in the interview.
Employee's views on performance for the past review period	Employee is requested to provide his or her own interpretation of his or her work performance of the past review period. Afford enough time to provide the necessary detail required to assess performance fairly.
Manager's views on employee job performance	The manager indicates how he or she perceived employee's job performance, substantiating perceptions with appropriate examples where possible. Indicates where he or she agrees and disagrees with employee's perceptions, and discusses issues where improvements are required.
Discussion of performance rating, using the performance appraisal instrument	Explain rating for each performance dimension and reason for providing said rating, afford employee opportunity to agree or disagree, and, finally, agree on a rating. Agree on an overall rating if one is required.
Discussion of action plans to improve job performance	Solicit suggestions from employee on job performance areas that need improvement, make own suggestions, and agree with employee on which suggestions to implement.
Discussion of action plans for employee development	Afford employee opportunity to state career goals and how he or she thinks these goals can be met. Agree on action plans for career development and suggest ways in which they can be implemented.
Discussion of performance objectives/goals for the next review period (if required by the system)	Agree performance goals for the next review period with employee if required by the appraisal system. Goals must be realistic, challenging, measureable and relevant.

Tips for conducting an effective performance appraisal interview include the following:

- Use the 'sandwich' technique. Mention areas in need of improvement in the employee's work between positive aspects.

- Emphasise the reason for the appraisal.

- Give the employee enough opportunity to voice his or her opinion about the appraisal, for it might explain the reason for performance that does not meet the requirements.

---

21 Bussin & Botha (2010).

- Never get aggressive during an interview, irrespective of what an employee says. **STAY CALM.**

- Provide enough time for the employee to accept the appraisal – acceptance of criticism does not always come immediately.

- Do not try to convince the employee of anything while he or she is aggressive.

- If remarks in respect of personality are made, they should never be vague – say exactly what is meant and substantiate with examples.

- Show interest in employee's work-related problems.

- Provide positive criticism. If an area for improvement is discussed, offer a possible solution or an improvement of the method.

- Ensure that the employee understands that the appraisal of his or her performance can change the next time around, but that the onus to improve is upon him or her.

- Be willing to listen and discuss, but be very firm.

- Ensure that the employee understands what is expected of him or her.

- Do not be afraid to praise good performance, as it can improve the employee's work satisfaction and positively influence attitudes.

- End the interview with a summary of strengths and areas for improvement, and summarise the plan of action.

In emerging markets, it is the performance conversation that is important. The forms and pieces of paper that need to be completed should never hijack the conversation. Sometimes, the forms are so long and cumbersome that they do hijack the conversation, and then it becomes a one-way talking 'at' the employee. Keep the form succinct.

3.8 Using Performance Management to Retain Talent in Emerging Markets

Increased demand for the limited supply of talent in emerging markets has driven employee turnover rates into the double digits. By actively and consistently focusing on personal and professional development, performance management supports employees' efforts to improve themselves. Development is an extremely effective retention strategy – it can be more valuable to employees than higher compensation, because it keeps their skills competitive. It also shows employees the organisation is willing to invest in them, which can influence their loyalty.[22]

Historically, organisations in emerging markets have focused development primarily on improving technical skills. In order to encourage a broader approach,

---

22 Sherman Garr (2011).

organisations are now putting processes and structures in place that support development planning, and they are seeing positive results. For example, Accenture has created a development planning tool that recommends specific development activities for employees based on their performance appraisals. Development activities vary based on an employee's job family and level within the organisation. Focused development support is helping the organisation to more effectively retain the 6 000-plus new employees it hires annually in emerging markets.[23]

The trend is to strengthen the link between performance and reward. Whether it is done individually or as a team, division or organisation needs to be considered in the context of the country, culture and industry. The next section sets out reward practices appropriate for emerging markets. Emerging markets have adopted a hybrid approach to reward – some parts are best practice from developed economies and some have been 'home-grown'.

4. Reward and Remuneration

Organisational reward systems – both financial and nonfinancial – are key elements in a company's strategic approach to human resource management, as these can influence a number of human resource processes and practices aimed at attracting and retaining high-performing staff.[24] Research has shown that the types of reward offered to employees reduce labour turnover, have a motivational impact, and positively influence the company's organisational culture and bottom line.[25] Remuneration or compensation also matters, because money spent on salaries, benefits, and other forms of reward typically amounts to well over half an organisation's total costs. Reward and remuneration are therefore major determinants both of profitability and of competitive advantage for a company.[26]

4.1 Purpose of Reward and Remuneration

Employers utilise employee reward and remuneration to achieve the following organisational goals:[27]

- **Recruiting high-quality employees and retaining their services in the organisation.** Prospective employees compare pay scales and will most likely choose those jobs that offer the higher salary. Employees expect to be treated fairly by employers, and part of this perception of fairness is influenced by the equity (fairness) that exists in the compensation system.

---

23 Sherman Garr (2011).

24 Guthrie (2007); Rubino (2006).

25 Guthrie (2007); Marchington & Wilkinson (2008); Nelson & Spitzer (2003).

26 Torrington, Hall, Taylor & Atkinson (2009).

27 Gilman 2009; Torrington et al. (2009).

- **Improving employee performance.** Employees expect to receive a certain level of remuneration for exerting a certain level of discretionary effort. They also expect that the compensation they receive for exerting a specified or determined level of effort will be fair. When the organisation recognises hard work and excellent performance, employees will be more willing to exert higher levels of discretionary effort in the expectation that this will also be rewarded in future.

- **Ensuring fairness.** Employees expect congruence between their effort levels and the compensation they receive. They also compare their own efforts and rewards with those of their colleagues, as well as with those of employees in similar jobs in different organisations. When employees perceive incongruence between their effort levels and compensation or that of their colleagues or other employees with whom they compare their situations, they experience dissonance and will react to that dissonance by changing their effort, their perceptions of the reward or the people with whom they compare themselves, or by leaving the organisation.

  Organisations establish fairness in the pay structure by ensuring internal equity through job evaluation and by ensuring external equity through salary surveys.

- **Ensuring legal compliance.** Compensation consists of more than money. All countries have specific legislation and regulations that affect components of compensation such as leave, overtime pay, and minimum pay levels. Unions often have a profound influence on employee compensation, and applicable union agreements must be considered in the determination of a compensation strategy.

- **Controlling labour costs.** Employee remuneration is often one of the main cost items in the organisational budget. Ensuring a sustained competitive advantage means engaging the best talent, but ensuring sustained profitability means creating and implementing a compensation strategy that gets the best value for money. Labour costs consist of the number of employees and the hours they work, the average cash compensation paid, and the average benefit costs.[28] All three of these components can be controlled in order to keep labour costs in the affordable region, although the increased use of a variable pay component may make tight management of labour costs more difficult.

- **Motivating staff.** Reward and remuneration systems are often used to direct effort and enthusiasm in specific directions and to encourage particular types of employee behaviour that lead to improved organisational performance. People value and are motivated by different rewards for different reasons, and therefore reward systems must be diverse to accommodate different and changing employee needs. Reward systems must be comprehensive and based on realistic

---

28 Milkovich & Newman (2009).

analyses of employee needs and work situations. Intrinsic and extrinsic rewards influence an individual's motivation and job satisfaction.[29]

Studies show that nonfinancial reward initiatives which are aimed at strengthening employees' intrinsic motivation have a positive impact on performance.[30] These nonfinancial rewards fulfil employees' need for challenge, responsibility, decision making, variety, social recognition, and career opportunities, either alone or in conjunction with financial rewards.[31] Additional research also suggests that, whereas financial and other tangible incentives such as pay, benefits and praise may be more motivating in the short term, in the long run, nonfinancial incentives such as challenging and interesting tasks are more motivating.[32]

4.2 The Impact of Globalisation on Remuneration

The emergence of the global marketplace is having a profound impact on the traditional ways in which work is managed, as well as on how employees are remunerated, which raises the issue of global pay. More and more companies are doing business internationally, which implies that they have employees in various countries, but also implies a squeeze on profits caused by intensive local and global competition.[33] So far, there has been a strong perception that the ways in which pay is determined and delivered constitute a well-defined marketplace that reflects a common set of values unique to each country. This perception, however, has frequently not been based on reality, since pay practices vary widely, based on a number of variables such as industry, geographical location, company size, location of the parent company, where a company is in its growth cycle, and the degree of creativity or risk-taking a company may exhibit in dealing with local, traditional pay practices and statutory requirements.[34]

A number of progressive multinational companies have started to view the global marketplace within the context of the company's own strategic plans and response to competition on a global scale. Rather than focus on each country individually, these organisations look at the global marketplace and seek to develop synergistic approaches that maximise the best remuneration practices and apply them to the highest degree possible in local markets. Quality of products and services, increasing

---

29 Weiss (2001).

30 Peterson & Luthans (2006).

31 Armstrong & Murlis (1994); Luthans (2005); Odendaal (2009).

32 Arnolds & Venter (2007).

33 Dessler (2009).

34 Coleman (1999).

market share, and sustaining a competitive edge are core goals that trigger a high level of interest in creative approaches to remuneration.[35]

4.3 The Reward System

Reward management is a key element in the strategic approach to human resource management. The actual remuneration system may require adjustment to develop employee motivation, effort and performance. The total reward system is essential to effective reward management and is a significant part of the company's financial strategy.[36]

The reward practices and reward criteria must be linked with the organisation's performance appraisal system.[37] stipulates the following criteria for an effective reward system:

- Rewards should be clearly defined and consistent with other rewards for comparable work and expertise.

Remuneration in Emerging Markets

Talent in emerging markets is not cheap. Constraints in the talent market drive salary inflation that works in tandem with the upward wage pressure already present in rapidly expanding economies. During 2011, workers in the United States, Canada, and Western Europe experienced some of the world's lowest base salary increases, around 3%, while some of their peers in emerging markets enjoyed average salary increases of twice that rate or more. According to the ECA International Salary Trends Survey, in 2011 Latin America was expected to see the world's largest average salary increases, as much as 27% in Venezuela. Salaries across Asia Pacific were expected to rise on average by 6% during 2011, with the largest increases being awarded to employees in Vietnam, India and Indonesia, each with expected gains of 9% or more. In the Middle East, employees were expected to see salary increases of around 5% in Saudi Arabia and the United Arab Emirates. Eastern European workers saw average salary gains of nearly 5% as well, with employees in Russia, Romania and Bulgaria enjoying the region's largest gains.[38]

- Employees should be informed about what exactly they are being rewarded for (eg quality or performance or innovation).

- Rewards should differentiate between different levels of performance.

- The criteria for giving rewards should be accurately and comprehensively communicated across organisations to ensure that employees perceive the rewards to be equitably distributed.

---

35 Coleman (1999); Dessler (2009); Torrington et al. (2009).

36 Marchington & Wilkinson (2008).

37 Weiss (2001:117).

38 CTPartners (2011).

- The organisation's rewards must be comparable with those of the company's competitors.

- Rewards must fit individual needs, be high enough to provide personal satisfaction, satisfy high performers, be related to job satisfaction, be related to performance, and fit other organisational requirements (management style, structure, and strategy).

4.4 Reward Strategy

The **reward strategy** of an organisation informs all employees of the direction the organisation wishes to take on reward management. It also describes the types of rewards that are offered to support implementation of the organisational strategy and accomplishment of organisational goals.[39] The strategy provides a well-reasoned and action-based framework for developing reward policies, practices, and processes. It also differentiates the components of total rewards and is based on the needs and values of the organisation and its employees. The reward strategy ensures that the organisation is directing its reward investments appropriately to achieve the greatest impact.[40]

The **total reward framework** evolves from the organisation's reward, human resources, and organisation strategy. Effective reward strategies positively influence employee behaviours by incorporating extrinsic and intrinsic motivators. Employees receive tangible and intangible rewards in return for their performance, while making a meaningful contribution to the organisation. As the organisation succeeds, so does the employee, and vice versa.[41]

It is important that a reward system clearly states the company's value proposition.[42] A **value proposition** is an analysis and quantified review of benefits, costs and value that an organisation can deliver to customers and other constituent groups within and outside of the organisation. It is also a positioning of value, where **Value = benefits – cost** (cost includes risk). The **value proposition statements** are not communicated externally. Rather, it is the **messages** created out of the value proposition statement that are communicated externally. These can be used in a variety of ways, such as in marketing communications material or in sales proposals.[43] In the context of reward and remuneration, a company value proposition is generally used to position value to prospective employees when recruiting new people or for retaining and motivating existing employees. This is also sometimes called the **employee value**

---

39 Luthans (2005).

40 Armstrong (2006); Gross & Friedman (2007).

41 Luthans (2005).

42 Barnes, Blake & Pinder (2009).

43 Kaplan & Norton (2004).

proposition (EVP). Examples of marketing messages, communicated as part of EVPs, of several well-known organisations are included in table 3.

Table 3: Examples of Marketing Messages Communicated as Part of Employee Value Propositions

Organisation	Marketing Message Communicated as Part of EVP	Impact
McDonald's (Singapore)	'Every crew member can be a manager'	Empowers restaurant employees who wish to make McDonald's a long-term career and communicates career path and longevity as employee benefits.
Kotak Mahindra Bank (India)	Focus on Results Leadership Active Involvement/ Inclusiveness Maximum Challenge Entrepreneurial Creativity	The EVP is called 'the FLAME' and is designed to 'ignite the spirit within' employees. It communicates a workplace characterised by challenge, innovation and reward.
Hewlett Packard (global)	'Stretch Strive Succeed'	Communicates a workplace that is inspiring and challenging, and characterised by simplicity, clear direction, and success.

4.4.1 Reward Categories

WorldatWork, the largest global not-for-profit professional association dedicated to knowledge leadership in total rewards defines total rewards as containing five core reward categories, which are illustrated in the following model:

Figure 3 not only positions the total reward strategy within the context of the business, the human resources strategy, and the organisational culture, but also illustrates the five core categories of a total rewards framework, which also form part of the company employee value proposition (EVP):

- Remuneration (Compensation).

- Benefits.

- Work–life balance.

- Performance and recognition.

- Development and career opportunities.

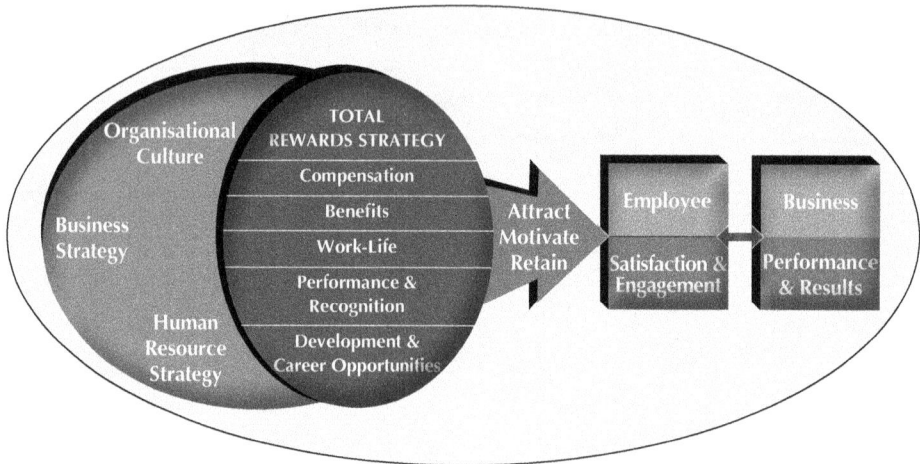

Figure 3: WorldatWork's Total Rewards Model[44]

Attitudes to reward systems are changing. Employers realise today that remuneration is no longer used only as a currency in exchange for effort, time and skill. Reward programmes are increasingly used to attract, retain and motivate employees.[45] It has also been shown that, where reward processes have been linked to key performance drivers in an organisation, employee morale, retention, engagement, and productivity have significantly improved. Furthermore, governance and compliance with organisational policies and regulatory requirements are enhanced.[46] This confirms that, although there appears to be a need for more flexible reward systems that align to employee needs, these systems should still be governed by policies, guidelines, and frameworks and should not lead to total flexibility at the expense of regulation.

4.4.2 Drivers of Reward Strategy

Four considerations contribute to making strategic reward and remuneration decisions. These include: (1) organisational (business) strategy; (2) organisation product life cycle; (3) remuneration policy; and (4) employee reward preferences and needs.

Organisational Strategy

The ultimate objective of the total reward strategy is to ensure that the company attracts and retains the right employees, and that it motivates them to do those things

---

44 WorldatWork (2007:7).

45 Gross & Friedman (2007).

46 Luthans (2005); Torrington et al. (2009).

that support the business plan, while also being legally compliant. Recognition for outstanding achievement is also an important part of the process. The **right** total reward strategy can deliver the **right** amount to the **right** people at the **right** time, for the **right** reasons.[47]

The organisational strategy refers to the fundamental direction adopted by the organisation. The broader organisational strategy gives rise to specific questions at different levels in the organisation. At **executive management level**, the question revolves round the kind of business the organisation should be involved in. At the **functional level**, the question revolves round how the strategy should be implemented in order to achieve organisational goals. Where remuneration is concerned, the question is whether the existing reward and remuneration strategy will encourage employees to behave in a way that will lead to the achievement of organisational goals.

Organisations can choose to follow various business strategies. The strategies that are most commonly used are the innovator strategy, cost-cutter strategy, and the consumer-focused strategy. These strategies require diverse and even contrasting behaviours from employees, so the compensation strategies should vary in each case. The business that decides to have an **innovative business strategy** must develop a total reward strategy that will reward innovative behaviour and decisions. The organisation that follows the **cost-cutter approach** should focus on efficiency and emphasise productivity in the compensation of employees, while the **consumer-focused business strategy** should be supported by a compensation strategy that rewards employee behaviours that ensure customer satisfaction.[48]

A reciprocal relationship exists between the business strategy and the total reward strategy. The organisational strategy informs the reward strategy, and the reward strategy enables employees to implement the business strategy by giving clear indications of the types of behaviour that will be rewarded. The **business plan** is used as a point of departure for developing the reward and remuneration strategy. This is followed by an assessment of how well the current, total reward system supports the objectives of the business. Gaps and any areas that are overfunded are identified. A pay or remuneration strategy which forms the basis of the total reward strategy is then developed. The reward and remuneration philosophy is then updated accordingly and aligned with the business strategy.

Organisation Product Life Cycle

Industry or product growth rate or life cycle stage has a significant impact on the remuneration strategy adopted. Figure 4 shows an example of industry maturity or product life cycle and sets out common organisational strategies that are used in each of these stages.

---

47 Gross & Friedman (2007).

48 Milkovich & Newman (2009).

Common business strategies used in specific life cycle stages

EMBRYONIC	GROWTH	MATURE	AGING
• Start-up • New product development	• Acquire market share • Find new markets	• Consolidate position • Find and protect market niches • Become low-cost producer	• Cost reduction • Withdraw from unprofitable market segments

Figure 4: Industry Maturity or Product Life Cycle

Each of these stages has a preferred remuneration strategy attached to it. Table 4 shows the most appropriate remuneration strategy for each stage.

Table 4: Common Approaches to Reward and Remuneration in Each Life Cycle Stage

Embryonic	Growth	Mature	Aging
• Less emphasis on salary, benefits and perks • Attention to share options and long-term incentives	• Continued emphasis on long-term incentives, with increasing attention to ways to promote short-term results • Catch up with salary and benefits	• Most attention focused on keeping salary and perks competitive • Reduced concern for long-term incentives • Bonuses oriented to productivity improvement	• Benefits and salary are king • Very little attention given to long-term, growth-oriented incentives

Remuneration Policy

The remuneration policy indicates how the remuneration strategy will be implemented (see table 5). It guides management decisions and should therefore be informative enough to ensure effective decision making, but also be flexible enough to allow for individual differences in pay should this be necessary. Organisations can choose between several competitive pay-policy options. The **match policy** pays employees salaries similar to those of the competition. This approach ensures that the organisation's remuneration costs are approximately equal to those of the competition, and, therefore, its ability to attract and retain talented employees will be similar to that of competitors. When an organisation pays more than competitors in the market, it follows a **lead policy**. This approach allows the organisation to attract and retain talented employees, but also increases labour costs. An employer who pays below the current market rate follows a **lag policy**. This may hinder the ability to attract and retain talent, except when the low basic salary is enhanced with other forms of compensation such as share options or high-performance bonuses.

Table 5: Typical Content of a Remuneration Policy

• Statement of intent and philosophy • Employee value proposition (EVP) • Purpose • Application and scope • Document control and versions
• Philosophy of guaranteed or fixed pay (GP) • Philosophy of variable pay (VP) • Remuneration mix • Comparative benchmarking • Links to performance management • Communication and the extent of transparency allowed • Annual remuneration reviews • Remuneration committee scope and guidelines

The total rewards strategy and framework are integral parts of an organisation's **employee value proposition (EVP)**.[49] When the framework is designed, the components offered by competitor organisations should be considered, as well as the value that employees attach to the respective components.[50] A sound reward framework positively influences the EVP, enhances the employer brand, and builds the organisation's reputation as an 'Employer of Choice' for current and prospective employees.

Research (cited by Bussin[51] and Arnolds and Venter[52]) shows that managers and employees tend to differ regarding their perceptions of a company's incentive scheme and their preferences for types of nonfinancial recognition rewards. In a study conducted by Arnolds and Venter[53], frontline employees ranked paid holidays, retirement plans, cash incentives, wage increases, and job security as the highest individual motivators. On the other hand, Grigoriades and Bussin[54] found bonus schemes to be mostly preferred by middle managers. It is recommended that organisations have the effectiveness of their incentive schemes evaluated by the people participating in the scheme.[55]

---

49 CLC (2008).

50 Harris & Clements (2007).

51 Bussin (2004).

52 Arnolds & Venter (2007).

53 (2007).

54 (2007).

55 Grigoriades & Bussin (2007).

4.5 Elements of Remuneration

Once the mechanisms for determining rates of pay for jobs in an organisation have been settled, the pay or remuneration package should be constructed. As shown in figure 5, the payment of an individual will be made up of fixed (or guaranteed) pay elements and variable pay elements. **Fixed or guaranteed pay elements** are those that make up the regular weekly or monthly payment to the individual, and which do not vary other than in exceptional circumstances. These include basic salary and employee benefits. **Variable pay elements** can be varied by either the employer or the employee[56], and include short-term and long-term incentives.

4.5.1 Incentives

Short-term incentives (STIs) are defined as incentives that are applicable for up to one year, such as **incentive target**, **discretionary bonus**, and **profit share**, and are tied to the performance of the company, team and/or individual. The **incentive target** is a bonus that is related to the achievement typically of a financial target such as turnover or profit, as well as other objectives. The **incentive bonus** is typically a percentage of the total guaranteed package. The **discretionary bonus** is a discretionary amount that bears some relationship to the individual's performance. **Profit share** is a predetermined percentage of the organisation's profits, usually also dependent on the achievement of other objectives. **Long-term incentives (LTIs)** refer to incentives that are applicable for over one year, such as a share option scheme, share grant scheme, share purchase scheme, or long-term cash incentive scheme. In pictorial format, the various forms of pay can be represented as follows:

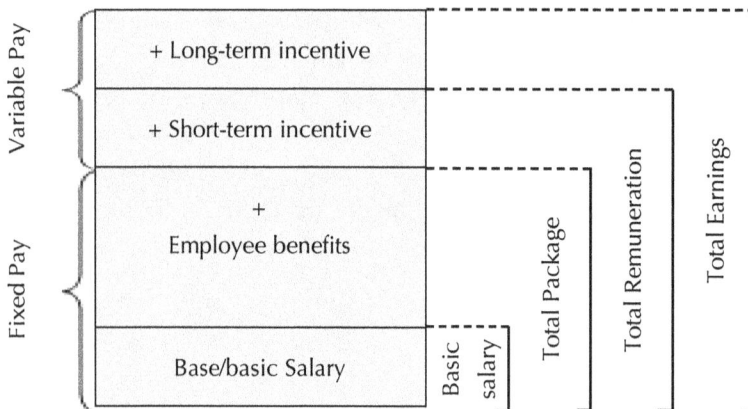

Figure 5: Typical Elements of Remuneration

Individual incentives reward individual performance. Sales commissions and once-off bonuses are commonly used individual incentive methods. **Team incentives** focus

56 Torrington et al. (2009).

on the performance of a work group or team. **Gain-sharing plans** are examples of a team incentive that is used, for example, when an employee team achieves specific goals such as reducing waste, reducing accident rates or improving productivity. **Organisational incentive schemes** reward employees based on the performance of the entire organisation. **Profit-sharing schemes** and employee share ownership schemes are commonly used organisational incentive schemes.

The incentive scheme should at least fit the organisational and reward strategies, reward the correct desired behaviours, and be managed effectively to ensure procedural and distributive fairness. The type of scheme implemented depends largely on what the scheme is supposed to achieve. It is a widely held view that there is no one best type of scheme – the scheme has to be designed to drive the desired behaviours. There are vast bodies of research showing that organisations with financial incentive schemes outperform those that have none.

Most organisations implement incentive schemes to incite superior individual, team and company performance, align with shareholder thinking (agency theory), share some of the wealth created in the organisation, tie the onerous salary bill to the fortunes of the company, reward participants for a job well done, drive company strategy, and create more shareholder wealth. The best-of-breed organisations use both short-term and long-term incentives in their remuneration mix. The primary purpose of this is that it encourages the long-term viability of the company, and executives are encouraged not to harm the company for short-term gains, because they would have too much to lose in the long term. A well-designed 'total earnings' scheme should prevent this from happening.[57]

The link between the performance management system and remuneration is most commonly experienced in three ways. The higher the performance score:

- The higher the fixed pay increase.

- The greater the slice of the STI pie relative to the pool.

- The greater the likelihood of receiving a larger amount of the share scheme pool and share top-ups.

4.5.2 Benefits

Benefits (fringe benefits) are indirect compensation that employees receive because they belong to the workforce of an organisation. These tend to be more prolific in emerging markets, and, in some countries, the tax treatment is still favourable towards this. As shown in table 6, these may be either cash or noncash additions to an employee's pay and must be taken into account in calculating the total package.

---

57 Bussin (2002a).

Table 6: Examples of Cash and Noncash Benefits

Examples of Cash Benefits	Examples of Noncash Benefits
• Car allowance	• Vacation leave
• Entertainment allowance	• Sick leave
• Housing subsidy	• Pension/provident fund contribution
• Professional fees	• Medical contribution
• Cellphone allowance	• Group life assurance
	• Accident insurance
	• Housing loan
	• Educational assistance
	• Travel abroad

Where trade unions are recognised, any changes to conditions of employment must be negotiated with the trade unions. Sometimes, organisations are subject to regulation through bargaining councils, which means that their remuneration practices are prescribed by industry-specific needs. It is unlikely that an application for exemption regarding the total package structure will be successful.

5. International Remuneration

5.1 Context and Linkage

The remuneration of international assignees tends to be a rushed, last-minute decision. The implications often arise only after the assignee arrives in the host country, and, when the assignment comes to an end, the new position in the home country, for example, pays less than the employee earned on assignment.

Few organisations spend sufficient time creating a well-designed, international-assignment remuneration strategy and policy, and this is a dangerous area to neglect given the latest research, which indicates very high employee turnover at the beginning and end of international assignments.

Most large global organisations have established a clear policy for remunerating international assignees. However, it is a complex area of remuneration fraught with issues such as volatile exchange rates, weak and strong currencies, differences in cost of living between countries, and attractive and less attractive countries to work in. This is an area where clear principles and policy are required to ensure fairness, equity and retention. Hopefully, this chapter will contribute to assisting in the management of international-assignment remuneration.

Global and, increasingly, regional organisations understand the value placed on and received from best-practice, international-assignment remuneration, along with the role of human capital in an organisation's success. International-assignment remuneration is no longer allocated to a human resources administrator, but is becoming a critical element in a total reward (TR) system and in reinforcing employees' commitment to organisation objectives.

5.2 Types of International Employment

The question of what constitutes an international assignment is one of the first issues to be established. Based on the length of stay outside the usual country of employment and the effect on the employee's tax position, five common types of international employment are distinguished.

Business trip: A business trip is classified as such if it has the following characteristics:

- From 1 day to 30 days in one location.
- Unaccompanied by family.
- No change in tax position.

Project assignment: A project assignment has the following characteristics:

- From 30 days to 6 months in one location.
- Unaccompanied by family.
- Normally, no change in tax position.

Fly-in, fly-out assignment: A fly-in, fly-out assignment has the following characteristics:

- Pattern of employment in a foreign location with regular home.
- Unaccompanied by family.
- Change in tax position.

International assignment: An international assignment has the following characteristics:

- Between six months and three years in a foreign location.
- Accompanied by family.
- Change in tax position.

Permanent transfer: A permanent transfer is classified as such if it has the following characteristics:

- Indefinite international change in place of work.
- Accompanied by family.
- Change in tax position.

The focus of this chapter is international assignments. Employees sent on international assignments are referred to as international assignees or expatriates.

Today's competitive global business climate means that employees increasingly have to work in various countries and return to the home base. Business leaders have to understand and use all of the tools available to ensure success. An effective, equitable approach to internal-assignment remuneration is one of these powerful tools.

5.3 Definitions, and Underlying Philosophy

A common reason for difficulty in understanding the value of an international-assignment remuneration policy is the lack of consistent definitions of each element of international-assignment remuneration and the underlying philosophy. The following definitions are all key elements of an international-assignment policy.

- **Home-based salary**

  This is the salary the assignee is normally paid in his or her home country. It is consistent with the home-country market and the home-organisation pay scales.

- **Home net salary**

  This is the home-based salary less hypothetical tax (the tax that the assignee would have paid in the home country).

- **Cost-of-living index (COL)**

  This is a figure that represents the difference in the cost of living between the two countries involved in an assignment (home country and host country). For example, the COL for an assignee sent to France from Africa may be 1.6. This information is based on the difference in the price of a similar basket of goods, and reflects that France would be 1.6 times more expensive than Africa. COL indices can be bought from consultants who specialise in the various areas.

- **Exchange rate**

  This is the currency exchange rate between the two countries involved in the assignment (home country and host country). The exchange rate is normally set at the beginning of the assignment and is reviewed annually or when there is a change in the rate which is greater than 10%.

- **International Premium Index**

  This is a figure that represents the difference between the two countries involved in the assignment (home country and host country) in terms of factors such as economic system, political system, religion, standard of living, security, and climate. The exchange rate is normally set for the duration of the assignment and is reviewed only if a major change occurs (eg the host country may experience a serious economic or political crisis).

- **Employee currency election**

  This is the percentage of the total assignment remuneration package which the employee elects to have paid in the host country and the home country.

Any discussion of an organisation's international-assignment remuneration policy must take cognisance of the following underlying philosophies in the aims, which are to:

- Provide consistent, equitable treatment for all international assignees, worldwide.
- Protect purchasing power against changed spending patterns.
- Recognise job size globally.
- Provide 'reasonable gain'.
- Offer flexibility within limits and where tax-effective.
- Be competitive.
- Address spouse-support issues.
- Have a simple structure to provide seamless coverage for different scenarios.

5.4 Approaches to International-assignment Remuneration

The application of the above philosophies has resulted in the emergence of three broad approaches to international-assignment remuneration. These are the following:

- **Build-up method:** This method uses the home-based salary as a base salary, minus hypothetical tax, and builds on this by adding an international premium, a cost-of-living index, and the exchange rate to deliver a net assignment package. The build-up method is used to maintain internal equity and to equalise the impact of host-country tax.

- **Local-market approach:** This approach uses the principle of applying the better of build-up or local market. It is used where a strong local market exists in the host country, and where the build-up method delivers less than the local-market remuneration levels (eg an assignee sent to a major First World country such as the United Kingdom or the United States).

- **Internationally mobile expatriate:** This approach is used by large, global multinational organisations, which often have a large pool of permanent expatriates who move from one country to the next on assignments. The internally mobile expatriate approach is used to put all expatriates on an equal footing, regardless of nationality.

5.5 Positioning International-assignment Remuneration in the Total Reward System

Figure 6 shows a typical positioning of the build-up method:

	Business objectives

	Total reward

❶	Home base-salary
	R750 000

❷	Less hypothetical tax
	–R306 181

❸	Home net salary
	R443 819

❹	Essential spending (40%)
	R177 528

❺	x Cost-of-living index
	1.46

❻	x Exchange rate
	R7.1200

❼	= Host-currency element
	R1 845 439

Host currency: Supa-Nova Peso

❹	Home net balance (60%)
	R266 291

❽	International premium 30%
	R225 000

❾	= Home-currency element
	R491 291

Home currency: Rand

Total: R750 482

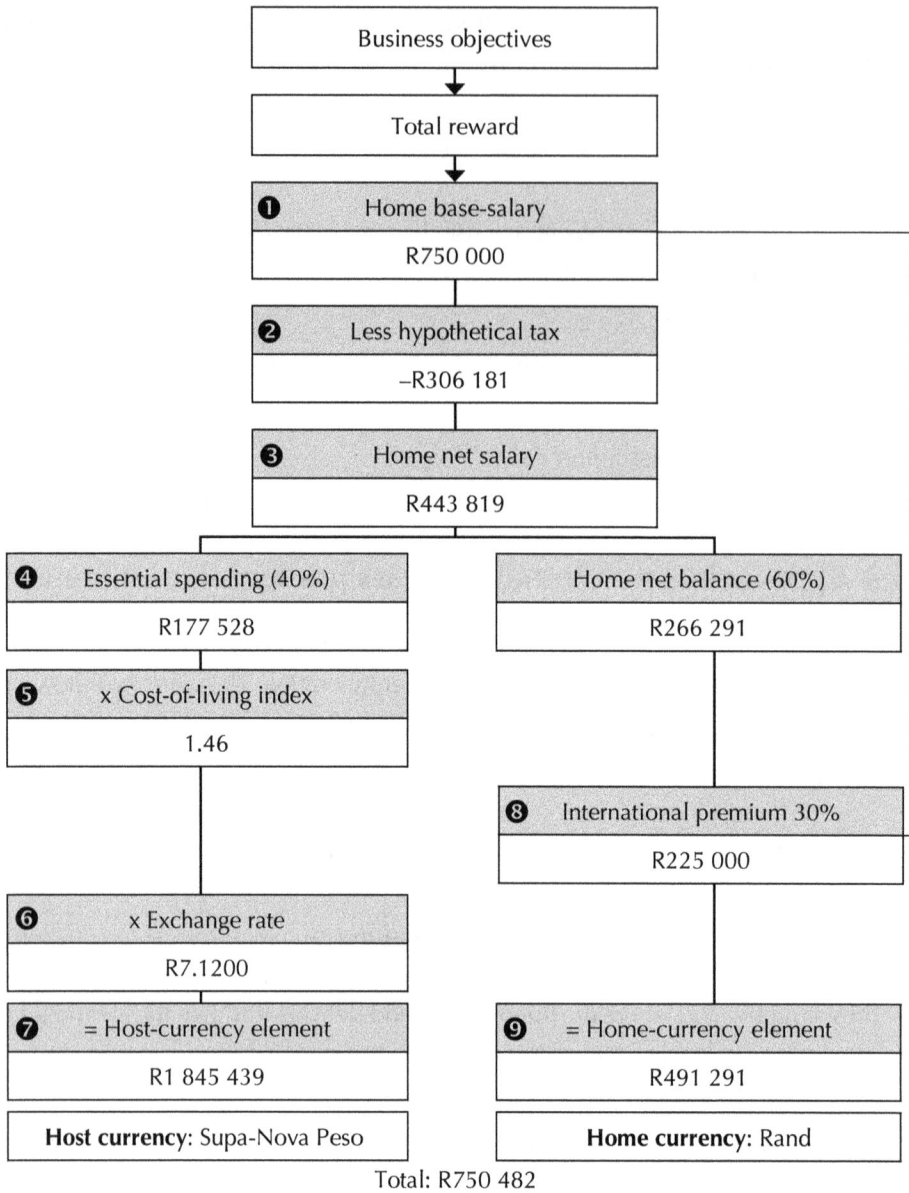

Figure 6: Build-up Method

5.6 Design Considerations

The approach to expatriate remuneration differs from one organisation to another, and within a single organisation, and depends on a number of factors such as:

- Length of assignment.
- Host country.
- Level of assignee.

Designing an international-assignment remuneration policy should include the organisation's position on each of the elements reflected in table 7. Typical applications of each element are shown for each of the three broad approaches:

Table 7: Comparison of Approaches for International Assignments

Remuneration	Build-up Method (BM)	Local-market Approach (LMA)	Internationally Mobile Expatriate (IME)
Purpose	Used to maintain internal equity and equalise impact of host-country tax. Used by approximately 70% of organisations.	Used where a local market exists and where the build-up method delivers less than local-market remuneration levels. Used by approximately 20% of organisations, most often for First World assignees, for example to Western Europe and the United States of America.	Used to put all group expatriates on an equal footing regardless of nationality. Employees resign from home country and relocate to group organisation, usually in tax-free country. Used by fewer than 10% of organisations, usually only by large global groups with large numbers of assignees.
Market relationship	Home-base salary in home country is market-related. Typically basic plus cost of all benefits, except car benefit (where car is provided in host country).	Host-country market determines level of remuneration.	International-base salary typically in US$. Benefits funded from group organisation in tax-free home country.
Tax philosophy	Assignees neither lose nor gain as a result of tax treatment in host country.	Taxed in host country. Net pay depends on tax laws and structure of package.	Taxed in host country, taking advantage of tax-free, home-country status.
Hypothetical tax	Generic model used to calculate home net salary.	N/A.	Generic model used to calculate home net salary.
Home net salary	Result of home-base salary less hypothetical tax.	N/A.	Result of home-base salary less hypothetical tax.

Remuneration	Build-up Method (BM)	Local-market Approach (LMA)	Internationally Mobile Expatriate (IME)
Cost of living (COL)	COL is used to neutralise the effects of COL differences between the home and host country. Applied to essential spending only (typically 40% of home net salary).	N/A.	COL is used to neutralise the effects of COL differences between the home and host country. Applied to essential spending only (typically 40% of home net salary).
Exchange rate	**COL is linked to exchange rate.** COL exchange rate used to deliver local amount of assignment salary.	Paid in local currency or US$ if allowed.	Paid in local currency or US$ if allowed. **COL is linked to exchange rate.** COL exchange rate used to deliver local amount of assignment salary.
International premium	Reflects amount of premium needed to compensate for assignee living conditions.	N/A.	Reflects amount of premium needed to compensate for assignee living conditions.
Car benefit	Excluded from assignment salary calculation and provided in host country in line with local host policy where appropriate.	In line with host-country policy.	Excluded from assignment salary calculation and provided in host country in line with local host policy where appropriate.
Housing	Housing typically provided in host country, often furnished, and includes utilities, water, lights, and housekeeper, depending on host-country policy.	Housing typically provided in host country, often furnished, and includes utilities, water, lights, and housekeeper, depending on host-country policy.	Housing typically provided in host country, often furnished, and includes utilities, water, lights, and housekeeper, depending on host-country policy.

Remuneration	Build-up Method (BM)	Local-market Approach (LMA)	Internationally Mobile Expatriate (IME)
Housing (continued)	No involvement by organisation in home-country housing arrangement, but caution against selling.	No involvement by organisation in home-country housing arrangement, but caution against selling.	No involvement by organisation in home-country housing arrangement, but caution against selling.
Assignment salary quotation	Two elements: (1) Local spendable (host currency), (2) Home-base element (home currency).	Local host-country currency only. Can remit an elected amount back to home country.	Two elements: (1) Local spendable (host currency), (2) Home-base element (home currency).
Employee currency election	Assignee elects, once a year, a mix of how much in host and home.	Assignee, elects once a year, a mix of how much in host and home.	Assignee elects, once a year, a mix of how much in host and home.
Variable incentive bonus	Remain on home-country scheme **based on home base**, but in line with host country and individual performance. Variable pay is designed to ensure that TR is competitive within home country.	Participate in host-country scheme. **Based on host base** in line with host country and individual performance. Variable pay is designed to ensure that TR is competitive within host country.	Remain on home-country scheme **based on home base**, but in line with host country and individual performance. Variable pay is designed to ensure that TR is competitive within home country / international market.
Retirement benefits (Overall, approximately 80% of assignees remain on home-country retirement plans)	**Remain on home-country retirement scheme.** Basis of retirement funding is home base, as assignee is expected to return and retire in home country.	**Remain on home-country retirement scheme**, where possible. Basis of retirement funding is home base, as assignee is expected to return and retire in home country.	**Remain on home-country retirement scheme.** Basis of retirement funding is home base (ie US$), as assignee is expected to return and retire in home country.

Remuneration	Build-up Method (BM)	Local-market Approach (LMA)	Internationally Mobile Expatriate (IME)
Retirement benefits (continued)	The most typical rate for approximately 67% of organisations is Employer 15%, and Employee 0% of Home-base Salary.	If the assignee converts to local by resigning from the home organisation, retirement funding reverts to the host country.	
Medical benefits	**Half of organisations allow assignees to remain on home-country medical scheme, and half provide offshore medical cover.** The majority of organisations provide assignees with emergency evacuation cover.	Medical cover and benefits are provided locally in line with host-country policy. The majority of organisations provide assignees with emergency evacuation cover.	**Half of organisations allow assignees to remain on home-country medical scheme, and half provide offshore medical cover.** The majority of organisations provide assignees with emergency evacuation cover.
Guaranteed 13th cheque	13th cheque is paid if it is part of the home-salary-structure policy. If paid, it is paid based on the gross, home-country base salary. Less than 10% of organisations pay a guaranteed 13th cheque.	13th cheque is paid if it is part of the host-salary-structure policy. If paid, it is paid based on the gross, host-country base salary.	13th cheque is paid if it is part of the home-salary-structure-policy. If paid, it is paid based on the gross, home-country base salary. Less than 3% of organisations pay a guaranteed 13th cheque for IMEs.
Guaranteed 13th cheque (continued)	In the majority of cases, 13th cheques are built into the build-up model and are incorporated in the total package so as to simplify administration.		

Remuneration	Build-up Method (BM)	Local-market Approach (LMA)	Internationally Mobile Expatriate (IME)
Disturbance allowance	Outward disturbance allowance of one month's net, home-base salary. Return disturbance allowance of one month's net, home-base salary.	Outward disturbance allowance of one month's net, home-base salary. Return disturbance allowance of one month's net, home-base salary.	Outward disturbance allowance of one month's net, home-base salary. Return disturbance allowance of one month's net, home-base salary.
Relocation allowance **(Approximately 80% of organisations pay for the storage costs of household effects that the assignee does not take to the host country)**	Relocation is generally paid for household effects and personal items, but only half of organisations pay for the removal of luxury / general items.	Relocation is generally paid for household effects and personal items, but only half of organisations pay for the removal of luxury / general items.	Relocation is generally paid for household effects and personal items, but only half of organisations pay for the removal of luxury / general items.
Education policy	Provide appropriate education support for assignees' children in order to minimise the disruption to their education caused by an international assignment.	Local education policy applies.	Provide appropriate education support for assignees' children in order to minimise the disruption to their education caused by an international assignment.
Partner-support policy	No attempt to compensate for loss of income of spouse. May provide partner support, eg budget to study or find a new job.	N/A.	No attempt to compensate for loss of income of spouse. May provide partner support, eg budget to study or find a new job.

Remuneration	Build-up Method (BM)	Local-market Approach (LMA)	Internationally Mobile Expatriate (IME)
Flights	Two flights per year for unaccompanied assignees. One flight per year for accompanied assignees. Additional flights are provided on compassionate grounds, typically on the death of a family member or next of kin.	Two flights per year for unaccompanied assignees. One flight per year for accompanied assignees. Additional flights are provided on compassionate grounds, typically on the death of a family member or next of kin.	Two flights per year for unaccompanied assignees. One flight per year for accompanied assignees. Additional flights are provided on compassionate grounds, typically on the death of a family member or next of kin.

Rigorous and careful benchmarking is often required in advance as the 'expat community' is sometimes small, and very often detailed notes are exchanged.

5.7 Critical Success Factors

As important as international-assignment remuneration is to an organisation, management often continues to undervalue the impact it has on assignees' morale, motivation and financial performance. The critical success factors for good international-assignment-package design involve the following:

- Include current and former assignees in the design process.

- Make use of research information and current best practice.

- Make use of tax experts regarding tax in both host and home countries (reciprocal tax agreements make this essential).

- Research shows that three- to five-year assignments provide optimum return on investment (ROI).

- Candidates' soft-skill abilities (emotional quotient – EQ) should be assessed before the candidates are assigned.

- Typically utilise international assignments as developmental opportunities for high-potential employees.

- Companies should invest time and effort in managing employee and spouse expectations.

- Companies should track employee career development over 10- to 15-year horizons.

- Most international companies use home-country base salary to calculate the international-assignment package.

- Increasingly, companies try to outsource the international-assignment administration function.

- Companies should double their repatriation efforts, as many assignees stay longer than required on high levels of assignment remuneration.

5.8 Benchmark Findings, and Lessons Learnt

When doing the research on best-of-breed schemes, one often comes across the following as typical benchmark findings. This could serve as a lessons-learnt check list for your scheme design:

- Companies generally assist with tax compliance.

- Companies strive to put international assignees on an equal footing with those at home.

- Most companies use external consultants for overall design, COL and parity.

- Half the companies allow the international assignees to complete 'location-ranking questionnaires' (typically 16 to 20 factors).

- Conversion to local conditions ranges from immediate to three years.

- The parent organisation is still responsible for the international assignee's career.

- Equity is managed by home base and job.

Other important design considerations include:

- Soft issues such as the spouse's loss of employment, repatriation, and reskilling.

- Volatile currency (such as the rand) against the major currencies in the past.

- Selling houses in the home country at a loss.

- Provision of a car benefit in the host country.

- COL index, particularly in high-inflation countries.

5.9 Current Issues

Any international-assignment remuneration policy must always take into account the fact that there are a greater number of dynamics involved with expatriate pay than with that of local employees. Many issues are still being grappled with by organisations that have been managing international assignees for many years. Some of the current issues being debated are the following:

- Hard-currency trend is on the decline (used only in highly unstable markets).

- Assignees from low cost-of-living/low-paying countries will always tend to earn less than assignees doing the same job in a host country and who come from higher cost-of-living/higher-paying countries, using the build-up model.

A few solutions to 'trailing-spouse' issues are the following:

- Help the spouse to find a job.

- Assist with the choice of a career by

  - preparing a résumé

  - obtaining a work permit

  - organising career counselling

  - reimbursing for tuition.

In addition, the following continue to cause problems:

- There is a significant trend towards a dual or hybrid approach to compensation.

- Home needs (to cover country commitment and incentive allowances, and fixed currency in the home country) are often overlooked or neglected.

- Host needs (to cover local, day-to-day living costs and fixed currency in local situation) are not adequately compensated for.

- Expatriate remuneration continues to be in a state of flux in response to the changing world in which we work.

The statistics of expatriates returning home and leaving the organisation within a few years are high. Organisations often do not take the time to focus on a repatriation programme. It is assumed that, because the person used to live here, 'he or she will be fine'. Suggestions to ensure a smoother repatriation and secure longer tenure include the following:

- Ensure that the person reintegrates into a real job of equal or higher complexity and status than was the situation when the person left.

- Ensure that the spouse and family are thoughtfully integrated back into the community.

- Avoid saying anything such as, "Things here are different now. Where have you been?"

- Be open to new thoughts and ideas the person may have learnt while away.

- Induction back into the organisation, focusing on what has changed, new strategies, and new focus areas, is of the utmost importance.

Many methods of paying expatriates exist, and this issue is a huge debate within remuneration committees. Whether to pay them in home-based pay or host-based pay must be decided on. A combination is often best. How to pay them often depends on their job, status and personal commitments. As a rule of thumb, expatriates should be neither better nor worse off.

6. Reward and Remuneration Trends

Having a good idea of global remuneration trends can be very helpful in setting an organisation's remuneration strategy and being prepared for what lies in the future. These trends reflect what leading organisations are currently doing or are contemplating for the future. Take note that a trend does not necessarily represent good or best practice; it indicates only that more and more organisations are considering it. In addition, with the rapid increase in the application of Western human resource practices in emerging markets, it is crucial to consider and investigate the impact of how non-Western employees react to Western human resource practices.

The following trends, where appropriate, could be used to guide an organisation's remuneration strategy. Trends should also be aligned with the organisation's operational strategy when they are implemented.

6.1 Global Remuneration

Glopats (globally mobile expatriates) want to know that their remuneration is competitive, that they will not be worse off (in other words, that hardship has been taken into account), that living standards are maintained, and that their purchasing power parity (PPP) index is upheld. Finally, they want to know that sufficient and adequate pension arrangements are made. Organisations are exploring 'global' retirement funds.

A real challenge in some emerging markets is to get closer alignment between Glopat pay and local employee pay. In some countries, there are laws stating that transfer of knowledge from the Glopat should take place from between three and five years to local employees. Work permits would theoretically not be renewed after this time frame. In practice, this is rarely achieved.

6.2 Retention of Employees

Retention of employees has been the single-biggest driver of remuneration policy for the past five years. The critical areas of shortage at the moment are in the fields of engineering, artisans, chartered accountants, information technology, and inspiring leaders. Organisations have explored and implemented many different mechanisms from a remuneration point of view, and the following points cannot be emphasised enough:

- People join companies and leave managers.

- Twenty-five per cent of the decision to remain in an organisation is influenced by remuneration.

- Inspirational leadership continues to influence employees' decisions to remain in an organisation, especially if they perceive their remuneration as fair.[58]

In developing markets, retention refers mostly to being retained in the country rather than the company. Often, this requires working closely with government policy makers to ensure that labour laws, tax laws and general labour relations laws are conducive to retaining skilled workers in the country. Being an 'investor-friendly' country also assists with employee perceptions of being a good country to work in. Sometimes, it is also a matter of safety – governments need to ensure safe countries and all citizens need to feel secure.

6.3 Media Scrutiny

Exorbitant remuneration continues to grab our attention by being used as headlines in the media. Remuneration reflects the values that guide employer decisions and influence its treatment of employees. It is a reflection of the organisation's image and reputation. A compensation manager must be proactive and knowledgeable about the accounting practices used in the organisation. This is especially important where variable pay is based on organisational performance in terms of profit.[59] Organisations need to ensure that their processes are extremely robust and can withstand any stakeholder scrutiny.

A strong and free press assists with governance. Governments should not underestimate the power of a free press relative to investor friendliness and citizen comfort levels.

6.4 Specialist Career Tracks

A fairly significant trend has evolved over the past few years. Organisations are acknowledging that superb skills in, or knowledge of, a technical position should also ensure advancement in organisations. Dual career paths, one for management and one for technical personnel, now exist in some organisations. The benefit of this approach is that the knowledge and skills of top-performing technical people can be retained where they can be utilised more effectively and profitably by the organisation. Employees who are technically above-average performers are not necessarily good management material, and it is in the best interest of the organisation to retain these employees where they can contribute to creating a sustained competitive advantage for the organisation.

58 Bussin (2002b).

59 Milkovich & Newman (2009).

6.5 More Flexibility

More than three-quarters of respondents to a recent survey which asked the question, 'Would you rather have a pay increase next year or more flexibility?', responded that they preferred more flexibility. There are a number of ways to introduce flexibility into compensation, two of which are the total guaranteed package and life cycle theory.

- **Total guaranteed remuneration packages** rest on three fundamental pillars: internal equity, structuring flexibility, and external-market competitiveness. The total-package concept is exciting and flexible, in that employees can choose, from a number of different options, those benefits that are most suitable to their lifestyles. The advantage of the total package to the employer is that it contains and defines the total fixed cost of employment and empowers its employees to structure more competitive packages compared with their peers.

- **Life cycle theory** shows that employees in various stages of their life cycle view reward differently. In order to obtain the most from your team, it is essential to remember the differences between each life cycle and understand what their preferences are, not only in terms of work but also in terms of reward and recognition.

6.6 Governance

Good corporate governance rests solidly on sound and effective communication. Learning to strike the balance between good governance and being too transparent is essential. The question being asked is, 'If we disclose all our remuneration data, schemes, and how they operate, are we giving away our competitive advantage?' The debate also continues as to whether non-executive directors should receive shares and bonuses in the organisation they serve. The general answer is – 'No'.

In emerging markets, particular attention needs to be paid to linking pay to corporate performance and publishing exactly how they are linked.

6.7 Branding

Is there a link between corporate branding and reward? Is there a remuneration discount if one works for a well-branded organisation? What is that discount? This is the trend about which the least information is available and that is least understood.

What is clear is that, in emerging markets, most people want to work for organisations that have big brands. This is an opportunity to be explored and emphasised.

6.8 Broad-banding

Broad-banding constitutes a pay structure that consolidates a large number of pay grades and salary ranges into fewer broad bands with relatively wide salary ranges.[60] A single band usually spans the pay opportunity formerly covered by several separate salary ranges. Most bands have a minimum and a maximum, but no midpoint.[61] Broad bands generally fall into one of two categories: salary bands or career bands.[62]

Salary bands represent a collapsing of the traditional structure into several overlapping bands. The purpose of salary bands may be to alleviate the 'topping out' of large numbers of employees who are at, or near, the maximum of their ranges.[63] **Career bands** are similar to salary bands, except that the purpose of the band shifts from an attempt to simplify salary administration to one of management development. Career bands are used to facilitate lateral moves, thereby reinforcing the fact that career growth can be lateral as well as vertical.

Reasons for implementing broad-banding include the following:[64]

- **Reducing the administration burden.** Many organisations spend an excessive amount of time trying to manage restrictive minimum, maximum and midpoint policies.

- **Accommodating a variety of market situations.** Organisations can compare themselves with a wider variety of competitors. Broader ranges accommodate a greater variety of market differences, functionally and geographically, for jobs that have essentially the same internal value.

Too few organisations have implemented this successfully in emerging markets. This is an untapped opportunity which needs to be pursued to alleviate the focus on miniscule changes to job descriptions and tying up job-grading committees for millions of hours doing non-value-add work.

6.9 Pay for Performance

Performance-based pay focuses on evaluating the performance contribution of an individual, a team or an organisation unit, and paying them accordingly. The emphasis here is on the value of the performance contribution rather than on the value of the job.[65] Pay for performance increases, in addition to general increases,

---

60 Economic Research Institute (2004).

61 Braddick, Jones & Shafer (1992).

62 Neubauer (1995).

63 Braddick et al. (1992).

64 Kanin-Lovers & Cameron (1994).

65 Torrington et al. (2009).

rewards individuals for doing their jobs well.

Performance-related pay (PRP) has many theoretical attractions when seen from the perspective of managers:[66]

- It serves to attract and retain good performers, creating incentives for the most talented and hard-working people to earn more than they would be able to earn under a system which pays a flat rate irrespective of personal performance.

- Since it distributes rewards according to the efforts and skills that people contribute, it is regarded as a fair system.

Pay for Performance in China

A research study on pay for performance (PFP) investigated its impact on 574 engineers in 22 domestic firms and 8 foreign firms in China. Results showed that PFP was positively associated with conscientiousness at the individual level, but negatively related to employees' organisational commitment and interpersonal helping at the organisation level. This study suggests that the impact of 'culture distance' associated with Western human resource practices may be more likely to manifest itself in the collective entity than at the individual level. Employees of domestic firms reported significantly higher levels of performance appraisal satisfaction and justice perceptions than employees of foreign firms, which might explain why PFP was more widely implemented in domestic firms in China. In addition to the culture distance, the 'context distance' between domestic and foreign firms may play a critical role in accruing benefits from PFP, indicating that PFP can be more beneficial to domestic firms than to foreign firms.[67]

- It motivates people by rewarding them for putting in additional effort for achieving specific objectives.

- It provides a means whereby managers can exercise control over people's priorities without the need for close supervision.

- It reinforces the individual employment relationship and undermines the influence of trade unions.

- It forces managers and staff to communicate directly and regularly about roles, duties, expectations, and development needs.

6.10 Skills-based Pay

A growing number of organisations, academics, and consultants argue that the traditional job-evaluation processes are easily abused and do not suit the needs of today's organisations. Traditional job-based approaches to evaluation support uncompromisingly hierarchical organisations that do not allow employees to be creative, and subsequently lead to their becoming demotivated. It also assumes that

66 Torrington et al. (2009:173).

67 Du & Nam Choi (2010).

people are commodities who can be made to 'fit' defined roles. For this reason, organisations are implementing skills-based pay to gain a competitive advantage.[68]

When skills are used as the basis, employees are paid for the number of skill units they can demonstrate. Pay is increased as new skills are acquired. An important assumption is that it is organisationally valuable for employees to be multiskilled, that is, to be able to perform several functions. In a traditional salary programme, it is assumed that employees have the required skills or are willing to develop them. By contrast, most skills-based pay plans incorporate formal processes to assess and certify skill attainment. In the skills-based compensation model, changing jobs or roles does not necessarily involve a promotion. Employees are expected to apply their skills as required. They do not move to a higher pay rate when they move to another job requiring the same skills. The acquisition of new skills is the basis for advancement. Skills-based pay plans, which can take several different forms, can support a company's focus on speed and flexibility.[69]

While skills-based pay is relatively new, a number of consequences have already been identified. Firstly, it creates an environment that facilitates worker rotation, which can reduce absenteeism and may ease job assignment pressures for management. Because workers are motivated to learn higher-level-skill jobs, an employee is likely to be paid more than the job evaluation rate of a specific job to which he or she is assigned. However, overall remuneration costs may be lower because of workforce flexibility and higher productivity.[70]

6.11 Market Pricing

Another approach commonly used in emerging markets is market pricing. This relies almost exclusively on rates paid in the external market when setting pay structures. Organisations that follow this approach collect as much market data as possible, and match as many of their jobs with this market data.

Following market prices as the approach to compensating the process of balancing internal and external pressures is a matter of judgement for the organisation. De-emphasising internal alignment may lead to unfair treatment among employees and inconsistency with the fundamental culture of the organisation. Neglecting external competitive pay practices, however, will affect the ability both to attract and to hire applicants who match the organisation's needs.[71] It is especially the market-driven company that must watch the market closely and act accordingly.

The market-pricing approach has a number of potential problems. Market rates are inconsistent, unstable and unpredictable. Relying on market-rate comparisons

---

68 Dessler (2009).

69 Vosloo (2005).

70 Schuler & Huber (1993).

71 Milkovich & Newman (2009).

alone will not necessarily result in the provision of an adequately reliable, stable basis for an equitable pay structure, although the market rates will influence rates of pay within the structure.[72] It may also be possible to get market prices for only some of the jobs in the organisation. Furthermore, it can be difficult to obtain information for uncommon or highly specialised jobs. It could be equally difficult to determine accurately the market worth of 'individual employees', whose value to the organisation depends more on their personal level of skill and competence than on their level of responsibility in a job hierarchy. Organisations which rely on market pricing still have to decide how these jobs fit into the pay structure.[73]

Salary surveys are not well developed in all emerging markets. This makes obtaining market rates particularly challenging. Steady inroads are however being made and this challenge will be obviated in time to come. In the meantime, building pay scales from an internal equity point of view and some benchmark jobs will need to suffice. Flexibility and quick response time are needed in these fast-moving markets. This is especially so when large multinational companies move into a country and are willing to pay top dollar to get established quickly. It throws the whole market out of sync and creates unrealistic pay levels, especially for scarce and technical jobs.

6.12 Team-based Pay

Teams have emerged as a widely used design approach in large organisations for a number of reasons: the changing nature of work, their match with employee involvement and total quality-management programmes, and the development of more and more knowledge about how to design and operate teams.[74] Teamwork has been widely commended as a means of encouraging employees to assume responsibility for identifying and solving the problems of poor communication, inappropriate coordination, low motivation, and slow response. Also, it is assumed that the self-interest of those with the highest skills will motivate them to train and assist team members with lower skills to increase their skills and effort, and thereby boost team performance and bonuses.[75] Team pay also enhances flexible working within teams.[76]

Many of these trends have been on the radar screen for a few years now. The order has changed, and some are more important in specific industries. Well-informed remuneration committees know these trends and are applying their minds as to which ones are appropriate for the organisations they serve. They should not be applied blindly.

72 Armstrong (1995).

73 Vosloo (2005).

74 Vosloo (2005).

75 Vosloo (2005).

76 Armstrong & Baron (2003).

7. Conclusion

Performance is the behaviour for which the employee is compensated, and therefore the evaluation of employees' job performance is a vital human resource function and of critical importance to the organisation. There has been a move away from pure performance appraisal to a performance management approach which looks at both current and future performance. In emerging markets where there is a scarcity of talent, performance management serves as a useful tool to identify, retain and develop talent. Reward and remuneration are closely linked to performance management and also play a pivotal role in attracting and retaining talent. It could be argued that performance management and reward and remuneration are two of the most significant bread-and-butter issues within human resource management. In emerging markets where the pace of development and growth adds an extra pressure to the complexity of the workplace, it is essential that these concepts are well understood and effectively implemented to ensure sustainable organisational success.

References

Aamodt, MG. 2007. *Industrial/Organisational Psychology: an Applied Approach*. Belmont, CA: Wadsworth, a part of Cengage Learning.

Appelbaum, SH, Roy, M & Gilliland, T. 2011. Globalization of Performance Appraisals: Theory and Applications. *Management Decision* 49(4):570-585.

Armstrong, M. 1995. *A Handbook of Personnel Management Practice*. 5th ed. London: Kogan Page Publishers.

Armstrong, M. 2006. *A Handbook of Human Resource Management Practice*. 10th ed. Cambridge, United Kingdom: Cambridge University Press.

Armstrong, M & Baron, A. 2003. *Performance Management: the New Realities*. London: Chartered Institute of Personnel and Development.

Armstrong, M & Murlis, H. 1994. *Reward Management. A Handbook of Remuneration Strategy and Practice*. 3rd ed. London: Kogan Page Publishers.

Arnolds, CA & Venter, DJL. 2007. The Strategic Importance of Motivational Rewards for Lower-level Employees in the Manufacturing and Retailing Industries. *SA Journal of Industrial Psychology* 33(3):15-23.

Barnes, C, Blake, H & Pinder, D. 2009. *Creating and Delivering Your Value Proposition: Managing Customer Experience for Profit*. London: Kogan Page Publishers.

Braddick, CA, Jones, MB & Shafer, PM. 1992. A Look at Broadbanding in Practice. *Journal of Compensation and Benefits* 27:28-32.

Briscoe, DR & Claus, M. 2008. Employee Performance Management: Policies and Practices in Multinational Enterprises, in *Performance Management Systems: Global Perspective*, edited by A Varma, PS Budhwar & A DeNisi. London: Routledge. [15-39]

Bussin, M. 1993. Broadbanding, Multi-skilling, Skill Based Pay: Any Connection? *Human Resource Management* 9:26-27.

Bussin, M. 2002a. *Choosing the Right Incentive Scheme – Guide 9*. The Nuts & Bolts Business Series – Remuneration Series. Johannesburg: Knowledge Resources.

Bussin, M. 2002b. *Retention Strategies – Guide 10*. The Nuts & Bolts Business Series – Remuneration Series. Johannesburg: Knowledge Resources.

Bussin, M. 2004. Total Remuneration Strategy. Paper presented on 27 February. [Online]. Available: www.sara.co.za/library/eventdocuments/eventdocuments2004/ [Accessed 23 April 2005].

Bussin, M. 2010. *The Remuneration Handbook for Africa*. Johannesburg: Knowledge Resources.

Bussin, M & Botha, J. 2010. Performance Evaluation, in *Personnel Psychology,* edited by M Coetzee & D Schreuder. Cape Town: Oxford University Press. [328-367]

Cascio, WF. 2006. Global Performance Management System, in *Handbook of Research in International Human Resource Management,* edited by GK Stahl & I Bjorkman. Cheltenham: Edward Elgar.

Chiang, F. 2005. A Critical Examination of Hofstede's Thesis and Its Application to International Reward Management. *International Journal of Human Resource Management* 16(9):1545-1563.

Chingos, PT & Marwick, KP. 1997. *Paying for Performance – a Guide to Compensation Management.* New York: John Wiley & Sons, Inc.

Coleman, NK. 1999. Global Pay and Results, in *Aligning Pay and Results: Compensation Strategies That Work from the Boardroom to the Shop Floor,* edited by H Risher. New York, NY: AMACOM Books. 259-273.

Corporate Leadership Council (CLC). 2008. CLC quarterly report on HR news and trends. [Online]. Available: www.clc.executiveboard.com [Accessed 16 June 2008].

Costello, SJ. 1994. *Effective Performance Management – the Business Skill Express Series.* New York: McGraw-Hill.

CTPartners 2011. Dynamic Markets Trend Talk. Retrieved from: http://www.ctnet.com/uploadedFiles/The_Firm/Trend_Talks/Dynamic%20Markets%20TrendTalk_Global_2011.pdf.

Dessler, G. 2009. *Fundamentals of Human Resource Management*. London: Pearson Education.

Du, J & Nam Choi, J. 2010. Pay for Performance in Dynamic Markets: Insights from China. *Journal of International Business Studies* 41:671-689.

Economic Research Institute. 2004. Economic Research Institute. 2004. ERI White Paper. Retrieved from: http://www.erieri.com/ on 16 December 2011.

Engle, AD & Dowling, P. 2007. State of Origin: Research in Global Performance Management – Progress or a Lost Horizon? Conference Proceedings of the VIII Word Congress of the International Federation of Scholarly Associations of Management (IFSAM) Berlin: Germany.

Evans P, Pucik, V & Barsoux, JL. 2002. *The Global Challenge: Frameworks for International Human Resource Management*. Boston: McGraw-Hill.

Gilman, NP. 2009. *Methods of Industrial Remuneration*. Charleston, SC: BiblioLife LLC.

Grigoriades, CA & Bussin, M. 2007. Current Practice with regard to Short-term Incentive Schemes for Middle Managers. *SA Journal of Human Resource Management* 5(1):45-53.

Gross, SE & Friedman, HE. 2007. Creating an Effective Total Rewards Strategy: Holistic Approach Better Supports Business Success. *Mercer Human Resources Consulting CD – Your Guide to the Age Of Talent*. United States: Mercer.

Grote, D. 2002. *The Performance Appraisal Question and Answer Book: a Survival Guide for Managers*. New York: American Management Association.

Guthrie, J. 2007. Remuneration Pay Effects and Work, in *The Oxford HANDBOOK of Human Resource Management,* edited by P Boxall, J Purcell & P Wright. Oxford: Oxford University Press.

Harris, S & Clements, L. 2007. What's the Perceived Value of Your Incentives? *The Magazine of World at Work: Workspan* 2:21-25. Scottsdale, United States: WorldatWork Press.

Hellqvist, N. 2011. Global Performance Management: a Research Agenda. *Management Research Review* 34(8):927-946.

Kanin-Lovers, J & Cameron, M. 1994. Broadbanding: a Step Forward or a Step Backward? *Journal of Compensation and Benefits* 9:39-42.

Kaplan, RS & Norton, DP. 2004. *Strategy Maps*. Boston, MA: Harvard Business School Press.

Latham, GP & Russo, SD. 2008. The Influence of Organisational Politics on Performance Appraisal, in *The Oxford Handbook of Personnel Psychology,* edited by S Cartwright & CL Cooper. Oxford: Oxford University Press. [380-410]

Latham, GP, Almost J, Mann, S & Moore, C. 2005. New Developments in Performance Management. *Organisational Dynamics* 34(1):77-87.

Lawler, EE. 2000. *Rewarding Excellence: Pay Strategies for the New Economy*. San Francisco, CA: Jossey-Bass.

Leonard, B. 1994. New Ways to Pay Employees. *Human Resource Magazine* 39:61-62.

Luthans, F. 2005. *Organisational Behaviour*. New York: McGraw-Hill.

Marchington, M & Wilkinson, A. 2008. *Human Resource Management at Work: People Management and Development*. London: CIPD.

Mathis, RL & Jackson, JH. 2004. *Human Resources Management*. 10th ed. Mason, OH: Thomson South-Western College Publishing.

Milkovich, G & Newman, J. 2009. *Compensation*. 9th ed. Boston: Irwin McGraw-Hill.

Milliman J, Taylor, S & Czaplewski, AJ. 2002. Cross-Cultural Performance Feedback in Multinational Enterprises: Opportunity for Organisational Learning. *Human Resource Planning* 25.

Nelson, B & Sptizer, DR. 2003. *The 1001 Rewards & Recognition Fieldbook: the Complete Guide*. New York: Workman Publishing Company.

Neubauer, RJ. 1995. Broadbanding: Management Fad or Saviour? *Compensation and Benefits Management* 11:50-54.

Nixon, A. 2011. Adapted from *A Handbook for Measuring Employee Performance*. Office of Personnel Management, US Government. Retrieved from: http://spectrain.wordpress.com/tag/cross-cultural/.

Odendaal, A. 2009. Motivation: from Concepts to Applications, in *Organisational Behaviour: Global and South African Perspectives,* edited by SP Robbins, TA Judges, A Odendaal & G Roodt. Cape Town: Prentice-Hall. [168-191]

Peterson, S & Luthans, F. 2006. The Impact of Financial and Nonfinancial Incentives on Business Unit Outcomes over Time. *Journal of Applied Psychology* 91(1):156-165.

Porter, C, Bingham, C & Simmonds, D. 2008. *Exploring Human Resource Management*. New York: McGraw-Hill.

Price, A. 2004. *Human Resource Management in a Business Context*. London: Thomson Learning.

Riggio, RE. 2009. *Introduction to Industrial/Organisational Psychology*. London: Pearson Education.

Rubino, J. 2006. *Principles of powerful Living*. Mumbai: Jaico Book House.

Schneier, CD, Beatty, RW & Baird, LS. 1987. How to Construct a Successful Performance Appraisal System, in *The Performance Management Sourcebook*, edited by CD Schneier, RW Beatty & LS Baird. Amherst, MA: Human Resources Development Press.

Schreuder, AMG & Coetzee, M. 2006. *Careers: an Organisational Perspective*. Cape Town: Juta & Co Ltd.

Schuler, RS & Huber, VL. 1993. *Personnel and Human Resource Management*. 5th ed. St Paul: West.

Schultz, D & Schultz, SE. 2010. *Psychology and Work Today*. 10th ed. Cape Town: Pearson Education.

Sherman Garr, S. 2011. Retaining Talent in Dynamic Markets. Retrieved from: http://talentmgt.com/articles/view/retaining-talent-in-dynamic-markets.

Shore, T & Strauss, J. 2008. The Political Context of Employee Appraisal: Effects of Organisational Goals on Performance Ratings. *International Journal of Management* 25(3):599-612.

Torrington, D, Hall, L, Taylor, S & Atkinson, C. 2009. *Fundamentals of Human Resource Management*. London: Pearson Education.

Vosloo, SE. 2005. Compensation, in *Personnel Psychology,* edited by PM Muchinsky, HJ Kriek & AMG Schreuder. Cape Town: Oxford University Press. [263-295]

Weiss, JW. 2001. *Organisational Behaviour and Change: Managing Diversity, Cross-cultural Dynamics, and Ethics*. Mason, OH: South-Western College Publishing.

WorldatWork. 2007. *The World at Work Handbook of Compensation, Benefits & Total Rewards*. Hoboken, NJ: John Wiley & Sons, Inc.

7 MANAGING LOCAL TALENT IN EMERGING MARKETS – FROM A GLOBAL COMPANY PERSPECTIVE

Richard Forbes

A set of approaches and practices recommended for implementation by global organisations for the management of local talent in emerging markets. This chapter is primarily an experiential perspective based on the author's 15 years of experience on assignment with a global employer in emerging markets.

Context

From a distance, it would be relatively easy to conclude that the talent environment in all emerging markets is similar, making for one-size-fits-all strategies, but, in reality, the differences are quite considerable. Take Brazil, for example, where top-level salaries have taken off at a phenomenal rate to the extent that they are, on average, 30 to 40% higher than in the already inflated markets of Peru and Colombia. And, in Colombia, where the overall view is that the domestic-violence problem has been largely resolved, 41 candidates standing for local positions in their November 2011 elections were murdered – 41!

Such factors do, of course, bring unique challenges to the management of talent in these markets, and there is, therefore, no substitute for developing local market knowledge. Notwithstanding such locality-specific uniqueness, there are undoubtedly a number of broad talent-related factors that are common to most emerging markets, the most important of which are the following:

- **Simultaneous increase in both demand for, and supply of, talent[1]:** As growth in emerging markets continues to forge ahead from anywhere between 5% and the early double digits, the demand for top talent is of course increasing. Consequently, the competitiveness of such talent markets has also increased. This is being alleviated to some extent by the second key trend, which is that there is a surge in the return of local executives, who have been living abroad in developed markets, to their home countries. This is happening throughout Latin America, with the exception of Venezuela, and is also certainly true of most Eastern European countries, whilst, in Africa, this trend has yet to be established. In most instances, however, the return of locals from abroad has not been

---

1   See footnote number 3 below.

sufficient to meet local demand – as evidenced by the spiralling executive pay levels in Brazil and elsewhere.[2]

- **Global businesses are becoming less attractive[3]:** Five or more years ago, the average aspirant executive, from one of the less-developed economies, would have leapt at the opportunity of moving abroad and working for one of the multinational companies. Often, this was done almost without regard to salary levels. Now, however, not only are global companies less attractive in their home, or developed, markets, due to the slump of developed markets, but they have also become less attractive employers in emerging markets due primarily to the growth of the many local **dynamic companies** that have large ambitions both domestically and internationally. Witness the rapid expansion, for example, of the Grupo Bimbo, the Mexican baker, and Vale, the Brazilian mining company that is now the second-largest mining business in the world. Their competitiveness as employers has taken off, not only because of their expansion aspirations, but also because of the nature of the working environment and potential challenges that confront a new recruit. They have the cash and the opportunities to grow and innovate and therefore typically present more of a compelling canvass to the executive who really wants to make his or her mark. Global companies, by contrast, typically offer a context in which the role is more orientated towards the less-compelling challenge of continuous improvement at best, and caretaking at worst.

With these two broad themes or developments in mind, we will now turn to the specifics on local talent management within the context of emerging markets.

Assessment and Selection

Language and educational differences: As a talent practitioner, the reader will know only too well that there is often a large difference between someone who speaks a good game and someone who delivers on the promise. We are, however, wired to assess people primarily as a result of their spoken performance, in meetings, one-on-ones, presentations, et cetera. Clearly, those who do not speak the language of

---

2 Data sourced from Maria Cristina Bautista, the Managing Partner at HAY Bogota, indicates that, in the 14 countries sampled in Latin America, the average executive increase, in 2011, outstripped the overall market increase by a considerable margin (often more than double) in 7 of those markets, whilst, in the other 7, there was little difference between these 2 reference points.

3 These two assertions (refer to the headings of the two bulleted sections) are original ones that do not have an alternative literature source. The observations originate from Carlos Rodriquez and Jose Fernando Calderon, the partners of the Bogota office of Egon Zender International. These assertions were subsequently confirmed by the author via verification conversations with other recruitment agencies and recruitment professionals from commerce and industry.

the global organisation, or, perhaps even worse, those who can speak it but are not fluent, are at a significant disadvantage. The author remembers his End Year 1 talent review on his first international assignment in Poland, where the list of top talents did not include a single individual who was not fluent in English! Clearly, there was something wrong with the assessment process. In fact, his anecdotal experience was that Polish people seemed to be, on average, significantly more intelligent than the norm, an impression that remains imprinted after he needed to arrange a quality assurance of the intelligence assessment instrument and process that was in use when three consecutive external candidates were assessed as being in the 140+ IQ range!

The point, however, is that one needs to have a robust and objective assessment and selection system in place that caters for language and educational differences. Certainly, no system that is based exclusively on interviews, where language is potentially a huge contaminant, will ever be adequate. It is consequently firmly recommended that an appropriate blend of cognitive, competence and ability tests be used. In the author's experience, the flagship of senior-executive ability tests, provided it is taken in the first language, is the **Career Path Appreciation** assessment.[4]

Care needs to be taken, too, when operating in a market that has previously had a severe form of authoritarian rule. In ex-communist regime countries, for example, the history, education, and other social systems have conspired to suppress the natural tendency to challenge conventional wisdom or authority. Even though communism officially collapsed more than 20 years ago, the experience of many Western managers in Russia is that there is still a strong tendency towards compliance and submissiveness. One of the author's sources, who majored in Russian literature and lived in Moscow for over 10 years, considers that the Russian psyche is characterised by a dimension of 'pathological submissiveness', paradoxically twinned with a clinical cynicism of authority figures. In his view, the origin of this cultural trait lies more in the teaching of the Russian Orthodox Church than it does in the communist legacy, and, consequently, its impact is unlikely to dissipate in the medium-term future. One would, therefore, need to exercise caution in selecting anyone who is either low or relatively low on the attributes of either dominance or independence.

It would also be advisable to train all recruiting and interviewing managers in the key cultural and educational differences, and also to sensitise them to their own potential biases and prejudices. The author, despite being a lifetime human resources (HR) professional, regularly caught himself on the verge of making inaccurate judgements based on personal paradigms ill-suited to a particular new context.

---

4   Developed by Elliot Jacques based on stratified systems theory. Commercial ownership of the instrument rests with BIOSS International. The instrument has been proven to be both highly reliable and to have predictive validity of circa 0.7, and therefore outperforms intelligence tests [average 0.5 Pv] and personality assessment [average Pv of 0.3]. For an exploration of the underlying theory, refer to: Jacques & Clements (1991). *Executive Leadership: a Practical Guide to Managing Complexity*. Library Binding.

1. **Relative performance:** Given that most emerging markets are currently experiencing rocketing growth, there is a concurrent swarm of commercial candidates who have flooded their CVs with stellar growth claims relating to market share, gross revenue and the bottom line. Since a rising tide does indeed tend to float all boats, one will need to exercise more keen judgement than normal when interviewing and making reference checks. This is further reason, too, for following a rigorous ability- and competence-based assessment process.

2. **The 'What' and the 'How':** Many global companies have invested heavily, and over a long period of time, in developing a customised way of doing business; a preferred manner of dealing with, and relating to, team members, peers and colleagues throughout the business. This blend of values and practices, commonly referred to as the **how**, is something that is quite often foreign to local employees who have only ever been assessed on the delivery of their hard goals – the **what**. Consequently, extra care should be taken in assessing fit in this respect. It would be advisable to have an experienced psychologist review personality profile reports to screen for fit and for possible dark-side attributes that, once flagged, could be more deeply explored in the interview and reference-checking processes. As the reader knows only too well, seldom do executives fail for reasons of technical or commercial competence; rather it is the set of softer competencies, or lack thereof, that is most often the cause of failure and/or suboptimal performance by the executive and his or her business unit.

3. **The X-factor:** By virtue of their emerging-market experience, most successful local executives will have had their resilience severely tested. The Colombians will have been through the cauldron of the narco and guerrilla wars of the 1980s and 1990s, the South Africans have lived through the pressure cooker of apartheid and global exclusion, and the Eastern Europeans have lived through the dark decades of suppression of individual rights and liberties. Those executives who have been successful in such contexts will typically have developed a superior capability for coping with restrictions and setbacks; their **resilience**, the X-factor, has been hardened on the anvil of uncertainty, instability and constraint. Such capability is of immeasurable value in today's globally competitive market in which surprises, shocks and setbacks are the order of the day. Further reason for stocking the talent pond from the local end rather than from the global reservoir.

On-boarding, Development and Engagement

If the author's experience of talent management is typical, then this is the area of the discipline in which specialists in the field typically invest disproportionately less time and effort, that is, most of their attention is swallowed by the processes of recruitment, assessment, calibration and balance-sheet calculations, and deployment. This is both understandable and regrettable, since this is the area in which we are likely to see the greatest impact on the performance of the business. The full power of discretionary effort is unleashed only when the executive feels thoroughly embraced by, and aligned to, the culture, practices and values of his or her organisation. Achieving such level of engagement within the context of local cultural differences can involve significant hurdles and complications. In fact, as the following insert demonstrates, culture can kill:

> On 25 January 1990, Avianca flight 52 crashed into the village of Cove Neck, Long Island, New York, killing 74 of the 158 people on board. There was absolutely nothing wrong with the aircraft – it simply ran out of fuel. The bottom line is that the Colombian Avianca crew was unable to convey the gravity of the situation to air traffic control (ATC). Had they been able to do so, the ATC would have granted them priority landing status and all would have been well. It is highly unlikely that the accident would have occurred if a crew from America, Australia or South Africa had replaced the Colombian cabin crew on board. How so?
>
> The cultural difference in play is that referred to as the power distance index, or PDI, one of the six key cultural differences identified by Geert Hofstede[5]. PDI refers to the manner in which people behave towards those in authority. In low-PDI-index cultures like those of Australia, South Africa and the United States, people typically behave towards authority figures with the highest level of directness and the least amount of deference. In high-PDI-index cultures like those of South Korea, the Philippines and most Latin American countries, the level of directness drops and the extent of deference increases significantly.
>
> Of course, cultural factors were not the only ones in play in the case of the tragic crash of flight 52. The crew was tired after a long flight during which bad weather had resulted in their being put into a fuel-burning holding pattern by ATC in three separate instances on their flight up the east coast of the United States. Additionally, there was strong wind shear on the approach to landing at JFK. The unavoidable conclusion, however, was that the cultural upbringing of the Colombian crew meant that, amongst themselves, and in their conversations with ATC, their mitigated, or indirect, speech resulted in them being unable to convey the gravity of their situation to the tough-talking ATC at JFK. A clear instance of where 'cultured killed'.[6]

The author is fond of sharing his view that cultural quirks make very little difference to how one runs a business. In his experience, such cultural differences exist as a

---

5   Hofstede (2001).

6   Gladwell (2008).

thin veneer beneath which the principal values of respect, responsibility, honesty, hard work and integrity are universally shared and accepted. However, the PDI issue is one clear exception to this dummying down of the impact of cultural differences.[7] One of the first rules of leadership is to 'confront reality', which is difficult to do if people are too deferential of authority figures to give them bad news. Granted, such tendency is universal, as people naturally feel reluctant to be the bearer of bad tidings if there is a chance that they might be held accountable or shot as the messenger. His experience has been, however, that there is a heightened tendency in Latin America to 'give the boss the news that he or she wants to hear', and that, in Poland, there was an extreme reluctance to reveal bad news for fear of being blamed – a clear hangover of the communist regime where self-preservation dictated that it was best to remain anonymous within the system.

The recommendations that follow are made within the typical context of the acquisition of a local business by a global organisation.

1. **Integration workshop:** This is something that should be held as soon as possible after the arrival of the new global managers and should be attended by the full, local senior management team, along with all of the global expatriates who are posted to the acquisition. The goals of the workshop are the following:

    a. A clear expression of the 'identity' of the global business. Identity includes values, work processes, leadership codes or behaviour competencies. It also includes the organisation's history, its current goals and its future ambitions. As indicated earlier, the core organisational values are universal and are likely to be accepted and readily adopted, provided that the context in which they evolved is understood. The principles of respect and decency dictate that a thorough, two-way introduction of bride and groom is made after the arranged marriage. This will eliminate later surprises, minimise second-guessing and generally facilitate the union.

    b. An exploration of the cultural differences between the global and local organisation. There are a number of instruments that will provide the necessary information for creating substance in this exploration; the one favoured by the author is that of the Barrett Values Survey[8]. Such surveys will clearly demonstrate the differences in approach and the weighting or ranking of values between the dominant global business and those held by employees in the local organisation. Clearly, the recommendation is that the unification of cultures needs to be a two-way process of accommodation.

---

7   Another such example of clear cultural differences is the respective approaches taken to negotiations. In Western cultures, the handshake at the end of negotiations signifies 'the deal is done and we are ready to work together as partners', whereas, in many of the Middle Eastern cultures, such first formal shaking of hands signifies 'and now we are ready to get down to really serious business'.

8   Refer to the following link for information on this instrument: http://www.valuescentre.com/.

Global organisations that have a black-box approach to management process and culture can accordingly skip this step, but only at their own peril!

William Bridges, in his seminal work on transitions,[9] explains how we need to make **explicit** that which we are losing or need to give up in such mergers (a clear example of a transition) and that which we need to take up or adopt. Furthermore, space and time need to be given to this transition; this initial integration workshop should thus take place within a series of such events held over the first 24 months post merger or acquisition. The agreed (give up and adopt or stop/start/continue) actions clearly need to find their way into team and individual goals and the agenda of all key governance structures. Additionally, the global organisation's values statement and leadership behaviours will probably require a degree of 'tropicalisation'.

2. **Leadership development programme** as a means for extending the integration process throughout senior management ranks – what follows is a recommendation for killing many birds with one stone. The objectives of such programme would be the following:

    a. To teach local employees the commercial and cultural language of the global company. This would include all of the company-specific ways or approaches that the global company has developed over the years towards the management of each of the functions and the management of people and work per se. Here, the programme leadership or teaching would be done by long-term senior executives from the global business.

    b. To combine such proprietary approaches with a review of the latest developments and trends within the industry. Here, programme leadership would be in the hands of a local university.

    c. The foundation of the programme would, however, be individual and collective leadership development[10] based on the global business's leadership competencies and values. Programme leadership should be shared by global long-term executives and the university faculty, with the former covering personal beliefs and experiences and the latter leading classroom and case study-based learning. To ensure that the classroom learning really has individual traction, it should be supported by individual coaching by certified external coaches.

    d. Among the more intangible of the objectives are the following: (i) To sow the seeds for the development of a relationship and knowledge management network amongst local managers which is simultaneously plugged into the global virtual community; (ii) To further personalise the local managers'

---

9   *Transitions* (1979) (2004).

10 By Ulrich & Smallwood (2007).

knowledge of the global business through their direct exposure to, and sharing with, long-term senior executives from the global organisation.

e. Logistics: This paragraph is a brief overview of the approach, towards such a programme, adopted by SABMiller in their Latin American operation that initially covered six countries and currently covers seven. The scope was all executive-level managers (country MD + 2 levels down), of which there were approximately 300 in the region. Classroom learning occurred in two, two-week sessions on campus at the Costa Rica University of the INCAE Business School, where all delegates stayed at a nearby hotel and were bussed in daily. There was a three-month break between the two sessions, during which time delegates continued one-on-one coaching that had been initiated in groups as part of the first academic block. Such coaching continued at the end of the second session until delegates had completed a programme of 35 hours of both group and individual coaching. It is interesting to note that the coaching component of the programme was consistently rated as the most effective element in the programme that is now in its fifth year, with approximately 200 delegates. The total cost of the programme, including accommodation, but excluding travel, was less than USD20 000 per delegate, of which the biggest component cost was that of coaching, where the individual rate was approximately USD300 per session. In order to graduate from the programme, all delegates were required to complete small group projects based on actual business problems back in their operations, with the idea being that their learnings would be applied in such projects. Of interest is the fact that the voluntary turnover rate in this target group over this five-year term was less than 3%; clearly, the credit for this is not exclusively attributable to the programme, but delegate feedback, both formal and informal, was very positive regarding the engagement and retention impact of the programme.

3. **Social responsibility – the path to both engagement and performance:** The authors of *Firms of Endearment*[11] have convincingly demonstrated the commercial case in favour of treating all stakeholders with the same degree of care and respect that is typically afforded only to financial investors. They have shown that organisations that have followed this model have, over a 10-year period, delivered total shareholder returns of 1 025% when compared with a 122% and 316% respective yield, over the same period, by the S&P 500 and the companies listed in *Good to Great*[12]. The talent management argument, therefore, is that it makes commercial sense to drive social responsibility and ethical management as a cornerstone of one's employment value proposition

---

11 Sisodia Wolfe & Sheth (2007).

12 Collins (2001).

(EVP), particularly since issues such as corruption and social upliftment or responsibility are already centre stage in most emerging markets.[13] There is in fact a third reason for exploiting this opportunity: which is that employees independently desire and value the assumption of accountability in this arena. Employees, in particular the younger ones, are increasingly showing their concern for social issues and are expecting their companies to take a lead on such key matters. In June 2008, SABMiller ran the Barrett Survey for its executive population of 293 people, in its Latin American operations. The relevant results were that the sample group (> 95% of the executive population) wanted the company to exhibit and manifest a 36% leaning towards values in the domain of the **common good**[14] (environmental awareness, ethics, social responsibility, etc.), whereas their then current rating of the business was that it had only a 21% weighting in that direction.

There is another reason, mentioned in the contextual introduction to this chapter, as to why global companies need to find segmented and distinctive approaches to their EVP: it is that emerging markets have become extremely competitive (recall the 40% pay premium in Brazil) and the lure of working for a global organisation has lost a lot of its lustre over the last three years. In particular, global organisations are up against dynamic local companies that are on an adrenalin-charged and cash-fuelled expansion trail.[15] What they have to offer as the jewel in their EVP crown is the Cullinan diamond of bottom-line accountability in new and unchartered territory. Such unfettered accountability remains the most attractive development option for any ambitious executive. Clearly, there are few global businesses that are currently in a position to counter directly on this score.

4. **'Globally owned and locally nurtured' and/or 'the best person gets the job':** Whilst there are many global organisations that have a global **approach** to talent management, in the author's experience, there are few organisations that truly **execute** globally. By this it is meant that, at a certain level and above[16], there

---

13 At the time of writing (November 2011), the theme of corruption is particularly dominant in India. The author wishes to clearly convey, however, that he does not see the challenge of corruption as one that is limited only to emerging markets – witness the United Kingdom's parliamentary allowances scandal of 2009 – but that it is merely more prevalent in emerging markets.

14 The Barrett categorises values into three broad ascending levels of social import, akin to Maslow's hierarchy of needs, namely **self-interest**, **transformation** and **the common good**.

15 Granted, this is not the case in all emerging markets, Africa being one of those instances where this is not currently a common trend.

16 This definition of the talent pool could differ according to the seniority of the job. For example, for jobs above 1 200 Hay points, the pool could be all executives in the global business, whilst, for jobs between 700 and 1 200 points, the pool could be limited to the business unit (whether defined by

should be a firm commitment to appoint the **best** candidate in the pool. Too many organisations continue to allow the fancies or whims of local business unit management, or short-term economic perspectives (expatriates are more expensive), to determine such appointments. The rationale for this is twofold: (i) In building a sustainably competitive business, there is no ingredient that is more important than the quality of the leadership; and (ii) executives who join global organisations expect to have fair and equal access to the global career channel. Clearly, local executives, who perceive that their opportunities are being constrained by appointment practices that do not follow this philosophy, will be motivated to consider alternative possibilities.

Attraction and Retention

1. **Deep breaths and deep pockets:** It has already been mentioned that pay rates for senior executives have taken off in a number of the emerging markets, with Brazil and Russia being examples in the extreme where base rates are now well in excess of those paid in both the United Kingdom and the United States. Besides inflating one's pay costs, this also creates the dilemma where local executives are likely to be more generously remunerated than global expatriates, even after allowances are taken into account (assuming, that is, that the global employer has a single pay scale and structure for all global expatriates, regardless of location). The suggestion in such instances is that one needs to swallow hard and stick to one's pay-positioning policy rather than being lured into a short-term and false economic perspective of attempting to save on base rates by developing a different, more cost-effective, pay line for a particular market. As far as the global expatriates are concerned, the employer needs to seize the initiative by briefing them up front about the nature of, and rationale for, the company's respective pay policies. Far better that it is done in this manner than on the back foot once the first complaint has been lodged.

2. **Exploit long-term incentives (LTIs):** In 2007, less than 10% of the participating companies in the Hay Executive Survey for Latin America reported that they were using any form of share scheme as part of their overall remuneration strategy. One of the global executive recruiters in the region has, however, seen the recent increased use of three- to five-year cash-based retention schemes[17]. Global companies with their already established schemes have an advantage here that they should seek to exploit. Since both options and performance shares are effectively a self-funding form of remuneration, there is huge scope to leverage them as significant components of the attraction and retention

---

geography or by product/servicing grouping).

17 Current Hay data from the Bogota office shows that the trend of using LTIs has certainly increased over the last few years, with Brazil showing the most marked increase, where nearly half the market now uses LTIs at the most senior levels.

strategy. Most schemes have a three-year vesting cycle, and, consequently, yield considerable sway over any executive who may be considering an alternative, greener pasture.

In some of the emerging markets, Russia being one such example, rapid turnover of executives and senior managers has become something of a headache for all employers. In Moscow, the current average tenure in a company for those in the 30- to 40-year age bracket is, according to certain sources, only three years[18]. This has, of course, been driven by growth-fuelled opportunities in the market. Global employers would therefore be well advised to consider the extension of their long-term incentive schemes to lower organisational levels than has traditionally been the level at which employees become eligible for such awards.

3. **Work–home balance[19]:** The author's experience in three separate emerging-market postings is that employees in such markets have a tendency towards working far later than is the norm in developed markets, something which is probably a legacy of either authoritarian or paternalistic employers. Global companies could potentially develop this into another means of distinguishing their EVP from those of local employers. Achieving such a cultural turnaround is, of course, no simple task. However, the implementation of two significant changes should serve to overcome the inertia of such habits: (i) the implementation of a performance management system that emphasises outputs and delivery rather than inputs and 'busyness'; and (ii) the active modelling of the expected work hours, along with employee sensitisation to the fact that the global employer fully expects, requires even, that its employees lead fully balanced lives, both for the inherent rightness of the proposition, and for the fact that balance is required in order for batteries to be completely recharged for full engagement once back in the office.

4. ***"Deja tu Huella, Muestra tu Marca":*** The literal translation of this Spanish expression is, "Leave your footprint, show your own brand." The Spanish version is a far more poetic expression of the essence of a high-performance and high-engagement organisational culture, which is **enabled self-management**. The point, in this context, is that, even though established global companies may not be able to compete head for head on an EVP basis on the issue of a clean entrepreneurial canvass, they nevertheless can choose **to run** their businesses in an **entrepreneurial fashion**. Any business can elect to implement

---

18 This data is very difficult to track and verify on a real-time basis. This particular data point is a best guestimate based on reports, from a number of the big specialist remuneration consultancies, made available to the SABMiller operation in Moscow.

19 More commonly referred to as 'work–**life**' balance, a term which the author avoids using since it implies that work is not, or cannot be, an **enjoyable** part of one's life.

the fundamental principles of a values-based culture in which employees are liberated to apply their maximum discretionary effort.

The 'how to implement such a culture' calls for more than another dedicated chapter within this book. Instead, it provides ample material for a dedicated publication and, indeed, many such books have already been published.

Expatriate Management

There are three specific considerations in this section: (i) whether or not to have a second category of expatriate employees, termed here **same-language** expatriates, in addition to the regular category, **global** expatriates: (ii) the approach to pay structure for such second category of expatriates; and (iii) the approach to be taken in the replacement of expatriates (both categories) with local executives.

1. **Language and culture/socioeconomic norms as a driver of expatriate categorisation:** The two most impactful challenges that confront an expatriate in a new assignment are the foreign language and all of the different socioeconomic norms and conditions with which he or she needs to become familiar in order to navigate everyday life. If neither of these factors is different, then the only difficulty that the expatriate faces, and for which he or she need be compensated, is the normal inconvenience (and suffering!) associated with selling a home and moving one's family to a new location.

   The only reason that an employer needs to consider the prospect of implementing a second category of expatriate is that there are considerable savings to be made in the payment of allowances. The logic for such differentiation is that, if schooling is available in the host country, in the same language as in the home country, then why should the employer pay for schooling? Similarly, if the language is the same, and it is therefore relatively easy (or within reach at least) to establish new friendships, then why should the employer pay for membership at a country club where the expatriate can meet other expatriates who speak the same language?

   If one accepts this distinction, then there are in fact only two obvious[20] geographical territories in which one could consider the implementation of a second category of expatriate employee, those being Latin America (where Spanish is spoken everywhere bar Brazil) and the Middle East, and those African countries in which Arabic is widely spoken (of which there are 12 countries).

   The suggestion, therefore, is that a second category of same-language expatriates be introduced along with a defined set of benefits, which would

---

20 There will be other specific instances where it may be applicable, for example a French company that operates in a number of African countries that were formally French colonies and where French is still widely spoken. (French is still one of the **official** languages in a significant number of African countries.)

typically include an overall mobility or inconvenience allowance (15% being the suggested minimum owing to the 'just noticeable difference rule') along with a housing allowance, which should be equal to that to which the global expatriates are entitled. In fact, all allowances to which both global and same-language expatriates are entitled should be exactly equal. If one sums all of the allowances paid that are related to language/cultural differences, then the total that can be saved per expatriate family will be in the range of $50 to 100k per annum for a family of two school-going children. Against this advantage must be weighed the potential damage that may be caused to the EVP if employees perceive the categorisation, and associated differential benefits, to be unfair. This, of course, is the key. If such differences, and the associated rationale, are openly communicated in advance, and if the policy is implemented with ruthless consistency, then the downside should be contained, particularly if the employer has established credibility in respect of all other aspects of employee terms, conditions and engagement.

A further recommendation is that there be a fixed duration over which employees are entitled to expatriate benefits. Should the benefits last too long, then it is inevitable that local employees will begin to feel an injustice is being done, in that certain of their colleagues, who speak the same language, are enjoying housing and other benefits after a period during which a reasonable person would have thoroughly adjusted to his or her new living conditions.

Expatriate replacement: Ceteris paribus, a local appointee will have a greater prospect of performing well than will an expatriate employee. In addition to the local knowledge advantage, the local employee does not have the potential liability of an unsettled family that will drain energy and detract from his or her ability to perform to his or her full potential. This, in addition to the fact that expatriates are more expensive, dictates that expatriates should be replaced by local employees as soon as is practical. Clearly, the primary factor determining such timing is the availability of a suitable replacement. In the author's experience, five years is too long a period, as it has three negative impacts on talent management, being: (i) the postponement of the replacement accountability beyond both the thought and accountability horizon of the responsible manager; (ii) it leads to a paradigm of entitlement of expatriate benefits such that, regardless of how well the policy has been communicated, it becomes very difficult to actually implement the withdrawal of the associated benefits; and (iii) the problem of 'local versus local' perceived inequity mentioned in the last paragraph of point 1 above.

Unilever has successfully practised a hard-and-fast, three-year rule: if the expatriate is still *in situ* after three years, then the localisation process is automatically triggered – no exceptions. The rigour with which this is applied forces pipeline development and/or rotation planning amongst the global expatriate population. Note, however, that Unilever has only one category of expatriate, and has therefore either rejected or not considered the concept of **same-language** expatriates.

2. **Pay structures for same-language expatriates:** There are three structural choices that confront the global employer: (i) home-based pay, (ii) host-based pay, and (iii) a separate structure for all same-language expatriates within the same geographical territory. What follows is a review of the pros and cons associated with each. Of course, the perspective will be dependent on the global employer's current approach to pay structure in the various countries in which it operates, which may vary from no standardisation whatsoever to full standardisation of both principles and benefits at the other end of the range. The following review is based on the assumption that there are variations in pay practices in the countries in which the global player operates:

   a. *Host-based pay:* This is arguably the simplest system with the least amount of administrative burden in establishment. Its other clear advantage is that it is the system most suited to converting someone from expatriate to local status, since the only change that need be made is that of the removal of the expatriate benefits. Whilst one may experience pressure from same-language expatriates for the implementation of both cost-of-living and foreign-exchange allowances, the firm recommendation is not to do so, since this runs counter to the key principle of home-based structures, namely that it is the competitiveness of the total pay package in the **local** market that is the only relevant factor in determining pay levels. What needs to be clearly communicated to newly appointed expatriates is that, once they have accepted the initial offer, which will clearly require a total package uplift, then, from then on, there is no basis for continuing to draw comparisons with developments in the pay structure back home.

   b. *Home-based:* Whilst this is administratively very complex and may attract the additional cost of withholding taxes if money is transferred between separate legal entities in different countries, it does alleviate the problem of the tendency to continue to make comparisons with the benefits enjoyed in the home country. Given that terms and conditions are different from those of local employees, it is also the least appropriate for the possible eventuality of localisation. Conversely, it is also the best suited to reintegration back into the home country should that occur at the end of the expatriate assignment. In the author's experience, the hidden factory requirements of such an approach completely outweigh any advantages that there might be. It is recommended that this system be considered only where repatriation is a certainty.

   c. *Independent system:* The clear advantage of a 'third-country system' is that it can be established on a tax-neutral basis, that is, the pay scale is set based on the net rate that the expatriate will receive independent of the applicable income tax rate in the country to which he or she is posted, as the employer picks up the tax bill directly. It is also the most suited to the ongoing mobility of any one individual who may be subject to a number of consecutive assignments in a range of different countries within the same territory. The clear disadvantage, however, is that it will be the most expensive system to implement, because the pay scale will have to be on a par at least with the rate applicable in the most competitive market in the territory, which means that one will be overpaying all of the expatriates in the territory other than those who originated from the most highly paid market in the region.

Retirement fund top-up: Regardless of which of these three options is implemented, it may be necessary, in certain geographies, to implement a supplementary retirement fund for same-language expatriates, given that, in certain countries, the transfer of contributions to another jurisdiction is not possible and access to benefits when one is living in a different country is uncertain at best. Certainly, in the Central American and Andean region, only El Salvador provides such access. Comprehensive guidelines for the establishment of such a fund would warrant a full, stand-alone chapter. Possibly, the most important issue to highlight here is the fact that the employer will incur a duplicate cost (since contributions will need to be made to both the statutory and supplementary funds). Consequently, this factor needs to be accounted for in the design and management of the scheme. For example, should employees be entitled to the duplicate benefit if indeed the statutory benefits become accessible in the future, or will such benefit be debited against the accumulated benefit in the supplementary fund – the so-called 'no double-dipping' approach?

Conclusions

As is the case with all new contexts or management challenges, the first rule of leadership is 'to know and face up to your reality'. Within this context, the first issue is that one must recognise that, whilst there are a few common themes in emerging markets, each one is unique in its own right. Consequently, there is no substitute for developing a full economic, demographic and sociological understanding of the particular attributes of the market in which one is operating.

Secondly, one cannot begin to manage one's talent pool unless the features and attributes thereof are known. Achieving such insight, particularly where a foreign language is spoken, has no short cuts and requires, as a minimum, a thorough objective assessment, which is achieved with the aid of psychometric evaluation.

The mining of such location-specific data will alert one to any potential, specific cultural mismatches (such as the PDI factor) that need to be addressed, and, conversely, to the existence of any heightened tendencies, such as the resilience or X-factor, that could be 'exploited'.

The next most essential and impactful action is to ensure that a thorough on-boarding exercise is conducted through which local employees develop an intimate knowledge of the corporate personality, values and ways of working of the global employer. Simultaneously, both local and global employees must be sensitised to, and equipped to deal with, any cultural differences that may exist.

In managing local talent, opportunities exist to compete against local, **dynamic companies** that have entrepreneurial contexts. Two features, in particular, were noted, namely that of differentiating on the (economically rewarding!) aspect of social responsibility and of adopting an entrepreneurial (enabled self-management) approach to management of the local operations.

The approach to pay requires, as always, thorough market knowledge. Typically, the global employer will need to align to a base pay rate that is high relative to First World benchmarks. The two potential areas in which pay can be used to differentiate (and attract and retain) are through the more leveraged use of long-term incentives and through retirement savings schemes that cater to the inadequacies of local state schemes.

References

Barrett Values Survey: http://www.valuescentre.com/.

Bridges, W. 2004. *Transitions: Making Sense of Life's Changes.* 2nd edition. De Capo Press.

Collins, J. 2001. *Good to Great.* Harvard Business Publishing.

Gladwell, M. 2008. *Outliers: the Story of Success.* Little, Brown & Company.

Hofstede, G. 2001. *Culture's Consequences: Comparing Values, Behaviours, Institutions and Organisations across Nations.* Thousand Oaks, CA: Sage Publishing.

Jacques, W & Clements, S. 1991. *Executive Leadership: a Practical Guide to Managing Complexity.* Library Binding.

Sisodia, R, Wolfe, D & Sheth, J. 2007. *Firms of Endearment.* Wharton School Publishing.

Ulrich, D & Smallwood, N. 2007. *Leadership Brand: Developing Customer Focused Leaders to Drive Performance and Build Lasting Value.* HBS Publishing.

8

PEOPLE PROFESSIONALS FIT FOR EMERGING COUNTRIES

Theo H Veldsman

Every organisation is embedded in a strategically chosen operating arena. Increasingly, emerging countries (ECs) are becoming the chosen operating arena for many global (or globalising) organisations as they look into the future, given the predicted, growing dominance and influence of ECs in the coming years in the globalising world. ECs are countries characterised as (expanded on below): being in a state of fundamental transition and transformation; undergoing rapid economic growth; experiencing the tighter integration of their localised, closed economies and societies into the global village; and experiencing the influx of high levels of foreign investment. In many quarters, the BRICS countries (Brazil, Russia, India, and China, and, more recently, South Africa) are regarded as the pre-eminent representation of ECs. South Africa is often seen as a proxy for sub-Saharan African countries and is used by many multinational companies as the gateway into the rest of Africa.

What are some of the vital facts, trends and predictions regarding the growing stature of ECs in the world at large? Fifty per cent of the world's current population live in ECs. As population growth slows down in developed countries, this percentage may even increase, although, currently, the population rates are also dropping in ECs.[1] For the first time in history, the economic recovery after the deep recession of 2008/2009 was fuelled, not by developed countries, which are still grappling to recover and are facing the growing, worrying probability of a further recession at the time of writing this chapter, but by BRICS, which is experiencing growth rates exceeding 6%, with China and India in the lead.[2] There is even a growing expectation, perhaps out of sheer desperation, that BRICS members must intervene financially to assist countries in the European Union to overcome their financial and economic woes.

It is expected that 70% of the world's economic growth over the next few years will come from the ECs, with China and India accounting for 40% of that growth.[3] Over the past decade, 6 of the world's 10 fastest-growing countries have been in Africa. In 8 of the past 10 years, Africa has grown faster than East Asia, including Japan.[4]

In 2000, ECs accounted for 37% of the world's economic output, which rose to 45% in 2011, of which the BRICS share was 22%. It is predicted that BRICS will dominate the world economy from about 2030. It is likely that China will

---

1   Smit (2011); *The Economist* (2010); Thirlwall (2011).

2   Sachs (2011); Van Zyl (2010).

3   Ernst & Young (2009); The Economist (2010).

4   Chironga, Leke, Lund & Van Wamelen (2011); *The Economist* (2011).

become the biggest economy in the world between 2020 and 2030, though not the richest country per capita. India may not be far behind China.[5] This is based on the assumption that both countries are able to address, in a constructive manner, their sociocultural and ideological challenges, problems and issues, and not implode whilst in transition. ECs had 70 companies in the Fortune 500 in 2007, up from 20 just a decade ago. ECs are likely to account for a third of the entire list within 10 years.[6] In 2011, 19 of the top 100 brands in the world were from BRICS.

Typically, predictions such as those given above are not realised exactly as estimated – they are frequently wrong in specific quantitative terms. However, what is clear from the above is the undeniable trend that ECs will be a major future force and player globally, although how the future size, shape, power and impact of ECs globally will unfold over time cannot be pinpointed exactly.

Within today's knowledge society, of which BRICS forms a part, it is estimated that 85% of the assets of an organisation are intangible instead of tangible.[7] Tangible resources refer to, for example, facilities, technology, and finance. Intangible resources include, for example, an organisation's reputation, brand, patent rights, organisational capabilities, and people expertise and skills. It could be posited that 70% plus of these intangible resources are resident in the people of the organisation in the form of creativity, innovation, expertise, knowledge, skills, and experience. People, and the destiny of their employing organisations, are thus intimately intertwined in the knowledge society. In this society people have become the predominant value-unlockers of the potential contained in the assets of the organisation by means of which they create sustainable wealth. People also contain and maintain the organisational memory of their employing organisation in a knowledge society.

People have therefore moved centre stage in the future, sustainable success of organisations,[8] and that of ECs as societies in transition.[9] Organisations with a formal people strategy perform 35% better than their peers.[10] The returns from leading and managing people in ways that build high commitment, involvement, learning, and organisational competence are typically in the order of 30% to 40% – substantial by any measure.[11] If people have moved centre stage, then the criticality of the role and contribution of the People Professionals in organisations, or those rendering consulting services to organisations, will correspondingly increase significantly.

---

5   Sachs (2011); Van Zyl (2010).

6   Ernst & Young (2009).

7   Lev (2001; 2004).

8   Boston Consulting Group and World Federation of People Management Associations (2010); Thite, Wilkinson & Shah (2012); Veldsman (2002).

9   Thite, et al. (2012).

10 PricewaterhouseCoopers (PwC) (2002).

11 Pfeffer (1998).

In the light of the growing importance of ECs and people in the future success of organisations, the purpose of this chapter is to consider the make-up of the People Professional fit for ECs as a rising, future global player. The term 'People Professional' is used in this chapter as an umbrella term to include all professions dealing with the people dimension of the world of work, for example Industrial Psychologists, Human Resource Practitioners, and Organisational Change and Development Practitioners.

The chapter endeavours to answer the following question: What are the critical features of ECs and, as a consequence of these features, the profile of the People Professional who will be able to function and contribute effectively from a people perspective to the success of his or her organisation that are embedded in the ECs context? The critical features of ECs, however, need to be considered first against the backdrop of the emerging order of the world at large. Consequently, the profile of People Professionals fit for ECs also has to be framed within the overall shifts in the emerging world order affecting People Professionals in general. In the first instance, then, what does the emerging world order at large look like?

The Emerging Order Infusing the World at Large

Figure 1 depicts the emerging order infusing the world at large.

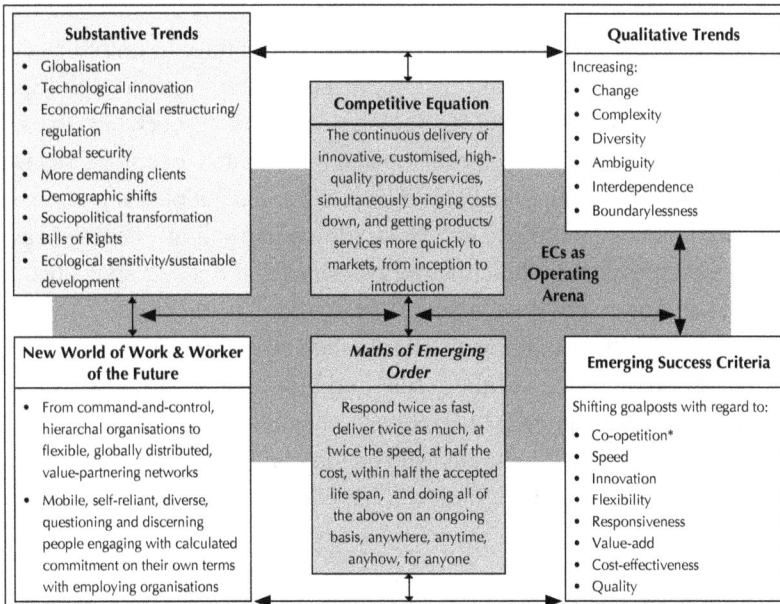

*   Co-opetition = Two or more organisations concurrently competing and cooperating.

Figure 1: The Emerging World Order[12]

---

12 Constructed by the author from the following sources: Boston Consulting Group and World Federation of People Management Associations (2010); Capelli (1999); Ernst & Young (2009); IBM Global Business Services (2008); Schwartz & DiMarzio (2011); Ukpere (2011); Veldsman (2001; 2007a; 2007b; 2008a; 2008b).

According to figure 1, organisations are facing a vastly different future in terms of expected substantive and qualitative trends, emerging success criteria, as well as the new world of work and the worker of the future. All of the aforesaid give rise to a 'recalibrated' competitive equation and reformulated competitive maths. The emerging order thus requires organisations to rethink radically the **Why? What? How? Who? Where?** and **Where to?** of their business, not only in the present, but also, in particular, whilst moving into the significantly different future of the emerging order. Playing fields, game plans, players, and rules have to be fundamentally reconsidered, reframed, and reinvented if organisations are to thrive sustainably in the future. The above implies that the future world of the People Professional also has to be reconsidered, reframed, and reinvented, which is the topic of the next section.

The Reconceived Future World of the People Professional in the Emerging World Order

Figure 2 depicts the building blocks inherent to the world of the People Professional. These building blocks are: (i) the expected, three-faceted scope of practice (eg effecting strategic business/people transformation) of the People Professional expressed in terms of (ii) three role types (eg People Generalist) regarding (iii) primary, internal stakeholders (eg line management) relative to (iv) the context (ie operating arena) within which the aforementioned are all embedded and have to unfold.[13]

The roles of 'People Generalist', 'People Leadership' and 'People Specialist' as given in figure 2, and as used in this chapter, refer respectively to: a People Professional who is client-facing, providing an integrated people service to line management and employees – the People Generalist; the People Professional(s) who is leading and directing the People Function of the organisation – People Leadership; and the People Professional who conceives, designs and delivers specialist, people-management solutions – the People Specialist.

It is suggested that the emerging order described above (see figure 1) will reinforce not only the importance of all of these building blocks making up the world of the People Professional (see figure 2) but, more significantly, will also affect the relative weighting of these building blocks, as well as the content awarded to them and the engagement mode through which they will have to be delivered.

---

13 Cf. Losely, Meissinger & Ulrich (2005); Morton, Newall & Sparkes (2001); Sparrow, Hird, Hesketh & Cooper (2010); Veldsman (2008a; 2008b) Wright, Bourdeau, Pace, Sartain, McKinnon & Antione (2011).

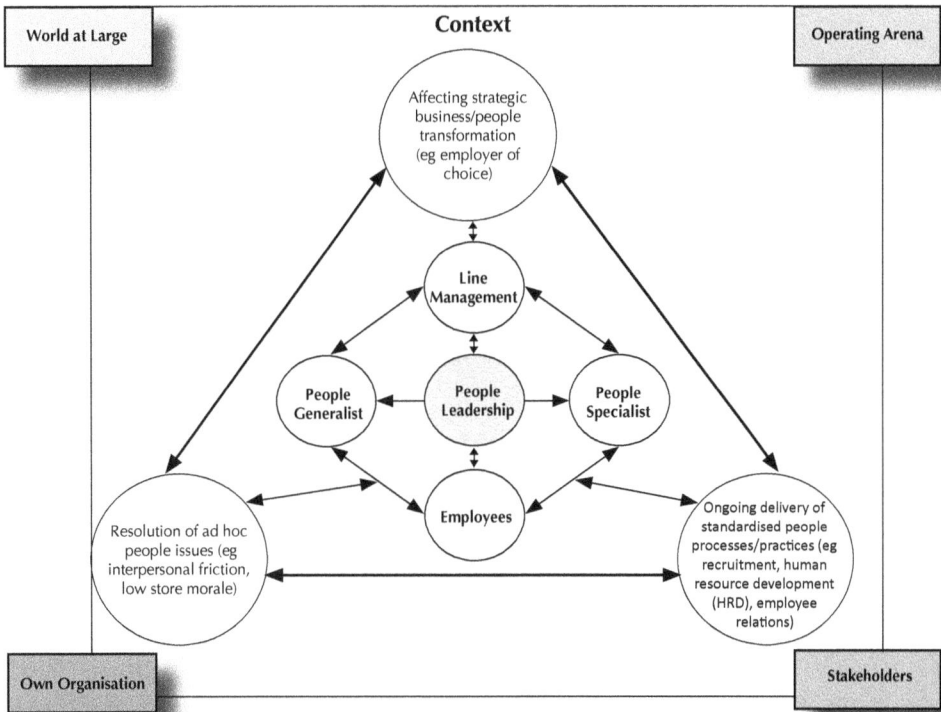

Figure 2: The World of the People Professional

In considering the emerging order discussed in the previous section (see figure 1) and the make-up of the world of the People Professional (see figure 2), at least the following five major, overall shifts will impact in general on the People Professional endeavouring to be future-fit:

- She or he will have to be much **more contextually aware and connected,** demonstrating in the process **good corporate citizenship.**

- A **good match will have to exist between him or her and the level of contextual complexity** he or she has to deal with, now and going forward into the future.

- She or he will have to **align and balance the three facets of the scope of practice** (illustrated by the triangle in figure 2, eg the ongoing delivery of standardised people processes/practices). This alignment and balance will have to be accompanied by a thorough understanding of the critical success factors associated with each facet from the vantage point of the specified facet that she or he is accountable for. More importantly, she or he will need to be able to function 'holographically' with respect to her or his facet. That is to say, the content and condition of her or his facet can only be fully understood and addressed through simultaneous insight into the content and condition of the other two facets. Holographically, the scope in its totality is contained and reflected in each and every individual facet. For example, the People Professional accountable for the ongoing delivery of standardised people processes/practices must see this delivery within the content and context of the strategic business/ people transformation the organisation is undergoing and actual/potential ad hoc people problems. This also implies that no one facet is more critical than the other. Facets must mutually support and enable one another.

- He or she must ensure that a **complete repertoire of People Professional roles** – People Generalist, People Leadership and People Specialist – exists in his or her organisation. Furthermore, the People Professional must **clearly understand the role** he or she has to fulfil (eg People Generalist), together with its requirements relative to the other two People Professional roles making up the repertoire. He or she must be able to execute his or her role in a teaming fashion, coherently, and in tandem with the other roles.

- She or he must be able to fuse, in a fair and equitable manner, the often divergent **needs, interests, and expectations of line management and employees** in forging a healthy and constructive psychosocial contract of partnering and identification, appropriate to the emerging order. A partnering contract encompasses a two-way relationship between employees and the organisation, based on everyone taking co-responsibility for the success of the organisation. An identification contract entails a two-way relationship based on meaningful and meaning-giving work.[14]

Within the future-referenced world of the People Professional, as illustrated in figure 2, the People Professional needs to make a fivefold contribution in order to be a 'shining star' in the constellation of the emerging order. Figure 3 depicts the fivefold contribution of the future-fit People Professional in the form of a star.

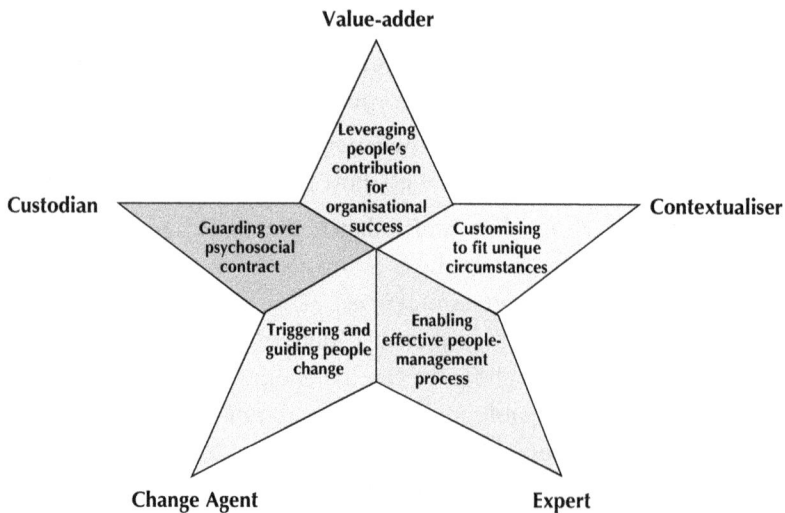

Figure 3: Being a Star: the Fivefold Contribution of the Future-fit People Professional[15]

---

14 Veldsman (2008a).

15 Source: Veldsman (2008b), as expanded from Ulrich (1997) and Ulrich & Brockbank (2005).

The fivefold contribution of the future-fit People Professional depicted in figure 3 needs to be made in a balanced and coherent fashion. This contribution in the emerging order will furthermore require shifts in the content of the engagement mode of the People Professional. These future expected shifts in the engagement mode of the People Professional are given in table 1.[16]

Table 1: Shifts in the Engagement Mode of the Future-fit People Professional

From	To
• Product-centric	• Client-centric
• Technical solutions	• Business solutions
• Functional specialist	• Business partner
• Risk avoidance, reactive	• Risk-seeking, proactive
• Transactional contributions	• Transformational contributions
• Activity focus	• Output, value focus

Against the backdrop of the emerging world order of the world at large – of which ECs form an inherent part – and the reframing of the world of the People Professional, what then are the critical features of ECs as the current or intended operating arena of an increasing number of organisations? These critical features of ECs set the specifications for the profile of the People Professionals who will be able to function and contribute effectively to the success of their organisations embedded in this operating arena. An in-depth understanding of ECs as the operating arena of one's organisation is in line with the first two shifts discussed above that will impact in general on the People Professional Requirements (PPR) endeavouring to be future-fit, namely: (i) to be much **more contextually aware and responsive (PPR1),** demonstrating in the process **good corporate citizenship (PPR2),** and (ii) **finding a good match between him or her and the level of contextual complexity (PPR3)** he or she has to deal with, now and going forward into the future.

Critical Features of Emerging Countries

For the purpose of this chapter, at least six critical features of ECs can be distinguished that are of crucial importance for organisations that have chosen ECs as their operating arenas. For at least the foreseeable future, these features will remain characteristic to a greater or lesser extent of ECs as a collective, although to different degrees for individual ECs.

---

16 Cf. Boston Consulting Group and World Federation of People Management Associations (2010); Ulrich (1997); Ulrich & Brockband (2005); Veldsman (2008a; 2008b).

Feature 1: A Fundamental Transformation is Occurring in ECs at the Foundational Layer of Society

Society can be conceived to consist of four interdependent layers, as depicted in figure 4. A deeper layer acts as the basis, and sets the frame of reference, for a later layer. The layers, according to figure 4, are given from normative-based, invisible to activity-based, visible:

- *Layer 1: Normative foundations* – the assumptions, beliefs and values forming the basis of the society. This layer provides the society with an identity, an ideology and a world-view.

- *Layer 2: Infrastructural arrangements* – the different types of entities, with their demarcated authority, rights, obligations, responsibility and accountability, making up the society and enabling it to function effectively and efficiently as a society (the 'organs of society'). For example public, semipublic and private organisations, regulatory agencies, profit and nonprofit organisations, business, as well as welfare and community organisations.

- *Layer 3: Accepted, everyday ways of doing things* – the rules, regulations, protocol, and etiquette guiding everyday living in a society. For example on which side of the road to drive, how to effect a business transaction, and how to treat and behave towards one another as citizens.

- *Layer 4: Actual everyday actions* – the actual daily conduct of citizens making up the society.

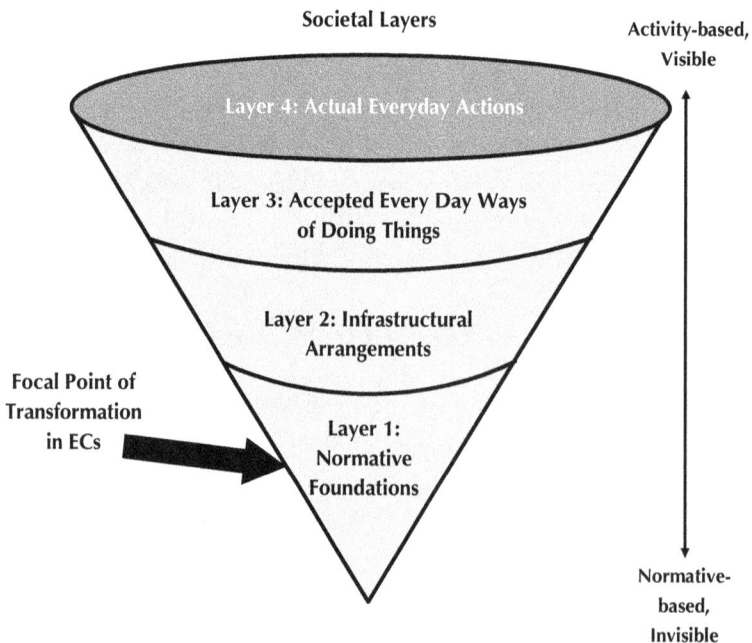

Figure 4: The Societal Layers and Focal Point of Transformation in ECs

ECs are experiencing a fundamental transformation of their foundational layer (Layer 1), that is, in the norms, values, beliefs, and assumptions informing these societies. Consequentially, this fundamental transformation is affecting, in a snowballing, destabilisation manner, their structural arrangements (eg legislative or regulatory arrangements) (Layer 2), their accepted everyday ways of doing things (Layer 3) (eg market competition rules and regulations), and, ultimately, actual everyday actions (Layer 4).[17] Diverse, competing ideological positions and camps exist in ECs about the 'right' foundational layer, normatively speaking, for these societies (Layer 1), appropriate to the new society coming into existence. Examples of such raging, intense debates are: a socialist versus a capitalist economic system; privatisation versus nationalisation; the role of the state in the economy; the relationship between the state and the church; and what should be included in the country's constitution. Commonly shared and unifying symbols, like a national flag, an official language, and public holidays and what they celebrate, are absent, weakly present, and/or hotly contested. This normative foundational ambiguity and fluidity in Layer 1 serve as a fertile ground for corruption and fraud to germinate, flourish and become endemic.[18]

These intense ideological debates and fiercely defended divides, often accompanied by violence, are frequently incubated by and/or result in unstable power relationships. Centres of power constantly shift through the ongoing reconfiguration of power groupings that represent opposing ideological and value positions. Sometimes, the state and/or the military are the only stable power base(s) in the transforming society. This results in the fierce jockeying by different groupings to gain political control of the state and/or the military. This is especially true if the state, and, sometimes, the military, control a significant portion of the available natural resources in the country, directly or indirectly through state-owned enterprises.[19] At present, one-fifth of the largest companies in ECs are state-owned.[20] Paradoxically, the endeavour to gain control of the state and/or military, in turn, may destabilise and weaken these institutions because of the power struggles. If the intense ideological dialogues and tensions are not sustainably resolved and the ideologically divisive positions taken become institutionalised in the society's fibre and DNA, the real risk to societies undergoing a fundamental transformation in their foundational layer is societal implosion, resulting in anarchy.

It is suggested that organisations operating (or wishing to operate) in the ECs typified by transformation at the foundational level have to be clear on what they stand for, as expressed in their values, beliefs, and assumptions (Layer 1 of the society), and that they communicate their stance uncompromisingly and openly, but

---

17 Agbakoba (2004); Bernstein (2010); Geldenhuys & Veldsman (2010); Thirlwall (2011); Veldsman (2002).

18 Iheriohanma (2011).

19 Schumpeter (2011).

20 Ernst & Young (2009); The Economist (2012).

diplomatically and with contextual sensitivity. They also have to be cautious where, when, how, and with which stakeholders they engage, given the ideological debates and power struggles raging in the EC society concerned.

Feature 2: The Lead/Lag Development of Infrastructure, and Systemic Imbalances

ECs are typified by the lead/lag development of their infrastructure (Layer 2 in the society), with commensurate incongruences and the absence of synergies across the country's infrastructure. For example the economy requiring skills which the educational system cannot supply or can only supply in insufficient numbers. Often, the population growth is too high relative to the growth rate of the economy, consequently creating vast pools of unemployed or semiemployed workers. Typically, in ECs, a limited pool of high-level skills exists alongside a vast pool of semiskilled and unskilled workers battling to find and retain meaningful, long-term employment, which contributes to socioeconomic class divides and significant income disparities.[21] In ECs, a highly active, informal economic sector exists in parallel with the formal economy as an escape valve for the high percentage of unemployed. (See also Feature 6 below.) The supply of high-level skills is also often detrimentally affected by a brain drain from ECs, particularly if the country's economy is struggling to expand, offers limited attractive career prospects, and/or the quality of life is poor in the country concerned.[22]

It is suggested that organisations operating (or wishing to operate) in ECs need to step in to smooth over and fill infrastructural mismatches and systemic imbalances in the society in which they are present, especially if the government of the day and/or the public sector is ineffective and weak or racked by political dissent as well as corruption and fraud. This may be done through the funding of infrastructural development and support, such as the construction/repair of roads, clinics, and schools, offering the use of training facilities to local communities to enhance skills, and joining forces with higher-education institutions to develop the higher skills needed in that country. Often, the hands-on involvement by organisations to address these infrastructural mismatches and systemic imbalances is a precondition to their ability to conduct their business efficiently and effectively in ECs.

Feature 3: Sophisticated Technology Pockets in a Sea of Low/Outdated Technology

Typically, ECs demonstrate an uneven mix of technologies of different levels of sophistication, varying from high to low, for example the widespread use of mobile

---

21 Chirongaet al. (2011); Thirlwall (2011); Ukpere (2011).

22 Benedict & Ukpere (2012); Doh, Smith, Stumpf, Tymon & Walter (2011); Iheriohanma (2011); Shah (2011).

phone technology in semi-industrialised/agricultural societies. Frequently, ECs leapfrog developed countries on the technology innovation curve by immediately advancing to the use of a more sophisticated technology, and not first adopting the less sophisticated technology. For example by bypassing land line communication and directly adopting the use of mobile phones, even smartphones.[23]

On the one hand, ECs often serve as dumping grounds for developed countries' sophisticated, yet dated, technologies, which ECs cannot always effectively deploy, use and/or maintain. On the other hand, ECs are frequently the suppliers of a variety of nonbeneficiated, natural resources to developed countries, which undertake the downstream beneficiation, the so-called 'curse of natural resources'.[24] Additionally, upcoming companies in ECs serve as outsourced manufacturing/service sites to provide the subcomponents of products/services to companies in developed countries because of their lower labour costs for skills levels comparable with those in developed countries. Concurrently, there is the growing emergence of home grown, aspiring multinational companies in ECs that are increasingly engaging in the design, production, and marketing of products for markets in developed countries and in technological innovations suitable for ECs. That is, affordable, fit-for-context consumer products appropriate to their countries such as cheap cars or mobile phones with limited functionality, the so-called frugal technologies.[25]

It is suggested that organisations operating (or wishing to operate) in ECs need to adopt fit-for-purpose technologies, appropriate to the skills levels available in ECs, and/or offer intensive, ongoing training and education to upgrade employees' knowledge and skills befitting more sophisticated technologies, and also, through alliances and partnerships, assist local, emerging organisations to build globally competitive capabilities (eg by assisting them to move downstream in the beneficiation of natural resources or deliver higher value-adding products/services.

Feature 4: The Dominant Presence of Multinational/Global, Capital-strong Companies in ECs

Frequently, the relatively unsophisticated economies of ECs are dominated by the presence of multinational/global, capital-strong companies or their local agents importing their products – especially if the host country is developing rather than emerging – to the detriment of local, upcoming, poorly capitalised companies unable to compete on an equal footing. This may pose a real threat in terms of bankruptcy and loss of employment to the local organisations, with a negative knock-on effect on local communities and individuals. Often, this real or perceived threat detrimentally affects the reputation and legitimacy of multinational/global companies, which are

---

23 Sachs (2011); *The Economist* (2010; 2011).

24 Chironga et al. (2011); *The Economist* (2011); Thirlwall (2011).

25 Sachs (2011); *The Economist* (2010); Thirlwall (2011); Thite et al. (2012).

perceived to be profiteering exploiters 'raping' these countries for their own narrow interests.[26]

It may even result in these organisations being expelled or only permitted restricted access in order to allow local companies to survive and expand. Import barriers may also be set up to protect local businesses. Local communities may also openly and aggressively mobilise and agitate against the presence of such companies or their products in their country.[27]

This situation is worsened if the multinational/global company which has a physical presence in the emerging country (EC) has an **ethnocentric attitude**.[28] This attitude assumes that there is only **one** way, and that is **their** way, as per their home country. Everything these organisations say and do takes on the flavour of how they do things 'back home'. This position is one of imported, imposed cultural imperialism. A multinational/global company may also adopt a softer, **polycentric attitude**. In this case, certain executive and senior leadership positions, especially those in critical functions, are reserved for individuals from the organisation's home country, whilst locals are given less important, more junior positions in less critical functions in the organisation. This attitude allows the organisation to 'localise' its approach in terms of *in-situ* demands and conditions.[29] The ethnocentric attitude, and also the polycentric attitude to a lesser extent, will result in the undermining and eroding of any shared sense of a common destiny amongst organisational members in the ECs, since local employees, their culture, and, by implication, their country, are seen as inherently inferior. A 'them' and 'us' divide will exist in the organisation, based on this superiority/inferiority categorisation.

It is suggested that multinational (or global) organisations operating (or wishing to operate) in ECs should rather adopt a **geocentric attitude**.[30] In this case, it is acknowledged that no single culture or management approach is superior, but that every person, and every culture, is equal and of value. The organisation should take the best from each and use what will work best within a specific context, and within the framework of shared, overarching goals and a shared destiny. From this vantage point, organisations need to seek out credible local partners with whom they can forge strong partnering relationships. They should also offer locals equal employment and career opportunities in their organisations, comparable with those offered to persons from their home countries, not only locally but also globally throughout their organisations.

---

26 Thite et al. (2012).

27 Bernstein (2010); Geldenhuys & Veldsman (2010).

28 Perlmutter (1969); Thite et al. (2012).

29 Perlmutter (1969); Thite et al. (2012).

30 Perlmutter (1969).

Feature 5: A Young, Unemployed Population with a Severe Drain of Top Talent

Typically, ECs have a rapidly growing population. In the order of 50% of their population is in the age bracket of about 15 to 35 years of age.[31] Because of systemic imbalances (refer to Feature 2 above), ECs also have a high proportion of unemployed post-high school and university graduates, because the economy is not expanding rapidly enough to provide them with employment. School-leavers in ECs also often do not have the financial means to further their education; not enough bursaries are available for such studies; insufficient educational capacity exists to satisfy the overwhelming demand for further education; and/or many of the ECs' public education institutions are of a poor quality, with poor infrastructure and insufficient resources.[32]

In contrast, most developed countries have aging populations due to a low population growth, causing a significant decrease in their economically active, high-level talented persons.[33] They also have ample financial resources for further education; have many outstanding educational institutions that set high standards; and offer attractive, lucrative career prospects. Consequently, developed countries lure the top talent of ECs, which depletes the skilled-talent pools in those countries, intensifying the war for skilled talent in ECs. The exception to this significant brain drain of top talent from ECs is where strong, local, aspiring multinational companies are emerging in ECs and/or attractive entrepreneurial opportunities are nurtured and germinated that lure local talent employed in developed countries back to ECs.[34]

It is suggested that the demographic dynamics in ECs require that, apart from the provision and/or enabling of good, widely accessible education and training (see above), organisations – local or foreign – in ECs also have to put together highly attractive, aggressive employee value propositions to attract, engage, and retain top local talent within these countries and entice back top talent currently employed in developed countries. Organisations may even have to consider differentiated employee value propositions for different talent segments that have different needs, aspirations, and values within their organisations.[35]

---

31 Chironga, et al. (2011); Smit (2011; Thirlwall (2011).

32 Benedict & Ukpere (2012); Thirlwall (2011); Ukpere (2011).

33 Benedict & Ukpere (2012); Boston Consulting Group and World Federation of People Management Associations (2010); Ernst & Young (2009); *The Economist* (2011); Smit (2011).

34 Benedict & Ukpere (2012); Doh, Smith, Stumpf, Tymon & Walter (2011); Ernst & Young (2009); Iheriohanma (2011); *The Economist* (2010).

35 Ready, Hill & Conger (2008).

Feature 6: The Wide and, in Many Cases, Widening Gap between the Haves and the Have-nots

Typically, ECs are characterised by significant socioeconomic class divides: the Haves and the Have-nots, the latter being in the majority in ECs, creating severe sociocultural and economic tensions and divides, especially as income inequality increases. Usually, the Have-nots feel marginalised and exploited, and see no positive future for themselves. Have-nots often do not have the knowledge or skills, resources, and/or opportunities to aspire to and realise a better future for themselves and their dependants.[36] Frequently, Have-nots are migrants moving from rural areas with fewer opportunities to cities that are perceived to offer more and better opportunities.[37] In developed countries, people usually feel they can have a different, better future as a result of taking personal initiative with respect to available opportunities (eg the 'American dream').

The severity of the ideological debates and divides in ECs, discussed above, is intensified significantly if they become societal fault lines along which the Haves and the Have-nots are divided. This adds a socioeconomic dimension to these debates and divides. The situation becomes exacerbated if Have-nots mobilise to gain political power through the ballot box as a means to impose their ideological agenda on society and, once they have gained power, deploy their cadres into key decision-making positions in state and semistate organisations. All of the above dynamics are worsened if corruption and fraud become endemic and acceptable ways of doing things.[38]

The severity of sociocultural and economic tensions and divides may be alleviated and countered, however, if an EC is expanding aggressively because of a high growth rate; a high influx of foreign investment; a vibrant entrepreneurial spirit with ample entrepreneurial opportunities infusing the society; and a fast-growing, emerging middle class that many can aspire to join; in conjunction with the emergence of rapidly expanding, resilient, EC-based, (multi)national companies that offer attractive employment opportunities.[39] These factors may provide greater stability for the country. Paradoxically, these factors can also accelerate the socioeconomic divide between the Haves and the Have-nots, but now more of the latter category, however, may believe that they can join the former.

It is suggested that organisations operating (or wishing to operate) in ECs have to consider how to bring the 'voices' of different socioeconomic segments of the community and society into their organisations, in this way tangibly and visibly

---

36 Geldenhuys & Veldsman (2010); Iheriohanma (2011); Smit (2011); Thirlwall (2011); Ukpere (2011).

37 Sachs (2011); Smit (2011); *The Economist* (2011); Thirlwall (2011).

38 Iheriohanma (2011).

39 Chironga et al. (2011); Ernst & Young (2009); *The Economist* (2010; 2011); Thite et al. (2012).

demonstrating their intention to be good corporate citizens. They therefore need to expand the restricted, conventional view of stakeholders (usually restricted to shareholders, employees, suppliers, and customers in the narrow Anglo-Saxon view), accompanied by a limited degree of engagement by stakeholders in organisational decisions, actions, and activities that impact on the communities in which these organisations operate. Additionally, organisations will have to go even further by concretely demonstrating their commitment to socioeconomic upliftment through publicly visible community-engagement projects in which locals are substantively involved. For example by enhancing the quality of life in communities; assisting the disadvantaged; funding the upgrading of the competence of teachers and/or upgrading schools; providing teachers at their cost to teach critical subjects in local schools; offering employment/training opportunities to new entrants into the job market and allowing them to gain the needed work experience; and providing well-planned graduate programmes and bursaries. The golden thread is organisational visibility and engagement where it matters, and making a real, sustainable difference.

Summary: Critical Features of Emerging Markets

A fundamental transformation is under way in the foundational norms, values, beliefs, and assumptions informing ECs, resulting in: intense ideological debates and fiercely defended divides, accompanied by unstable power relationships with the commensurate risk of societal implosion; the lead/lag development of infrastructure and systemic imbalances in ECs, with commensurate incongruences and the absence of synergies across their infrastructure; the presence of sophisticated technology pockets in a sea of low/outdated technology in ECs, with ECs sometimes leapfrogging developed countries on the technology innovation curve by immediately moving to more advanced technologies, especially with respect to information/communication technology; and the dominant presence of multinational/global, capital-strong companies to the detriment of local, upcoming companies that are unable to compete on an equal footing with the former, causing local resentment and resistance to their presence.

Demographically, there is a young, unemployed population concurrently with a severe brain drain of top talent from ECs, countered somewhat in instances where strong, local, (multi)national companies are emerging in ECs and/or attractive entrepreneurial opportunities are germinated and nurtured that lure local talent employed in developed countries back to ECs. Finally, the wide (and, in many cases, widening) gap between the Haves and the Have-nots in ECs creates severe ideological, sociocultural, and economic tensions and divides. The severity of the sociocultural and economic tensions and divides may be alleviated and countered, however, if an EC is expanding aggressively because of a high growth rate, if a vibrant and strong entrepreneurial spirit and ample entrepreneurial opportunities exist, and if there is a fast-growing middle class that many can aspire to join, alongside the emergence of rapidly expanding, resilient, EC-based, (multi)national companies that offer attractive employment opportunities.

The major implications of these features for organisations with ECs as their chosen operating arena in general and for People Professional Requirements (PPRs) in particular are the following:

1. The need for a visible, clearly articulated and communicated **values and beliefs stance**: "This is who we are and what we stand for" (**PPR4**).

2. The need for a well-thought-through **stakeholder engagement strategy**, given the power struggles and ideological debates raging in the society (**PPR5**).

3. The need to find effective ways and means to bring the **'voices' of different segments of the society and communities into the organisations**, in the process expanding the organisation's view of its stakeholders and engaging both the Haves and the Have-nots (**PPR6**).

4. The need to visibly and concretely demonstrate good corporate citizenship through real, sustainable **social upliftment interventions** in which local stakeholders are directly involved in a real and meaningful way, again engaging both the Haves and the Have-nots (**PPR7**).

5. The need to step in to smooth over and **fill infrastructural underdevelopment/ mismatches and systemic imbalances** in the society (**PPR8**).

6. The need to adopt a **geocentric attitude** by finding credible local partners with which strong partnering relationships can be formed, and by giving locals equal employment and career opportunities across all organisational levels and areas in their organisations, both locally and globally (**PPR9**).

7. The need to craft a highly attractive, aggressive **employee value proposition** to attract, engage, and retain top local talent and local talent that is currently abroad (**PPR10**).

8. The need to adopt fit-for-purpose technologies, appropriate to the skills levels available in ECs, and/or offer intensive, ongoing **capacity building** through training and education to upgrade prospective and current employees' knowledge and skills befitting more sophisticated technologies (**PPR11**).

9. Through alliances and partnerships, assisting local, emerging organisations to build **global competitive capabilities.** For example by assisting them to move downstream in the beneficiation of natural resources (**PPR12**).

Given the features of ECs, with their implications for organisations operating (or wishing to operate) in these countries, what, then, should be the profile of the People Professional able to function and contribute effectively to the success of his or her organisation within the EC context?

Suggested Profile of People Professionals Able to Function and Contribute Effectively to the Success of Their Organisations with ECs as Their Operating Arena

The discussion on the crafting of the suggested, desired profile of People Professionals fit for ECs as their organisations' operating arena will proceed along the following lines: **first**, the key performance dimensions of such People Professionals will be distinguished; **secondly**, these performance dimensions will be translated into the required competency domains; and, **thirdly**, the competency domains, in turn, will be unpacked in terms of specific personal attributes, knowledge, skills, expertise, attitudes, and conduct.[40] From a broader perspective, the desired profile of the EC-fit People Professional is made up of all of the above elements. From a narrower perspective, the profile could consist of only the last element, namely personal attributes, knowledge, skills and expertise, attitudes, and conduct. The suggested profile of EC-fit People Professionals also needs to incorporate the demands imposed by the emerging order infusing the world at large and accompanying shifts in the People Professionals' world as discussed above.

Figure 5 depicts the **proposed key performance dimensions** of People Professionals able to function and contribute effectively to their organisations in the emerging world order in general, and, more specifically, in ECs as their operating arena, making them 'EC-fit' People Professionals.

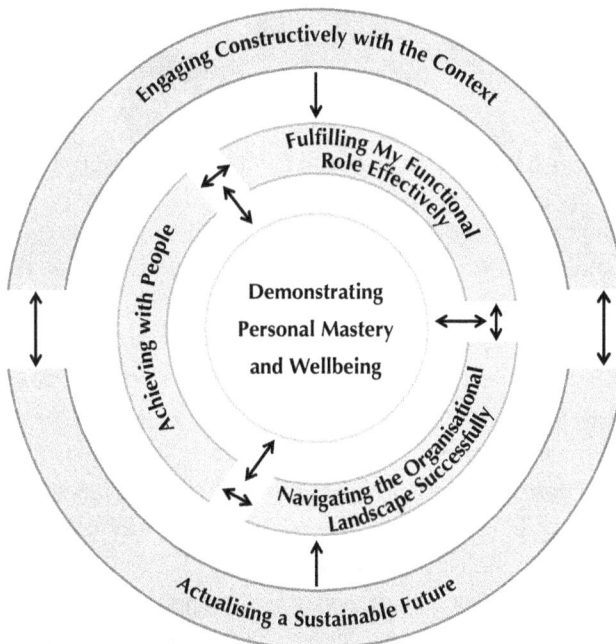

Figure 5: What It Would Take to Succeed as an EC-fit People Professional: Proposed Key Performance Dimensions

---

40 Veldsman (2012).

The proposed key performance dimensions depicted in figure 5 form a systemic and integrated whole. Success as an EC-fit People Professional is therefore the outcome of the metacompetence of holistically integrating all of these key performance dimensions, simultaneously and synchronously in a synergistic and coherent fashion.

Figure 6 gives the translation of the proposed performance dimensions for an EC-fit People Professional into the **required, commensurate competency domains**.

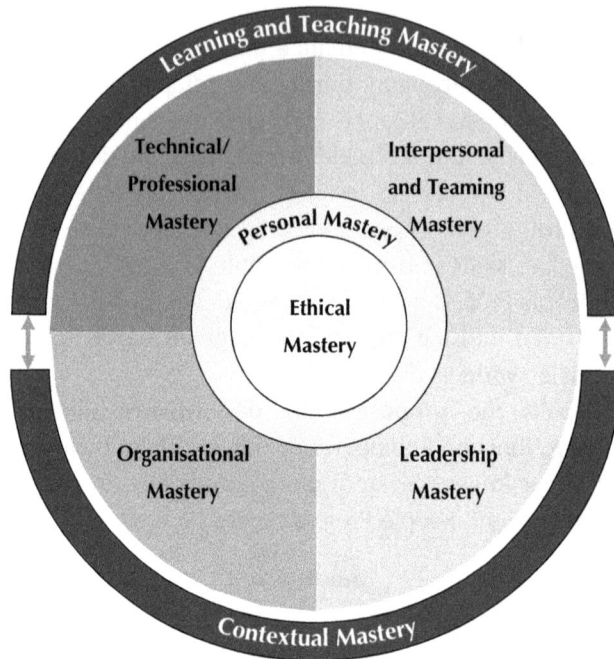

Figure 6: Suggested Competency Domains of an EC-fit People Professional

With respect to figure 6, important to note is the relative positioning of the respective competency domains to one another. According to figure 6, Ethical Mastery forms the centrepiece of the competency landscape of the People Professional and infuses all of the other competency domains. Personal Mastery, in turn, provides the basis from which the other competency domains are leveraged delivery-wise. The Contextual and Learning Masteries set the frame of reference for all of the other competency domains. The competency domains given in figure 6, like the proposed key performance dimensions depicted in figure 5, also form a systemic and integrated whole. Success as an EC-fit People Professional is therefore also the outcome of the metacompetence of holistically integrating all of these competency domains, simultaneously and synchronously, in a synergistic and coherent fashion.

The suggested competency domains contained in figure 6 can be defined as follows:

- **Ethical Mastery:** the ability to act consistently and coherently in accordance with one's moral convictions.

- **Personal Mastery:** the ability to manage oneself in terms of who and what one is and wishes to be.

- **Technical/Professional Mastery:** the ability to apply the knowledge, skills, and expertise associated with a discipline/practice area.

- **Interpersonal and Teaming Mastery:** the ability to interact in a constructive and conducive manner with others.

- **Organisational Mastery:** the ability to get things done in the organisation with the support of stakeholders.

- **Leadership (including Management) Mastery:** the ability to develop and mobilise people around a shared vision and values, lead them towards actualising the vision and living the values, and direct and lead the organisation on a daily basis.

- **Contextual Mastery:** the ability to function at the requisite level of complexity as set by the requirements of both the external and internal contexts of the organisation.

- **Learning and Teaching Mastery:** the ability to learn/teach, and to use one's learning/teaching effectively by changing oneself and the setting in which one operates.

In terms of the competency domains given in figure 6, it is proposed that People Professionals in EC-based organisations will need at least the following specific mission-critical competencies in terms of personal attributes, knowledge, skills and expertise, attitudes, and conduct, as given in table 2. The PPRs informing these competencies, as identified in the above discussion of the emerging world order and features of ECs, are given in the last column of table 2.

Table 2: The Recommended Mission-critical Competencies of an EC-fit People Professional

COMPETENCY DOMAIN	PERSONAL ATTRIBUTES	KNOWLEDGE, SKILLS, AND EXPERTISE	ATTITUDES	CONDUCT	PEOPLE PROFESSIONAL REQUIREMENT (PPR) ADDRESSED
Ethical Mastery	• A clear stance regarding their values, beliefs, and norms • Integrity	• An understanding of/insight into local cultural values, beliefs, norms, customs, and traditions	• Social conscience • Corporate citizenship	• Integrity • Honesty	PPR2: Corporate citizen PPR4: Values and beliefs stance

COMPETENCY DOMAIN	PERSONAL ATTRIBUTES	KNOWLEDGE, SKILLS, AND EXPERTISE	ATTITUDES	CONDUCT	PEOPLE PROFESSIONAL REQUIREMENT (PPR) ADDRESSED
Personal Mastery	• Systemic ('big picture') thinking • Convergent (ie synthetic) and divergent (ie analytical) thinking	• Fun orientation • 'Can do' orientation • Curiosity		• Self-driven • Courage • Perseverance	PPR1: Contextual awareness and responsiveness PPR3: Contextual complexity match
Personal Mastery (continued)	• Resilience • Responsiveness • Agility (or Flexibility) • Internal locus of control • High tolerance for ambiguity • High risk-taking • Creativity and innovation				PPR8: Infrastructural and systemic balancing
Technical/ Professional Mastery	• Future-driven	• An understanding of, and ability to effect, changes in mind-sets and world-views • Strong technical/ professional base with the ability to localise/ customise • Multilingual • E-technological savvy	• Geocentric approach	• Large-scale, systemic change ability	PPR7: Social upliftment PPR8: Infrastructural and systemic balancing
Interpersonal and Teaming Mastery	• High emotional intelligence • Persuasiveness • Strong diversity sensitivity	• A deep understanding of interpersonal and teaming dynamics within a multicultural setting	• Diversity-friendly • Inclusivity and Teaming	• Caring • Good listener	PPR5: Stakeholder engagement PPR6: Inclusivity

COMPETENCY DOMAIN	PERSONAL ATTRIBUTES	KNOWLEDGE, SKILLS, AND EXPERTISE	ATTITUDES	CONDUCT	PEOPLE PROFESSIONAL REQUIREMENT (PPR) ADDRESSED
Leadership Mastery	• Personal presence and stature	• A sense of a purpose which is bigger than merely the pursuit of profits	• Consultative and co-determinate styles	• Transformational (ie vision- and values-driven) **and** Transcendental Leadership (ie purpose- and meaning-driven)	PPR4: Values and beliefs stance PPR5: Stakeholder engagement PPR6: Inclusivity
Organisational Mastery		• A deep understanding of organisational dynamics and culture within a multicultural setting • Cross-functional organisational insight	• Entrepreneurial	• Partnering • Network and coalition building • Organisational branding	PPR6: Inclusivity PPR10: Employee value proposition PPR11: Capacity building
Contextual Mastery	• Intergenerational and intercultural sensitivity	• EC business acumen • Intergenerational and intercultural literacy	• A global mind-set	• Risk mitigation • Being intergenerationally and interculturally streetwise	PPR1: Contextual awareness and responsiveness PPR2: Corporate citizen PPR3: Contextual complexity match PPR9: Geocentric attitude
Learning & Teaching Mastery		• Multiple learning approaches, eg learning to learn, learning by reframing	• Learning and teaching attitude	• Learning and teaching	PPR7: Social upliftment PPR8: Infrastructural and systemic balancing PPR11: Capacity building

According to table 2, the EC-fit People Professional will need to be a much more rounded, contextually connected, culturally and values-attuned person, with deeper, more complex competencies, and able to make things happen with diverse stakeholders in spite of *in-situ* challenges, issues and problems. The challenges, issues and problems need to be seen within an integrated localised/global frame of reference, and be clearly linked to a clear vision of where the organisation wants to go. In other words, technical/professional competencies are necessary, but are not sufficient to be effective as a People Professional practising in an EC. Contextual, stakeholder, and intercultural wisdom and intelligences will be significantly more important.

Conclusion

If ECs are going to be a force to be reckoned with in the future world order, organisations will need to have People Professionals who fit the demands and requirements of this operating arena. In the light of the growing importance of ECs and people in the future success of organisations, the purpose of the chapter was to consider the make-up of the People Professional fit for ECs as a growing, future operating arena.

The chapter endeavoured to answer the following question: What are the critical features of ECs and, as a consequence of these features, the profile of the People Professional who will be able to function and contribute effectively from a people perspective to the success of his or her organisation embedded in the EC context? The critical features of ECs were considered against the backdrop of the emerging world order. The profile of People Professionals fit for ECs was also framed within the overall shifts affecting People Professionals in general, because of the emerging world order.

The profile of the EC-fit People Professional set against the backdrop of the emerging order will differ significantly from that of current People Professionals, who will increasingly become future-unfit as ECs grow in global importance. The challenge to higher-educational institutions and organisations operating (or wishing to operate) in ECs is how to identify, assess and develop People Professionals who are EC-fit. Specifically, the challenge is to shift the conventional focus and emphasis on the Technical/Professional Mastery of People Professionals to the masteries essential to a well-rounded, contextually, value- and culturally attuned People Professional. If higher-educational institutions and organisations do not rise to this challenge, People Professionals will be unable to assist their organisations in turning their people into true value unlockers and wealth creators, which is essential to organisations wishing to thrive in the knowledge society with ECs as their operating arena.

Acknowledgements

Inputs by my colleagues in the Department of Industrial Psychology and People Management, University of Johannesburg, and by members of the Department's Advisory Committee regarding the profile of the EC-fit People Professional are gratefully acknowledged.

References

Agbakoba, JC. 2004. Transitional African Political Thought and the Crises of Governance in Contemporary African Societies. *Journal for the Study of Religions and Ideologies* 7 (Spring):137-154.

Benedict, OH & Ukpere, WI. 2012. Brain Drain and African Development: Any Possible Gain from the Drain? *African Journal of Business Management* 6(7), 22 February 2012:2421-2428. DOI: 10.5897/AJBM11.2385. Available online at http://www.academicjournals.org/AJBM.

Bernstein, A. 2010. *The Case for Business in Developing Countries*. Johannesburg: Penguin Books.

Boston Consulting Group and World Federation of People Management Associations. 2010. *Creating People Advantage 2010. How Companies Can Adapt Their HR Practices for Volatile Times*. Boston: Boston Consulting Group.

Capelli, P. 1999. *The New Deal at Work*. Boston: Harvard Business School Press.

Chironga, M, Leke, A, Lund, S & Van Wamelen, A. 2011. Cracking the Next Growth Market: Africa. *Harvard Business Review* May 2011:177-122.

Doh, JP, Smith, RR, Stumpf, SA, Tymon, WG & Walter G. 2011. Pride and Professionals: Retaining Talent in Emerging Economies. *Journal of Business Strategy* 32(5):35-42.

Ernst & Young. 2009. *Global Trends 2009*. Cleveland: EYGM Ltd.

Geldenhuys, CA & Veldsman, TH. 2010. A Change Navigation-based, Scenario Planning Process within a Developing World Context from an Afro-centric Leadership Perspective. *SA Journal of Human Resource Management* 9(1). DOI:10.4102/sajhrm.v9i1.265.

IBM Global Business Services. 2008. *The Enterprise of the Future. IBM Global CEO Study*. Somers, New York: IBM.

Iheriohanma, EBJ. 2011. Capacity Building, Leadership Question and Drains of Corruption in Africa: a Theoretical Discourse. *Asian Social Science* 7(3) March 2011:131-138.

Lev, B. 2001. *Intangible Assets: Values, Measures and Risks*. Oxford: Oxford University Press.

Lev, B. 2004. Sharpening the Intangibles Edge. *Harvard Business Review* June 2004:109-116.

Losely, M, Meissinger, S & Ulrich, D. 2005. *The Future of Human Resources Management*. New Jersey: John Wiley.

Morton, C, Newall, A & Sparkes, J. 2001. *Leading HR*. London: Chartered Institute of Personnel and Development.

Perlmutter, H. 1969. The Tortuous Evolution of the Multi-national Corporation. *Columbia Journal of World Business* January/February 1969:9-18.

Pfeffer, J. 1998. *The Human Equation. Building Profits by Putting People First*. Boston: Harvard Business School Press.

PricewaterhouseCoopers. 2002. *Global Human Capital Survey 2002/3. Executive Briefing: Effective People Management and Profitability.* London: Global Centre of Excellence, PriceWaterhouseCoopers.

Ready, DA, Hill, LA & Conger, JA. 2008. Winning the Race for Talent in Emerging Markets. *Harvard Business Review* November 2008:2-10.

Sachs, J. 2011. *The Price of Civilization. Economics and Ethics after the Fall.* London: The Bodley Head.

Schumpeter column. 2011. Khaki Capitalism *The Economist* 3 December 2011:67.

Schwartz, J & DiMarzio, M. 2011. *Human Capital Trends 2011. Revolution/Evolution.* Deloitte Consulting LLP.

Shah, JI. 2011. Brain Drain: Why People Leave their Motherland? (Implications for the Developed and Developing Economies). *Journal of Managerial Sciences* V(1):63-74.

Smit, F. 2011. Mirror Image of the World. SA Follows Trends, but Can It Overcome the Challenges (title translated from the Afrikaans). *Beeld* 12 July 2011:13.

Sparrow, P, Hird, M, Hesketh, A & Cooper, C. 2010. *Leading HR.* Houndmills: Palgrave Macmillan.

The Economist. 2010. *Special Report: the World Turned Upside Down* 17 April 2010.

The Economist. 2011. *Briefing. Africa's Hopeful Economies* 3 December 2011:68-70.

The Economist. 2012. *Special Report: State Capitalism* 21 January 2012.

Thirlwall, AP. 2011. *Economics of Development. Theory and Evidence.* Houndmills: Palgrave Macmillan.

Thite, M, Wilkinson, A & Shah, D. 2012. Internationalization and HRM Strategies across Subsidiaries in Multinational Corporations from Emerging Economies – a Conceptual Framework. *Journal of World Business* 47:251-258.

Ukpere, WI. 2011. Globalisation and the Challenges of Unemployment, Income Inequality and Poverty in Africa. *African Journal of Business Management* 5(15):6072-6084.

Ulrich, D. 1997. *Human Resource Champions.* Boston: Harvard Business School Press.

Ulrich, D & Brockbank, W. 2005. *The HR Value Proposition.* Boston: Harvard Publishing Company.

Van Zyl, A . 2010. Emerging Countries 'Are Centre of Future Economic Growth' (title translated from the Afrikaans). *Sakebeeld* 4 June 2010.

Veldsman, TH. 2001. To Have a Future or Not? Reinventing People Management to Fit a Different Competitive Reality. Top HR Conference, August 2001, Midrand.

Veldsman, TH. 2002. *Into the People Effectiveness Arena. Navigating between Chaos and Order.* Johannesburg: Knowledge Resources.

Veldsman, TH. 2007a. The People Effectiveness Compass: Holding a Steady Course in Worsening Weather Conditions (Part 1). *Management Today* 23(8):58-60.

Veldsman, TH. 2007b. The People Effectiveness Compass: Holding a Steady Course in Worsening Weather Conditions (Part 2). *Management Today* 23(9):58-60.

Veldsman, TH. 2008a. People Management in the New Order. In Pursuit of Leading World-class Practices (Part 1). *Management Today* 24(8):56-60.

Veldsman, TH. 2008b. People Management in the New Order. In Pursuit of Leading World-class Practices (Part 2). *Management Today* 24(9):60-64.

Veldsman, TH. 2012. An Organisation Person-fit Competency Model Appropriate to a Newly Emerging World of Work, in *Managing Performance in Organisations,* edited by J Herholdt. Johannesburg: Knowledge Resources, 53-76.

Wright, PM, Boudreau, JW, Pace, DA, Sartain, E, McKinnon, P & Antione, RL. 2011. *The Chief HR Officer.* San Francisco: Jossey-Bass.

Part 2: Managing Talent in Emerging Markets: Case Studies

Chapter 9:   The Role of Talent Management in SABMiller's Globalisation

Chapter 10: Global Talent Management Case Study: Talent Management in AngloGold Ashanti

Chapter 11: Case Study: Pick n Pay – the Upside of Exporting Values

Chapter 12: Unilever Brazil: a Story of Organisational and Personal Renewal

Chapter 13: Standard Bank – Leading the Way in Africa

Chapter 14: Transitioning from a State-owned Factory to a World-class Operation: British American Tobacco Prilucky Factory

Chapter 15: From Fossil to First-in-Class: Transforming Corporate Culture in British American Tobacco Heidelberg Factory

9 THE ROLE OF TALENT MANAGEMENT IN SABMILLER'S GLOBALISATION

Steve Bluen, Tony van Kralingen & Lara Hirschowitz

South African Breweries (SAB) grew from being a dominant player in the South African market to becoming the second-largest brewer in the world in less than 20 years. Today, SABMiller (SABM)[1] owns more than 200 beer brands and employs 70 000 people in over 75 countries. It is also one of the world's largest bottlers of Coca-Cola. For the year ended March 2011, beer sales were over 217 million hectolitres and soft-drink sales represented a further 46 million hectolitres.[2] Over the past decade, SABM's global beer sales grew from 3.8% of the total market in 2000 to 12% in 2010. SABM currently has garnered 20% of the global beer-profit pool.[3]

In the early 1990s, when SAB started globalising, a critical component of the business model was to acquire businesses, initially in emerging markets, and to send hand-picked expatriates to run these businesses. To do so, the South African operation provided talent to fill global positions, while continuing to perform optimally locally – sufficient managerial depth needed to be maintained to ensure that all key SAB positions were filled with competent leaders. There thus had to be sufficient bench strength to meet local and international demands. The size of this challenge was impressive: Some 200 executives – 40% of the senior management ranks – were expatriated over a 10-year period. To become an effective global talent nursery, talent management became a critical business strategy at SAB. In this chapter, we describe the role that talent management fulfilled in SABM's transition from local to global brewer. In doing so, the following topics will be covered:

- Contextual factors supporting SAB's globalisation.

- SAB's historically strong people focus.

- Establishing people processes to ensure a strong talent pool ready to move offshore.

- The global geographic footprint: Africa, Europe and the Americas.

---

1   While 'SAB' refers to the South African operation, in 2002 the Group's name changed, with the acquisition of Miller Brewing Company, to SABMiller (SABM).

2   SABMiller (2011a).

3   Bank of America and Merril Lynch, 2010.

- The challenge of scale.

- Managing the emerging-market talent challenges.

- Entrenching a global business: Global Talent Management.

Contextual Factors Supporting SAB's Globalisation

Prior to the 1990s, anti-apartheid sanctions resulted in South Africa's economic isolation. The geographic landscape of many local companies, including SAB, was limited to South Africa and expansion was confined to domestic growth. At the time, SAB's beer-market share was over 98%, with little room for organic growth. Consequently, SAB adopted a strategy of growth through diversification, investing in other consumer-related industries, such as furniture, matches, hotels and retail. SAB became South Africa's major consumer-based conglomerate, accounting for R1 in every R20 spent by South African consumers.

In the late 1980s, early 1990s, the following geopolitical events enhanced SAB's transition to a global brewer:

1. **Transformation in South Africa.** Nelson Mandela was released from prison in 1990, previously-outlawed political parties were unbanned and the first free and fair elections were held in 1994. South Africa was readmitted into the global community and SAB was free to expand beyond South Africa's borders.

2. **The rise of globalisation.** Globalisation, liberalisation, and deregulation had gained great impetus by the late 1980s.[4] The world had opened up more rapidly and SAB was well positioned to take advantage of this trend, to grow globally.

3. **Collapse of the Berlin Wall.** The Berlin Wall came down on 9 November 1989. This heralded a dramatic breakdown of communist regimes across Central and Eastern Europe. "In Poland the transition (from communism to democracy) took 10 years; in Hungary 10 months; in East Germany 10 weeks; and in Czechoslovakia 10 days![5]" This paved the way for previously state-owned enterprises to privatise via joint ventures with foreign partners.

4. **The end of African socialism.** The downfall of the socialist regimes in Eastern and Central Europe contributed significantly to the demise of African socialism.[6] As with Europe, African governments sought joint-venture partners for their previously state-owned enterprises. SAB embraced this opportunity on both continents.

---

4   Jones (2006).

5   Timothy Garton Ash, 1993.

6   Pitcher & Askew (2006).

5. **The Chinese government's move towards economic liberalisation.** In the 1990s, as part of its revised economic policies, China experienced rapid growth and international trade and foreign direct investment mushroomed from 1992.[7] This created opportunities for joint ventures with Western companies such as SAB.

6. **Greater political stability in South America.** Increased foreign direct investment in South America was positively correlated with economic stability, growth and trade openness and led to the improvement of the political and institutional environment[8]. This paved the way for SABM to acquire Grupo Empresarial Bavaria in 2006.

7. **Diversification falls out of favour and SAB recognises its core competencies.** In the late 1980s, early 1990s, the view emerged that corporate diversification destroyed shareholder value.[9] With the opening of global markets, growth in SAB was no longer limited to local diversification. During the mid-1990s, SAB divested from its noncore assets in retail and manufacturing, disposing of 10 companies, 7 of which were listed on the Johannesburg Stock Exchange (JSE). This enabled SAB to focus on its core beer and beverages capabilities and to free up capital to purchase offshore acquisitions.

These contextual changes presented great opportunities for SAB to globalise. As mergers and acquisition prospects presented themselves in Africa, Central and Eastern Europe, China and South America, many of the established brewers in developed countries shied away from emerging markets. This left a clear path for SAB to acquire operations, largely across the developing world in the 1990s, thereby obtaining 'early mover' advantages; and then enter North and South America and Western Europe in the next decade (see figure 1).

While the context favoured globalisation, SAB faced some serious challenges. The company had limited acquisition funds. Tight foreign exchange controls restricted the amount of money the company could take out of the country to make these purchases. Also, while many multinational companies had strong global brands to drive international expansion, SAB had no global brands upon which to base its international drive.

What SAB had in its favour was an exceptionally strong talent pool comprising experienced people who were eager to apply their expertise across the world. Also, SAB had developed extremely effective management practices that helped drive performance across the Group in subsequent years. Many factors contributed to SAB's strong people focus over the years, and it is to these issues that the attention now turns.

---

7   Foreign direct investment in China increased from $12 billion in 1991 to $58 billion in 1992 and to $111 billion in 1993 (Dang 2008; Huang 2008).

8   Amal, Tomio & Raboch (2010).

9   Martin & Sayrak (2003).

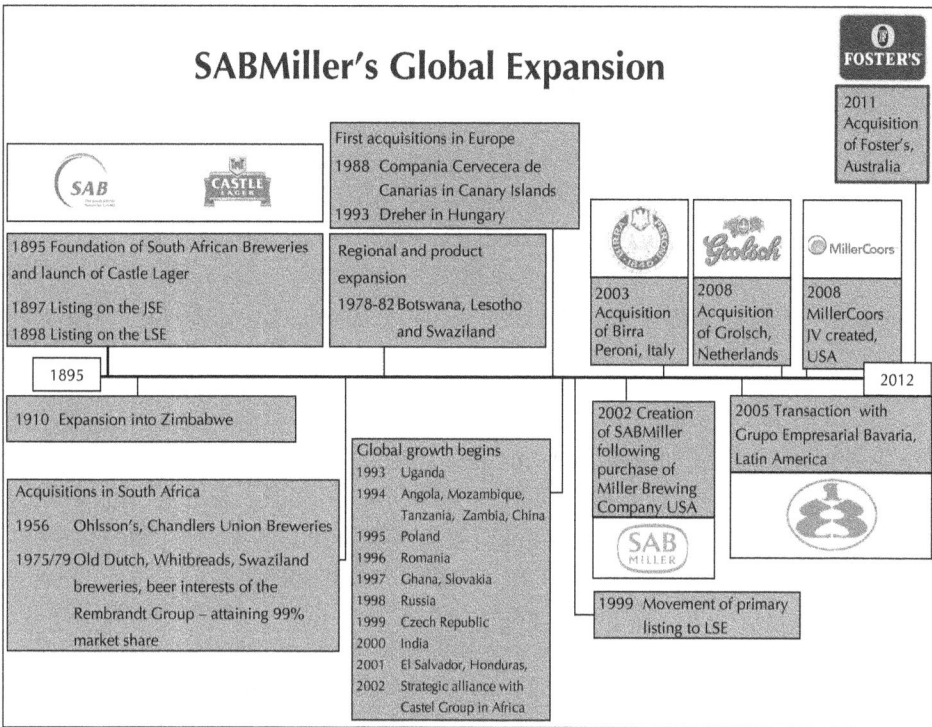

Figure 1: SABMiller's Global Expansion

SAB's Historically Strong People Focus

Many of the human resource (HR) practices SAB pioneered in the late 1980s and in the 1990s to lay the groundwork for globalisation have subsequently become common talent management practices in multinational corporations today. At the time, however, they were considered ground-breaking practices. SAB leaders have always believed that success as a business is linked to the calibre of its people. As Meyer Kahn, SABM's past Group Chairperson, said, "In the short term, business is all about achieving the numbers, but in the medium and long term, it's all about people." Some examples of SAB's historical, people-focused approach are listed below.

Psychometric assessments to select for potential. One example of the historical importance that SAB placed on HR is that it was the first South African company to appoint a Human Resources Director[10], namely Dr Simon Biesheuvel, to its Board in 1962. Biesheuvel had previously headed up the National Institute for Personnel Research, which, under his leadership, pioneered psychometric assessment in South Africa. Biesheuvel established psychometric assessment as a cornerstone upon which SAB's stringent selection criteria were based. The tradition of using psychometrics as

---

10 At the time, termed 'personnel director'.

a non-negotiable selection tool has remained central to SABM's talent approach ever since. When Graham Mackay moved from Managing Director of the South African operation to take on a Group role in 1994, he stated in his farewell speech: "There are many features that make SAB a great company but there is only one characteristic that is uniquely excellent and that is the quality of its people." A key contributor to this feature is the stringent and universal use of psychometric assessments. Psychometric batteries have been compiled to assess candidates in all job categories. By making psychometric assessments central to selection, entry into SAB is limited to people with high potential, intellectual capability, and the psychological make-up to succeed.

What continues to differentiate SABM from other companies is **how** psychometric assessments are used. Many organisations base selection decisions on candidates' skills and abilities to do the **current job**, which has a clear short-term benefit. SABM, on the other hand, focuses on hiring people for their **potential**. This yields a much longer-term talent benefit and enhances the future leader pipeline. The SAB psychometric model focuses on three components, namely personality, cognitive ability, and judgement, which enhances the accuracy of predicting potential and thereby feeds the company's future leadership talent pool.

Recruiting for potential. As mentioned above, people with exceptional potential were recruited to become part of a talent pool in order to learn about the business and be deployed as the need arose. Typically, these high-potential people were slotted into the company as 'trainees'. They would be assigned to a senior manager and were required to run projects and undergo rigorous training in areas where competence gaps were identified. As trainees, they learnt the business while giving the company the opportunity of assessing where best they would fit. Within 12 to 18 months, they were ready to perform a mainstream role. Recruiting above headcount was extremely brave and expensive and broke all the rules of cost-cutting. Nevertheless, it provided an ongoing source of new, high-calibre talent and remains a cornerstone of SABM's talent approach to this day.

Striving to be an authentic employer of choice. To attract high-calibre talent, the company had to offer something special. Indeed, the aim of SAB's talent strategy was

> ...to attract, retain and develop a disproportionate number of top calibre people to enhance its high performance, high engaging, diverse culture, which enables the company to achieve spectacular and sustainable business results.

To achieve this ambitious goal, it was critical that the company was consistently regarded as an **employer of choice** by current and prospective employees. Comprehensive surveys were undertaken to understand what employees wanted and a Total Employment Offering was designed accordingly. Also, an aspirational employment value proposition was crafted to depict SAB's unique talent selling proposition. To obtain external validation of SAB's aspired **'employer of choice'** status, it entered both the Deloitte's Best Company to Work For Survey and CRF's Best Employers South Africa competition and was consistently rated as one of South Africa's top employers to work for. These external employer-of-choice endorsements enhanced SAB's talent drive to attract and retain top-calibre talent.

Taking risks with gifted talent. The development of exceptionally talented people in SAB involved moving them into unfamiliar roles across functional, industry and geographic boundaries. This yielded the mutual benefit of broadening and stretching them beyond their comfort zones in preparation for senior roles. It also benefited SABM by providing a fresh, creative approach to managing the jobs unfamiliar to the high-flyers into which they were appointed. One such example is Alan Clark. He was previously a professor of clinical psychology at Vista University, brought into SAB to manage the Learning and Development function. His potential recognised, he was soon promoted to General Manager of Alrode, the largest brewery in SAB. From there, he became Operations Director and then Marketing Director. He then moved to Amalgamated Beverage Industries, as Managing Director. These diverse functional, industry and geographic moves prepared him for his current role, namely Managing Director: SABMiller Europe, and for his designated roles: he has been appointed as Chief Operating Officer of SABM from July 2012 with the intention that he succeeds Graham MacKay as Chief Executive of the Group from mid-2013.

Diversity. SAB embraced employment equity as a core business strategy in 1971, aimed at significantly increasing the number of black people in salaried ranks which, at the time, was 1%. The equity strategy has evolved to keep pace with company and societal changes. These equity initiatives were directed at attracting, retaining and developing a critical mass of black people into senior jobs and were designed to ensure that the organisational climate embraced diversity. Also, lessons learnt in the various SAB equity initiatives have subsequently informed localisation and diversity initiatives across SABM.

Line management buy-in to the strategic importance of talent management. The historic importance SAB placed on people stemmed from an enduring leadership commitment to the central role people fulfilled on the strategic agenda. As part of the overall business strategy, talent management was the responsibility of every line manager, not just an HR function. A key feature of the SAB culture was a clear understanding that investing time, money and resources in talent was critical if business results were to be achieved. For example:

- Managers were expected to actively and consistently attract high-calibre people into the business. Every external social event represented a potential recruitment opportunity.

- When high-potential candidates were identified, money was always found – even where no formal budget existed. This, in a company where cost leadership was sacrosanct, underlined the importance of recruiting talented people.

- Each line director was held accountable for setting and meeting stretch employment equity targets.

- A characteristic feature of the SAB culture was just how well every line manager knew his or her people – not just in terms of their working lives, but also their family circumstances – something that was important when making global career decisions.

Establishing People Processes to Ensure a Strong Talent Pool Ready to Move Offshore

When SAB expanded geographically, it had no obvious international beer brands. Instead, the business model of the 1990s was based on the following approach:

- Aspire to become a global player, in the top five brewers in the world.

- Scour the brewing world (initially focusing on emerging markets in Africa and Eastern/Central Europe and China) to find attractive beer businesses to buy.

- Negotiate favourable merger/acquisition deals, often resulting in joint-venture arrangements with the local governments as business partners.

- Inject the necessary capital to upgrade plant and equipment.

- Irrespective of the equity acquired, secure management control[11] (SAB's key competitive advantage was that it knew how to run breweries in emerging markets. Management control meant that, with suitable local adaptations, it was able to replicate this capability.).

- Expatriate a small team of experienced SAB managers to fill key positions in the acquired operation to transfer and adapt SAB's best practices, culture and leadership styles to suit local conditions, turn the operation around, and quickly create a sustainably profitable operation.

The centrality of securing the right talent to deliver on this business model was clear. Talent management, then, was at the heart of SAB's globalisation drive.

To capitalise on SAB's strong people focus, the company established various people-related processes to harness a talent pool that addressed South African needs **and** served as a global nursery, at least for the first decade of global expansion. A factor that contributed to the calibre of talent and management practices in SAB was the drive to improve manufacturing in SAB in the late 1980s, which gave rise to the World Class Manufacturing Initiative.

World-class manufacturing: the quest to improve production. Maurice Egan, Group Head of Manufacturing for SABM, recounts how a series of symbiotic

---

11 With the exception of China and, initially, Uganda.

interventions laid the groundwork for the improved production capability that supported subsequent global expansion via talent expatriation.

In the late 1980s, Graham Mackay, then Managing Director of SAB, was concerned that the large breweries were not performing optimally, despite numerous efforts to address the problems. If this was not rectified, SAB would be forced to build additional breweries at huge cost. He initiated the Quality and Production Upgrade Project to analyse the talent bench strength in Manufacturing. The investigation revealed that SAB had limited technical talent. In particular, many senior technical positions were occupied by older people who were not up to speed with latest techniques. There was a dearth of young, upcoming, high-calibre talent to introduce the latest thinking into the operation and fill key positions to enhance production.

What followed was a drive to attract high-potential technical talent. Line managers were dispatched to tertiary institutions and overseas to recruit the brightest and best. Only the top candidates were appointed. Again, the focus was on employing technical leaders with potential.

Focusing on developing talent. At the same time, the Technical Training Institute was built to develop technical competencies. To turbo-charge technical advancement, SAB embarked on an aggressive 'industrial tourism' drive. Experts were sent across the world to ferret out global best practices and import them to SAB. These learnings were harnessed into a World Class Manufacturing Initiative which was implemented across SAB.

Once acceptable technical competence levels were attained, the learning and development emphasis was broadened and the Technical Training Institute was renamed the Training Institute. Its focus covered learning across all functions. A comprehensive learning and development department was created that mirrored the SAB value chain.[12] Successful line managers were recruited as Training Managers to create learning solutions for every job at every level in their function.

Competency standards were developed for all relevant positions. Each person's competence was formally assessed and individual development plans were created to close competence gaps. Individual development plans went beyond closing job-related competence gaps to address performance-related, career, leadership and personal development needs. Performance against individual development plans was regularly monitored. Competence targets were set for all key positions to ensure that everyone was 100% competent. This resulted in a tightly integrated curriculum that accelerated learning and time to competence.

A comprehensive suite of leadership interventions was created for all leadership levels. Learning solutions included executive development programmes at major international universities, global action learning, in-house leadership programmes, coaching and mentoring.

---

12 That is, Training Managers dedicated to run the training for each of the functions, respectively.

Given the skills shortages in South Africa, pipeline development was a major focus. This included identifying and recruiting talented people at various entry levels across the business and placing them on accelerated learning programmes. Pipeline positions included bursars, apprentices (an active apprentice programme was established at the Training Institute), trainees and executive assistants. These programmes developed new talent at all relevant levels.

Where there were no suitable tertiary qualifications to meet SAB-specific skills gaps, the company partnered with tertiary institutions, including Nottingham University, Brunel University, City and Guilds, Natal Technikon and Heriot-Watt University to craft unique, accredited curricula to meet these needs.

Introducing performance management. To enhance world-class manufacturing, performance management was introduced in 1991, which aligned the business strategy with functional, team and individual goal setting and attainment. Key to SAB's performance management was

> ...to focus performance management strongly, directly, and explicitly on core business drivers by infusing a customer perspective and customer-related metrics into all performance goals in the organization ... This approach differs from standard 'goal cascading' practices in two critical ways. First, the infusion of a customer element into each and every performance goal embeds in performance management and measurement a close and direct focus on key business drivers. Second, by placing responsibility for meeting customer expectations with the individual employee, the practice enfranchises employees directly in the goals of the business.[13]

This feature was considered so significant that the Corporate Leadership Council (2002) included it as a benchmark in its global book on performance management best practice.

A benefit of performance management was that it would serve to engage, and therefore retain, the new generation of technical experts that had been recruited. The resultant high-performance culture – created by challenging them, setting them stretch individual and team targets, and, then, when they achieved the outputs, rewarding them handsomely – appealed to most high-flyers, and the SAB Group was no exception. Many of the hand-picked recruits of the early 1990s, who were young, bright, resilient graduates with an undergraduate qualification in mechanical, chemical or industrial engineering, are still with the company today, occupying top technical positions in SABM across the globe.

Career development. A career-development process was introduced to optimise each person's career growth, while simultaneously maximising company value-add. Because SAB defined career development as the acquisition of diverse competencies, career growth implied lateral and vertical growth. It entailed determining each

---

13 Corporate Leadership Council (2002:109).

person's strengths and weaknesses, current job challenges, and career aspirations. The individual, his or her manager, and the Executive Committee all participated in the career-development process to arrive at a consensus view of the talent available in the company.

Career development produces benefits for both the employee and the organisation. The individual receives honest, person-specific career advice, and unrealistic career aspirations are tempered. The process yields an individual development plan – a customised learning needs analysis, based on the person's consolidated career development data, which is then actioned. From the company's perspective, the process generates information used for training needs analyses, succession planning, and determining company bench strength. This information, in turn, informs broader regional and national People Balance Sheet and talent planning decisions.[14]

The strategic people review. Once career information had been gathered, verification, via strategic people reviews, was conducted at successively higher organisational levels to ensure consistency. Like many other organisations, SAB adopted a performance-potential grid to categorise employees. Strategic people reviews allowed for one version of the truth to be created and ensured business-wide calibration of ratings. The grids were closely linked to the business strategy, informing whether the business had the talent to achieve its objectives and what steps to take to rectify any identified gaps.

The People Balance Sheet. Talent cannot be managed as a key strategic priority if information about people is not treated with the same rigour and importance as financial, sales or marketing data. A key component of talent management is the People Balance Sheet.[15] It is the 'people bottom line' aimed at consolidating and interpreting data in a consistent manner to maintain an ongoing people focus and to alert the business to current and future people-related gaps and trends.[16]

Every year, each business unit populated a People Balance Sheet comprising critical HR measures, and compared them with previous years' performance and against benchmark scores. They then identified gaps and specified how they intended addressing those gaps. Once all business units had been covered, consolidated action steps were outlined to ensure the ongoing health of talent in line with business strategies.

Multiple benefits accrued from the People Balance Sheet. First, it provided a comprehensive analysis of the talent health throughout the business and allowed for early problem identification and resolution. Secondly, it ensured that accountability for talent management was located at the right place, namely local line management. Thirdly, the People Balance Sheet highlighted organisational bench strength. Cover/

---

14 See Bluen (2004).

15 See figure 2, which outlines the information used to construct the People Balance Sheet and the outputs of the process.

16 Hirschowitz (2004).

succession lists were created for each key job. Where cover ratios were low, they were bolstered, either by targeted external recruitment or by accelerated learning and development of 'cover' employees. Fourthly, given SAB's role as a talent nursery for the wider group, the People Balance Sheet reflected talent needs for South African and global operations.

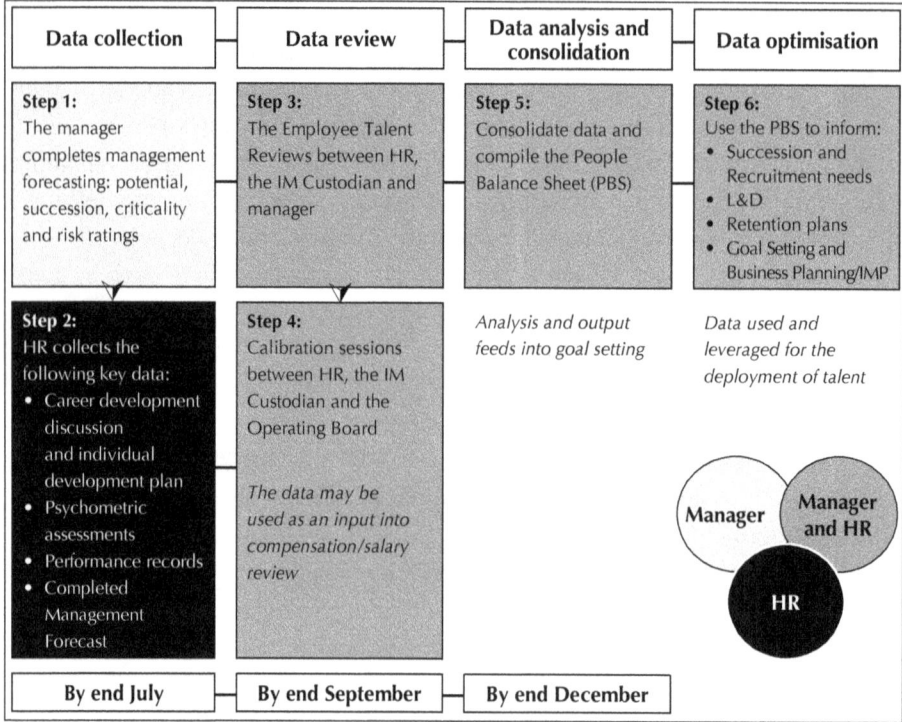

Data collection	Data review	Data analysis and consolidation	Data optimisation
Step 1: The manager completes management forecasting: potential, succession, criticality and risk ratings	**Step 3:** The Employee Talent Reviews between HR, the IM Custodian and manager	**Step 5:** Consolidate data and compile the People Balance Sheet (PBS)	**Step 6:** Use the PBS to inform: • Succession and Recruitment needs • L&D • Retention plans • Goal Setting and Business Planning/IMP
Step 2: HR collects the following key data: • Career development discussion and individual development plan • Psychometric assessments • Performance records • Completed Management Forecast	**Step 4:** Calibration sessions between HR, the IM Custodian and the Operating Board *The data may be used as an input into compensation/salary review*	*Analysis and output feeds into goal setting*	*Data used and leveraged for the deployment of talent*
By end July	**By end September**	**By end December**	

Figure 2: Processes Surrounding the People Balance Sheet[17]

To access real-time talent data, a comprehensive HR system was required. The company therefore implemented an enterprise-wide SAP system, which included an end-to-end solution covering all talent management activities, thereby providing real-time talent data for every manager in the business.

A unique feature of SAB's talent management approach was its focus on the individual and the organisation. Some companies focused solely on the organisational approach to talent management – how to deliver value to the business – where the main tool used was a performance-potential grid. Little emphasis, however, was placed on engaging the individual. Other companies adopted an individualised approach, focusing on employee engagement by mainly using individual development plans. SABM adopted a blended approach where both organisational and individual needs were addressed, extracting value simultaneously for both.

The world-class manufacturing production upgrade drive, along with performance management, learning and development, and talent management, provided a sound

---

17 SABMiller (2010a:27).

talent base to launch global expansion into emerging markets. The seasoned, experienced brewery leaders, who, in many cases, had reached their ceiling in the rapidly changing South African environment, were ideally suited to move into the newly acquired operations. Global expansion, certainly into Africa, presented a serendipitously positive outcome. Those professionals jumped at the opportunity of a reinvigorating 'second career', pioneering SAB's expansion across Africa. This gave the Young Turks new opportunities. Having had a few years of finding their way in SAB, they were now ready to take on more senior leadership positions.

The Global Geographic Footprint: Africa, Europe and the Americas

What were the specific talent needs of the different regions across the globe? SAB's first global moves were predominantly into Africa in the early 1990s (see figure 1). There, the most pressing challenge was to improve manufacturing operations, which were typically in a poor state. Processes needed were world-class manufacturing, performance management, talent management, and management accounting. In most cases, local talent lacked the authority and wherewithal to rectify the situation. The talent needed was seasoned manufacturers with hands-on experience who could design and implement turnaround plans to add value to underperforming and undervalued assets across Africa. As mentioned previously, this created an ideal opportunity for experienced technical experts who were seeking new careers beyond South Africa's borders.

The business challenges in Central and Eastern Europe were very different from those of Africa, and, consequently, European talent requirements were different. Unlike Africa, where technical skills were in demand, European technical skills were readily available. However, although different, the European talent challenges were equally demanding.

The years spent under communist rule had impacted business practices and, therefore, talent management.[18] For example, management styles were typically militaristic, with great respect for rank. The various levels of management wanted instruction from their managers and were reluctant to make any decisions themselves, resulting in most decisions cascading up to the managing director. This presented the requirement for SABM to change culture and leadership style in Europe. For European managers, the number of people reporting to you was seen as a measure of importance. In addition, the businesses were supply- rather than demand-driven. The focus was on how much to produce, and, thereafter, the businesses made plans to sell the beers. SABM's priority was to shift the mind-set from supply- to demand-driven and create a demand for beer in the market. However, the communist legacy

---

18 These views were expressed in an interview with Rob Priday, who was the Vice President: Sales and Distribution Development: Browary Tyskie, Poland, from 1997 to 1999, and provided some valuable insights into talent management in Europe.

yielded few suitable marketers to build strong beer brands. SABM Europe needed people who thrived in competitive environments. Given SAB's market dominance, these competitive skills were not available from South Africa, so talent searches went broader and heralded a new approach to expatriate recruitment, namely from external sources. The European cultural landscape comprised different nationalities that did not necessarily mix well with one another, and the movement of talent across countries in Europe had to be handled with great cultural sensitivity. To enhance the demand drive, the sales force needed bolstering. In Poland, in 1997, the number of sales representatives was increased from 17 to 143 in 6 weeks – all in an effort to stimulate demand for SABM beers in the market.

In South America, although companies employed good marketing talent, they lacked processes to perform effectively. This was true across functions: there was an abundance of well-educated talent that was keen and quick to learn, trusting of SABM, and open to change. The resultant expatriate requirements were to recruit high-calibre, experienced SABM leaders who could drive the SABM ways of working with these talented people. Given the expatriate skills required, most SABM expatriates recruited into South America were drawn from SABM Europe, rather than from South Africa.[19]

Thus SABM adopted talent requirements and expatriate strategies that differed from region to region, rather than a one-size-fits-all approach.

The Challenge of Scale

By 2005, SABM had established a strong presence in five continents. Globalisation brought increased size and complexity. Following the dot-com crash, movement of SAB's primary listing to the London Stock Exchange (LSE) in 1999, and a heightened global anti-alcohol lobby, governance and compliance were receiving increased attention. The beer industry was rapidly growing and consolidating, and competition was increasing in both emerging and mature markets. SABM's strategy shifted from being an international operating business to a global branded business that sought to build global brands, reputation and talent. Increased emphasis was placed on organic growth (without sacrificing merger and acquisition growth), moving into mature markets (ie Italy and the United States), and building strong regional hubs in Europe and (with the acquisition of Grupo Empresarial Bavaria) South America. The focus was on increasing operational excellence. To do this, core management disciplines were needed to enhance quality, drive efficiency in manufacturing and distribution, reduce supply chain and overhead costs in each country, and build local marketing and sales capabilities.[20]

---

19 After spending time in Europe, Rob Priday moved to South America where he was the Managing Director of Cerveceria Hondurena, Honduras (2001-2005), and President of SABM Peru (2006-2011). He provided some of the input into talent management in South America used in this chapter.

20 For a full account of the different operating models adopted by SABM over time, see Smith et al. (2009).

This increase in complexity and change in operating model needed to be supported by defining and building new strategic capabilities. In 2005, Graham Mackay observed that SABMiller had expanded dramatically, primarily through the export of people to foreign countries. These people had had a way of working that was not written anywhere, but existed in their heads. He wanted to know how this way of working could be defined and rolled out to the business to ensure the business sustained high performance. He asked Tony van Kralingen (who worked with Steve Bluen, Brian Ireland and Nicola Jowell) to find a way of expediting learning and standardising best practice.

What followed was the identification of eight areas of strategic advantage, against which capability was to be built across SABM. These eight 'Ways of Working' were developed and disseminated.[21] The purpose of each Way was to codify knowledge considered core to sustainable competitiveness (that had not previously been written down) for Group-wide adoption and to build capabilities in defined areas of strategic relevance. Specifically, the aims of the Ways were: (a) to be a single, credible point of reference on how to operate, manage and leverage best practice that enabled ownership of profitable growth; (b) to build Group-wide capability in defined areas of strategic relevance through deliberate implementation and anchoring; and (c) to continuously codify, implement, anchor and refresh best practices that represented real competitive advantage.

Pertinently, talent management was included as one of the eight core Ways. It was clear from experience that SABM could no longer rely on SAB expatriates to satisfy its talent needs, since the South African talent pool had been depleted. Also, capabilities needed elsewhere in the Group (eg commercial capabilities sought in Europe) were different from the South African skills set. South Africa was no longer the sole source of talent and learning supply. Also, SABM expatriates who had successfully completed one assignment needed to be redeployed where their international experience could best be used. To herald this new approach to talent management, whilst not losing the years of developing best practice in the field, the Talent Management Way was developed and implemented (see figure 3).

The Talent Management Way ensured that consistent, leading-edge talent processes that addressed the increasingly complex talent needs of SABM, were universally adopted. Consistency was crucial to enable a common, calibrated set of standards by which to compare talent from all parts of the world when making global appointment decisions. The Talent Management Way also ensured that the various components of the comprehensive talent management system did not operate in silos. Instead, they were integrated into a holistic, systemic approach.

---

21 The eight SABM Ways developed were the Marketing Way, the Global Brands Way, the Manufacturing Way, the Operations Finance Way, the Talent Management Way, the Performance Management Way, the License to Trade Way, and the Sustainable Development Way (see SABMiller 2010c).

The Overall Objective	To manage talent effectively to ensure that we are attracting, retaining and developing motivated people who deliver high performance and are succession for the future.				
	1 Talent Acquisition	2 Psychometric Assessment	3 Career Development	4 Talent Engagement	5 Talent Analysis, Deployment and Optimisation
The Five Pillars of the Talent Management Way	The way we source, select, on-board and integrate talent and enable early impact and sustainable performance	The way we use valid and reliable psychometric assessments to ensure sound development and selection decisions	The way we manage individual learning, development and progression over time in order to drive competence development and provide succession	The way we enable commitment and engagement of employees to enable performance and the retention of talent	The way we integrate information for insghtful analysis as a basis for planning development and development of people
Examples of Enablers	Business/strategy planning			Organisational effectiveness surveys	
	Employment policies			Functional/leadership development	
	Performance management			Triumph/local systems	
	Job evaluation/grading			Talent Coordinating Committees (TCCs)	

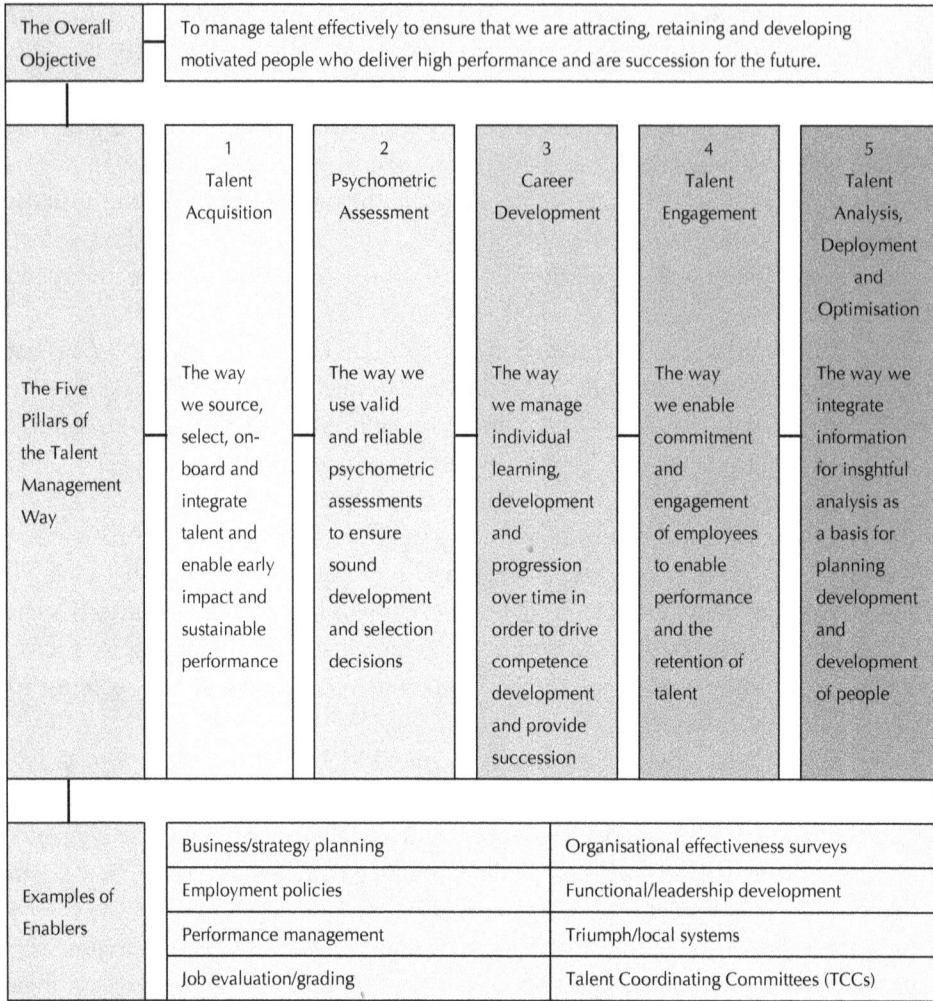

Figure 3: SABMiller's Talent Management Way[22]

Managing the Emerging-market Talent Challenges

Over the past two decades, the transformation of SAB – the local brewer to SABMiller, the world's second-largest brewer – has been nothing short of spectacular. This journey for SAB in general, and for talent management in particular, has yielded many lessons. Set out below are some of the typical problems encountered, and how SABM dealt with them.

Selecting the Right Expatriates

One of the first joint ventures SAB entered into was with the Tanzanian government in 1994. SAB identified one of its top young executives, who had been earmarked as

22 For a full account of the Talent Management Way, see SABMiller (2010a).

a future business leader, as the potential Managing Director of Tanzania Breweries. He was sent on a 'look-see' visit. He embraced the visit with enthusiasm, energy and a strong leadership style, making many suggestions of how things could be improved once he took over; clearly the man for the job. Yet, at the end of the visit, the head of Tanzania Breweries, Arnold Kulwewa, called aside SAB's visiting Technical Consultant, with whom he had established a relationship, and cautioned: "If this is SAB's candidate there will be no deal." Flabbergasted, the Technical Consultant, who thought the potential Managing Director had acquitted himself superbly, asked why. Kulwewa responded: "...we want someone with a little grey hair on the temples, someone with age, wisdom and humility, who can work with us and show us new and improved ways of jointly creating a great company."

A valuable lesson had been learnt: do not assume that what makes a successful leader in South Africa will necessarily be the same in emerging countries. In fact, when asking Danie Niemandt (who was then appointed as Managing Director of Tanzania Breweries and emerged as an exceptional leader) what he considered to be important for success as an expatriate, he mentioned the following five criteria:

> First, develop a simple strategy. Unpack it clearly so that everyone can understand and follow it. Also, you need the patience not to try change the world overnight. Rather, set achievable stretch targets. Second, be clear about the company values and the consequences of not living up to them. Third, invest huge effort into developing local talent. There are many talented local employees. As an expatriate, you need to help locals individually to realise their potential. Similarly, embrace a localisation mindset. This entails identifying talented people, mentoring and coaching them to take over from expatriates. Fourth, mix with local leaders and establish meaningful, enduring relationships, not just when there is a problem to solve.[23] Fifth, be humble. Mix with people at every level and respect the local people, their customs and practices. Never forget that you are a visitor in someone else's home.

The importance that SABM now places on forming down-to-earth relationships as part of doing business starts way before the expatriates arrive – with concluding the deal itself, as the story in the box reflects.

Other factors that contribute to expatriates being successful include cultural flexibility, being resourceful and resilient, driving performance, having the maturity to get beyond 'own egos', and deep technical and managerial experience in order to operate independently and with minimal support or backup. Richard Forbes, immediate past Senior Vice President: Human Resources for SABM South America,

---

23 A clear example of this is that Castel, SABMiller's partners in Francophone Africa, sends expatriates to destinations for extended periods of up to 20 years so that they can develop enduring local relationships. Also, in Zambia, the head of Zambian Breweries Plc would send the country's President a weekly letter informing him of the company's performance. He regularly got a reply from the President.

observes that a key characteristic of a successful expatriate is being tough: "Nothing prepares you for an expatriate life and, once on assignment, you receive minimal support. Therefore, you need to be tough and resourceful to survive." Also, a useful skill is being able to speak the local language.

> While you can get away with speaking only English in some Central European countries, in Ecuador no-one in the business speaks English. So learning Spanish is essential. Being able to speak Spanish in South America makes a big difference. Local people make you feel at home, your understanding of the culture and people is greatly enhanced and your credibility as a leader improves dramatically.

Meyer Kahn, past Chairperson of SABM, tells the story of how the Hungarian business, Dreher Breweries Ltd, was acquired:

> The Hungarian government was looking to privatise Dreher and had short-listed two potential partners, [Company A] and SABM. They gave each company a day to present their case in whichever way they preferred. On Day 1, Company A's private jet landed at Budapest Airport, the rear under carriage opened and out rolled two luxury cars, accompanied by body guards and fanfare. Company A's delegation spent the day with members of the Hungarian cabinet. The head of Company A spent much time telling the Hungarians what was wrong with Dreher and how they intended fixing it. On Day 2, Malcolm Wyman, the then Chief Financial Officer, and I arrived from Johannesburg, via Frankfort to Budapest. We waited for about a half hour for someone to fetch us but no-one arrived. Eventually, we approached a group who could speak English and asked them about transport to the city. It turns out that they were the government officials sent to fetch us but they had expected the same fanfare as the previous day and mistook us for regular tourists. Instead of meeting cabinet ministers, we asked to visit the brewery and spent the day discussing the business, touring the brewery and chatting to people at all levels. After a great day of relationship building we shook hands on the deal which was to become SAB's beachhead into Eastern and Central Europe. The rest is history.

Regarding technical expertise, there is no 'one size fits all'. Instead, needs vary from one country to the next, and from one continent to the next. For example, in Africa, the initial skills needed were manufacturing. Conversely, in Europe, the main skills required were marketing and sales, while, in Latin America, the most difficult skills to source were technical.

Prejudice is unacceptable. Not only should expatriates be 100% fair in their treatment of all people, regardless of race, gender, religion or nationality, but their partners should also be equally nondiscriminatory. In one instance, an expatriate's wife was soon identified as being racist and the locals targeted the expatriate, who was sent home within weeks.

The Role of the Expatriate's Spouse

Since many of the SABM expatriate destinations present challenging living conditions, a key consideration when choosing expatriates is to ensure that both members of the couple are suited to undertake the assignment. If the spouses are not happy, especially given the relative isolation from their regular social network, the chances of expatriates succeeding are slim. Furthermore, the adaptation required of expatriates when settling into host countries can be relatively minor: Working in a brewery – whether it be in Arusha or Alrode – is familiar. But spouses are expected to leave their jobs, families, friends and even their children behind. They cannot work and, in some cases, are prohibited from driving or from moving around freely without a bodyguard. Furthermore, their lifestyles and resources are completely different. For all this, in almost every case, expatriate spouses have not only survived – they have thrived.

Preventing Informal Talent Broking

An undesirable practice that occasionally took place was informal talent broking. Certain expatriates would contact their favoured employees directly and ask them to work with them offshore, making them unsupported promises. This practice had several negative consequences, including disrupting strategic people-resourcing planning, increasing the potential for conflict between countries (which were already competing for scarce skills), and unrealistically raising expectations, leading to inevitable disappointment for the person being contacted. To overcome this practice, strict expatriate-recruitment processes were implemented and transgressors duly disciplined.

Localisation

The business model was to send expatriates to disseminate SAB's practices and culture and blend these with the local operation. Once the business was running successfully and the SAB practices had been anchored, the expatriates were tasked to identify and train local managers to replace them. Besides the huge cost to company incurred by expatriates, there were government pressures to localise.[24] Most importantly, the multiple benefits of local leaders running the breweries were enormous. However, localisation was a challenge, since expatriates became accustomed to the generous financial benefits they earned and were reluctant to find their replacements.[25] In

---

24 In certain countries, expatriate work permits were granted on condition that local talent would replace them within a defined time.

25 In Botswana, the government has grown impatient with the slow pace of localisation and stopped issuing new work permits, and will not extend current permits. This forced Kgalagadi Breweries to implement urgent localisation plans.

most African countries, the drive to localisation is being tackled in much the same way as South African companies address the challenges of employment equity – top management sets targets and proactively identifies local talent to take over from the expatriates, ensuring they receive the necessary development and support to replace expatriates within a set time.

Secondments versus Transfers

When SAB first went offshore, no-one knew what to expect in these unfamiliar environments. To encourage expatriation, SAB offered a secondment safety net: at the end of the assignment, the expatriate's contract would either be renewed by mutual consent or she or he would return to a guaranteed job at SAB. This allayed expatriates' fears of the unknown and ensured that all expatriate positions were filled with suitable SAB talent. However, it created a new problem: what to do with returning, seconded expatriates, especially those who had been out of the country for several years, and who were out of touch with SAB's latest technological developments? The suboptimal solution was that they were re-employed by SAB and then, relatively soon, separated. A more enduring solution was to phase out this type of secondment. When people accepted offshore assignments, they were transferred to the host businesses and the home operation had no further obligation to re-employ them when the contracts ended.

Understanding Local Headcount and Staffing

The first talent challenges confronting leadership was to understand local staffing and the calibre of the workforce. What emerged was that organisational design and staffing were very different from what occurred in South Africa. Danie Niemandt, Managing Director of the Tanzanian operation, explained that, "with nationalisation, companies operated for the benefit of employees, rather than to compete in the market. People were not employed to produce profits. Instead, they were there to look after themselves and their families. This occurred at all levels in the company." One consequence was that organisations were grossly overstaffed. Niemandt said that, in Tanzania Breweries, they found that there were several hundred people who were being paid but had no real jobs. Because the business had been state-owned, it had been difficult for management to reduce the workforce. Also, many employees were moonlighting, running their own businesses when they were supposed to be at work. Dave Pieterse, the then Tanzania Breweries HR Director, said that, to unravel the organisational structure, "we had to scrutinise organisation design, reporting structures, job descriptions and rewards from scratch. We literally took one weekend to line up everybody on a football field and physically started a top-down approach to get managers and supervisors to identify who worked where." Once headcount and structures were clarified, a retrenchment exercise followed. The workforce was reduced to about 1 200, all filling legitimate jobs, and was trained accordingly. Employees received liveable wages and no longer operated small businesses on the side.

Alternatively, increasing headcount in targeted areas has also been used to great effect in Europe and South America. Rob Priday observed that, when he took over as head of both SABM operations in Honduras and Peru, there were many long-serving employees who were 'tired' and resisted the changes he was implementing. They were 'anchors slowing up the ship'. Instead of dismissing them and thereby losing valuable corporate memory and local employee sympathy, he recruited a critical mass of young, energetic, local MBA graduates who were eager to work for a multinational company.[26] These young talents quickly adapted to the high-performance approach and set new performance standards that served as a 'wake-up call' for their older, jaded counterparts, who ratcheted up their performances and invariably became great assets to the company over time. Such was the success of recruiting a critical mass of 'Bright Young Things' that Barry Smith, the then Managing Director of SABM South America, adopted it across South America with great success.

Recruiting for Talent, Not Just to Fill Vacancies

The cornerstone of SABM's success in talent management had been recruiting for potential, rather than focusing on current skills needed. By bringing in creative and different talented people, novel solutions to old problems had consistently been found. Also, the high-potential recruits, who typically rose rapidly in the SABM ranks, perpetuated the recruitment of exceptional talent, thus enforcing the high-calibre talent attraction cycle. They were confident and not threatened by the prospect of hiring young, bright people who may well have challenged them.

While recruiting for talent had long been established in SAB, many new businesses were operating on tight budgets. Employing additional people was a luxury. This was problematic, since finding suitable people to fill demanding brewery jobs was difficult. The SABM HR Director for Africa attended a Careers in Africa recruitment summit in London. African delegates, who had successfully completed degrees in Europe, were interviewed. Ten candidates were short-listed and their CVs circulated to country Managing Directors. Despite repeated efforts, none were placed. In each case, the Managing Director acknowledged that they were superb talent, but, because there were no suitable vacancies at the brewery, they would not hire them. To avoid this mistake the following year, a budget was established to absorb additional headcount costs and the Operations Director accompanied the HR Director to the recruitment summit. All short-listed candidates were placed in the business.

---

26 In Honduras, Priday recruited 20 MBA graduates within 2 months of his appointment. In Peru, he appointed 40 MBA graduates when he took over in 2006. Six years later, four of them are now heading up breweries in Peru.

Appropriate Use of Psychometric Assessments

Given the central role psychometrics fulfilled in SAB, country managers were keen to use psychometrics offshore. However, this posed certain challenges, including: (a) local legislation preventing the use of certain instruments; (b) ensuring the tools were culture-fair; (c) overcoming language barriers; (d) the availability of appropriate, local norm scales; and (e) the availability of suitable psychologists. SABM South America represents a good example of how these challenges were met. Shortly after acquiring the business, a network of assessors was set up. Fifteen qualified external psychologists across South America were recruited and a validated Spanish version of the executive assessment battery was compiled. Within 15 months, comprehensive psychometric assessments were obtained for over 90% (478 out of 526) of the senior level of South American managers. This provided comprehensive data upon which to base talent-related decisions.[27]

A hallmark of talent management in SAB was attracting high-calibre talent and ensuring they were competent. The aim was to replicate this model globally. In South America, the workforce was extremely well educated. In Europe, there were highly intelligent and well-educated local people working for SABM. Thus brewery-specific competence development was relatively easy.

Conversely, in Africa, the workforces typically lacked competence to perform effectively. Over time, initiatives were implemented to increase competence. Examples included ensuring that the expatriates' goals incorporated coaching local employees, sending key people to South Africa to gain on-the-job experience, accrediting satellite institutions to run SABM courses, sending experienced SAB trainers into Africa, and establishing strong, local learning and development functions. However, competence levels remain low. To address these competence gaps, the Global Technical team has developed a technical learning and development strategy. Instead of focusing on competency building for **all** jobs, the strategy focuses on 14 critical manufacturing jobs (eg Brewer, Packaging Unit Manager, and Engineering Manager). For each of the 14 jobs, global competencies will be defined, technical criteria and learning solutions will be developed, and learning solutions will be delivered as required. "It is anticipated that the benefits of such a strategy will include a significant focus on building technical capability, and developing depth of talent. The output will be a discernible improvement in sustainable Manufacturing performance."[28]

---

27 Unfortunately, the Mexican norms used for the intelligence test were derived from an elite university sample that proved to be too stringent for the target population. This resulted in a further comprehensive exercise to recalibrate and adjust scores accordingly.

28 SABMiller (2011b:3).

Focus on Employees AND the Community

An early lesson learnt by SABM leaders operating in developing countries was that, because the breweries were often located in areas where infrastructure is lacking, being an employer of choice entailed focusing on the workforce and the communities in which the brewery operated. For example, in all African operations, the company clinics are open to employees, their families and members of the broader community. At those sites where access to clean running water is a problem, the breweries have set up taps outside the company where local community members queue to fill buckets with fresh water. SABM's approach to handling HIV/AIDS is a clear example of successful community involvement (see box below).

Managing HIV/AIDS in the Usuk Community, Uganda

Jenni Gillies, SABM's Group HIV Manager, states that the company has taken education and training with regard to HIV/AIDS and other major diseases beyond focusing on employees and their families, into the company's supply chain. The focus is on at-risk groups, including female bar tenders, truck drivers and small farmers supplying the sorghum, maize or barley to the company. As Jenni says:

> A great example is the work done in Uganda. Given that HIV/AIDS is sexually transmitted, the first step was to ensure that both the employees AND their spouses were entitled to voluntary counselling and testing (VCT) to determine their HIV status. Then we focused on a particular community in our supply chain, namely Usuk, a small sorghum farming district supplying Nile Breweries with sorghum. The goal was to provide access to health care, including testing for HIV to farmers in remote areas. SABMiller launched a rigorous health campaign: Farmers trained as community health educators went out into the Usuk community and educated the people on the benefits of knowing their HIV status. Besides HIV/AIDS, they gave them general health education and trained them on other diseases, including tuberculosis and malaria. To incentivise participation, couples agreeing to have an HIV test together received a malaria bed net. The testing was carried out by staff from the local health clinic in the couples' own homes. In addition, any children were also tested for HIV and treated for malaria. Those people who tested positive were given the necessary treatment, including anti-retroviral medication at the clinic. This partnership was funded by SABM, the local Department of Health and USAID [United States Agency for International Development] working in conjunction with a local NGO [nongovernmental organisation]. Of the 5 000 residents in the Usuk district, approximately 4 700 participated in this campaign. Having been so successful in Usuk, we are turning our attention to other communities in Uganda and have received funding from USAID to do this. The programme is being further expanded to include nutrition, deworming of children and male medical circumcision. This expanded programme is currently underway.

Entrenching a Global Business: Global Talent Management

As SABM grew over the years and as the business model evolved, it became evident that a new approach to managing talent on a global scale was required. With SABM's executive population now spread across six continents and talent resources at a leadership level becoming increasingly stretched, a model that focused deliberately on the global, executive talent pool was required. Although SABM's talent management was highly effective and fit for purpose, an evolutionary step was required to enhance current processes and take them to the next level. This gave rise to the implementation of a global talent model, launched in 2010, which represents the next chapter in SABM's talent management story.

Besides the company's increased size and complexity, several other factors precipitated the need for a supplementary talent management approach:

- At a senior level, there remained instances of informal, internal networking as a means of agreeing international talent moves. This was a legacy of the company's rapid expansion, but was no longer a desired or practical means of making critical talent decisions.

- With SABM's increased scale, the company's Executive Committee was no longer familiar with many senior executives. This necessitated a greater consistency of quality information at the top-tier level to inform decision making.

- As a decentralised organisation, there remained a reticence amongst some senior line managers to 'share' talent with the rest of the business; a protectionist approach was evident which was counterproductive to embedding a global talent pool.

- SABM's dramatic increase in size had resulted in less than optimal succession for certain key global positions and functions in particular.

- The organisation's increased complexity and ongoing centralisation of some functions increased the need to move talent in a more agile way to support business priorities.

- There was a perceived risk that executives would become increasingly reluctant to accept international assignments, especially to the less desirable locations.[29]

As Graham MacKay noted in 2010:

> The crucial question is how we ensure that we make the right appointments, across such a broad sweep of operations. At some stage we have to centralise the decisions because we are one company, and to achieve what we need to achieve we have to promote our best people and move them across countries and regions. It is difficult to make the whole process of consideration fair and

---

29 SABMiller (2010b).

open. Knowledge of people is imperfect and it is spread unevenly around the world. The new Global Talent Management process will help us assemble enough knowledge and will give us a clear enough perspective on all our top people at one point in order to make the right decisions.

Consequently, a detailed research project was undertaken to establish how best to enhance SABM's approach to managing the global, executive talent pool. Based on the research, several best-practice success factors were identified:

- Global ownership of senior executives by the Executive Committee or chief executive officer (CEO).
- A focus on succession management and driving bench strength of key functional competencies.
- The success of leaders to include a measure of their ability to develop talent.
- Talent planning that is fully integrated with business planning.
- The use of international transfers as the principal method for accelerating development.
- Talent management processes which are globally consistent and are aligned to the organisation's culture and value system.[30]

These factors were considered as part of the formation of the new model and resulted in six key operating principles:

1. SABM's senior-executive talent pool is 'owned' by the Executive Committee.
2. The approach will focus on the critical positions[31] that are key to delivering business strategies.
3. Development of talent is accelerated through deployment in challenging, diverse and international job experiences.
4. Interregional experiences are a prerequisite for those who aspire to the most senior positions, and these expectations are clearly communicated.[32]
5. A stronger, executive talent pool is developed by taking full advantage of the diversity available in the global talent pool.
6. Talent development is a key responsibility of senior managers. Their success is measured by their ability to develop talent as well as business performance.[33]

---

30 SABMiller (2010b).

31 These positions are defined as those senior-executive roles which are most critical to achieving business priorities.

32 Less mobile executives are not precluded from enjoying rewarding careers, but will not be considered succession for the most senior leadership roles.

33 Hirschowitz (2011); SABMiller (2010b).

To entrench this new approach, operating rules were developed for the new global talent model:

- No decisions for positions or candidates within the scope of the model will be made outside the global talent management process.

- Informal networking or 'talent broking' is no longer tolerated.

- Global talent management processes are coordinated centrally with support from each region.

- Disputes around releasing candidates and priority between critical positions will be resolved at Executive Committee level.

- If a candidate is identified as succession in a role, the relevant line manager must interview and provide feedback.

- Talent newly appointed into a role will remain 'owned' by the region for three years unless a transfer/move is agreed by the Executive Committee. Thereafter, there is no automatic right of refusal.

The objective of the new model is the creation of a talent pool comprising those senior executives who occupy the most critical positions in the company and a governance system which ensures that the movement of talent supports individual development and organisational priorities.

This represents a shift away from a proudly decentralised approach to managing talent. However, the creation of an executive talent pool should also address many of the challenges inherent within a wholly devolved approach to talent management. It still places the accountability for individual management and people development with the local country and line manager. Furthermore, the new, global talent management model is well positioned to cater for the talent needs of SABM as it moves into its next exciting phase of growth in the international brewing arena.

Finally, the common thread underpinning talent management in SABM is that, based on its dynamic culture and enduring commitment to its people, the company has always been able to attract, retain and develop a disproportional number of high-calibre people who have helped build SABM over time. As Meyer Kahn states: "The Company is filled with talented people – people who are intelligent, practical, have the right personality to lead and are driven, dedicated and committed, not just to the Company but to their jobs. Many of them are trained executives who have gone through tough times with the Company and are ready to be unleashed across the globe."

References

Amal, M, Tomio, BT & Raboch, H. 2010. Determinants of Foreign Direct Investment in Latin America, *Journal of Globalization, Competitiveness and Governability* 4(3):116-133.

Bluen, SD. 2004. Global Human Resource Management: the SABMiller Story, in *Building Human Capital: South African Perspectives,* edited by I Boninelli & T Meyer. Johannesburg: Knowledge Resources.

Corporate Leadership Council. 2002. Closing the Performance Gap: Driving Business Results through Performance Management. Washington DC: Corporate Executive Board.

Dang, X. 2008. Foreign Direct Investment in China. Master's dissertation submitted to the Department of Economics, Kansas State University, Manhattan, Kansas.

Garton Ash, T. 1993. *The Magic Lantern: the Revolution of '89 Witnessed in Warsaw, Budapest, Berlin and Prague.* Vintage Books.

Hirschowitz, L. 2004. People Balance Sheet Guidelines. April, SAB.

Hirschowitz, L. 2011. Global Model for Talent Management (TM) 2011. SABMiller internal company document.

Huang, Y. 2008. *Capitalism with Chinese Characteristics: Entrepreneurship and the State.* United Kingdom: Cambridge University Press.

Jones, GG. 2006. The Rise of Corporate Nationality, *Harvard Business Review* October.

Martin, JD & Sayrak, A. 2003. Corporate Diversification and Shareholder Value: a Survey of Recent Literature, *Journal of Corporate Finance* 9:37-57.

Pitcher, MA & Askew, KM. 2006. African Socialisms and Postsocialisms, *Africa: Journal of the International African Institute* 76(1):1-14.

SABMiller. 2010a. The SABMiller Talent Management Way: an End-to-end Guide. Internal company document.

SABMiller. 2010b. Elective Session: Global Model for Talent Management (TM). Presentation at the SABMiller Global Leadership Conference, United States of America.

SABMiller. 2010c. The SABMiller Ways: Strategic Context and Introduction. Internal company presentation, November.

SABMiller. 2011a. SABMiller plc. Annual Report.

SABMiller. 2011b. Technical Learning and Development Strategy. Internal company document.

Smith, D, Davies, R, Woodward, S, Bluen, S, Lumsden, G & Buko, C. 2009. Operating Model and Leadership Requirements. Internal company document.

10 GLOBAL TALENT MANAGEMENT CASE STUDY: TALENT MANAGEMENT IN ANGLOGOLD ASHANTI

Italia Boninelli

The Company: AngloGold Ashanti

AngloGold Ashanti is a gold-mining company with about 63 000 employees. It has a portfolio of many assets and differing ore-body types in key gold-producing regions. The company's 20 operations are located in 10 countries (Argentina, Australia, Brazil, Ghana, Guinea, Mali, Namibia, South Africa, Tanzania and the United States of America), and are supported by extensive exploration activities. The operations are run as four distinct regions – Southern Africa, Continental Africa, Australasia, and The Americas. The company is well positioned for future growth through substantial greenfields and brownfields exploration project pipelines.

AngloGold Ashanti's primary listing is on the Johannesburg Stock Exchange (JSE). It is also listed on the stock exchanges in New York, London, Paris, Brussels, Australia and Ghana.

Our Vision is 'To be the leading mining company'. We will achieve our business goals through our five core strategies:

- Recognise that People are the Business – organisational development will be a strategic value driver for the business.

- Maximise margins – manage revenues and costs to ensure delivery and protection of returns through the price cycle.

- Manage the business as an 'asset portfolio' – allocate capital to support delivery of return targets within a balanced risk profile.

- Grow the business – look for value-adding targets across all value-adding dimensions, including exploration, organic improvement and growth, and through targeted acquisitions.

- Embrace sustainability principles – understand and focus on creating value for both business and social partners to manage risk and opportunity.

Implicit in achieving our Vision and Mission is the development of people, with our primary core strategy to recognise that 'People are the Business' and that Organisation Development is a strategic value driver.

Our emphasis that people are not assets is not random. Instead, 'People are the Business' was intentionally ranked first amongst our five core strategies for a number of reasons.

First, it is testament to our conviction that the people working at AngloGold Ashanti are central to our success. In our operating environment and across the global mining industry, there are known practical and potential human-capital risks. In general, these relate to: acquiring and retaining key skills; training and developing people; and how we relate to individuals by not relying on others to deliver our leadership message. These are identified and tracked each quarter as we seek to design and implement region-specific solutions to minimise our exposure and to maximise engaging, and constructive relationships, with relevant stakeholders.

Secondly, it reflects our focus on: practising our values; caring for ourselves and one another, particularly with regard to our safety and health; treating everyone with dignity and respect; valuing our diverse cultures, ideas, experiences and skills; being accountable for our actions and doing what we say we will do; and positively building up the communities, societies and natural environments in which we work. We commit to people currently and to leaving behind a notable legacy for future generations.

Thirdly, it articulates our Mission to create value safely and responsibly for all people. 'People' includes: our employees; the local communities and societies in places where AngloGold Ashanti (AGA) has a presence; our shareholders; and our and other business and social partners.

And, fourthly, it is aimed internally to draw attention to the fact that how we deliver on our Vision is as important as the outcome.

How 'People are the Business' Fits into Our Operating Model

When Chief Executive Officer (CEO) Mark Cutifani joined AGA in 2007, the business was in a slow but steady decline. The business projections for the next three years showed the same inexorable trend. The CEO implemented a strategic change programme called Project ONE, which saw the projected results for 2008, 2009 and 2010 drastically improve (see figure 1 below). (Final audited results for 2011 were not yet available at the time of writing this article, but were expected to exceed those of 2010.)

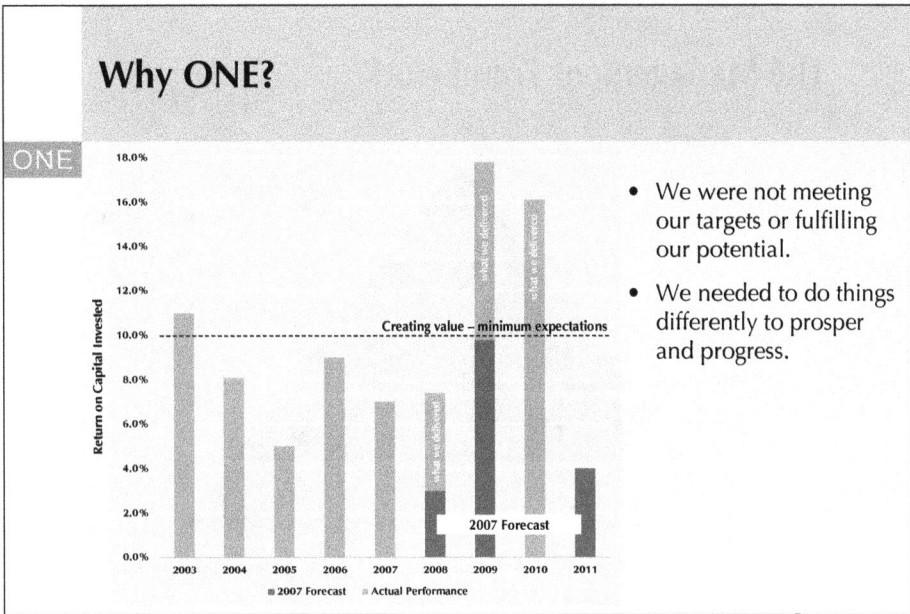

Figure 1: AGA Performance

The broad strategic direction of AGA as it was defined in 2008 in our business framework – namely our Vision, Mission, values and five core strategies – compelled a new approach to leadership that supports people doing the right work. AGA has adopted a Management Framework that sets the approach to how we conduct our business. It places the required emphasis on strong leadership, line ownership of the work, the bringing together of employees and technical systems, and the importance of continuous improvement through ongoing measurement and review. The Management Framework is not a change model – it is a total management system with a focus on strengthening both our people and our work systems (technical, commercial and operating) so that, through our constantly changing business and risk contexts, we can always reflect an aligned and consistent working model to achieve results and engagement.

The Management Framework

ONE

Management Framework

Mission

Vision

Values

Strategy

| Leadership | Line Ownership | HR Systems | Technical Systems | Measure & Review |

- The management framework brings people and systems together to realise our vision to be the leading mining company
- It sets the framework of how we do things – delivering consistency and efficiency to enhance operating performance and control

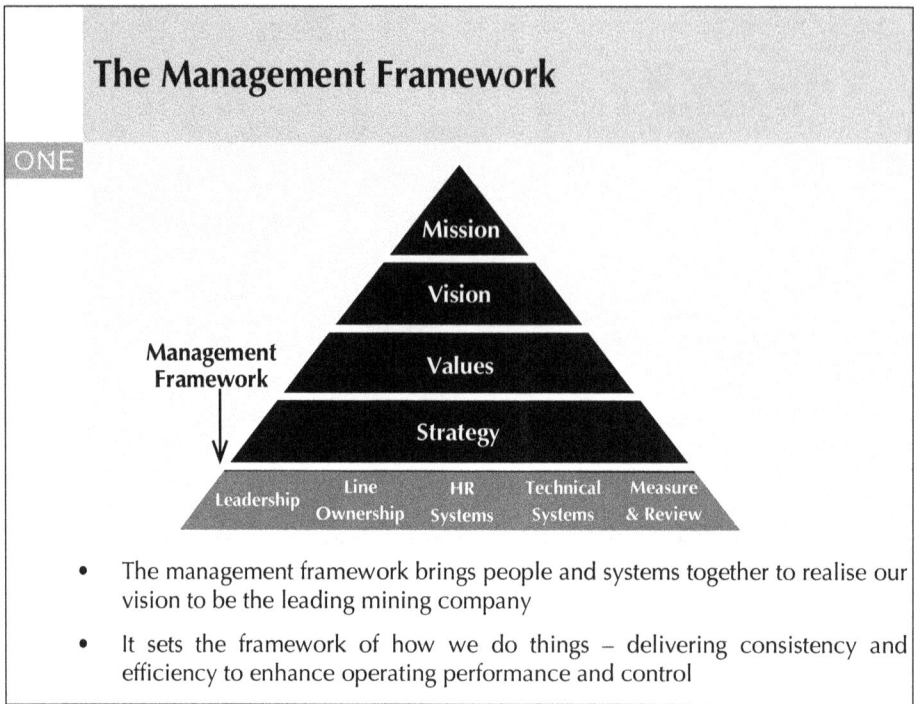

Figure 2: The Management Framework in AGA

We have also focused on the implementation of Project ONE, our change programme. In terms of Project ONE, we have rebuilt our business processes quite deliberately through the System for People (SP) based on the work of Elliott Jaques[1], the technical process re-engineering called the Business Process Framework (BPF) based on Deming's[2] model of Plan/Do/Check/Act, and Employee Engagement systems based on the work of Maurice Driscoll and Rob Evans in order to change our working environment and the work of people.[3] These ensure the integration of People and Systems of Work as in figure 3 below:

---

1 Elliott Jaques (18 January 1917-8 March 2003) was a Canadian psychoanalyst and organisational psychologist. He developed the notion of requisite organisation from his 'stratified systems theory', running counter to many others in the field of organisational development.

2 William Edwards Deming (14 October 1900-20 December 1993) was an American statistician, professor, author, lecturer and consultant. He is regarded as having had more impact upon Japanese manufacturing and business than any other individual not of Japanese heritage.

3 Much of the information on the AGA Management Framework, SP and BPF comes out of documents prepared by AGA's internal teams that have worked so diligently with these systems for the last few years and whose pioneering efforts I hereby acknowledge.

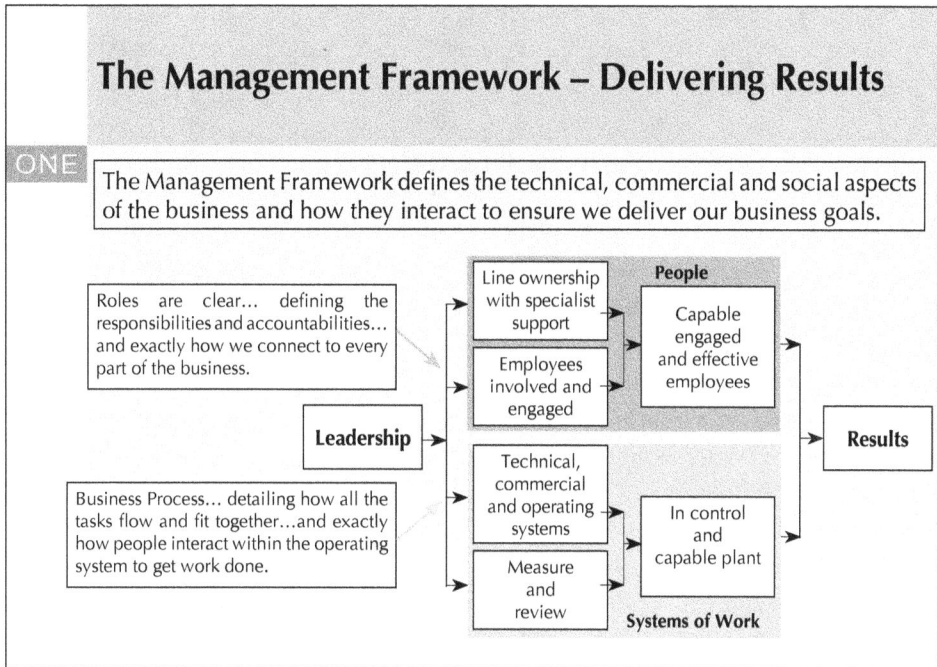

Figure 3: The Management Framework – Delivering Results

These three systems are integrated approaches to operating, and, together, they give effect to all our core strategies, but particularly to People are the Business. The SP begins with organisation design in order to describe clear structures and hierarchies based on levels of work, roles, and associated accountabilities and authorities that clarify exactly how we connect every part of the business. The SP, specifically, is a top-down implementation of Jacques's Requisite Organisation[4] and is aimed at ensuring AGA has the right people in the right roles doing the right work. The BPF details our business processes and how all tasks fit and flow together to explain exactly how people interact within the operating system and with one another to get work done. And the Engagement system encourages line ownership of people processes and teamwork, as we each have to step up and engage, ask the right questions, listen and connect, thereby further enhancing, systemically, the way in which employees do their work.

Simply put:

- The **System for People** (SP) is about making sure we have the right people in the right role doing the right work.

- The **Business Process Framework** (BPF) is about making sure we are doing the right work at the right time in the right way.

---

4   Jaques (1996).

- **Employee Engagement** – or how we connect with people – is focused on making sure that we involve the right people in the right way to ensure we deliver the right outcome.

The Skills Challenge

The shortage of skills is one of the biggest constraints to achieving aggressive growth plans in AGA. The resources boom is both a blessing and a curse. While a higher gold (or other mineral resource) price drives up margins, it also lands up in higher input costs – which partially explains why the profit margin never widens as much as one would expect. It also intensifies the war for talent. Many companies used to think of globalisation from a very ethnocentric perspective, asking questions such as: "In which countries should we pursue our growth objectives, selling which suite of products?" Today, of course, globalisation is a double-edged sword, in that companies with names that were not well known just a few years ago, and which were once viewed as fledgling operators in obscure regions, are now recognised as serious competitors, not only for mature companies' best customers but also for their top talent. Poaching is also not limited to direct competitors. Mining companies such as AGA lose top talent not only to other mining companies, but also to other sectors – sometimes, before graduates have worked even a day in mining! The three nonmining sectors which account for the bulk of lost mining engineering-related skills are the petrochemical, finance and consulting sectors.

What has been the traditional response of Human Resources (HR) practitioners in AGA and in other companies? There are many sound HR practices which are applied, and these include the following:

- Conduct exit interviews and stay interviews.

- Place more creative advertisements in newspapers.

- Do climate surveys to understand the cultural levers that could be pulled to both attract and retain top talent.

- Participate in 'Best Company to Work For' surveys.

- Do employment branding to better position the image of the company.

- Ensure all staff have Individual Development Plans (IDPs) and development opportunities.

- Design better retention bonuses.

- Convince the Compensation Committee to move from paying at the 50th percentile of the marketplace to the 60th or the 70th.

- Make sure we spend 3 to 5% of payroll on training (in the good times!)

Most importantly:

• Let's see how we can poach from our competitors!

Unfortunately, these traditional responses very often do not prove sufficient to ensure an ongoing pipeline of skills, often serving only to chase the same small pool of talent with ever-increasing pay packages. While I am not suggesting that HR practitioners abandon these practices, I am suggesting that a more strategic approach is necessary.

Talent Management in AGA: How It's Practised

To enable AGA to realise the full potential of its employees, become the employer of choice in the industry, and be considered by investors to be a leading corporate citizen with one of the industry's most outstanding management teams, the company requires a systemic talent management strategy that transcends a generic approach to individual and organisational development.

Inherent in this approach are the following:

• Leadership commitment – without which we would not be able to establish a culture of accountability or trust, the success of talent management being driven and practised by the manager and 'manager once removed' (the manager's manager) role holders.

• Change management – Project ONE is integrated, iteratively growing and a huge, all-encompassing change programme. Sustainability of the implementation approach receives ongoing attention, the principles of the system now being embedded in the implementation of AGA's SAP project called oneERP (enterprise resource planning).

• Risk management to reduce and manage exposure to human-capital risks.

The company views all its employees as talent and will provide the opportunities for them to learn and develop to their maximum capability, and into higher-level positions should these match potential capabilities and personal aspirations. As a global mining company, we offer opportunities to work in different countries and contexts. We value cultural adaptability.

In addition to technical skills, we look for prospective employees whose behaviours are aligned to the six organisation values of AGA. This requires: embracing a zero-harm culture which ensures the safety of all AGA employees; treating one another with dignity and respect by promoting an environment of trust, transparency and equality; valuing the diversity of each of the individuals within the company from across the globe, ensuring that our differences are understood and respected; being accountable for our actions and delivering on our commitments by acting in accordance with the AGA Code of Business Principles and Ethics; and respecting the environment in which we operate, ensuring that we build productive and mutually beneficial partnerships within the communities in which we operate.

Strategic talent management starts with the principle that AGA's talent pool includes all of its 63 000 employees, the communities in which AGA operates, and the broader resources industry.

As provided for in the SP, the process starts with the Human Resources Planning Subsystem in order to establish a systematic approach for matching human resources with the short-, medium- and long-term future needs of the organisation. The objectives of the Human Resources Planning Subsystem are:

- To ensure consistency between the strategic plan and the anticipated human-resource requirements.

- To identify future challenges and provide human resources to match.

- To identify candidates for current and future roles.

- To be proactive in attaining and developing human resources to effect these future strategies and challenges.

The strategy focuses both internally and externally, with the **internal focus** on effectiveness of the SP to date, technical skills demand and supply, and country-/region-specific challenges and needs; and the **external focus** on skills supply and development, industry collaboration, and the use of technologies such as social media and e-learning. While the development of all AGA's employees is considered essential, it is also acknowledged that special initiatives may be required when ensuring a pipeline for scarce and critical skills. This starts with identifying which are the truly scarce and critical skills, and then crafting a strategy for the development of both an internal and external pipeline.

Defining the Scarce and Critical Skills

It is important to set objective criteria for defining scarce and critical skills, as, in my experience, every line manager who has experienced some turnover will consider the roles in his or her department or business unit as requiring 'scarce and critical skills'. The following are some suggested criteria for defining this category of employees in a way that is both replicable and transparent:

1. **Turnover:** The analysis should start with a list of where turnover has been significant, that is, over 10% in the last year. This should then be broken down into categories, for example 10 to 15% (cause for concern); 15 to 20% (serious); and 20%+ (requires urgent attention). Particular attention should be paid to any roles where turnover has been over 15% in the year. (Ironically, very low turnover may also be a signal for concern, as young talent lower down the ranks may grow impatient at the perceived lack of promotion opportunities above them and start looking for external opportunities.)

2. **Vacancy period:** The length of time that it takes to fill a job is another indicator. If the job remains vacant for three months or longer from the time the previous incumbent left the company to when the new incumbent joins, this is often an indication of scarce skills. Keep in mind that this excludes notice periods, which, at lower levels, could be one calendar month (ie four months in total to fill the job), and, at senior levels, notice periods could be three calendar months (ie six months in total to fill the job). If vacancy factors are longer than six months, then this requires special attention.

3. **Criticality to the business:** This should be defined by some measure of impact on the business, for example production would be brought to a standstill (most severe), to there would be a significant impact on production and the bottom line (medium severity), to there would be a noticeable impact on production and this would also affect the bottom line (some impact). Different companies could attach different metrics to this definition, as long as the metrics are used consistently and are well understood by the key players in the business.

4. **Internal pipeline:** This is an indicator of the 'health of discipline' for each key discipline in the business. One of the ways to measure this is to look at the ratio of internal promotions to external appointments to vacancies. While it is always desirable to have a certain number of new people join the organisation, as they bring different experiences and fresh perspectives, AGA would ideally target a 1:2 ratio of external appointments:internal promotions.

5. **External pipeline:** Analysing the external pipeline can be done on the basis of anecdotal information from line managers and from recruitment agencies, and then be defined in broad terms with **descriptors**, such as: (i) This role is fairly easily filled from local or in-country sources; (ii) This role requires skills which are scarce in-country or available regionally at some premium; (iii) This role requires skills which are available only internationally and may only come on expatriate conditions; (iv) This role requires skills where it is virtually impossible to find a competent person to fill this job even internationally, and an international premium will have to be paid. Alternatively, the external pipeline can be defined far more accurately with **detailed studies** of actual numbers of different types of graduates available in different countries measured against the projected needs of the company, its direct competitors and other industry players who may recruit these skills. AGA has gone the latter route, commissioning a study of the availability of global mining engineering and artisan skills which is informing the specific strategies needed to address specific gaps.

Future Demand for Skills

Understanding how to address specific gaps requires a detailed understanding not only of current vacancies, but also of the drivers of future demand. These include the following:

- **Economic cycles:** In previous, long cycles of economic boom, unprecedented growth has meant for almost everyone in the workforce, but particularly for those with key skills, a period of nothing but prosperity, good jobs, easy promotions and easy salary increases. We are currently in a period of economic recession and, as a result, the attraction and retention pressures on most companies become less intense and poaching activity should decrease. We may experience a temporary respite in the talent war. Companies are restructuring and downsizing, and there is a short-term increase in people available in the market compared with what has been the case in recent years (but not necessarily in key skills). Voluntary turnover is dropping as people stay put in an insecure job market where 'last in, first out' may see you on the retrenchment list. However, it is to be expected that, as soon as the economy turns and employment markets open up again, these individuals will move on very quickly. One of the other negative trends in times of economic crisis is that one of the first budgets to be cut in most companies is the training budget. Many companies have not learnt from previous cycles where the kneejerk reaction of cutting training budgets and even closing down training academies completely in hard times drastically reduced graduate and technical pipelines, leaving very little capacity for the upswing when it inevitably occurred.[5] AGA has one of the largest training academies in the industry and has striven to maintain its training capacity consistently through all economic cycles.

- **Innovation and technology:** With new technology comes increased production efficiency and often progressive labour savings. However, this is often accompanied by the reliance upon a new set of potentially scarce skills and the difficulty of reskilling existing staff.

- **Productivity factors:** Critical to understanding the need for skilled labour is the understanding of the productivity of that labour. Where the productivity can be improved, it will often prove the case that less of that labour is needed to deliver the same outcomes. The opposite is of course also true. Key factors that impact the productivity of labour in the mining industry include the following:

  o   *Age:* While a decline in productivity related to age might only occur in office-bound roles from the late 50s onwards, the more manual the role the greater the impact of age on productivity. This is further exacerbated by environmental conditions such as heat, humidity and long travelling time

---

5   Boninelli (2009a).

to the workplace often found in mining – resulting in a rapid, age-related decline in productivity from the early 40s. Retirement is furthermore posing a serious threat to the industry's talent base, with 50% of the employee base being over 40 years old. In Canada, 60 000 employees in the mining sector are expected to retire by 2020. In Australia, a labour shortage of 195 000 workers is estimated by 2012 as increasing 'baby-boomer' retirements and the development of new projects with huge new skills demands coincide. In South Africa, the average age of mining professionals is estimated to be 50 to 55 years old. In the United States of America, 58% of industry members were already 50+ years old in 2005.[6]

-   *Health factors:* Health factors in the workforce can have a serious impact on productivity. For example, South Africa has one of the highest prevalence rates of AIDS in the world, and the negative effects of AIDS are further compounded by other diseases such as tuberculosis (TB) and silicosis leading to as much as a 10% loss of productivity in the workforce.[7] There seems little option but to continue to educate, to administer antiretroviral therapy (ART), and to actively manage TB. In other African countries, diseases such as malaria have a serious impact.

-   *Lifestyle:* While lifestyle choices in the First World have led to a greater need for work–life balance and to companies being forced to accommodate this in their work rosters and fly-in, fly-out arrangements, different challenges face the Third World. Many workers in Third World communities live in overcrowded conditions with poor sanitation and poor nutrition, which are compounded by the abuse of alcohol and cannabis. The impact of this is seen in biomedical and psychological issues. Prevention of issues is better than cure, and enhancing employees' lifestyles has a positive effect on productivity, supporting the return on investment (ROI) in company wellness programmes.

-   *Competence:* The mere presence of a qualification does not in any way guarantee competence. The declining standards and shortage of qualified teaching staff in many educational institutions have meant that many graduates of universities or technical colleges come with some degree of skills gap. In addition to this, a qualification may be only the starting point for true competence, as success in a role may require knowledge of many other things (the particular equipment used by the company, safety procedures, company policies, etc.). Existing internal skills need to be identified and assessed to determine competency levels and potential for ongoing training and development. Skills audits put together with the input

---

6   Deloitte UK Report.

7   Munday (2008).

of the relevant line managers and technical consultants which are then conducted on the staff in the discipline often render surprising and often disappointing results.

– **Utilisation of skills:** Often, skills are not appropriately utilised in the workplace. In a study conducted in a company I previously worked for, we established that professional nursing staff were spending less than 43% of their time on activities that actually required a nursing qualification.[8] This reinforces the need for companies to look carefully at productivity and review how jobs are designed and resourced. In cases of severe skills shortage, it may require re-engineering of the workplace to get away with less high-level skills.

– **Workflow efficiency:** Workflow efficiencies often leave a lot to be desired: the positive is that there are often many real opportunities for improvement. For example, travel time to the workplace in deep-level underground mines in South Africa can be as much as 24%. The re-engineering work done in AGA under the BPF has shown that, "if production and maintenance processes are effectively aligned and managed through a coordinated planning and scheduling process, improvements in productivity can be realized in excess of 30%", and "if processes are moved from high to low variation performance, output can be increased by 15% to 30%, without significant capital inputs".[9]

• **Employee engagement:** Employees should perform optimally when the job is well designed, they are properly trained, and the outcomes of the role are defined and resourced per the BPF/SP model. But the right managerial leadership practices will enhance the personal commitment of employees and their willingness to go the extra mile. Many companies strive to 'maximise shareholder wealth' – a goal that is inadequate in many respects. As an emotional catalyst, wealth maximisation lacks the power to fully mobilise human energies. It's an insufficient defence when people question the legitimacy of corporate power. And it is particularly true in an economic recession when retrenchments and other cost-cutting inevitably result in poor employee morale and anxiety around job security. In turbulent times, we look to organisations that share our concerns, manage anxiety and take the lead. In these difficult times of economic crisis, leaders play a central role in not only attracting new talent, but also in retaining and motivating the remaining talent within the organisation. It has been said that people join an organisation, but leave their manager – if the assumption can be made that people come to work motivated, then the question is what prevents them from working to that full motivation? AGA has embarked

---

8   Thomas, Venter & Boninelli (2010).

9   Cutifani (2010a).

on several initiatives around employee engagement utilising the work of Maurice Driscoll and others.[10] Their work is based on the belief that the lift from satisfactory to scintillating workforce performance is based on the connection between managers, supervisors and employees being built upon: (i) managers setting the right context; (ii) managers and supervisors creating relationships of trust founded on requisite leadership practices, personally earned authority, beneficial decision-making influence and supportive behaviour; and (iii) supervisors and managers being enabled to deliver the leadership's message to the workforce. The results of their initial pilots have been most encouraging. Another benefit is that the very process of engagement helps to develop talent that has hitherto remained latent.

- **Legislative and other pressures:** The strategic management of HR always occurs within a broader sociopolitical and business context. Legislation may create affirmative action or employment equity targets (sometimes called localisation in African countries where the intent is to replace expatriate staff with staff of local origin), increasing the pressure to develop people from designated groups. Community agreements (such as those AGA has in Brazil) may require that a minimum percentage of staff be recruited from within the community immediately surrounding the mine (which may prove difficult in areas that have not previously had a mining culture). Sustainability pressures may result in stricter governance on environmental or other controls, simultaneously creating a need for the skills to manage in those situations.

- **Company and industry growth projections:** AGA has five-year targets of 20% increase in productivity and a 20% increase in production to 5.5 million ounces of gold. AGA is extremely well positioned for high-value growth. Having invested heavily in exploration, AGA has one of the strongest greenfield and brownfield expansion portfolios in the industry. Expansion is concentrated in Australia, the Americas and West Africa, with combined, proved and probable ore reserves currently estimated as 75 million ounces. AGA will grow the production by 1 million ounces within 5 years. But the growth projections of the mining industry, and neighbouring industries such as oil and gas, are equally aggressive. For example, in Australia, a record $76 billion in mining-led business investment is expected in the next year, creating around 61 500 new jobs by 2015.[11]

All of the above factors clearly indicate the need for a strategic talent management strategy which focuses on developing both the internal and external pipeline of talent.

---

10 Driscoll & Evans (2009).

11 National Resources Sector Employment Taskforce (2011).

Developing the Internal Pipeline

AGA's SP is considered a critical component for supporting the repositioning of the organisation. The SP, with its interrelated subsystems, is based on the work of Elliott Jacques, and, more specifically, his later developments of 'Requisite Organisation' (RO). The RO management system proposes that most problems in organisations are caused by poor structure and systems, not deficient employees. Therefore, interventions which focus on fixing the organisation, free employees to work to their full potential, increasing efficiency, effectiveness and employee satisfaction. The SP model has been specifically developed to ensure integration of the critical managerial effectiveness subsystems to be implemented on a global basis. The three key objectives of SP are:

1. Creating the right organisation design.

2. Ensuring the right people are in the right jobs.

3. Developing effective working relationships.

What is Talent Pool Development? When we at AGA talk about 'talent', we're not referring to a small, elite group, but to all of our 63 000 employees, who are essential contributors to our success. Therefore, Talent Pool Development is the AGA process for providing each and every employee with the opportunity to work to their maximum potential to fulfil our business needs.

Why is Talent Pool Development important to AGA? Talent Pool Development seeks to facilitate an understanding of how every individual can best contribute to the achievement of our goals, enabling us to match the right people to the right roles, providing all employees with the right balance between challenge and capability. This is critical in order to:

- Increase effectiveness, because business goals are assigned to people who are best capable of reaching them.

- Improve efficiency, because people are working at a level which matches their capability.

- Enhance trust, because people are being recognised for their capability and are not overstretched or underutilised, and both manager and subordinate can count on each other to do what is being committed to.

By understanding the capability and aspirations of our people, we will be able to determine whether we have the talent necessary to deliver on our current and future strategic objectives and to develop our own pipeline of talent, through which candidates can be sourced internally for role vacancies.

What does it mean to the individual employee? Talent Pool Development also provides for the development and implementation of appropriate career development plans for all employees, thereby facilitating the growth of our talent and supporting individuals' aspirations to become the best they can be, within the scope of what is viable for the organisation.

The AGA talent management strategy incorporates all aspects of Project ONE, namely the SP, Employee Engagement and the BPF, and recognises that one of the key principles is that every employee is part of the talent pool – defined by the direct subordinates and subordinates once removed (SORs) reporting to that employee's manager once removed (MOR).

Talent management in AGA is an integrated system that is underpinned by:

1. The right organisational structures (Organisation design) and work complexity (accountabilities and authorities).

2. The right people in the right role (Role accountabilities and Individual Capability).

3. Doing the right work in the right way (supported by BPF), with clearly assigned tasks that have a clear line-of-site up and down the organisational goals.

4. Effective working relationships (laterally and vertically – supported by our Engagement initiatives).

5. The right processes (supported by SP subsystems such as Talent management, Performance management, etc.) and measures (standardised in SAP).

The purpose of the Talent Pool Development Subsystem is to provide all employees with the opportunity to develop to their maximum potential capability so as to meet current and future business needs. The objectives are:

• To match individuals to appropriate roles based on current and future capability.

• To identify employee development needs in line with likely career progression and company objectives.

• To identify company-wide development needs.

• To support our individual employees in their aspirations to perform to their potential, within the scope of what is viable for the organisation.

All employees are included in the talent pool; this includes employees who are working under long-term contract to the company and who have an existing or potential career with the company, and/or if the contractor is a manager to subordinate employees.

The system is designed to adhere to the following principles:

• Work for everyone at a level consistent with their level of current capability, values, and interests.

- Opportunity for everyone to progress as his or her potential capability matures, within opportunities available in the organisation.

- Fair and just treatment for everyone, including fair pay based on equitable pay differentials for the level of work and merit recognition related to personal-effectiveness appraisal.

- Managerial leadership interaction between managers and subordinates, including shared context, personal-effectiveness appraisal, feedback and recognition, and coaching.

- Clear articulation of accountability and authority to engender trust and confidence in working relationships.

- Opportunity for everyone individually or through representatives to influence policy development.

Every manager within the organisation is fully accountable for the outputs of the people who work directly for us; we are accountable for their safety performance, their production, their costs, and every other facet of measurable output, including their behaviour towards every individual inside and outside the business. Given that we are accountable for every aspect of their output, it is our specific accountability to select the right person for the role, provide them with the right training, give them the right tools, and coach and advise them to ensure that they deliver the required outputs for the business. How does it work? AGA has adopted a formal Talent Pool Development process based on a three-tier management structure in which the manager once removed (MOR) performs both an in-role performance management calibrating role to ensure fairness, and a career development mentoring role to guide the development of the subordinate once removed (SOR).

But talent management does not exist separately from other managerial practices.

The 10 Managerial Leadership Practices

At AGA, you'll come across the term 'accountability' often, as opposed to 'responsibility'. It is one of our stated organisational values: "We are accountable for our actions and we undertake to deliver on our commitments." It's also one of the founding principles upon which the SP was designed and is being implemented at AGA. Accountability is an obligation to honour a commitment made to someone else. Unlike responsibility, which resides in the person, accountability is attached to the role. Within our working context, accountability is the obligation of each employee to deliver all elements of the value that he or she is employed to deliver. Employers themselves are also accountable for delivering elements of value (such as, for example, proper working conditions and remuneration).

Managers have two types of accountabilities: those as an employee and those specifically related to managerial roles; and the 10 managerial leadership and engagement practices.

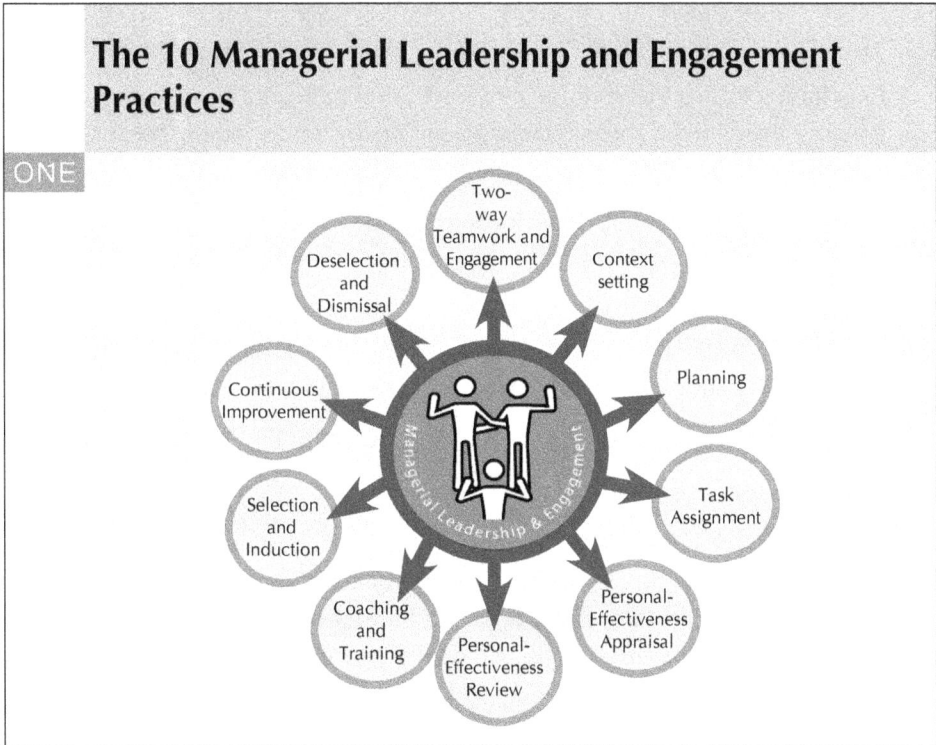

Figure 4: The 10 Managerial Leadership and Engagement Practices

All managers are held accountable by their managers for exercising leadership using these practices:

1. Developing a **two-way, manager–subordinate working relationship** that takes into consideration the input of subordinates.

2. Managers must provide their subordinates with an up-to-date **context** to ensure that they have a clear understanding of why they are doing what they have been tasked to do.

3. Managers must engage their subordinates in **planning** which could be

    (i) delegated plans or those set by a manager, or

    (ii) personal plans, or those set by individuals for themselves within the context set by their manager.

4. Chief among the managerial accountabilities is the **assignment of tasks** and being clear with subordinates about what they have to deliver (quality and quantity of required outputs), and the time and resources that they have to deliver it.

247

5. **Personal-effectiveness appraisals** refer to the ongoing and often informal managerial accountability of providing subordinates with constructive feedback on their performance.

6. **Personal-effectiveness reviews** are the annual process when managers meet with their subordinates to formally appraise their performance and remuneration.

7. **Coaching** refers to that training provided to subordinates by their managers to enhance their effectiveness in their role and help them work as close to their full potential and the role's maximum required effectiveness.

8. Managers are accountable for **selecting** capable subordinates who can perform the work required of them, and for personally ensuring that they are inducted into the role.

9. Managers are accountable to their managers for **continually improving the processes** that they control and delegate to their subordinates to use.

All these processes play a role in talent management, but the coaching and mentoring require further discussion.

- **Manager Coaching** is focused on developing the subordinate within his or her current level of work and focusing on his or her Current Applied Capability (CAC) and the way he or she is applying himself or himself in his or her role. Coaching has shown itself to be an equally effective, but more direct, form of development in areas where a manager is

  - providing specific direction, interim support and ongoing feedback during new or difficult work assignments

  - providing ongoing feedback on specific performance areas that need improvement

  - covering sensitive areas where tactful and/or direct input is necessary, ie in the case of inappropriate behaviour, etc.

  - covering any areas where work assignments or education courses are either not available, or are available but need local reinforcement or clarification in order to be meaningful

- **MOR Mentoring** is used to help an SOR to understand her or his potential and how that Current Potential Capability (CPC) might be developed to achieve as full career growth as possible. Mentoring can also assist in the development of knowledge and skills.

The accountabilities are as shown in the following table:

TALENT POOL	PERFORMANCE MANAGEMENT
– MOR accountability	– Managerial accountability
– Focus on Current Potential Capability	– Focus on Current Applied Capability
– Mentoring on career development	– Coaching on personal effectiveness in role
– > 1 year	– < 1 year

The SP ensures that individuals work at the level (or stratum) of work that corresponds to their abilities, and their developmental and aspirational needs, and that match the organisation's requirement to get work done at appropriate levels of complexity. The terms 'Current Potential Capability' and 'Current Applied Capability' are referenced to the level of work described in the RO.

Level of work (ie the felt weight of the role) and the term 'stratum' (ie measurement of the role in time span of the longest task) describe the complexity of work in a role and a person's corresponding ability to handle the complexity. Stratum 1 is the first level of work and is concerned with the day-to-day provision of services or the manufacture of goods. Workplace collaboration in the form of teamwork and on-the-job training are characteristic of this level of work, which is usually routine in nature. Each next stratum requires additional cognitive capability and maturation to handle additional complexity. Stratum 4 and 5, for example, are responsible for adding value for the future. Stratum 4 requires the holding together of business in the present, whilst at the same time building for the future; it signals a shift away from central operational concerns to managing both continuity and change. Stratum 5 is accountable for the viability of the business over a 5- to 10-year time frame, taking into account the external environment.

Current Applied Capability (CAC) therefore refers to an individual's ability to do a certain kind of work in a specific role at a given level at the present time. It depends not only on the individual's Current Potential Capability (CPC), but also upon the extent to which she or he values the work (V), whether she or he possesses the necessary skilled knowledge (K/S), and her or his working within the boundaries of the required behaviours established for all employees, and the specific required behaviours established for the role, both of which are essential components of (RB). This is expressed in the formula:

$$CAC = f\ CPC \bullet K/S \bullet V \bullet RB$$

Current Potential Capability (CPC) is then defined as the maximum level at which an individual could work in a role at the present time, given that they value the work and possess the necessary skilled knowledge.

'Potential' refers to how large a role someone could handle if he or she were to acquire the knowledge, value the work, and apply the required behaviours at a particular level.

In matching employee capability to role complexity, it is important to understand that Work Complexity defines the complexity of decision making required in a role. 'Complexity' refers to the number of variables operating in a situation, the clarity and precision with which they can be identified, and their rate of change. This is then compared with Individual Capability, which defines the mental capacity to handle the complexities of a particular role, and the actual ability of an individual to complete tasks – or solve problems – of a specific complexity in a specific time span (see figure 5 below).

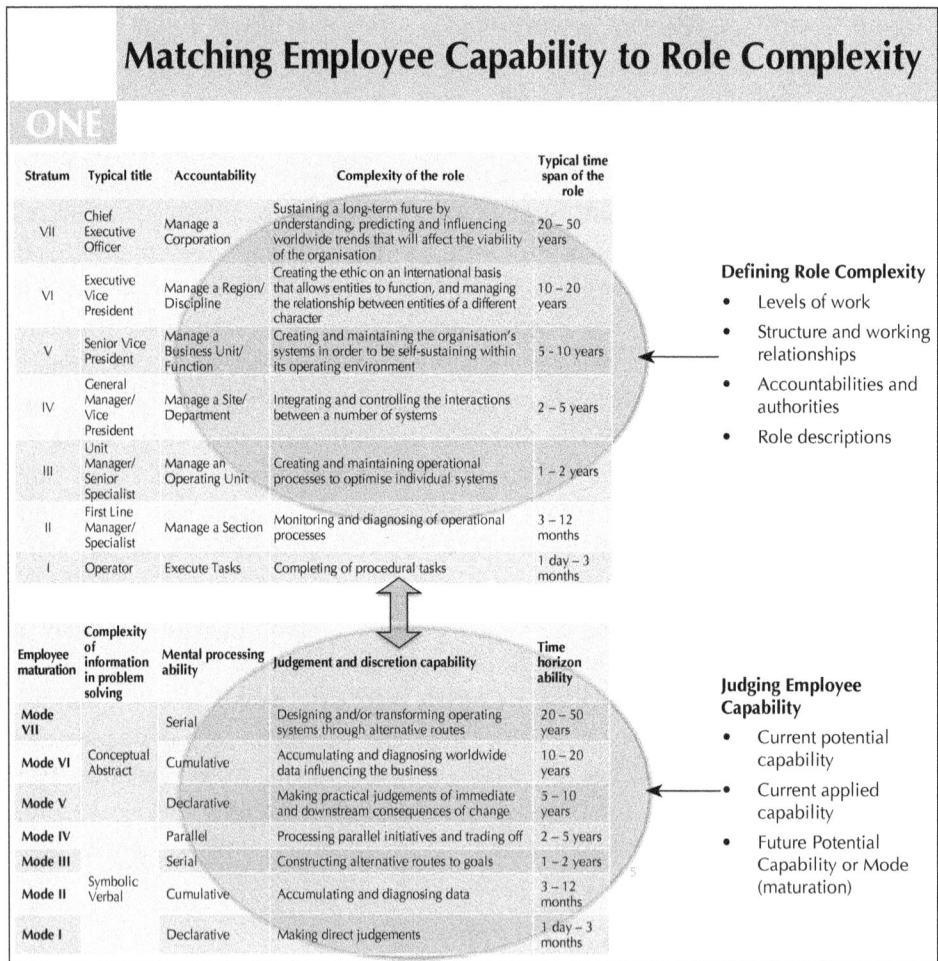

Matching Employee Capability to Role Complexity

ONE

Stratum	Typical title	Accountability	Complexity of the role	Typical time span of the role
VII	Chief Executive Officer	Manage a Corporation	Sustaining a long-term future by understanding, predicting and influencing worldwide trends that will affect the viability of the organisation	20 – 50 years
VI	Executive Vice President	Manage a Region/ Discipline	Creating the ethic on an international basis that allows entities to function, and managing the relationship between entities of a different character	10 – 20 years
V	Senior Vice President	Manage a Business Unit/ Function	Creating and maintaining the organisation's systems in order to be self-sustaining within its operating environment	5 - 10 years
IV	General Manager/ Vice President	Manage a Site/ Department	Integrating and controlling the interactions between a number of systems	2 – 5 years
III	Unit Manager/ Senior Specialist	Manage an Operating Unit	Creating and maintaining operational processes to optimise individual systems	1 – 2 years
II	First Line Manager/ Specialist	Manage a Section	Monitoring and diagnosing of operational processes	3 – 12 months
I	Operator	Execute Tasks	Completing of procedural tasks	1 day – 3 months

Defining Role Complexity
- Levels of work
- Structure and working relationships
- Accountabilities and authorities
- Role descriptions

Employee maturation	Complexity of information in problem solving	Mental processing ability	Judgement and discretion capability	Time horizon ability
Mode VII		Serial	Designing and/or transforming operating systems through alternative routes	20 – 50 years
Mode VI	Conceptual Abstract	Cumulative	Accumulating and diagnosing worldwide data influencing the business	10 – 20 years
Mode V		Declarative	Making practical judgements of immediate and downstream consequences of change	5 – 10 years
Mode IV		Parallel	Processing parallel initiatives and trading off	2 – 5 years
Mode III		Serial	Constructing alternative routes to goals	1 – 2 years
Mode II	Symbolic Verbal	Cumulative	Accumulating and diagnosing data	3 – 12 months
Mode I		Declarative	Making direct judgements	1 day – 3 months

Judging Employee Capability
- Current potential capability
- Current applied capability
- Future Potential Capability or Mode (maturation)

Figure 5: Matching Employee Capability to Role Complexity

All employees' CPC will be judged and equilibrated at least once annually; and employees' career development needs will be assessed, recorded, actioned and monitored. The integrity lies in the process. The first assessment of the individual is done by the individual's manager. A separate assessment is done by the individual's

MOR. These judgements are taken into an equilibration session for the MOR's talent pool, that is, in a session chaired by the MOR. The CPCs of all his or her SORs are reviewed and compared by the MOR together with all the managers reporting to the MOR. The idea behind this is to have as many inputs as possible, for example the individual whose CPC assessments are being reviewed may have previously worked for another manager or other managers on the review panel of the MOR team of managers who may have different working experiences with the individual in question.

Once input from all those participating has been received and the MOR has reached a decision on the CPC, this is plotted on a maturity chart against the individual's age, thus allowing a projection of future potential (sometimes called 'Mode') using the graph to read at what level the individual could be capable of working in their 60s and even 70s (assuming that Knowledge and Skills, Valuing the Work and Required Behaviours are in place). The results of the equilibration session are then translated into Individual Development Plans (IDPs) which are actioned through the MOR for mentoring and through the manager for on-the-job coaching, with the guidance of the HR Department as needed.

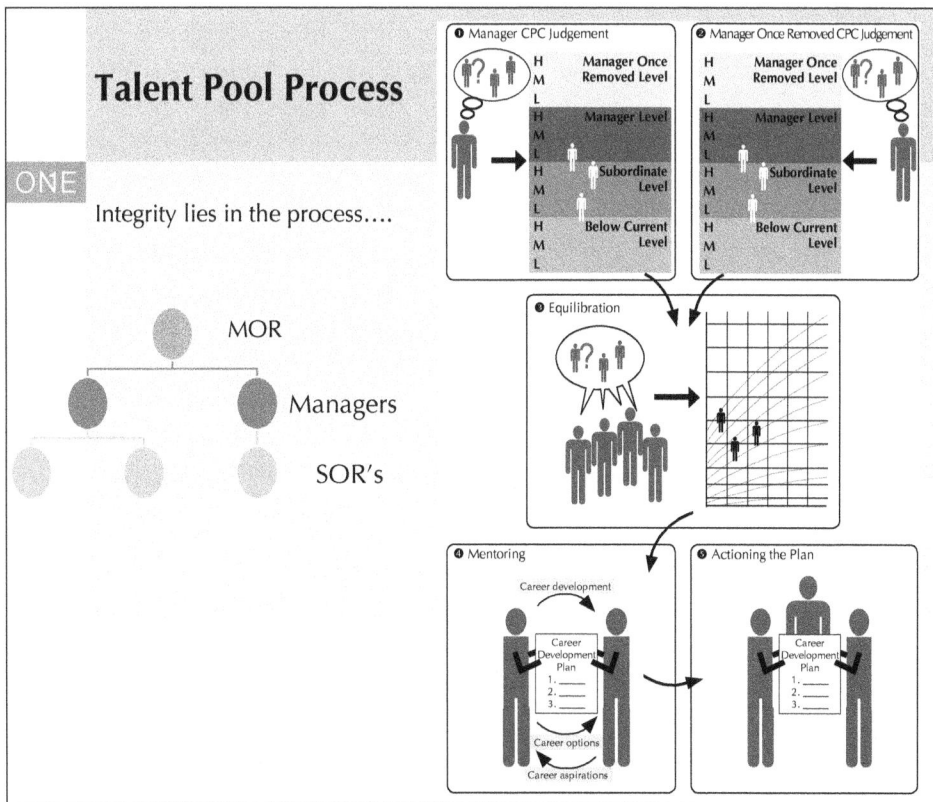

Figure 6: The Talent Pool Process

Just about any organisation will have some great natural judges of talent, but none have enough to ensure the assessment and development of all talent will take place as it should. AGA has focused on training all managers in the principles of SP and in how to make judgements of CPC and CAC with the assistance of trained practitioners as part of a process to institutionalise this expertise in the company. Those managers making the judgements have to know the talent they are assessing well. They have to know all about the job the person is being considered for. This particular form of talent management and talent assessment is practised, tracked, and learnt by all leaders until it becomes second nature – part of the established processes and daily routines. Through this process, AGA will create our own supply of good judges of capability. They calibrate individuals through a myriad of dialogues, using information collected through many observations of decisions, actions, and behaviours, and refined in group discussions. The discipline of pooling managers' judgements about talent is comprehensive, continuous, and part of the culture. It integrates the development of people with the running of the business, and connects their capability with the business results. The judgements continue to improve with practice and experience; hence the importance of internally developed systems such as the SP which maximise the likelihood of a systemic and sustainable way of managing employees.

This significant investment of managerial time in talent management is considered essential to the success of the system. Ram Charan and Bill Conaty (2010) say:

> Getting to the core of a person's values, behaviours, beliefs, and talents may seem like a lot of work, but masters understand that the return on time is huge. It's like analysing a business problem or opportunity: we drill down to find the causes, understand the context, and assess options. Similarly, when we get to know a person, we are able to develop insights and options to speed his or her growth and development. This is especially important for companies that rely on specialized knowledge and need to quickly develop the leadership potential of their experts. The right decisions build organizational capacity. Insight into an individual's talents and foresight into where the leader could go turn traditional succession planning on its head. Rather than finding people to fill positions, it puts the emphasis on opening paths for leaders to grow their talents and become ever more capable.[12]

Succession planning in AGA, then, is fully aligned to the particular approach to talent management described above. We have the traditional charts that show possible successors 'Ready now', 'Ready in 1-3 years' and 'Ready in 3-5 years', but these are closely aligned to the maturation charts of successors so that we can match when the individual will transition to a new level of work to when he or she will be ready for the next role. Clearly, manager coaching and MOR mentoring are also applied

---

12 Charan & Conaty (2010).

to addressing any gaps identified in Knowledge and Skills, Valuing the Work and Required Behaviours.

In addition, AGA also focuses on **Health of Discipline** for key functions. A discipline development committee is formed consisting of the head of discipline together with senior specialists in the discipline, supported by internal HR and Training and Development specialists, and, in some cases, even by external academic resources. This committee will set standards for the discipline by applying BPF principles to the processes of the discipline.

It will set technical and people targets for the discipline to be achieved and monitor recording of best operating practices to ensure:

- Capturing of discipline-specific technical knowledge.

- Safekeeping and accessibility of technical knowledge.

- Establishing the best way to transfer knowledge.

- Consistent transfer of best practices.

- Retention of technical/institutional memory.

It quality-assures the SP practices to ensure:

- SP and levels-of-work application.

- Qualification and standards setting (industry versus AGA requirements).

- Curricula development in the AGA training academy, in consultation with local colleges and universities.

- The approval of role and competency profiles.

- That skills matrixes and competency frameworks are in place.

- That skills audits are conducted.

- The supporting of coaching and mentoring practices.

- Performance management application and practices.

- IDP application and practices.

- Career paths and learning pathways application and practices.

- The tracking of pipeline delays from training.

But no amount of work on the internal pipeline would suffice to fill all our talent needs. AGA also has a strong focus on the external pipeline dynamics.

External Pipeline

The challenge for the global mining industry is twofold: expanding tertiary training institutions for mining in absolute terms, while simultaneously considering a range of (often region-specific) measures to make mining careers socially more respectable in order to build a sustainable pipeline of candidates from the schooling level upwards.

One of the things to be considered in looking at the external pipeline dynamics is the attractiveness of the industry and the profession to new, young talent. A recent survey by Deloitte (2011)[13] showed that mining ranked last in familiarity and attractiveness of 12 major professions considered (behind Hospitality, Healthcare, Information Technology, Transportation, Business Services, Construction, Government, Finance, Agriculture, Manufacturing, and Utilities).

Quite apart from the attractiveness of the profession, there may not be enough entrants to mining engineering-related degrees because the basic mathematics, science and computer proficiency skills (and, sometimes, even the basic language literacy skills) are not in place coming out of high school. The 'feeder' line is broken in many countries, for example South Africa is in a particularly bad state with respect to skills, where only 4% of matriculants have higher-grade mathematics and 65% of these come from just 7% of the schools.[14] In 2009, one South African university estimated that 47% of first-year students had sufficient English language skills, and only 7% of students had sufficient mathematics skills to successfully pass the engineering degree in the prescribed time[15]. The skills set demands are also changing with the entry of new technologies, and university curricula are traditionally slow to change.

In First World economies, we also face the reality of the disappearing 'boomers' with a greying of the workplace. These retirements, combined with the exit out of the profession for personal or other reasons of more experienced staff, not only leave vacancies which are difficult to fill, but also leave the young talent in the organisation relatively exposed without sufficient mentors and without the organisational memory that assists decision making in difficult times. This has a major impact on the transfer of skills, many of which can only be acquired tacitly and on the job from experienced mentors.

As AGA is active in more than 20 countries and skills are very mobile, AGA conducts research on the global supply of mining engineering graduates. A summary of the trends of mining engineering-related graduates is supplied in table 1, and the conclusion is that demand far outstrips supply!

---

13 Deloitte UK Report.

14 Howie (2005).

15 Boninelli (2009b).

Table 1: Summary of trends with regard to mining engineering-related graduates

Country	Mining Engineering Graduate Supply
South Africa	Numbers of mining engineering graduates are increasing, but demand still far exceeds supply. Many graduates are lost to other industry sectors.
Southern Africa	The only country with any real numbers is Zambia – all graduates are absorbed into the Copperbelt.
East Africa	Produces only small numbers.
West Africa	Only Ghana and Nigeria produce any significant numbers of mining engineering-related graduates – mostly absorbed into the oil and gas sector.
Canada	Until recent years, a net exporter of graduates, but tar sands project demands will exceed local supply.
United States of America	Produces only 30 to 40% of its graduate needs!
South America	Brazil produces the largest number, but all graduates are absorbed by companies that partner the universities. Chile, Peru and Colombia produce fewer graduates than their national needs.
Europe	Best numbers from German-speaking countries. United Kingdom universities have high percentages of students from the Commonwealth or Asia – who return home after graduating. Most other European nations experience declining interest in mining as a career owing to the poor image of the industry.
Australia	Produces large numbers of mining engineering-related graduates, but heavy poaching from petrochemical sector means it cannot meet its own needs.
Russia/China/India	Growing number of graduates, but insufficient for their needs – and do not contribute to the global skills pool. This might change as numbers grow and English-language skills improve.

Depending on the success of continental European, South American and South African institutions in boosting their graduate and postgraduate throughput, an absolute decline in mining engineers of between 15 to 25% by 2020 is nevertheless a realistic scenario. Areas to potentially focus recruitment efforts on could be Germany, Turkey and Eastern Europe.

Then there is the issue of the 'defectors' or those mining engineering graduates who leave the sector after only one or two years of work, or, in some cases, graduate and never spend a day in the mining industry. Three sectors account for the bulk of lost mining engineering-related (MERS) skills – the petrochemical, finance and consulting sectors.

Based on recent research conducted on behalf of AGA[16], key initiatives we will be driving are the following:

- **Addressing teaching capacity constraints:** Development and retention of competent teaching staff have proven a global challenge. To structurally overcome this challenge, two types of industry professionals should be deployed: lecturers teaching the basic (boring) courses required for the general first degree, and professionals seconded for longer periods from industry with an explicit mandate to develop the curricula for the postgraduate specialisations that the industry requires for the longer term.

- **Poaching from sectors to which MERS conventionally are lost:** Three sectors account for the bulk of lost MERS – the petrochemical, finance and consulting sectors. Recovering skills from each of these sectors will require different strategies, but, generally, will contribute to payroll inflation.

- **Lengthening the shadow of the headgear:** The industry and its career options remain poorly understood, except in the very few societies where it is the dominant sector. To broaden the pool of potential recruits, the industry should bring awareness of the career-path options within mining to communities not traditionally familiar with it. This would also require the mining HR departments to take a more long-term, holistic and active approach to broadening, securing and nurturing the skills pipeline all the way from primary to tertiary.

Another strong trend is the global growth in mobility, as evidenced by our own statistics in AGA. In the financial year 2011, the talent AGA employed just at senior management level and above came from 22 different countries. Some months ago, I was paging through the *Sunday Times* newspaper (in South Africa) and worked out that the ads represented no fewer than 78 different countries, all trying to recruit skills out of South Africa. Changes in the psychological employment contract have increased mobility and decreased loyalty. Expatriate assignments are no longer the domain of the career expats, but we have had cases where local talent in African countries that was being trained up under localisation policies to take the place of expats left the company before that transition could take place – to go on an expatriate assignment themselves!

More flexible working practices are now also the order of the day. This might be by employing skills on a temporary basis for a particular project, allowing a permanent support employee to become part-time or bringing back retired staff on short-term contracts to meet certain needs. Not only do talented individuals expect to be given international assignments as part of their working experience, but experienced individuals with scarce skills are also demanding to work out of the city of their choice and 'telecommute'. AGA has top technical specialists working out of cities as far afield as Melbourne, London, Washington, et cetera, but we have

16 Reichardt (2011).

no offices in these places. They work from home, telecommute and only physically travel to a mine site as and when required.

We have also had to become more flexible in our employment contracts. Based on a preferred candidate's unique situation, AGA can create an offer that will best suit their needs and wants.

AGA has also invested increasing effort into defining its employee value proposition and building an employment brand. While this is a work in progress, AGA considers it essential to defining what makes our company unique and what it stands for. In association, it communicates to potential employees what it is like to work for our organisation and why long-term employees are retained.

In 2010, Generation Y outnumbered baby-boomers – and 96% of Generation Y have joined a social network.[17] AGA has recently experimented in social networking with channels such as Twitter and professional networking sites such as LinkedIn. What we have learnt is that these channels require experienced and dedicated resources to drive them properly. One can never forget that social networking gives candidates the opportunity to share their interview and job-search experiences with a global audience – whether positive or negative.

Retention

Of course, no discussion on talent management is complete without a reference to retention strategies. It is difficult to attract and keep top talent, but AGA believes that our company's culture and climate are key to creating a system that works. In terms of Project ONE, we have rebuilt our business processes by landing the people (SP), technical (BPF) and engagement systems quite deliberately to change our working environment and the work of people. While Base salary, Bonus, Incentives and Benefits have a higher short-term impact, the factors driving longer-term retention are Recognition, Career opportunities, Feedback and Development, Leadership and Coaching, and, last but not least, Culture, Values and Brand.

As the CEO of AGA, Mark Cutifani said:

> First, money is not a positive motivator in terms of delivering outstanding results. However, it can be a major demotivator if you do not pay at market – or at a level people believe is reasonable. Second, people look for a reasonable degree of autonomy – to be able to be innovative to deliver results they can own. In this context the key is to provide a degree of structure so that they can be innovative within certain limits. The use of the BPF actually opens up the ability to be more innovative, as we are able to open up degrees of freedom through involvement and a clear definition of boundaries (which can be broader if well defined and integrated across the activity chain). Third – the concept of Engagement. By involving people in the planning of their work

17 HAYS Resources & Mining Report (2011).

we start to liberate their creativity. By giving more autonomy as part of the process it is amazing to see how quickly they respond to the challenge and how innovative they will become.[18]

Conclusion

There is no more fitting conclusion than the words of AGA's CEO, Mark Cutifani, who said:

> I live by a simple leadership philosophy: the business is ours to manage ... the future is ours to create. Taking this starting point, the most important thing to understand about our business is that it is not grades, processing plants and headgears. It's actually about people: **People are the Business ... Our Business is People**. In recognition of the importance of our people to the success of the business, AngloGold Ashanti is committed to helping each and every employee to realize their full potential.

References

Boninelli, I. 2009a. Recession and the War for Talent. Is the War for Talent Over?, in *The State We're in: the 2010 Flux Trend Review*, edited by D Chang. Johannesburg: Pan Macmillan.

Boninelli, I. 2009b. Preliminary Findings of Review of Mining Engineering Faculties in South Africa. Gold Fields Internal Executive Report. Johannesburg.

Charan, R & Conaty, B. 2010. *The Talent Masters*. New York: Crown Business.

Cutifani, M. (CEO of AGA) 2010a. AngloGold Ashanti Business Improvement Strategy. Internal AGA Paper.

Cutifani, M. 2010b. Extract from an internal AGA e-mail sent to a group of senior managers after a strategy off-site.

Deloitte UK Report. Tracking the Trends 2011 – the Top 10 Issues Mining Companies Will Face in the Coming Year.

Driscoll, M & Evans, R. 2009. *The Engagement Phenomenon*. Brisbane: Frontline Planning Pty Ltd.

HAYS Resources and Mining Report. 2011. Recruitment and Retention in Mining. Australia.

Howie, S. 2005. *DoE Teachers for the Future 2005: Meeting Teacher Shortages to Achieve Education for All*. Pretoria: Department of Education, 46/47.

Jaques, E. 1996. *Requisite Organization*. Arlington VA: Cason Hall & Co.

Munday, N. 2008. Strategic Skills Supply. Gold Fields Ltd Internal Report. Johannesburg.

National Resources Sector Employment Taskforce. 2011. Resourcing the Future http://www.deewraaa.gov.au/Skills/Programs/National/nrset/Pages/ResourcingtheFutureReport.aspx.

Reichardt, M. 2011. Mining-related Engineering Skills – a Global View. Report prepared for AGA. Johannesburg.

Thomas, A, Venter, AB & Boninelli, I. 2010. Addressing the Nursing Shortage at Netcare: a New Remedy or the Same Prescription? *SA Journal of Labour Relations* 34(1).

---

18 Cutifani (2010b).

11

CASE STUDY: PICK n PAY – THE UPSIDE OF EXPORTING VALUES

Tamra Veley

Pick n Pay's foray into Africa beyond its immediate borders has been criticised by many retail analysts as too slow, too cautious and subject to the muting effects of competitor acceleration.

But nothing quietens the critics quite like success. Although Pick n Pay does not report segmentally, it is common cause that its operations outside South Africa are beginning to deliver some very pleasing results for a company currently in deep transition.

Its measured approach to expansion in Africa is gradually being appreciated as a canny one; Pick n Pay's key to success in Africa has been a deliberate, planned campaign of expansion through which the company's central operating ethos and values system, critical to its 45-year success story, have been exported effectively north of the Limpopo.

Setting the Culture

Described as one of Africa's largest retailers of food, general merchandise and clothing, Pick n Pay's history really began in 1967, when a recently fired Raymond Ackerman purchased four small stores with a staff of around 250, and listed it a year later with shares issued at R1 each. As a measure of rapid growth, the company was ranked 42nd in the South African *Sunday Times Business Times* Top 100 Companies ranking, just one year after listing and two years after the initial Ackerman acquisition.

The operating philosophy that guides the company and gives it a unique character is driven by the values and principles that reportedly inspired Raymond Ackerman to establish Pick n Pay in 1967. Those values and principles are genuinely considered sacrosanct at the company, and, irrespective of technological, operating and social change, they have remained deeply ingrained.

The company's culture takes its cue from its mission: 'All of us are here to serve, regardless of which level of the organisation we occupy. We are all here to make a contribution.'

This is underpinned by Pick n Pay's vision, which is focused on creating an 'environment conducive to people realising and achieving their dreams'.

This results in a milieu that tends to foster personal growth, nurture leadership and reward innovation. Pick n Pay wants people to feel safe in taking risks; to know that it's acceptable to make mistakes. This is carried forward to its African operations as a central operating ethos.

Values and Core Principles

Pick n Pay's values were formulated from the bottom up – comprehensive interviews with large groups of staff from around the country formulated ideas on what they thought the company's values should be, and a list of 'timeless values' was then drafted with input from employees.

Says former Chairman and now Company Ambassador, Raymond Ackerman: "Besides being a useful predictor of performance, I believe that values are the very lifeblood of an organisation. In time of constant and fairly rapid change, the values and principles of a company determine how it will behave, and, therefore, how it will perform."

Pick n Pay's 'Timeless Values'

- We are passionate about our customers and will fight for their rights.

- We care for, and respect, each other.

- We foster personal growth and opportunity.

- We nurture leadership and vision, and reward innovation.

- We live by honesty and integrity.

- We support and participate in our communities.

- We take individual responsibility.

- We are all accountable.

The core principles that constitute Pick n Pay's business activities include the following:

- Maintaining abiding values, in spite of business practices changing with time.

- Fostering respect for individuals, not as a strategic advantage, but because it is morally correct.

- Acknowledging the difference between timeless principles and daily business practices.

- Sticking to values – even if this appears to put the company at a competitive disadvantage.

Pick n Pay maintains that its growth and success are attributable to two fundamental principles:

- An unwavering belief in consumer sovereignty.

- The application of the 'four legs of the table' principle.

These principles were put into practice at its founding and continue to be the cornerstone of the business.

The Four Legs of the Table

The 'four legs of the table' principle follows a simple analogy, but one which finds easy resonance with employees.

The business is essentially likened to a table supported by four legs, on top of which the consumer is positioned. Each leg is required to be equally strong so that the table may remain balanced and upright. The four legs comprise the following:

- Administration.
- Merchandise.
- Promotion and social responsibility.
- People.

Each leg is equally important to the success and continued sustainability of the business. Each requires, and continues to receive, equal focus and management support. Thus, merchandising enjoys no advantage over concentration on people at Pick n Pay – each 'leg' is equally weighted in order to achieve balance.

Pick n Pay's philosophy is particularly recognised in its social activities – from championing consumer rights to investment in communities and family activities. While this is laudable, what is particularly instructive is the way in which its people are encouraged to become involved, and the degree to which this approach of 'doing good is good business' is deeply entrenched in those who work at the company. Thus, emergency relief given to communities in times of disaster will not take the form of a company cheque, but is more likely to see Pick n Pay employees being driven to the site of a crisis to deliver emergency food and fresh water, or putting on overalls and cleaning up mud and debris and offering its customers the ability to participate by giving donations of food, blankets and fresh water.

Says Raymond Ackerman:

> Our people know what we stand for and, therefore, how to make the right decisions. Whether it is giving food and blankets following a flood or fire in the community, or subsidising the price of bread and meat in the face of steep price hikes, or buying forward on rising prices and holding prices for consumers, our people make a difference.
>
> It is our values that cause us to regard social responsibility and environmental responsibility as a corporate duty. It is our values that cause us to invest in our people and graduate thousands at all levels of the company. It is our values that cause us to spend vast sums on social responsibility programmes, and it is our values that force us to be open and honest.

Pick n Pay supports the view that it – and other businesses – should be working together towards securing the economic security and social wellbeing of generations to come as an act of enlightened self-interest. Employees are encouraged to recognise and accept that it is a privilege for communities to allow Pick n Pay to operate in their areas, and, because of that, it has a responsibility towards them.

Employee Approach

Pick n Pay set the tone from 1967, when, in contravention of South Africa's apartheid laws, it sought to promote people of colour in its stores. A number of well-documented, high-profile clashes between founder, Raymond Ackerman, and successive apartheid leaders followed throughout the 60s, 70s and 80s, and, more often than not, Ackerman got his way.

Apart from rejecting the Job Reservation Act in place at the time, Pick n Pay has also scored a number of notable 'firsts' with its human resources (HR) policy. It was the first company to offer 11 months' maternity leave for its employees. Paternity leave was first introduced in South Africa by Pick n Pay. It also argued successfully for the opportunity for its black managers (who were only allowed by special dispensation to Ackerman in the first place to hold such senior positions) to have access to proper, formal housing with 99-year leases, beating off the first official response from the apartheid-era President Vorster that government policy mandated that blacks were considered 'temporary sojourners and hewers of wood' and therefore not entitled to housing.

But its philosophy goes a lot further than that. Families of employees are often assisted with bursaries and other educational assistance for employees' children, and further education for employees themselves has also been widely encouraged. These innovations took place well before they became popular – and sometimes mandated – in South Africa. It was one of the first companies in South Africa to award shares to employees of all races based on performance and service.

The company has proved itself uniquely able to muster support and loyalty from employees, illustrated not only by length of service, but also by examples of employees acting to protect the company.

A good example was when Pick n Pay was the target of an extortionist in 2003. When the company faced this very real crisis and began recalling products from shelves, it took the decision to communicate as widely as possible, with employees in particular being kept up to date. In understanding that while the media, government, shareholders and others were crucial stakeholders, employees were the interface with its consumers and needed always to be kept in the information loop. This paid off handsomely and employees rallied around the company, with Chairman Gareth Ackerman saying that the support they received from employees was "nothing short of incredible". Pick n Pay earned significant public kudos for its handling of the crisis and its level of transparency.

As a point of departure, Pick n Pay welcomes people whose values are aligned with its own: honesty, integrity and accountability. Pick n Pay HR Director Isaac Motaung emphasises that the company works hard to ensure employees abide by its values and primary behaviours, and, as a last resort, procedures are in place for those who either can't or won't.

Natural leaders tend to flourish at Pick n Pay, where those who have spent over 25 years at the company are not uncommon to find, and many employees are company 'lifers'. Many in top management started life packing shelves, and a large number of families have more than one or two members working for the company.

The company works from the premise that it cares about relationships, and people should work for it if they are looking for a career, not a job. A culture of promoting from within wherever possible pervades the company, and occasionally has caused a degree of myopia, which is now being corrected by bringing in new blood with new thinking.

The career-pathing system is designed to create a clear sense of future growth and reassure employees of their place and future in the company. Because all store and regional managers are promoted from within the organisation's ranks, staff turnover is kept to a minimum.

Diversity is viewed as a competitive advantage.

Primary Behaviours

- Greet everybody with whom you come into contact, in a warm, friendly manner.
- Do not scream or shout at anybody.
- Do not swear at people or call them offensive names.
- Do not practice racism by word or action.
- Confront bad behaviour and poor performance.
- Do not gossip, rumour-monger or talk behind anyone's back.
- Attend to people's problems at once, listen carefully, and provide a well-motivated response that same day.
- Communicate clearly, accurately, timeously and regularly.
- Do not reprimand people in front of others, especially not in front of customers.

Moving into Africa

Today, Pick n Pay has about 50 000 employees and 775 stores.

The company had made three disappointing foreign expansions – two large investments in Australia, one in which it was forced to withdraw owing to political activism in the 1980s, and the other in the next century (Franklins), which was sold in late 2011 – and a small investment in the Philippines in partnership with Shell, which lasted a very short time.

Its African expansion started just after the end of apartheid when it acquired a strategic stake in Zimbabwe-based TM Supermarkets in 1996. This was followed by Namibia (1997), Swaziland (2001), Botswana (2002) and Lesotho (2009).

But its African acceleration really began in early 2009 with the appointment of an Exco member directly responsible for, and focused on, Africa, after appreciating that expansion beyond South Africa's borders was more likely to realise a return closer to home and not in Australia or other developed markets. This was especially the case given low penetration of formal retail.

This focus on Africa resulted in the opening of its first Zambian store in June 2010, in Mozambique in June 2011 and in Mauritius in September 2011. Expansion into the Democratic Republic of Congo (DRC) and Malawi has been confirmed, and the company is investigating both Angola and Ghana. There are now 94 stores in Africa.

Its African strategy included the following guiding principles:

- Always take the company's values and operating ethos into all operations, irrespective of where they are and whether they are franchise or corporate-owned stores.

- Invest in countries that showed a lack of formal retail penetration.

- Build the company in Africa deliberately and strategically for the long term.

- Bring the best of Pick n Pay to new customers.

- Price goods fairly with good but never exploitative margins.

- Focus on local procurement to build economic growth and entrepreneurial development.

- Build a new business from the ground up without any loss of focus on South African operations.

- Always invest in surrounding communities.

- Attract top talent by paying above-average wages to employees.

- Retain top employees through new and better benefits, advancement opportunities and cultural belonging.

In understanding Pick n Pay's way of thinking, Ackerman believes that, because the company is steadfastly long term in its thinking, values, principles and policies, so too will be its endurance. He also believes that family-controlled businesses greatly facilitate long-term thinking.

Says Dallas Langman, the Exco member responsible for Africa and head of Pick n Pay's Group Enterprise operations:

> We have long maintained that Africa held challenging but at the same time enormous opportunity. We believe that if we can locate a local

franchise partner who will buy into our value system and ethos, this would be the preferred way of taking our brand throughout Africa. Franchising is not a given and we will open corporate-owned stores, Zambia being a notable example. However, whether franchise or corporate, we will always ensure that, where possible, local farmers, suppliers and employment remain in the country of expansion and that we employ and develop the people of our host nation; this makes our presence in the country of origin far more acceptable and endeared to the local communities we serve.

In each country we look at for possible investment, we visit with government and explain exactly who we are and what our values and principles are. Of course financial investment is important, but we need for the leaders of African states to understand that this is about our values system as much as it is about our ability to invest. In our discussions, we always focus on the way we treat employees and the way we try and build entrepreneurs. We always receive an outstanding response and huge co-operation. There's too much exploitation in Africa and we wanted to make it clear that we weren't that type of investor.

When we opened in Zambia in 2010, Pick n Pay focused on local employment and employed 130 people just for the first store. This was critical given the high unemployment rate in Zambia. We also made sure that we worked closely with the Zambian Development Agency as a point of consolidation for local small-scale farmers to help grow and improve the farming community in Zambia. Local suppliers have been used as far as possible, and our Zambian operation is working with the local farmers in a bid to grow the local farming base.

We also took a strategic decision to employ locally, and only a very small percentage of our workforce in Africa constitutes expatriates, who in any event are there to transfer skills and train our people in the country concerned.

Addressing the Challenge

Hiring, on-boarding and retaining talent in Africa have presented some key challenges, including the following:

1. **Attracting the top talent available**

    Pick n Pay's strategy was to focus on key attractors:

    *   Very competitive salaries, that is, salaries above the national average and those of its competitors.
    *   Providing benefits for its employees, something not common to most countries in Africa.

- Providing clear career-pathing information.
- Overtly making its mission, values and principles known to communities so that prospective employees would want to belong to a responsible and caring company.

The result was that Pick n Pay has been able to attract the 'cream' of available people in its African operations. In some countries, graduate applicants were willing to start as cashiers, not only because of the competitive wage and benefit structure, but also because they understood that advancement would come to those who showed the potential and worked hard, and that they

Key Employee Challenges in Africa

1. Attracting the top talent available

2. Training not only in retail but the specifics of each job, mostly from scratch

3. Reacculturating staff coming from competitor companies

4. Preparing new employees to assimilate Pick n Pay's values and core principles

5. Managing the talent pipeline to 'home-grow' those worthy of promotion, and retaining top talent

6. Providing evidence that Pick n Pay's values were underpinned by actual performance

would be working with a company with high operating ethics.

An important differentiator was the method of employment. Competitors have a high proportion of temporary or casual labour – as high as 70% in some countries. Research showed seemingly endless industrial relations problems and that employees were being retained by its main competitor by dint of having little alternative. Pick n Pay instituted permanent employees, and introduced contract workers, but with guaranteed hours per month and with pro rata benefits too.

The issue of pensions was also important. Although the law in many countries mandated the payment of pensions, many of Pick n Pay's competitors weren't doing so. The company made this a non-negotiable, offering pensions immediately not only to its full-time employees, but also pro rata to its contract employees, which was not common practice in Africa.

A sense of excitement also served to attract and retain the top talent. In each country, Pick n Pay didn't simply look at the retail environment and then replicate it in order to compete. It reinvented the retail environment in each case. As an example, the company opened in Lusaka on Christmas Day, the first time this had ever been seen in Zambia. Trading was phenomenal and employees were amazed at how ordinary citizens responded.

For every store opening, jobs are advertised in the local papers and agencies are briefed. While each store may eventually employ only 300 people, thousands apply.

Being accepted to Pick n Pay is seen as an achievement on its own.

2. Training not only in retail but the specifics of each job, mostly from scratch

Africa has a dearth of formal retail operators. That meant that training, from fresh-produce handling to cashiering to shop floor management to dry-groceries management and procurement, had to be provided from scratch. All of this had to be done without assistance from head office in South Africa, but Pick n Pay made its training manuals and training modules available. However, as Langman and Motaung point out, each module had to be made relevant and customised to each country concerned. A cookie-cutter approach to training in Africa was rejected and a national bias introduced in training for each country – brand Pick n Pay is customised for each country to make it relevant.

Says Langman:

> When we open our first store in a country, we can only really train the fresh employees two or three days before the store opens because that's when the fresh produce arrives in store. We put together a concentrated training programme and the employees concerned responded extremely well. Those with experience are then moved up the pipeline to other stores to transfer their knowledge.

Getting employees and suppliers to understand why the company was different was done in terms of information provision, but also practically. Pick n Pay demonstrated its commitment to good quality, fresh food, proper air conditioning, reliability of supply, and consistency. These are taken as read in South Africa, but are key differentiators in Africa.

The issue of expatriates is a sensitive one in Africa. It is all too often the accusation that foreign-based companies reserve all the top jobs in management for expatriates. Gareth Ackerman says that Pick n Pay was determined to keep this at a minimum, so it made it clear that few jobs would be reserved for expatriates once skills transfer had taken place – and this was at a fairly rapid pace. As an example, Zambia now has four stores open, employing 760 people. Only seven are expatriates.

3. Reacculturating staff coming from competitor companies

According to Langman, this was, surprisingly, quite a key challenge. Although those wishing to come across from its key competitor had been trained in formal retail, the need to migrate their thinking to Pick n Pay's way of operating was actually quite difficult. Employees of competitors in Africa have been very keen to cross over to Pick n Pay as it became clear not only that Pick n Pay was a good employer and that their benefits would be better, but also because of the kind of company it was. Word travels fast in Africa, and, before long, Pick n Pay had many more applications than jobs available, even considering the rate of unemployment in many countries like Zambia, for example.

On-boarding with a focus on company culture and values was key (see below) to get their thinking in line with Pick n Pay's operating ethos.

4. Preparing new employees to assimilate Pick n Pay's values and core principles

Motaung stresses that Pick n Pay's timeless values are at the centre of everything it does.

> Pick n Pay's employees are inducted before they put a foot into the stores about being passionate about our customers and fighting for their rights. And while our business practices and strategy might change in the future, our values absolutely wouldn't. They were shown at inception about our commitment to nurturing and fostering personal growth and we entrench these values by living them every day. Employees had to see very early that we meant what we said.

Says Langman:

> Getting employees to understand who we are and what we're about was absolutely critical – and quite difficult given that the 'mother ship' was so far away and they couldn't actually see this in action before they started at the company. Many of our top performers in Africa travel to South Africa now to spend time with our teams, in training courses and community projects so that they can spread the word back home.

Motaung explains that, culturally, Pick n Pay had to be aware that things seen as self-evident in South Africa were not necessarily the case elsewhere. As an example, he notes that Zambians are highly educated, have no sense of entitlement and are very respectful – all good qualities. But the culture of respectfulness means that questioning one another is not common practice and can be seen as rude. Zambian customers likewise tend not to be too overt in their demands, while South Africans are far blunter. Getting Zambian employees to learn how to handle tricky – even aggressive – customers was a key challenge.

5. Managing the talent pipeline to 'home-grow' those worthy of promotion, and retaining top talent

Fairly rapid store roll-out provides excellent opportunities for promotion and growth. As its top performers in its first stores show their potential, so Pick n Pay promotes them in a move to another new store. Employees witness the rewards of hard work, commitment and potential first-hand, so they know exactly what they are able to achieve at the company if they perform similarly. Progress through the company is visible and delivered promptly, enabled through Pick n Pay's philosophy of promoting from within, its commitment to local employment and, operationally, through its store roll-out. Pick n Pay offers a hybrid of its South African trainee manager programme to those who show potential, with notable success.

Says Langman: "Our employees see evidence of high performers in the company being promoted. As an example, we've had store managers being rapidly promoted to procurement managers as we've expanded and new opportunities have opened up, and this is highly motivational for our employees everywhere." Some of the high performers are also brought to South Africa to study at Pick n Pay's Fresh Food Academy or visit stores and the company's buying teams to learn more about their jobs. Apart from learning job-specific information, they are made to feel part of a broader family.

An example was in Zimbabwe, where certain TM-branded stores were to be converted to Pick n Pay-branded stores. There was much scepticism from the TM team, so Pick n Pay flew the top management to Lusaka to look at the new stores, asking them what they liked and didn't like. The process showed transparency and a willingness to consult, and the team was completely won over, surprised at the standards Pick n Pay had introduced in an African country outside South Africa. Says Langman: "It's not about South Africanising our African operations; it's about taking the best and adapting it to local conditions."

These examples illustrate the value of Pick n Pay acknowledging employees – it has a business benefit and makes employees feel appreciated and part of the team at the same time.

6. Providing evidence that Pick n Pay's values were underpinned by actual performance

Pick n Pay Chairman Gareth Ackerman says that values are inextricably linked to business strategy, which applies in Africa as it does in South Africa: "It's crucial that all employees support the company's strategy and buy into its values. They are, after all, responsible for implementing strategies and ensuring that our dream becomes a reality."

Talking the talk is one thing. Walking the talk is quite another. Says Langman:

> When you look at local procurement, about 70% of our goods are local in Zambia for example, which is significantly more than the 50% we guaranteed the government of Zambia. This takes effort, including having special supplier days to brief them on our standards and requirements, but it's worth it, not only financially, but in building loyalty.

When we say that 'doing good is good business', it's easy to prove. Procuring locally and getting local suppliers to manufacture and produce to our quality standards not only means we are developing the expertise of locals, but it also means it's cheaper, which makes us more competitive. An added upside is the knock-on to our employees and to government players – they see very clearly what we're doing.

Our commitment to communities is no different to what it is in South Africa and completely in line with our values. Before we even opened, our Zambian team was already involved in community upliftment initiatives in the region, most notably with one of the local orphanages, as well as the renovation of the Woodlands-A Basic School library and in the distribution of lap desks to schoolchildren.

Another important issue was that of pricing. Pick n Pay's research showed profit margins in Africa way beyond what they are in South Africa. Langman calls this 'blood food – like blood diamonds' – and says that Pick n Pay deliberately set out to make a fair, but never extortionate profit, in keeping with its consumer sovereignty principles set at the company in South Africa at foundation. Thus Pick n Pay's pricing philosophy, and principled approach to consumer sovereignty, has had a direct financial benefit to consumers in Africa. The added benefit is that employees can see the difference in pricing very clearly, another proof-point to the company's values system.

Even store design provided evidence of the company's values system. Many operators treat African countries as poor relations of their South African operations. Stores in Africa are often poorly lit, with little or no climate control, and with poor-quality goods and poor standards. It was very clear by the time Pick n Pay opened its first store that every quality control standard from South Africa would be brought into Africa – and would sometimes exceed the standards of the home country. Employees were amazed at the level of quality introduced in Africa, which created not only a sense of pride, but also encouraged yet more employees from competitors to want to come across to Pick n Pay.

Leading by example has been crucial to success and instils company pride. Employees live Pick n Pay's values and see the company and its management doing the same. As an example, says Langman:

> We not only procured locally beyond what we set out to do, but are now involved in 'backhauling' – taking local suppliers' products like tilapia from Kariba in Zambia and sweet potatoes from Zambia and exporting them for sale at our stores in South Africa. Employees see what we're doing, and they're highly motivated by the evidence that we walk the talk.

Conclusion

In 2011, Pick n Pay won the Federation of Zambian Employers' 'Employer of the Year', despite having only four stores on the ground.

News not only travels fast within countries; it also travels fast among them in Africa. Pick n Pay's growing reputation in Africa means that new host countries have already heard about the company's operating ethos in Africa, and thus the welcome and interest shown by new countries grows all the time. The company's values, ethics and honoured commitments translate into a perceived humility and lack of arrogance, seen as foreign by many African countries when experiencing South African and other Western investors.

Chris Gilmour, an analyst with Absa Investments and one of South Africa's foremost retail analysts, sums up Pick n Pay's adherence to values and its ability to export these across borders:

> Pick n Pay has always stood out among its retailing peers in SA as 'the retailer with a conscience'. This is not to say that other South African retailers don't have a conscience but Pick n Pay has walked the talk with respect to doing good in the broader community. Raymond Ackerman certainly did this, especially in the dark apartheid era, when he risked being imprisoned for his forthright views on the welfare of his workers in the company.
>
> This ethos has stayed with Pick n Pay to this day, even though Raymond Ackerman is no longer on the board. It is embedded in the DNA of the company in everything it does, whether it be treating customers fairly, looking after the environment, in corporate social investment or in the broader field of good corporate governance.
>
> And it has also stayed with the group as it has moved into Africa. It would be the easiest thing in the world for a foreign retailer to exploit workers in the rest of Africa, as few if any other African countries have the same degree of rigid labour legislation as South Africa. But that's not how Pick n Pay operates.
>
> Says Langman: "We've built a legacy in South Africa over the past 45 years. Now we're building the new legacy in Africa."

12 UNILEVER BRAZIL: A STORY OF ORGANISATIONAL AND PERSONAL RENEWAL

Rob Mallick & Marcelo Williams

This is a case study of the renewal of Unilever's business in Brazil. It is the story of a leadership team's journey when faced with the need to reignite the growth of a proud company whose performance had disappointed in recent years while it focused on a very complex reorganisation to merge five different divisions.

The issue from a talent management perspective was less one of enhancing or importing best practices, because Unilever Brazil was already a mature business that had benefited from being part of a prestigious fast-moving consumer goods (FMCG) corporate. It was more about renewal, both personal and organisational. It was more about igniting existing talent and using the brand and an exciting story of corporate growth and renewal to attract high performers from outside the company. All of this, on a battleground for the emerging middle-class consumers in a huge market for FMCGs.

This is a personal account of the journey from the Vice President (VP) of Human Resources (HR) (Marcelo) and the Organisation Development (OD) Consultant (Rob) who assisted Unilever Brazil. It includes the inspirations for their actions, the interventions they undertook, as well as sharing the Voices of others who participated in the journey.

Introduction

Unilever Brazil is the Brazilian operation of the Unilever Global FMCG business. It is the second-largest company of Unilever worldwide and the number one in developing and emerging countries. In 2007, it was a €2.9 billion operation, covering Personal Care (eg deodorants and shampoo), Home Care (eg detergents), Ice Cream and Foods (eg packet soups and fruit juices).

Between 2001 and 2007, Unilever's businesses in Brazil underwent a series of consolidations. Between 2001 and 2005, a Home and Personal Care business (HPC) was created with the integration of the Home Care and Personal Care businesses with the National Management function. At the same time, the Foods business was busy integrating its recent acquisition of the Best Foods business, while the Ice Cream business continued to run as a separate business, isolated from the rest of the organisation. Throughout this period, growth rates continued to be strong, particularly in the HPC business. The years 2005 to 2007 saw the next phase of the

273

integration with the objective of creating a ONE Unilever Organisation, and this period saw the integration of the three different businesses (HPC, Foods and Ice Cream) into a single business.

From a talent management perspective, there was much to be proud of. For example, Unilever's companies had consistently been among the most admired companies and desired places to work. In 2003, the Brazilian business magazine, *Exame*, deemed Unilever Brazil "one of the three best companies in Brazil for a graduating student to start their career". According to Cia de Talentos and Lab SSJ pesquisa 2002 to 2007, Unilever Brazil was described for five years in a row as one of the top three companies where a student would want to work.

Furthermore, Unilever Brazil's management trainee programme was attracting an increasing number of applications from young talent. For example, between 2001 and 2007, applications doubled. And it was difficult to get in, with an acceptance rate of only 0.1%! Unilever Brazil was also regarded within Unilever plc as a source of talent for its global operations. In 2008, for example, 90 Brazilians held senior positions outside of Brazil, 50% in the Americas, 40% in Europe and 10% in Asia.

And what of the macrotalent situation in Brazil? Over the last five years or so, Brazil has become one of the most competitive markets for FMCGs in the world, if not the most competitive. The market has been growing consistently and the dynamic of the business world has accelerated, with new players coming to the market and Brazilian companies becoming multinational or at least expanding horizons beyond the Brazilian frontier.

Many multinational companies are coming to Brazil without deep knowledge of the Brazilian market. Many Brazilian companies were beginning to do business abroad without talented people with multicultural experiences.

In this competitive environment, competitors looking to attract executive talent were targeting companies like Unilever Brazil that had a strong reputation for developing talent. By 2009, Brazil was becoming a battleground for executive talent. It was clear that, in this emerging reality, Unilever Brazil was both a strong player and one that was also vulnerable.

This challenging situation confronting Unilever Brazil coincided with a difficult time for the Unilever Brazil business. Notwithstanding the track record of growth and demonstrated strengths in talent management, the period between 2005 and 2007 was difficult for the business. After many years of strong growth in most of its categories, growth slowed and, in late 2007, a new Chairperson (Chief Executive Officer [CEO]), Kees Kruythoff, was appointed.

Framing and Diagnosing the Talent Management Issue

Kees's brief was simple – **Reignite Growth!** Kees immediately saw the need for a strategic review to provide greater clarity of direction and a much-needed, long-term perspective. But he sensed that this would not be sufficient. He felt intuitively that energy levels were low and that the culture was not supportive of an effort to grow the business.

The first step was to explore the leadership and cultural reality of Unilever Brazil. Upon exploration, including the use of a values assessment tool that we describe below, it became clear that Kees's intuition was correct. Illustrated below (see figure 1), and using a systems dynamics approach, it was clear that the exertion in integrating the businesses had kicked off a train of events that had created significant dysfunction in the organisation that would surely undermine efforts to grow the company.

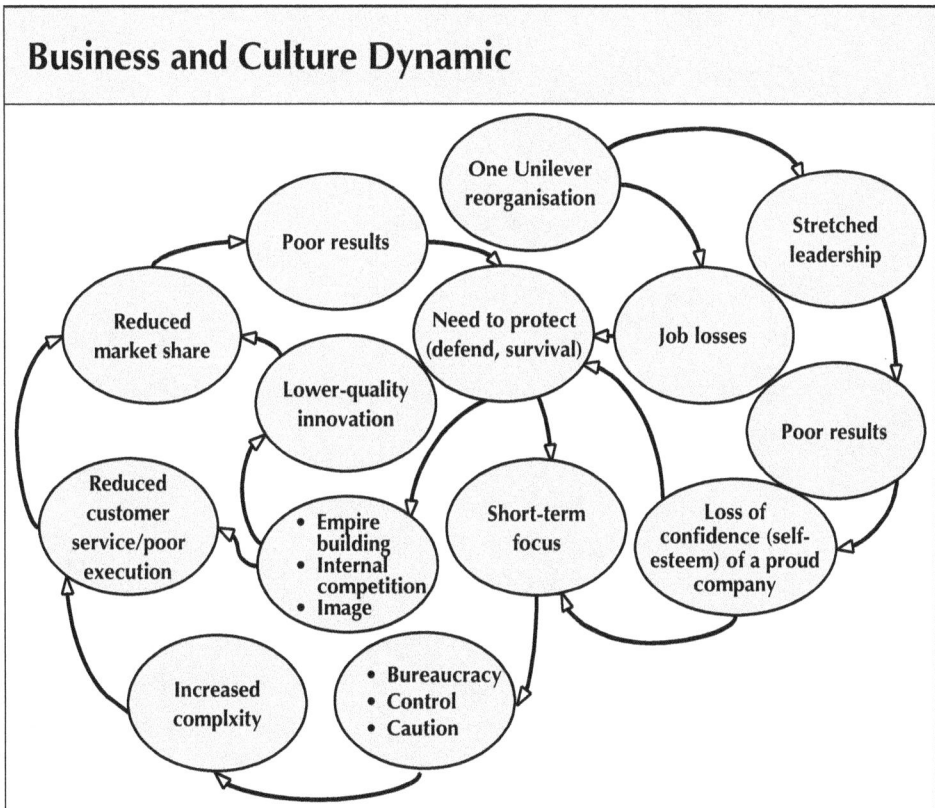

Figure 1: Business and Culture Dynamic

Faced with this reality, the Unilever Brazil leadership team concluded that this was not something that could be fixed in a technical manner. From a talent management perspective, for example, as we saw above, there was a strong tradition in attracting and developing talent, and Unilever Brazil already had good systems in place. For instance, it already had in place Performance Assessments Systems, Competency Models, Formal Succession Plan Discussions, Personal Development Plans and strong Leadership Development Programmes. There were some improvements that could, and would, be made, but it was clear that process enhancements would not generate the magnitude of improvements sought. The issue was more fundamental than that. The real leverage was in the more subtle domains of the energy, culture, confidence and spirit of the place.

What was required was a fundamental transformation that got to the heart of the contraction in the business and helped unleash the talent that was going to waste in the business. In thinking about talent in Unilever Brazil, we found inspiration in the Prophet's evocative account of parenting children (Gibran 1980:20-23):

Your children are not your children.
They are the sons and daughters of Life's longing for itself.
They come through you but not from you,
And though they are with you yet they belong not to you.

You may give them your love, but not your thoughts,
For they have their own thoughts.
You may house their bodies, but not their souls,
For their souls dwell in the house of tomorrow,
Which you cannot visit even in your dreams.
You may strive to be like them, but seek not to make them like you,
For life goes not backward nor tarries with yesterday.
You are the bows from which your children as living arrows are sent forth.

The archer sees the mark upon the path of the infinite,
And He bends you with his might that
His arrows may go swift and far.
Let your bending in the archer's hand be for gladness;
For even as He loves the arrow that flies,
So He loves also the bow that is stable.

The challenge to reignite growth in Unilever Brazil was not so much about improved talent management, but about unleashing the creative potential in talented people who had somehow lost their way.

In 2012, our sense is that Unilever Brazil is not alone in this, certainly among divisions of global companies operating in emerging markets. General Electric (GE) is acknowledged globally as the frontrunner with regard to talent management. Susan Peters (2012:1), GE's VP of Executive Development and Chief Learning Officer, reported recently on the outcomes of GE's recent reflection on ways to attract, develop and retain talent in the future. She says:

We named the effort 'Global New Directions' and we knew we'd picked the right people (to lead the review) almost immediately when they told us that they didn't want to retain employees, they wanted to inspire them. The generation entering the workforce today is uniquely connected digitally and socially attuned to the forces of change and common purpose. But what is the best way to unleash their potential?

What Has Been Achieved So Far?

So, in early 2008, Unilever Brazil launched what was called UB2012: Let's Build a Company That Is Greater Than Great. Led by Kees, his HR VP, Marcelo Williams, and the Board of Vice Presidents, the programme was marked by investment and unrelenting focus on both strategic clarity and a revitalisation of a culture that was feeling tired and beaten after the massive integration efforts along with low rates of growth.

What has been achieved? By the end of 2011, a very significant transformation was evident, both in terms of business performance and the quality of the leadership and culture. Growth, both revenue and margin, had returned to the business and customer service had improved significantly. For instance, in the 2010 Advantage study, Unilever Brazil went from sixth to second, with customer development number one in all measures except one.

Quantitative evidence also pointed to the emergence of a genuine performance culture. For example, from the survey tool discussed below, the levels of dysfunction in the organisation had fallen by over 35% and the alignment between the current and desired culture had improved significantly Also, in late 2011, the respected AON Top Companies for Leaders[1] gave special recognition to Unilever Brazil for the first time, ahead of its major competitors.

From a talent management perspective, Unilever Brazil had also regained much of its strength and lustre.

- As never before, Unilever Brazil executives are taking over key positions around the world. More than 70 Brazilian executives are working abroad, and many of them in very senior positions having great strategic impact in the business.

- Unilever Brazil's gender approach has started to show significant signs of success. Around 50% of Unilever Brazil's managers are women, and more than 40% are in Director and Vice President positions.

- In spite of the fierce war for talent in the Brazilian market, Unilever Brazil has succeeded in keeping attrition rates below the average of the market.

- Unilever Brazil has introduced an Agile Working approach, and the Flexible Work and Home Office policies are creating a better Employee Value Proposition for Women and the 'Y' generation.

Just as important, the spirit has also returned to the business, with talented young executives feeling energised, challenged and fulfilled – as their stories below demonstrate:

---

1   Cited in 2011 Top Companies for Leaders: Winners and Special Recognition http://www.aon.com/ human-capital-consulting/thought-leadership/leadership/reports-pub-topcompanies-2011-winners. jsp.

Robert Hein Schermers, a Dutch national, is in his late 30s and is Director of the Ice Cream Division:

> I joined Unilever The Netherlands in 1995 as a trainee, and I have worked in numerous roles in marketing, sales and category management. The last 8 years I have been working in various director roles in The Netherlands, Germany, South Africa and Brazil, in regional brand development and local management roles in various categories.
>
> What struck me in my early interactions with my colleagues was the frightening silence I felt during the plenary sessions, when Kees asked for feelings, thoughts, and ideas when we were all together. Nobody was responding and people looked away, which led to eerie silences and an awkward feeling. The team was far more hierarchical than I expected it to be and people were apparently afraid to say something wrong in front of bosses and peers. This was a reflection as well – I discovered later – of the way of working in the business at the time: avoiding risks, not speaking up and, for sure, not saying something which was not in line with the boss's opinion.
>
> This changed, fortunately. I feel that we have made a giant jump from a top-down led organization, with little initiative from the teams below the board, to an organization in which the board takes a facilitating role, responding to the expressed needs to deliver the agreed plans by the teams below. We have, for sure, made the step from individuals with totally socialized minds to more independent minds, taking ownership and responsibility, driving our teams to work in the same way.
>
> I am convinced that we have learned to see the benefits of speaking up, of expressing our confidence and/or doubts about the plans and challenges we face. I am convinced that we have – as an extended leadership team – learned from working closer, sharing experiences and best practices and that this has made Unilever Brazil a far stronger organization, responding quicker to the challenges we face, deciding with more courage and willing to take risk. And I am convinced that within certain teams, the DNA of the team has changed fundamentally and has evolved from socialized behavior to really acting on what the business and team need, realizing that this demands real ownership and courage.
>
> Personally, the journey has given me the great luxury to step back, look and learn on where I am at, with the help of great colleagues in fantastic settings in this impressive country. Personally I have grown a lot!

Bruno Francisco, a Brazilian national, is in his mid-40s and is Director for Deodorants:

I rejoined Unilever 3 years ago after a long period in other FMCG companies.

I am passionate about what I do and completely sure I made the right decision to rejoin Unilever culture, which I found quite different from the previous times: more results oriented without losing the passion for developing people, always respecting their characteristics and opinions.

I rejoined the company at the beginning of the Journey and I felt people were adapting to the new moment. There was a lot of excitement to get things done but also a question like 'Are they really true about the change?' Coming from other companies, which are very down to earth, I could not believe the opportunity the company was giving us to be authentic and to make the personal growth the true driver of professional growth. I was so passionate about this moment that sometimes I even got feedback from people that I believed too much.

I was experiencing some dynamics I never had the chance to experience in other companies. The feeling was of participating in one process that other companies would take years to have the same dynamic. It was also interesting to see that when you just have one professional experience, you tend to get very skeptical and critical about what you have in your hands. I felt at that time there was a lot of understanding of the issues but we needed the energy to flow to criticize and also solve the issue at the same time.

The journey we have been on has been based around very candid discussions and also making the link between your personal characteristics and the way you behave professionally. These conversations have been an immense source of growth. People were open to discuss dreams, issues, opportunities, building visions as a team and creating a passion to deliver results.

We have been able to drive this energy through the entire organization, never linked to one person or leader but to yourself as a leader and how you create the environment for people to behave as true leaders, authentic and delivering results.

The growth comes from all interactions, from debates, difficulties, from working in teams. The very positive side is that it gives you the opportunity to get where you want and do not depend on somebody else. I believe the biggest risk in a company is when you only get highly dependent on one charismatic leader.

I can feel the value of the cultural change every week. We had a change of president in the company, with lots of changes happening but we have the same energy to accept questions and also make sure that we keep doing the right stuff that we developed in the last few years.

This is coming from all levels of the organization, stepping up as a team to accept the constant need to evolve as an organization, avoiding defensive and denial style. I feel we are ready to really get the positive moment and accelerate growth.

Every week I try to work with my team and also with functional areas to develop new ideas, talents and face the facts with a solving issue mindset, with ability to accept others opinion but also with a results and drive orientation to get things done.

From my side, I am also getting a much higher understanding of the constant need I have to develop myself, creating instant links to situations and my behavior related to that, and how do I learn and change to a personal growth. I am doing that mainly for me, as a person and delivering results are just the consequence. Important to say that in doing that I am enjoying the moment, different from older times when I tended to get highly self-critical. Really a great moment.

Jessica Hollaender, an HR Director in her mid-30s:

I'm a Psychologist, with an MBA in Business Management. I have 11 years working in Unilever. I joined as an intern and one year after my internship I was hired as a Trainee. I experienced a variety of jobs within this period in Unilever in the most diverse context: Regional scope, Local scope, an international experience, Organization Development area, different projects, etc.

When we started the Journey, I felt we had a culture with some strength but also with some qualities that were holding us back. Our strengths included high ethical standards, informality and an openness to teach and to learn. On the other hand, I felt we had a consensus culture, were overly concerned with our internal image and how good our PowerPoint presentations were. We were too disposed to intellectual argument and debate and too little to action and taking intelligent risks.

One of the most important lessons for me has been about linking personal and professional growth. I believe that we started our turnaround in the cultural transformation when we embraced this statement. We were explicit in linking leadership and culture with our business strategy. I have never seen, in these 11 years of Unilever, such a strong people agenda as part of the business agenda. This has been a highlight.

I think we have taken great steps in a short period of time. One thing I really learned was that 'God doesn't play dice', so where we put our full attention was where we had a significant change. And for me that was the journey itself. Unilever is much better in some aspects; the ones we wanted to eliminate because they were bad in our current culture (consensus, feuds, image, etc.). And also we accelerate other values that really care and would drive us for the success (openness, leadership, stand up to speak your truth, etc.). Of course, there is room to improve some other aspects such as bias for action, performance driven, external focus, etc. But we know that it is a long journey, and it would be unrealistic to believe it would take less time than it has taken.

> From a personal perspective, I started this journey somewhat lost and lacking energy I normally bring to my work. Today I feel enthused and excited and bring these qualities to all that I do. I am grateful for what I have experienced and how I have grown.

How was this journey of renewal and growth undertaken? Let us first introduce ourselves and then share with you the interventions and lessons we have learnt along the way.

Marcelo and Rob

Marcelo's story: Marcelo is an Argentinian who joined Unilever 20 years ago from another multinational company. He worked for seven years in HR at Unilever River Plate (Argentina, Uruguay and Paraguay). After that, he moved to London to be part of the Latin American Business Group, as one of the HR Directors, having projects in different countries in the region. In January 2001, he arrived in Brazil with the main challenge to integrate three Unilever divisions into a single Home, Personal Care and National Management responsibility in HR. He was there in 2005, ready to move to a destination in Europe when Unilever requested him to stay in the country to merge all the divisions in ONE Unilever Organisation. In early 2008, when our story began, he could not imagine that he would be part of what, in his own words, would have to be the most significant experience of cultural transformation that had starred in his 22-year career at that time. He is currently responsible for Unilever Latin America, in addition to his responsibilities at Unilever Brazil. Having a college degree from the Faculty of Economic Sciences at the University of Buenos Aires, Marcelo confesses to being professionally fortunate in being able to devote his entire professional life (more than 26 years) to what he loves most, that is, making a positive difference in and through the lives of people.

Rob's story: In mid-2007, Rob left a prestigious management consulting firm, having chosen to set himself up as a sole practitioner focusing on organisation development work. The last two years with the consulting firm had been spent working in South America, where Rob lived with his young family in Rio de Janeiro.

It was not an auspicious time to be setting up a consulting practice. The world was just entering what became known as the Global Financial Crisis, and organisation development work was surely a nice-to-have as the corporate world imploded. In a moment of stress and vulnerability, Rob found himself on the second floor of The Coop book store in Harvard Square. Seeking inspiration of any sort, he glanced through the recently released Deepak Chopra book, *Buddha*. There on the second page of the author's note was just what Rob needed to know: "Whoever sees me, sees the teaching," said the Buddha, "and whoever sees the teaching, sees me."

It was a sharp but gentle reminder to stay true to do the work he loved to do, **and** a promise that clients were out there. And, sure enough, through contacts with his former employer, Rob was introduced to Kees in early 2008 and spent the next three years helping Kees, Marcelo and the Unilever Brazil team on their Journey. From a practical perspective, the stakes for Rob were high. With his first major client, it had to work!

The Monks

The Journey started with a short parable about a monastery, four monks and an abbot (sourced from Zander & Zander 2002:52-53).

> A monastery had fallen on hard times. It was once part of a great order which, as a result of religious persecution in the 17th and 18th centuries, lost all its branches. It was decimated to the extent that there were only five monks left in the mother house: the abbot and four others, all of whom were over 70. Clearly, it was a dying order.
>
> Deep in the woods surrounding the monastery was a little hut that the rabbi from a nearby town occasionally used for a hermitage. One day, it occurred to the abbot to visit the hermitage to see if the rabbi could offer any advice that might save the monastery. The rabbi welcomed the abbot and commiserated. "I know how it is," he said. "The spirit has gone out of people. Almost no-one comes to the synagogue anymore." So the old rabbi and the old abbot wept together, and they read parts of the Torah and spoke quietly of deep things.
>
> The time came when the abbot had to leave. They embraced. "It was wonderful being with you," said the Abbot, "but I have failed in my purpose for coming. Have you no piece of advice that might save the monastery?"
>
> "No, I'm sorry," the rabbi responded, "I have no advice to give. The only thing I can tell you is that the Messiah is one of you."
>
> When the other monks heard the rabbi's words, they wondered what possible significance they might have. "The Messiah is one of us? One of us here, at the monastery? Do you suppose he meant the abbot? Of course – it must be the abbot, who has been our leader for so long. On the other hand, he might have meant Brother Thomas, who is certainly a holy man. Or could he have meant Brother Elrod, who is so crotchety? But, then, Elrod is very wise. Surely, he could not have meant Brother Phillip – he is too passive. But, then, magically, he's always there when you need him. Of course, he didn't mean me – yet supposing he did? Oh Lord, not me! I couldn't mean so much to you, could I?"
>
> As they contemplated in this manner, the old monks began to treat each other with extraordinary respect, on the off chance that one of them might be the Messiah. And, on the off chance that each monk himself might be the Messiah, they began to treat themselves with extraordinary respect.

Because the forest in which it was situated was beautiful, people occasionally came to visit the monastery, to picnic or to wander along the old paths, most of which led to the dilapidated chapel. They sensed the aura of extraordinary respect that surrounded the five old monks, permeating the atmosphere. They began to come more frequently, bringing their friends, and their friends brought friends. Some of the younger men who came to visit began to engage in conversation with the monks. Then another, and another. After a while, one asked if he might join. Then another, and another. Within a few years, the monastery became once again a thriving order, and – thanks to the rabbi's gift – a vibrant, authentic community of light and love for the whole realm.

Unilever Brazil was not in decline, but something of the spirit had left the place. There was a sense of 'stuckness' and not much hope. When we shared the story of the monks with senior leaders in early 2008, they immediately saw the relevance to their own situation.

Deeper down, the story of the monks was the initial source of inspiration to commence the journey of renewal, because it offered people new language, encouraged them to look with new eyes, and invited them to explore new places.

New language: The 19th-century philosopher, Wittgenstein[2], said: "You cannot enter a world for which you do not have the language." Business today has a language, and, if a business is to move and to renew, it needs new language. What is the language of business today? It's a language that emphasises the measurable, data, process, replication, and scale.

What is needed is language for a new age, what Dan Pink (2005) calls the Conceptual Age. In the Conceptual Age, new capacities will be needed to survive, let alone prosper. These include what Pink calls Story, Symphony and Empathy. Story includes, but goes beyond, providing skilful, fact-based argument. It evokes persuasion, communication and self-understanding, and the ability to fashion a compelling narrative. Symphony is the ability to go beyond analysis and see the big picture, cross boundaries, and combine disparate pieces into an arresting new whole. Empathy is the ability to understand what makes others tick, to forge deep relationships, and to care for others.

We see a new language emerge among the monks. We see the language shift in the internal dialogue each monk has with himself, and we see it shift in the language and communication among the monks. It is a language marked by more respect, more compassion, and more possibility than the defeatist language that had preceded it. This is a language that could be deemed touchy-feely and airy-fairy. But it is not this. In the case of Unilever Brazil, a new language was a prerequisite for renewal and growth.

---

2   As cited in Kenny (1974).

A little language goes a long way. What is important is that it does not take much to stimulate renewal and growth. Dan Pink reminds us of EM Foster's observation that a fact is: "The queen died and the king died." A story is: "The queen died and the king died of a broken heart." – same facts, and yet very different energies from only a few different words.

New places: For the monks, as for many in Unilever Brazil, they initially looked for the answers from outside when, in fact, so much of the leverage lay inside. As the old indigenous saying puts it: "The faraway stick never killed the snake."

New places go beyond looking closer to home. As Ralph Waldo Emerson[3] said, "What lies ahead of us and what lies behind us are tiny matters compared to what lies within us." The monks also inspired leaders in Unilever Brazil to explore domains that they had not really grappled with before. This is the domain of the invisible aspects of the organisation – the mind-sets, beliefs and assumptions. The culture of Unilever Brazil is like an iceberg. The behaviours and results – the things we can see, touch and measure – are at the top of the iceberg. But so much lies below that is invisible. And the invisible matters. The *Titanic*, after all, did not have a problem with the tip of the iceberg.

New eyes: The late psychiatrist, RD Lang, reminds us (as quoted in Zweig & Abrams 1991:xix):

> The range of what we think and do
> is limited by what we fail to notice.
> And because we fail to notice
> that we fail to notice
> there is little we can do
> to change
> until we notice
> how failing to notice
> Shapes our thoughts and deeds.

We see in the monks' story how their awareness expanded – of themselves, of others and of their surrounds. Huge amounts of energy and insight are aroused when one's attention and awareness are expanded. And, equivalently, energy is wasted when attention is spent on churning through the same issue, over and over again. We can see how new eyes – in the case of the monks, an appreciative and enquiring eye – were crucial for the renewal of the monastery.

It is also important to have new eyes in order to reframe experiences. The foibles of Brother Phillip can be reframed from being a character flaw to something enduring that makes him whole. What was once seen as a problem might in fact be a source of enlargement, of learning. This involves a vulnerability that many are not comfortable

---

3   Ralph Waldo Emerson (1803-1883) was a famous American poet, lecturer and essayist.

within business. It asks us to see as whole what was once separate. To the extent that we do not open our eyes because we are scared of what we might find, it asks us to be courageous.

So, the monks were the initial inspiration for the cultural and leadership renewal of Unilever Brazil. What was done of a more practical nature, that is, what was the perspiration to complement the inspiration?

What Was Done?

Over the course of the period 2008 to 2011, we undertook many interventions to facilitate and prompt the cultural and leadership renewal of Unilever Brazil, and, in doing so, attracted, developed and excited talented executives.

Let us first outline how we thought about sequencing the programme, and then outline the framework that held our interventions together in a coherent way. We conclude this section with a summary of a few of the most important interventions we undertook.

Sequencing

We chose not to adopt a particular process map or prescribed sequential set of steps. For those who find this approach helpful, we would recommend the steps outlined in Richard Barrett's (2006) *Building a Values Driven Organization*. Instead, an unlikely source – Martin Luther King – inspired the way we sequenced and choreographed the work.

In 1963, Martin Luther King was imprisoned for his early efforts at direct action to ignite the civil rights movement. From prison, he wrote a note in defence of direct action, as a rebuttal to those who said he should pursue civil rights in the courts.

He wrote in his Letter from Birmingham Jail[4]:

> In any nonviolent campaign there are four basic steps: collection of the facts to determine whether injustices exist; negotiation; self-purification; and direct action.

As illustrated in the chart below (see figure 2), we found these steps to be helpful in very practical ways.

---

4   Martin Luther King Jr. 1963. Letter from Birmingham Jail.

Sequencing

Collection of facts	Negotiation	Self purification	Direct action
• Cultural and business metrics • Quantitative and qualitative data • "See, feel" as well as "Analyze, think"	• Dialogue • Reflection • Courageous conversation	• Accountability • Master, not victim • Where am I in this? • Fearless vulnerability	• Technical and adaptive • Small enough to matter, big enough to win • Symbolic actions

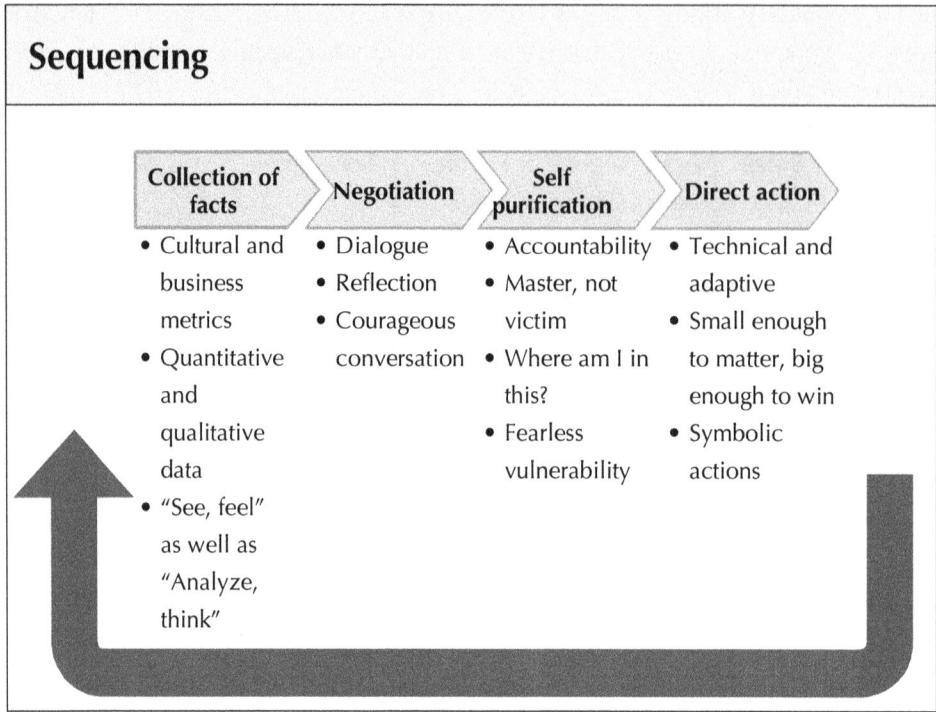

Figure 2: Sequencing (Source: MOHAN VEENA Consulting)

It provided us with guidance as to the steps to take **and** as to what was needed at each step. As in the more widely known Plan, Do, Check, Act, there is a circular sequence to the steps, but, at any point, we found it was important to evoke each step. At any particular point, one of the steps might be most relevant, but it is best undertaken in partnership with all the steps. We found this, time and time again, to be a very helpful discipline.

We also found that the process was not linear. In fact, it was more of a spiral. For example, the period March to December 2008 saw us work through each of the steps and we began to see improvement in the business. For example, growth returned to many parts of the business that had been struggling, customer service began to improve, and the spirit seemed to be returning to the business.

In the early part of 2009, we took the time to check in and hear from people – Step 1. We were shocked to discover that all was not well. The Voices we heard are summarised in the chart below (see figure 3).

Clearly something was amiss and there was a feeling of 'stuckness'. This entailed some tough conversations and soul-searching. As the senior leadership talked about this (Step 2), we discovered the power of Step 3 – self-purification.

What we discovered was that, while good progress had been made, much of the momentum was 'out there' and, to progress further, we had to go 'in here', and, in particular, to another level of personal accountability. The antidote to a feeling of 'stuckness' was to face into the sense of vulnerability and work through it. Up to this point, the 'easy things' had been done. Now, tougher things needed to be done, and personal risk-taking was required. This made people feel unsafe, and it required people to reflect on their own very personal leadership challenges.

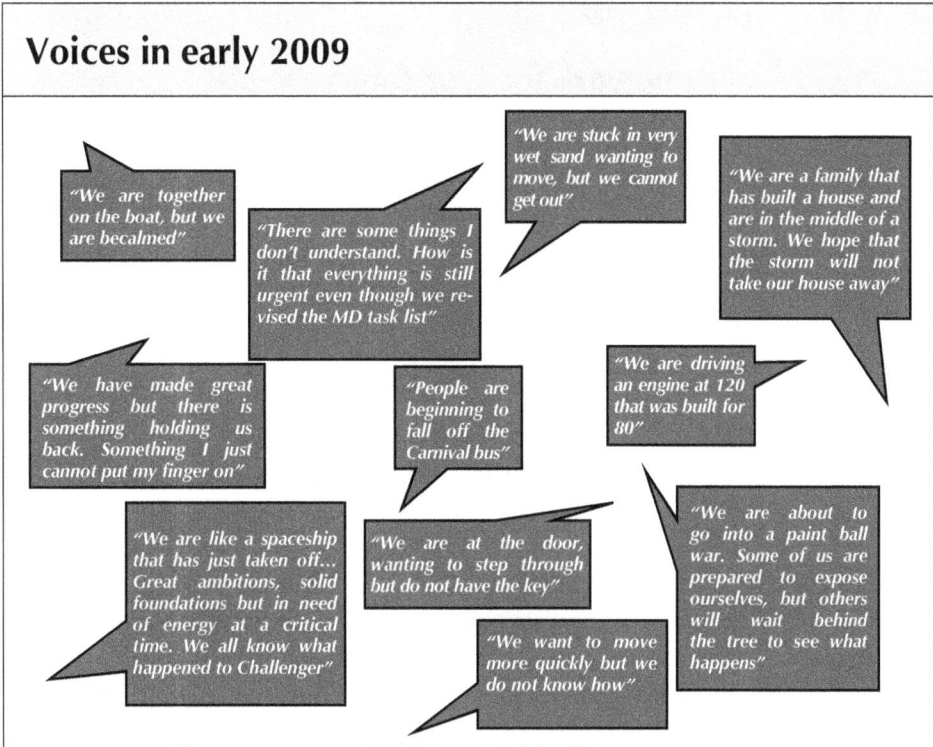

Figure 3: Voices in Early 2009 (Source: MOHAN VEENA Consulting)

One such example was a member of the leadership team reflecting positively on how he felt he had been taking many more risks over the last year. When asked to give an example, he said: "Just last week I shared a PowerPoint slide with the Board that I had not seen before." As soon as he said it, he and everyone else knew that we had a lot of work to do regarding risk-taking! It became clear to many leaders that the most important source of entropy was how they showed up each day. In the words of the cartoon character, Pogo, "We have met the enemy...and he is us!"

From a talent management perspective, we do not think it is a coincidence that it was soon after this period of intense reflection and 'self-purification' that we began to attract a new range of talented executives, with some joining Unilever Brazil for the first time, and others drawn back by what they sensed was happening to the business. It was as if we were beginning to attract just the sort of talent that we needed, and that talent was being attracted to us. Jung called this "**participation mystique**" (Corlett & Pearson 2003:19).

So, in a sense, we had come full circle. We were back where we started in early 2008, but we were different. It was the same 'stuff', but we could see it a bit more clearly. This was an experience we would have many times over the next few years, and we were constantly reminded about the critical role of the self-purification step.

And what of Step 4, direct action?

Framework for Our Interventions

Two models inspired our interventions, the first being a simple formula for change from several early organisation development thinkers, and, the second, a framework from the contemporary American philosopher, Ken Wilber.

The formula for change – originally proposed by David Gleicher, published by Dick Beckhard and Reuben Harris, and simplified by Kathie Dannemiller – is simple but quite profound and very helpful (Jacobs 1994:123).

Dissatisfaction (D) *Vision (V) *Interventions (I) > Resistance (R)

When trying to shift an organisation (or an individual for that matter), you need to purposefully increase the sense of dissatisfaction with the current state of affairs. This may be straightforward, but it might not be. How often are we in denial? What about various forms of fatalism? How comfortable are we when people express dissatisfaction?

In addition to generating dissatisfaction, one also needs to provide a picture of a better future. This is not controversial today. And, then, one needs to offer practical steps and interventions to help bridge the gap. Because each variable is multiplied, you need to attend to all three variables. It is not enough to focus exclusively on one, your 'pet' variable.

The sum of these aspects needs to exceed the resistance to change that is often so significant in individual and organisational change efforts. How many of us know that we are overweight? We don't like it. We have a picture of what we want to look like, and are inundated with help regarding diets and gym memberships. But why are we unable to lose weight?

Sidney Howard[5] once said: "One half of knowing what you want is knowing what you must give up before you get it." But what we fear most is loss, and this leads to resistance. For, as JK Galbraith noted, "Faced with the choice between changing one's mind and proving that there is no need to do so, almost everybody gets busy on the proof."

Ken Wilber (2001), the philosopher at the centre of the Integral Movement, has popularised the second model. In many of his publications, including *A Theory of Everything*, Wilber works with what he calls the Four Quadrant Model. Illustrated

---

5   The American playwright and screenwriter, Sidney Coe Howard, received a posthumous Academy Award in 1940 for the screenplay of *Gone with the Wind*.

below in figure 4, it proposes that, at any moment, the world (and, in our case, an organisation) can be experienced in all of the four quadrants. The Upper Right (UR) is the domain of individual behaviours (the 'tip of the iceberg' to use that metaphor again). The Lower Right (LR) is the domain so familiar in business language today – process, budgets, and strategies. The Upper Left (UL) refers to what lies below the waterline in the individual icebergs of people in an organisation, while the Lower Left (LL) refers to what Edgar Schein (2009) defines as culture – the underlying collective mind-sets and assumptions made in the organisation.

Wilber's point is that, to shift a system, you need to intervene in all four quadrants. To focus on only your 'pet' domain will lead to imbalanced development and you will end up being 'stuck' and disappointed with your change efforts. We suspect that the fact that most (70%+) change efforts fail is down to this oversight.

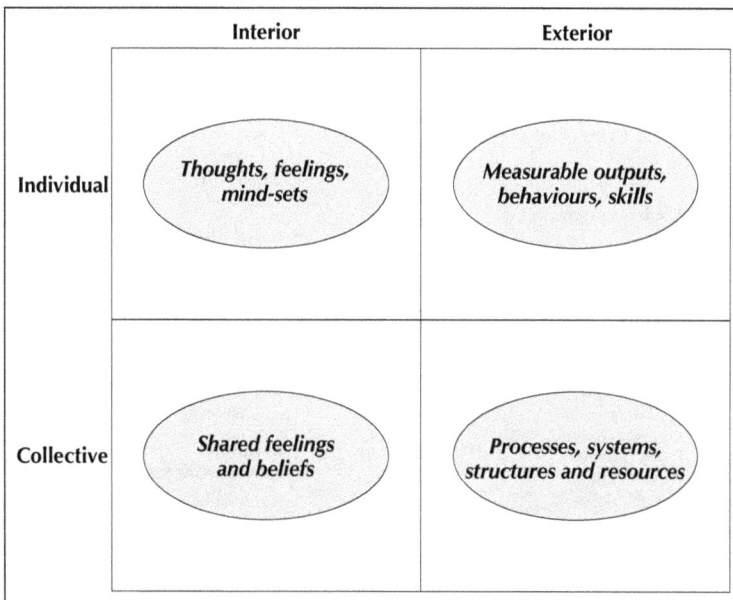

Figure 4: The Four Quadrants

In figure 5 below, we combine the two frameworks. The horizontal dimension is the four quadrants applied to an organisation. The UL and UR are combined and relate to leadership development, while 'Infrastructure' refers to the elements of the LR. We find that teams exist at the centre of the four quadrants, as they combine all four elements simultaneously, while culture sits squarely in the LL.

Our interventions were framed by the intersection of these two models. Essentially, we sought at all times to work across all the domains, purposefully looking to increase D, increase V, provide practical steps **and** reduce resistance.

Figure 5 summarises the 'cookbook'. Now, we hasten to add that a cookbook is not about cooking, and that there are lots of recipes that work for different occasions. Practically, this means the transformation journey is not a road map, but a series of unfolding interventions. There is an art to knowing what intervention or combinations of interventions are required at any particular time. There are times when the focus of attention might be in a particular domain (eg building a high-performing team), and, at others, in a different domain (eg a strategic review). Some interventions are more focused on a particular variable (eg resistance), while others work on all variables simultaneously. What is important is the discipline to cover all the bases and integrate as much as possible.

Cookbook

Levers	Domains			
	Leadership development	**Teams**	**Culture**	**Infrastructure**

D (X)	• Personal insight e.g.
	  - 360 feedback tools e.g. LVA, Disc, MBTI
	  - Group feedback e.g. Circle of fire
	  - Reflective exercises e.g. FLE
	• **Ladders for growth e.g.**
		• **Foster desire e.g.**
		  - Barrett
		  - Voices
		  - 4 ways or knowing
		  - mirror galleries
		  - U process
		  - Appreciative Inquiry
		  - Visioning
		  - Fish bowls
		  - Peak experience
			• **Surface data e.g.**
			  - Schein's three levels analysis
			  - *Barrett corporate values assessment*
			  - See, feel events
			  - *Collective 4 columns*
			  - *Voices*
			• **Social rituals e.g.**
				• **Strategic and operational alignment e.g.**
				  - Meaningful strategy
				  - Restructuring
				  - Resourcing and budgets
				  - Measurement of culture
				  - 3, 3 and 3

V (X)	- Voice dialogue
	  - Somatics
	  - Personal mastery
	  - Inner game
	  - Mindfulness
	  - Clinical approach
	  - Archetypes
	  - Shadow work
	  - Vision quests
	  - 4 Columns
		• **Get unstuck e.g.**
		  - Four player model
		  - Maister trust equation
		  - 5 Powers of a team
		  - Collective 4 columns
			- Values jams
			  - Workout and CAP
			  - Whole system summits
			  - Town halls
			  - *Big Journeys*
			  - Corporate University
				• **Formal business processes and systems e.g.**
				  - RASCI
				  - Delegations
				  - Governance
				  - Planning/budgeting

FS (<)	- Meditation/contemplative practices
	  - Calling/True North Corporate Athelete
	• **Support and encourage "deliberate practice" e.g.**
		• **Embedding e.g.**
		  - Team journeys
		  - Team coaching
		  - Meeting observations
		  - Team charters
		  - Rituals
		  - Reflective moments
			• **Linguistic interventions e.g.**
			  - Metaphors
			  - Symbolic actions
			  - Reframing/story telling
			  - Organizational "mantras"
			  - Feed forward
			  - Vital/unacceptable behaviors
				• **Core HR systems e.g.**
				  - Behaviors embedded in performance management, talent management and recruiting incentives and recognition
				  - Attention to social aspects

R	- Skill building and training e.g. Conversations Wellness programs
	  - Holistic personal plans
	  - 1:1 Coaching
	  - On-line reminders/prompts
	  - 3+1... because
	  - Field work
			• **Viral interventions e.g.**
			  - Positive Deviants Champions
			  - Social network analysis
			  - "Give a Gorilla"
				• **Artefacts e.g.**
				  - Office collateral
				  - Physical layouts
				  - Organization structures
				  - Meeting agendas

Figure 5: The Cookbook (Source: MOHAN VEENA Consulting)

Sample interventions: Let us describe five of the most powerful interventions, and how they worked to renew the effectiveness of talent and the culture of the Unilever

Brazil organisation. There are both technical and adaptive interventions discussed here.[6] Heifitz et al. describes technical interventions as processes and systems enhancements designed to address issues and encourage the desired behaviours. Technical interventions are akin to a heart transplant to address heart disease. These interventions exist 'outside of the people', and 'the experts' do the work. Adaptive interventions, on the other hand, speak to the underlying behaviours, mind-sets and values of the people in the organisation. Adaptive interventions for the heart patient might include changes to diet and addressing sources of stress. It is the person who does the work, not the experts.

Barrett Values Survey. There is a wide variety of survey tools to help interveners in organisation development work. One of the best we have found is the Barrett Values Survey. This is a tool inspired by the work of Abraham Maslow, and we used this tool as part of the initial diagnostic and then annually to track progress. The tool has a number of strengths.

First, with its focus on values, it addresses the invisible domain below the surface of the iceberg, and so it helps make visible the invisible, and makes tangible the intangible. It is therefore especially helpful in framing adaptive interventions. Secondly, it is a simple online tool that takes only 15 to 20 minutes to complete. Thirdly, it provides a quantitative measure of wasted energy and dysfunctional behaviour in the organisation. Best practice is 5 to 10%, and, in early 2008, Unilever Brazil's entropy was 37%, confirming the need for fundamental transformation.

Fourthly, it distinguishes between personal values, values in the current culture and values in the desired culture. Dissonance between prominent values in these three domains brings home accountability to where it belongs. If much of what people in the organisation value personally is not showing up in the current culture and/or there are big discrepancies between the values in the current and the desired culture, there is only one place to look and that is the leadership of the organisation. This is because what is valued in an organisation is what is valued at the top. As Robert Frost[7] said: "Something we were withholding made us weak. Until we found it was ourselves."

As you can imagine, the process of reviewing, discussing and making meaning of this sort of data with the leaders of Unilever Brazil was a powerful way to increase dissatisfaction, and the data about the desired culture also stimulated energising conversations about vision and what was possible in Unilever Brazil.

Surfacing and managing behaviours. One of the first and most important initial steps we took in mid-2008 was to move from a focus on values to also attend to behaviours. Behaviours, unlike values, can be observed and hence managed. Using an Appreciative Inquiry (AI) process, we surfaced what came to be called Unilever Brazil's Vital Behaviours. These were the behaviours that people would

---

6   Heifitz, Grashow & Linsky (2009).

7   Robert Frost (1874-1963) was one of America's most popular 20th-century poets.

hold themselves accountable for and would be enablers of the new strategy that was being shaped at the time. We also took the time to face the brutal facts and gave language to what we called the Unacceptable Behaviours, or how it was that high levels of entropy were being experienced in the business.

By mid-2010, we felt that it was time to review the Vital Behaviours. We were seeing growth in the business and entropy levels were now well under 30%, and it felt like the behaviours were vital then but less relevant now. So, we undertook another high-engagement exercise involving some 1 000 senior leaders, and crafted what we called the Winning Behaviours. These felt qualitatively different from the first generation of behaviours – sharper, more externally focused, and more aspirational in keeping with the fact that the darkest days were behind us.

A very important step was to incorporate the Winning Behaviours in Unilever Brazil's performance management process (a Lower Right [LR] intervention). In the performance conversations that were being had, explicit recognition was given to the extent to which each person was living the Winning Behaviours. We also published print materials throughout premises and factories promoting Winning Behaviours so that there was no doubt about which behaviours were expected. Finally, in another link into the organisational infrastructure of Unilever Brazil, the Winning Behaviours were formally integrated into the annual awards that recognised outstanding achievement in the business.

Developing talent through personal growth. The Barrett survey highlighted the importance of how leaders conducted themselves in creating the culture and the high levels of entropy. The data suggested a big discrepancy between the values that they espoused and those that they actually demonstrated that they cared about. Closing this gap and having leaders live more often into their espoused values needed more than a training intervention. It called for more profound personal growth.

We found the title and book cover of Marshall Goldsmith's book, *What Got You Here Won't Get You There* (2007), captured this idea perfectly (see figure 6). It invites leaders to reflect on who they have become, on their strengths and weaknesses, as well as on their personal vision and aspirations. Most importantly, it draws attention to the white space between the ladders. At the end of the day, the move to the next ladder involves taking risk, a letting-go, a vulnerability. And this lies at the heart of personal growth.

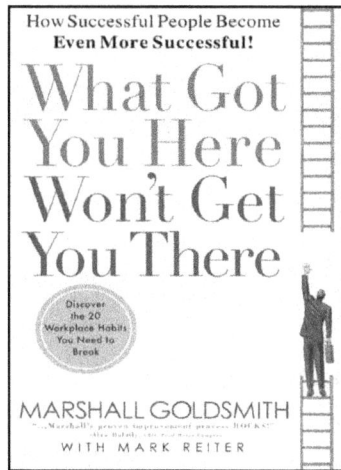

Figure 6: What Got You Here Won't Get You There

One tool we found particularly useful in helping leaders attend to their personal growth is the work of Bob Kegan and Lisa Lahey (2009). Their Four Columns process is a simple, but profound, tool to help people uncover unconscious sources of resistance and hence tackle head-on the Resistance variable in David Gleicher's equation (see Jacobs 1994).

The reason why there was a gap between Unilever's actual and espoused values was that, in addition to the espoused values on the Barrett Values Survey, people held other values or competing commitments. These other values are held unconsciously and typically relate to basic needs and self-preservation. They act as a foot on the brake, no matter how determined one is to press the accelerator and live the higher-order espoused values.

To help lock down the importance of personal growth, each leader took time each year to shape what we called their 'holistic personal plan'. This was a chance for each person to reflect on the key roles they played in life, not just as a businessperson, but also as a father, a mother, a friend, a soccer coach, et cetera, and to define the goals for each role. The personal plans were a fixture in the discussion in the regular journeys that we discuss below.

Journeys. Another very important intervention was what we called 'Journeys'. These were off-sites that were held regularly each year, and they formed the backbone around which the cultural shifts were managed. Einstein once said, "God does not play dice." What he was referring to was the power of attention – in culture, you get the culture that you pay attention to. These Journeys were a discipline to help us maintain attention on the culture we wanted as an enabler of the growth ambitions of the business. They also created safe spaces for courageous conversations and for trust-based relationships to be established that were a precondition for reducing entropy.

As the work was getting under way in 2008, Kees and his top team would meet every quarter, and this was followed immediately by a working session with the top team and their direct reports. This pattern continued for the next three years, although the frequency of the sessions was reduced as things became more settled. In addition to these Journeys, we held what we called the Big Journey once a year where we invited some 250 of the most senior people in the business. In addition to these Journeys led by Kees and Marcelo, each VP would take time out to meet with his or her team in regular 'mini Journeys' (see figure 7 below).

Unilever Brazil Journey Design

Domains

Journey	Description	Time/frequency	Learning
Board journeys	• 10 person board • Offsite locations • Aim for depth	• 2–3 days • Quarterly initially and now twice per annum	• Don't claim victory • The right people will come and go
ELT journeys	• 45–50 directors • Replicate the experience of the preceding board journey	• 2 days • Quarterly initially and now 2–3 hours after quarterly Town Halls	• Heavy investment initially and then can taper off. Don't linger
Big journeys	• – 160–180 Managers and key interfaces	• Once per annum	• High engagement dynamics • Barrett data for THEIR direct reports
Mini journeys	• Functional teams down to front line	• 1–2 a year in third year of transformation	• VP and HR led • Vital to widening and deepening agenda

Figure 7: Unilever Brazil Journey Design (Source: MOHAN VEENA Consulting)

A number of features distinguished the Journeys from more traditional corporate off-sites:

• They were a formal item on the corporate calendar. We knew that the culture shifts we were after needed more than a once-off off-site or team-building intervention. What was needed was disciplined attention, as a senior leadership team would attend to other things it valued. A senior leadership team would not think twice about taking regular time out to review pressing business issues, so why not culture and leadership?

- Attention to physical spaces. We took great care to ensure that the locations were well chosen and, ideally, involved nature. We were constantly amazed about the impact that the location and the physical spaces had on the quality of conversation and insight. As Churchill[8] once said, "We shape our buildings, and, from that moment, our buildings shape us."

- Semistructured but emergent agendas. In the weeks prior to each Journey, we would take the time to discuss which issues needed to be discussed. At the same time, in each and every Journey, we would always come back to conversations under three headings: Where am I on my personal journey? Where are we as a team on our journey? Where are we as a company on our journey to build a company greater than great?

- Integration across the quadrants. The Journeys were not just about culture. In fact, they were a great opportunity to ensure that we very consciously integrated things across all four quadrants. For example, in addition to regular reviews of personal plans (UL and UR), the Journeys were an opportunity to review major strategic issues (LL).

3+1...because. Like many mature companies operating in emerging markets, Unilever Brazil had the benefit of drawing on the best thinking around performance and talent management processes. One feature of the process was that following the annual planning cycle: all executives would clarify what was called their '3+1'. The '3' refers to their three biggest objectives for the year, and the '1' refers to their most important developmental goal, typically something of a leadership nature.

What we realised was that, while this was very good and focused, it was missing a very important aspect – the '**Why bother**?' We believed that more explicitly integrating personal meaning into the performance and talent management systems would be a source of great energy. As Nietzsche[9] said, "He who has a why to live for can bear with almost any how."

Many of us had seen an example of the performance impact of a strong 'why' in the recently released movie, *Blindside*, the story of Michael Oher. Adopted into a well-off family from a very impoverished background, he is attending his first American football training session. His imposing physique marks him out as a perfect offensive lineman whose objective is to protect his quarterback from onrushing defensive linemen seeking to sack the quarterback. Only one problem! The X and O's coaching style was not getting through to Michael, and he was floundering. Up steps Michael's adopted mother, played by Sandra Bullock. "Watch this," she says to the coach. She walks up to Michael and points at Michael's quarterback. "Michael, see him? He is a 'goodie'. He is like your little brother, SJ. See these guys over there

---

8   As stated by Sir Winston Churchill in the House of Commons (during a meeting in the House of Lords), 28 October 1943.

9   Friedrich Wilhelm Nietzsche (1844-1900), German philosopher.

[pointing to the defensive linemen]? They are the 'baddies' and they are trying to hurt your brother. Your job is to protect SJ. Got it?" Michael nods and, from that moment, Michael Oher performed exceptionally, and, as the story unfolds, signs as a professional footballer for the NFL team, the Baltimore Ravens.

What Sandra Bullock has done was touch Michael's '**Why?**' She recognised what gave him meaning. We wanted to capture the same idea in the way objectives were set in Unilever Brazil.

We settled on a very simple innovation. Each conversation had the 3+1 **and** a 'Why?'. Why is it that you want to achieve these objectives? What are you fighting for? Where does your passion lie? If there was not a strong 'why', you could be sure that it would be a struggle to achieve the 3+1. So, as a result, much richer conversations occurred, and objectives were set that had much more meaning behind them.

The Next Phase of the Journey

"Historic continuity with the past is not a duty, it is only a necessity." So said Oliver Wendell Holmes Jr.[10]

As we write this chapter, Kees has moved on to a new Unilever business, and a new CEO has been appointed to run Unilever Brazil. We see it as a moment of transition and a never-ending process of **inheritance and growth**.

In 2007, Kees inherited a business with great strengths and great challenges. His team of VPs and the leaders of Unilever Brazil have made significant improvements and the business is now on a different trajectory. As Kees had received the gift of a divisionalised organisation that had been converted into a fully integrated ONE Unilever organisation, so the new CE inherits a business with great strengths and great challenges. Brazil is one of the fiercest battlegrounds for FMCGs in dynamic, emerging markets, and the business has to continue to renew in order to grow. Unilever Brazil has invested heavily to build capabilities and processes to succeed in the marketplace. Now is the time to put the whole organisation on the street, winning in the marketplace, with all the assets we have accumulated in our handbags in the last few years.

When we reflect on the Journey to date, there is much we are proud of and there are things we would do differently. We achieved many of the goals we set, and failed to meet others. Just as the business enters a new phase, so we do too. And, like the business, we feel enlarged. Not perfect, not the finished item, but more capable and more resourceful having participated in this phase of the Journey.

We conclude with Marcelo's own Voice in April 2012.

---

10 Justice Oliver Wendell Holmes Jr (1841-1935) was the longest-serving member (30 years) of the United States Supreme Court.

Marcelo Williams:

> From the personal side, this was the deepest journey in which I have been involved. I could say that what strikes me most is to see the legacy of a team of leaders with the confidence to write this new chapter in the history of the organization. In the Brazilian day to day, I can see our people delivering extraordinary results and gaining market share and our major competitors are suffering. And I know nothing of that would be possible without our journey. It is like the transformation is inside the individuals and they are paying back all the investment we have made in each other and ourselves.

> Being completely honest and perhaps more selfish, I would say that this journey transformed myself as a person and allowed me to find my calling. I discovered the power to transform individuals in a leadership team, confirming that my real calling is to impact positively the lives of people and through them produce significant impact on organizations. The tremendous pleasure is to make a difference through people.

References

Barrett, R. 2006. *Building a Values Driven Organization*. USA: Butterworth-Heinemann.

Corlett, J & Pearson, C. 2003. *Mapping the Organizational Psyche*. USA: Center for Applications of Psychological Type.

Gibran, K. 1980. *The Prophet*. Great Britain: William Heinemann.

Goldsmith, M. 2007. *What Got You Here Won't Get You There*. USA: Hyperion.

Heifitz, R, Grashow, A & Linsky, M. 2009. *The Practice of Adaptive Leadership*. USA: Harvard Business Press.

Jacobs, R. 1994. *Real Time Strategic Change*. USA: Berrett-Koehler Publishers.

Kegan, R & Lahey, L. 2009. *Immunity to Change*. USA: Harvard Business School Publishing Corporation.

Kenny, A. 1974. *Philosophical Grammar*. Oxford, England: Blackwell Publishers.

Peters, S. 2012. How GE Is Attracting, Developing and Retaining Global Talent. *Harvard Business Review* Blog Network, 8 February 2012 http://blogs.hbr.org/cs/2012/02/how_ge_is_attracting_and_devel.html.

Pink, D. 2005. *A Whole New Mind*. USA: Riverhead Books.

Schein, E. 2009. *The Corporate Culture Survival Guide*. USA: John Wiley & Sons.

2011 Top Companies for Leaders: Winners and Special Recognition http://www.aon.com/human-capital-consulting/thought-leadership/leadership/reports-pub-topcompanies-2011-winners.jsp.

Wilber, K. 2001. *A Theory for Everything*. USA: Shambhala.

Zander, R & Zander, B. 2002. *The Art of Possibility*. USA: Penguin Books.

Zweig, C & Abrams, J. 1991. *Meeting the Shadow*. USA: Jeremy P Tarcher/Penguin.

13

STANDARD BANK – LEADING THE WAY IN AFRICA

Jennifer Morris & Shirley Zinn

A Truly African Bank

Standard Bank started life 150 years ago in Port Elizabeth as the brainchild of John Paterson. Funded and supported by a group of local businesspeople, The Standard Bank of British South Africa was officially incorporated and registered in 1862, with capital fixed at one million pounds and with 10 000 shares of £100 apiece.

The Group's expansion into Africa began just 10 years later when a subsidiary was formed to carry business into South Africa and South West Africa (now Namibia). By 1917, Standard Bank was operating in 12 African countries. Standard Bank's Africa focus was brought to an abrupt halt in 1987 when its parent company, Standard Chartered, sold its controlling interest in Standard Bank and it once again became a purely South African bank. Standard Bank had to start again.

In the late 1980s, a branch was opened in Swaziland. Standard Bank's Africa growth strategy was further enhanced in 1992 when it acquired ANZ Grindlays Bank, a small bank which had operations in eight African countries: Botswana, Kenya, Uganda, Zaire, Zambia, Zimbabwe, Ghana and Nigeria. By the 2000s, Standard Bank had grown its African presence to 17 countries, as well as acquiring a foothold in Russia, Argentina, Turkey and Brazil. In 2008, the world's largest bank, the Industrial and Commercial Bank of China (ICBC), acquired a 20% shareholding in Standard Bank for R36.7 billion, which was the biggest-ever Chinese foreign direct investment at the time. Today, the company has total Group assets of more than R1.49 trillion, and more than 50 000 employees across 30 countries. But, as Chairperson, Fred Phaswana, recently stated: "We have chosen to focus on a strategy that recognises and participates in the great opportunity that is unfolding on the African continent. Africa remains at the heart of the Standard Bank Group's strategy."

Terry Moodley, Head of Personal and Business Banking in Africa, agrees: "Because we have a long history on the continent, we enjoy the brand equity of trust. Africa is our core business, which sets us apart from our international counterparts."

This emphasis on long-term relationships and a focus on the continent has seen Standard Bank named as the 2011 Bank of the Year in Africa and the Best Bank in four African countries – Botswana, Lesotho, Malawi and Zimbabwe – by leading industry journal, *The Banker*. In early 2012, Standard Bank Group was named as the best investment bank in South Africa and Africa by *Global Finance* magazine. In a recent Ask Afrika Trust Barometer Survey, Standard Bank was recognised as the most trusted company in South Africa and the top-ranked organisation in the Ask Afrika Sustainability Index.

The Standard Bank Talent Management Strategy

Effective talent management is critical to the delivery of our business strategy, ensuring that Standard Bank has the right people with the right capability in the right roles to deliver on its business plans both now and in the future. While always regarded as important, 2010 saw the establishment of a Talent and Capability team to ensure that the talent strategy is driven both Group-wide and within the individual business areas as a priority.

The talent strategy of the bank is rooted in the Standard Bank Strategy and Values (see table 1). It seeks to deliver an employee value proposition, built on its Africa focus, the recognition that the quality of people can differentiate in a highly competitive market, and a commitment to investing in growing its people.

Table 1: Standard Bank's Strategy and Values

Our Strategy	Our Values
• We aspire to build the leading African financial services organisation using all our competitive advantages to the full. • We will focus on delivering superior sustainable shareholder value by serving the needs of our customers through first-class, on-the-ground operations in chosen countries in Africa. • We connect other selected emerging markets to Africa and to each other, applying our sector expertise – particularly in natural resources – globally. • Our key differentiator is people who are passionate about our strategy, wherever in the world they are based.	• Serving our customers. • Growing our people. • Delivering to our shareholders. • Being proactive. • Working in teams. • Guarding against arrogance. • Respecting each other. • Upholding the highest levels of integrity.

Inherent to the approach to talent management is a capability strategy which seeks to ensure close alignment between the organisation's strategic priorities and the longer-term human capital demands of the bank. To support this, Standard Bank aims to build both broad bench strength and provide competitive advantage through attracting and retaining superior talent, build capability in strategic areas, and ensure we have the agility to deploy talent quickly and effectively in line with changing business needs and growth in key markets. The Group places a premium on leadership capability that enables high-performance insight into the markets that it operates in and collaboration across the business to serve our customers.

The five pillars of our talent strategy are as follows:

1. **Leveraging our brand and unique position in Africa** to attract the right skills and calibre of talent into the organisation.

2. **Providing an environment for that talent to thrive** through teamwork, values, and providing space to exploit opportunities.

3. **Actively growing capability** through leadership development and building technical depth in key strategic areas for competitive advantage.

4. **Formalising the talent review process** to better identify and provide visibility for high-potential talent and 'game changers' among a staff of over 50 000.

5. **Proactively deploying our talent** to meet business requirements and ensure that they gain critical career experiences that are aligned to future business plans and succession pipelines.

Leveraging Our Brand and Unique Position in Africa

As an emerging-market-focused bank headquartered in Africa, it is critical that we have a deep understanding of the markets in which we operate. A commitment to serving our customers, collaboration, growing our people, and upholding the highest standards of integrity are values which Standard Bank holds dear (see table1). They are at the core of the bank's employee value proposition.

These values play an important role in our recruitment and selection process. We are looking for people who are passionate about Africa and the values we stand for. We invest heavily in building relationships around the world with organisations and networks that are focused on the continent, and with university campuses and alumni who will provide us with a pool of talent to achieve our strategy of building the leading African financial services organisation.

We have leveraged this focus and positioning to provide us with differentiation as we compete with many of the global banks for talent, particularly among members of the African Diaspora who have worked in the international financial services sector and are looking to return to the continent.

Providing an Environment for Talent to Thrive

Collaboration and relationships are core to the Standard Bank culture and to operating effectively across multiple geographies. Standard Bank is built on a teamwork philosophy which prizes collaboration over individual superstars. We believe in the abilities of the team as a collective to bring a solution to a client and to build sustainable capability across the organisation.

This approach is embodied in Group Chief Executive (CE), Jacko Maree. He constantly challenges his managers to unearth and grow 'hidden talent gems'. "We believe in growing our own talent. A diverse talent base is essential, because we are an organisation that operates in many different places and we must be reflective of the countries within which we operate," says Maree.

The Standard Bank Group is proud of its legacy in developing and growing its own talent. Its graduate development programmes have been core to the strategy and have grown in stature and importance over the 10 years they have been in place. We believe our programmes enable us to identify high-potential talent and develop them into well-rounded bankers, while also instilling our values.

We recognise that we also need to constantly bring new talent into the business, particularly as we look to ensure that we maximise competitive advantage. The requirement for a diverse talent base in an increasingly competitive talent market makes the development and search for talent management a constant challenge. In response to this, we have focused on the following five areas to enhance our agility in not only sourcing and deploying talent, but also in ensuring we retain that talent and give them space to lead:

- We have focused on enhancing our own internal resourcing and search capability to improve ongoing access to market data about talent in critical skill areas, which speeds up time to hire when gaps exist.

- Our graduate programmes and learnerships are core to building our talent pipeline. Graduates typically have a 12- to 18-month programme to orientate them to banking and build their skills before being deployed into the business where their progress is tracked as part of our ongoing talent management process. We have had over 1 200 talented youngsters enrol in our formal SBG graduate programme over the past 12 years, with a retention rate of approximately 60%. We are also increasing our focus on and presence at local university campuses across Africa to improve our access to local talent, while also building our employment brand.

- In emerging markets, one is constantly balancing formal organisation requirements with being opportunistic in finding great talent and nurturing that talent. We therefore place emphasis on line managers and talent teams being 'talent magnets' able to find and deploy great talent across the business. The year 2012 has seen the introduction of a formal talent scorecard measuring bench strength, movement and diversity, which increases our ability to track and recognise line managers who develop others.

- Getting under the skin of our best people and playing to people's strengths is crucial if we are to engage and retain them. Our talent process is structured around career-planning conversations and facilitating appropriate career sponsorship for identified talent to improve career mobility, particularly across business areas and geographies. We need to differentiate and focus on those who have the potential to have the greatest impact on the business in the future. We can only do that if we form a deep connection with talented individuals. This, combined with regular reviews of vacancies, high-profile projects and those requiring opportunities (an insight learnt from the big consulting firms), has helped us to better manage career movement and exposure in a flatter, matrixed structure. We do not believe we have yet fully mastered this, but it remains a key priority as we move forward.

Actively Growing Capability

In order to fully align the talent strategy with the business strategy and culture of the business, it is essential to grasp the dynamism which underpins the organisation's history in Africa. Our initial phase of expansion onto the continent was characterised by balancing quite deliberate and planned growth with some opportunism. Over time, this African thrust exposed some very real requirements in terms of leadership capability. Gradually, a particular type of Standard Bank leader began to emerge: leaders who can spot opportunities in complex markets, who can bring deep, local market knowledge and global expertise to deliver for their customers, and can work effectively in cross-cultural environments.

One of those executives, Guido Haller, Head of Global Markets Africa and Group Head of GM Sales, is quick to identify the range of qualities that are core to success on the ground in Africa. "Confidence in your technical skills and intuition is usually an absolute core leadership quality in managing a Global Markets business," he says, outlining the following skills as critical:

- **Communication skills** and the ability to distil and articulate experiences and technical knowledge from learnings in one market to another.

- An **instinctive understanding** of the markets that allows the manager to adapt more developed procedures, trading strategies and products to suit market conditions and trading processes.

- Ability to **network effectively across the global organisation**, given the importance of the cross-border transactional flow.

- A talent for **listening**.

- **Humility**. "The right answer is often not your smart idea – but a home-baked solution," says Haller.

These qualities, combined with a rigour in adhering to global good practices and building a robust platform that will create integrated management information and controls, require leaders with soft hands but strong determination. "This will allow us to make informed decisions in Africa based on the integrity of the data we are getting out, such as reporting capabilities," says Sim Tshabalala, Deputy Group CE. "It's a very important step to enable more effective governance and decision making, but it also hinges on the input of top executives to determine where potential risks and opportunities lie," he says.

The importance of leadership development was recognised early by Maree, and 2006 saw the opening of the Global Leadership Centre (GLC) in Morningside, an impressive facility in which the Standard Bank Group has invested substantial resources in building our leadership capability, ensuring that leaders have access to world-class development programmes and providing a forum for leaders to network with one another across the Standard Bank Group.

Standard Bank is proud of its investment in developing leaders, and the leadership and learning strategy within the bank has been both broad and deep. From its early days, the GLC had a dual strategy of delivery of core programmes that built managerial and team leadership skills right across the Group, supplemented by customised action learning programmes considered more leading-edge at the time such as its International Consortia and Wings Programmes. The latter programmes were targeted at high-potential executives and emerging talent who worked on key business projects sponsored by senior executives with the support of faculty and involving benchmarking trips to other organisations. This improved both the return on investment of leadership development activities and the sponsorship it enjoyed from senior executive across the Standard Bank Group.

In addition to leadership development, the bank has focused on building core technical capability through the bank's various academies. The Academy Initiative, which began three years ago with the 'credit' academy proved so successful that, in 2011, three more academies were launched for business, working with high-net-worth individuals and specialist banking skills. The year 2012 has seen an increased focus on building academies for the enabling functions as the Group seeks to create scale and efficiency through the creation of Group-wide enabling functions. These academies have been key in embedding the 'Standard Bank way'.

Over time, the pendulum swung to greater focus on consistency in delivering programmes for each stage of the leadership pipeline (executive, senior and foundations leadership) to create scale and efficiency in the development of leaders. However, with that came some distancing of the development agenda from the heart of the business agenda.

Competition from international banks is becoming more fierce and we are mindful of the need to be systematic about a capability strategy that will take the Group forward and differentiate it from competitors. More recently, Standard Bank has sought to reharness the benefits of both core programmes for management and leadership capability, while also enhancing the focus on supporting specific business initiatives and delivery through global action learning programmes which enable leaders to 'move the dial' on strategic initiatives and thus fast-track change across the bank.

An example is the recent Strategic Leadership Programme run for Personal and Business Banking both at the GLC and in-country with a strong action learning and immersion bias. Central to this approach is an understanding that not every branch in Africa looks like a high-end Sandton outlet. If we're going to be a truly African bank, our business leaders need to understand the markets in which we operate. Our leaders need to go out and experience what it's like for some of our entrepreneurs who are in the markets, in the fields, in the spaza shops, and in the Kariakoos (markets) of Tanzania. We need to understand that these operations may sometimes look different, but they are critical clients.

Formalising Talent Management

While talent management and development have always been deemed important within the Standard Bank Group, the importance of a more formalised and systematic approach has been recognised to enable the degree of growth expected by our shareholders.

Ensuring quality personnel across 18 diverse African countries is a challenge which requires the proactive identification and development of talent, says Haller. "This involves a recognition that talent sits not only in the generalist management ranks but often in specialist functions. And, increasingly, the critical realisation that talent is available to us onshore in Africa if we are more proactive in identifying it."

Roy Ross, Head of Business Banking for Africa, echoes this view, saying that the bank's maturing strategy has called for a 'narrow and deep' staffing focus. This requires focusing on people development in chosen strategic areas, such as credit or portfolio management. He believes Standard Bank is currently in the 'eye of the storm' when it comes to talent management. "Developing people at speed and scale has never been more important. There is war for talent like never before," he says. "In many African markets the talent pool is shallow and if we want to be the No 1 bank on the continent this will only be achieved by having the best people. Our ability to attract, develop and retain our talent is vital."

Bearing these nuances in mind, the Group is embarking on a process that will create an integrated management information system across its global footprint. In the early days, because we were much smaller, our leaders' informal knowledge of talent was deep. As we grow, it is as critical – though more difficult – for our senior executives to have an intimate knowledge of the talent we have in order to best utilise that talent and also to ensure that talent feels valued by the business. It is our role as a talent function to ensure that is enabled through effective talent review processes across the organisation, ensuring visibility of the talent identified.

While the starting point of talent management is still encapsulated in the performance management process, leaning heavily on the input and insights of line managers, the renewed talent focus has necessitated a clear definition within the Group of the two main types of talent being sought.

First, we're looking for people who will be future leaders, whether they'll be building franchises or leading products and functions. They are people who can lead and inspire, they have commercial acumen, and they learn quickly. Secondly, we are also looking for those who are our value creators. They may not be people who have strong leadership or general management skills, but are the people who are revenue generators and are specialists who bring thought leadership to the bank and have the potential to be game changers in the business.

"A very good example of this is what our Tanzanian team has done in the SME [small and medium enterprise] market," says Ross.

> We've turned our branch banking model from a reactive one to a proactive one and we now take the bank to our customers. This has required us to change our focus on the quality of talent recruited and to invest heavily in developing critical scarce skills. As a result we've seen a remarkable turnaround in our branch staff in terms of their ability to communicate with clients, understand their needs and provide a banking solution.

Formal talent reviews focusing on talent demand and talent supply are held biannually across the organisation to ensure the potential successors, leaders and value creators coming through the pipeline are in line with our business requirements over the next few years. We have to be fairly futuristic given how fast-paced the world has become and how competitive this area is going to become. This is an ongoing challenge.

Some of the key shifts in processes and thinking include:

- **Deepening our understanding of core capability requirements** and **strategic workforce planning** to understand talent demand now and in the future.

- **Formalising the talent review process** to better identify and provide visibility for high-potential talent and 'game changers' among a staff of over 50 000.

- **Implementing a formal talent management system** to improve visibility and career mobility of talent across the Group.

However, talent reviews are insufficient if they do not result in tangible talent strategies aligned to particular business strategies. While we have a macrotalent strategy, we have learnt that real traction only comes through business area delivery. Sitting in China, Craig Bond , CE of Standard Bank China, is also dealing with the nuances of the Chinese market and reflects that "one has to get very close to what drives behaviour in specific markets".

Case Study: Angola

A good case study of this has been our Angola start-up. In September 2010, South African-based Standard Bank launched operations in Angola, making it the largest African bank to enter that dynamic market.

The move was in keeping with Standard Bank's entrepreneurial approach to growth on the continent, a philosophy which has served the bank well over the past 150 years. However, this time, an extra ingredient was added: the ability to leverage off Standard Bank's existing talent pool to uniquely equip Standard Bank de Angola with the skills, people and leadership needed to fast-track growth. Just 16 months into operation and Standard Bank de Angola already boasts six branches – five in Luanda and one in Lubango. The intention is to have 20 branches and a staff complement of 160 by the end of 2012.

While Standard Bank de Angola CE Pedro Pinto Coelho, is the man steering the ship, he is mindful of the benefits his start-up operation is reaping from Standard Bank's experience, history and Africa focus. Being part of the large Standard Bank franchise has offered significant advantages. "It's given us the right momentum and we've benefited from having procedures in place. Also being part of a large network enables us to interact with other parts of the continent and the world," says Coelho. That said, the start-up has not been without its teething problems, chief among which has been the need to adapt the model to the Angolan way of doing things and ensuring a sustainable talent strategy.

The human resources (HR) and talent team worked closely with the leadership team to develop a recruitment and development strategy to source talent, particularly internationally in order to find Portuguese-speaking bankers with the relevant experience and a more sustainable development strategy. "Angola lost a number of people to emigration due to the civil war [which ended in 2001], so we have a lack of skills," explains Coelho. "Furthermore we are in competition with the oil and gas sectors, so we have to fight for talent." This has seen the start-up pull in more expatriates than is ideal, "but we're busy fast-tracking young, local talent through a series of programmes which will see them emerge in five years, as opposed to the usual 10," says Coelho. Moulding this younger generation according to Standard Bank values is central to Coelho's plans and he's looking for attitude, effort and capability in his future leaders.

Deploying Our Talent

Ensuring we are agile enough to deploy talent to meet business needs as well as providing stretch experiences to develop and grow our talent are a key part of our strategy, and often the most challenging. In doing so, we need to balance the needs of the organisation with the needs of the individual, as well as balance mobility and opportunities for international assignments with the very real need to build local talent and ensure we retain local market insights.

While Standard Bank is seriously focused on growth and consolidation in Africa, this strategic resolve is tempered with a fundamental understanding of the associated challenges. While the logistics and cultural and regulatory obstacles have been well documented by the World Bank and the McKinsey Global Institute in their 2010 Lions on the Move report, less has been written about the local push to build African talent and leadership.

In our view, the need to build local leadership in Africa is critical. This requires a sensitive hand at Group level when moving people within the organisation. There must be a balance between providing individuals with experiences and career development opportunities, getting the best possible person for a position, and meeting localisation demands. In the past, there has been too much emphasis on deploying talent from South Africa, our head office, rather than ensuring movement of talent across countries and from countries into head office, as well as vice versa.

The Group's approach to deploying expatriate talent in key markets has certainly not waned, but – along with a more strategic African focus – the importance of such staff movements is being treated as part of the need to build local capacity.

The talent mobility policy ensures that assignments are distinguished between those requiring an experienced hire or expatriate who is there to build capability and future succession, and those who are high potential and are being deployed for development purposes either on a short-term or longer-term assignment and clear assignment objectives are agreed. Cultural agility is a key criterion in placement, and building local succession is often a key performance objective in the former category.

This is echoed by Craig Bond, who, for years, 'ran' Standard Bank in Africa. Bond believes in building capacity and talent at a local level, while leveraging global capability. "In all the countries in which Standard Bank operates we have more than 95% local staff, while international banks still employ loads of expatriates," he says. "Where we do place expatriates, we stress the importance of their being good connectors – who understand how to navigate the internal system and who are culturally adaptive. They act as a link between the local market and head office. This has been a very conscious decision."

Recent years have seen a greater focus on using short-term placement and project experiences, thus enabling us to balance the need to build the cross-border capability required for future leaders with our localisation commitments. One popular solution is the use of 'virtual' teams, which allows local talent to gain project experience, interact and learn from other global leaders. Deploying people to new areas is expensive, so utilising virtual teams certainly forms part of our deliberate skills transfer process enabling us to deploy experienced talent with emerging talent to provide on-the-job experience and mentorship, as well as providing that emerging talent with exposure to deals across geographies.

In making decisions as to filling roles locally or via expatriates, the biannual talent review process provides a starting point for these decisions, but can only be brought to life at Group and Business Exco meetings where vacancies and those needing opportunities are reviewed. Internal talent maps and succession plans are compared with external talent maps, and the needs of the business are closely considered. The focus on succession pools rather than job-based succession and our emphasis on building future leaders have enabled greater flexibility in ensuring backfill for positions vacated.

Another challenge is how to reward managers for not only building their own talent but, when necessary, also being prepared to release that talent into other parts of the Group. We have found that our focus on teamwork and collaboration has provided a good cultural starting point for this, but that is insufficient. We hope that the recent introduction of the talent scorecard will provide more formal recognition of line managers who facilitate talent movement and development.

Squaring up to Talent Challenges

Moodley believes that the work Standard Bank is doing in terms of talent spotting and development has a downside. "We can become the feedstock for the industry because our middle managers are being poached," he says, while admitting that many do return. He also feels that, while impressive work is being done at senior management level, more needs to be down lower down the corporate ladder.

"We've spent a lot of money and continue to invest in both high-end and middle levels, in order to grow talent from within, but we still need to design a system where the people who service our customers are at this high level too," he says.

Standard Bank has a long and proud tradition in Africa, one which puts the Group at an advantage as the world turns its attention to the continent. While past experience will stand the Group in good stead, the organisation's executives are mindful of the need to formalise this dynamic entry into the market and carefully manage talent across the Group to develop, grow and innovate within existing and new markets.

Rapid growth and a time of change place a greater premium on employee engagement. This has seen the recent appointment of a Group Communications Head who is working closely with the Talent team in driving employee engagement and improving communication channels across the Group. The induction and orientation programmes are being revamped and greater use of social media should enhance people's connectivity to the organisation.

Developing local leadership, growing talent in Africa and providing unique career opportunities across the Group give Standard Bank a compelling edge on the continent. How the Group maintains that focus comes down, in part, to the delicate balancing act of talent management and learning lessons from our successes and failure in this regard. We believe that greater formalisation of the talent management process is critical as we grow in size and complexity, but hope that, in doing so, we do not lose our agility to respond to the needs of the business and the dynamic nature of the markets within which we operate, factors which proved successful in building a strong pipeline in the past.

14 TRANSITIONING FROM A STATE-OWNED FACTORY TO A WORLD-CLASS OPERATION: BRITISH AMERICAN TOBACCO PRILUCKY FACTORY

Bernd Meyer

Introduction

The town of Prilucky lies in the eastern part of the Ukraine, a two-hour drive from the capital city, Kiev. The town is small, by any standard; the 60 000 inhabitants had hardly any restaurants until the turn of this century, and supplies were bought from the local market. Even since independence in 1991, hardly any major industry has been attracted to the town.

British American Tobacco (BAT) acquired the Prilucky factory in 1993. Although the production volume was significant (over 20 billion cigarettes per year), production tended to concentrate on local brands, which were sold for very low prices. With low profit margins and infrastructure dating back to Soviet times, the factory was far from the world-class operation expected by multinational companies.

This case study outlines the implementation of a transformation process undertaken in a country in which linguistic and cultural challenges far outstripped those relating to infrastructure and technology. It highlights the importance of courage, risk-taking, assertive but inclusive leadership, authenticity, and continuous consultation and collaboration. This is Prilucky's story.

Background

The Ukraine is a country in Central and Eastern Europe, bordering on the Russian Federation to the east and the northeast; Slovakia, Poland and Hungary to the west; Belarus to the northwest; and Moldova and Romania to the southwest. The Ukraine became independent when the Soviet Union dissolved in 1991, and then it began its transition towards a market economy. Despite various economic downturns, Ukraine is an important supplier and market. For example, in 2011, it was rated as the world's third-largest grain exporter. It is a country with a large, heavy-industry base, but is also known for its technological and transport products. It is regarded as a developing country which has a significant potential for economic growth.

The population is made up predominantly of ethnic Ukrainians (78%) and Russians (17%). Over two-thirds of the population speak Ukrainian as their home language, and nearly one-third speak Russian. Russian tends to be the second language of the majority of Ukrainians.

The dominant religion in the Ukraine is Christianity, which tends to influence many of the local customs. Gender roles continue to be quite traditional, and extended-family structures are commonplace.

The Challenge

In 2004, Bernd Meyer was invited to take on the biggest challenge of his life to that point: to replace the existing administration and production infrastructure of the Prilucky factory with state-of-the-art facilities, whilst continuing existing production until such time as world-class productivity objectives could be achieved.

This proved to be the easy part; the greater challenge was the social, political and people-management issues emanating from the transfer of the 600 staff from a mainly local enterprise to the demands of a multinational company. Not only had virtually none of the managers had any exposure to other countries or factories in the BAT organisation, let alone to business generally, but also a hierarchical, top-down approach was predominant at the factory at the time. Moreover, the Production and Engineering managers were apparently in competition with each other for the post of the first Operations Director of BAT Ukraine, which led to a defensive attitude and reluctance to share information. The old adage that 'information is power' enabled them to feel in control and to breed insecurity amongst both colleagues and staff alike.

One of the immediate challenges Bernd Meyer, the new Operations Director, faced was an inability to speak the local language. Although most of the managers were quite fluent in English, consultation with the shop floor was severely curtailed. However, this was a challenge which had to be overcome, not only to gain the trust of shop-floor workers, but also to ensure a commitment to the change strategy. The competence, experience, expertise and commitment of the shop floor would be the foundations of the business strategy's success. So, one of the first solutions was to assign an interpreter to the Operations Director on an ongoing basis.

Interventions

Tone at the Top

Another immediate, and very obvious, challenge was the management style of the Production and Engineering managers. This style seemed to have been exacerbated by a belief that one of them would be promoted to a Director position, an expectation that had been fostered by a previous Operational head seemingly because of his aspiration to appoint a local Operations Director. After assessing the dynamics for the first two months, the newly appointed Operations Director called a one-on-one with the Production Manager and presented his observations to him. He was also told unequivocally that, in order to qualify for future promotion, he would have to change his behaviour significantly. This message was reiterated on a number of occasions in the coming weeks, but no action was taken by the Production Manager, and he soon tendered his resignation. The Engineering Manager was also asked to leave following allegations of mishandling the construction works at the factory. With the filling of these posts with more dynamic and trustworthy managers, the atmosphere in the factory changed significantly, especially as the remaining managers were also well disposed to adopting a more open and consultative style.

On-boarding the Shop Floor

A significant plus factor for businesses operating in the Ukraine is the level of professionalism of the workforce. Because of the compensation packages offered by multinational companies, well-educated staff chose to work in factories on the machines. A scarcity of materials during the previous political dispensation also meant that workers had often had to improvise and use their ingenuity, which stood them in good stead for the technological changes which were introduced. The majority of employees were also hugely experienced and their efficiency was praiseworthy. The incoming Operations Director soon realised that day-to-day operations in the factory were being handled by genuine experts. This realisation and the respect and trust shown to shop-floor workers enhanced not only their levels of trust, but also engagement and motivation.

It was with a sigh of relief that Bernd Meyer realised that his major areas of focus could be organisational culture and leadership development. New corporate values were introduced and spread through regular meetings with the leadership team, encouraging staff to question and challenge. Despite the difficulties in communicating with the shop floor, a culture of information-sharing and open feedback was established. These simple actions helped overcome initial mistrust and prejudice, and demonstrated a leadership commitment to change and to a world-class production environment.

Symbolic and (Not Simply Just) Cosmetic Changes

As the construction of the new facilities neared completion, changes were made to the original plans and open-plan offices instead of enclosed offices were introduced to reinforce the value of transparency. The new canteen provided a friendly and accommodating environment, which was complemented by the high quality of the food it provided. Colourful meeting rooms replaced their shabby forerunners, whilst revamped lighting created a warmer atmosphere in the administration block and the new production building. The inauguration party was held here; a fact which did not go unnoticed by the workforce, which could be justly proud of their new environment.

A commitment to consultation and information-sharing was reinforced by the installation of plasma screens, notice boards and displays which all reported on key performance indicators on a monthly basis. Numerous workshops on the BAT guiding principles (values) were organised, and workers were encouraged to nominate employees who demonstrated these values in their daily working lives. It was especially encouraging for the new Operations Director to be nominated by the workforce as an example of someone living the values!

Regular briefing get-togethers, in English and Ukrainian, were also instituted. Initially, employees were reluctant to participate in the question-and-answer sessions. However, slowly but surely, they began to air their views. A suggestion scheme also allowed employees to make proposals and put forward their ideas. These were then evaluated and the best rewarded.

Attracting, Developing and Retaining Talent

The new Prilucky factory gives the visitor the impression of a spaceship docking in a remote backwater. For local employees, it was a place of work to be proud of. The modern and imposing structure also assisted with the initial attraction of Graduate Management Trainees. However, after their development phase was over, many of these young people were attracted by the sights and sounds of Kiev and other large cities. Retaining all but local talent in the factory proved a major headache. One solution was to invite overseas trainers to present courses to managers and nonmanagerial staff alike. This helped to motivate and retain some staff, and also assisted with the embedding of the BAT culture. When factories in Germany and Poland urgently required staff to meet increased production demands, the idea was also born to send 30 to 40 operators and technicians to assist. This proved to be a major success and generated huge excitement in the plant; very few of the employees had a passport and the majority had never travelled outside of the Ukraine. The local staff proved to be highly competent on 'foreign' soil and returned to Prilucky with many tales about their experiences 'abroad' – this challenge clearly increased their levels of self-confidence and engagement dramatically.

The 'Sting in the Tale'

All good things potentially come to an end: tough market conditions and increased competition led to lower production volumes at the time, which meant that more than one headcount-reduction exercise had to be undertaken. However, the initiatives outlined earlier assisted with obtaining the cooperation of the trade union in the reduction of headcount by a total of approximately 200. Nevertheless, the mood in the factory remained positive, as confirmed by the year-on-year improvement in the Prilucky results of the BAT global culture survey, 'Your Voice'.

Also important during these redundancy waves was that employees were treated with dignity and respect, and their contribution to the business honoured through fair redundancy packages. The Operations Director remembers being really touched at a party for those made redundant, where those who had been laid off were generally still positive about the company and still proud to have been part of the BAT family.

Moving Forwards

Over the next few years, the 'Your Voice' results continued to improve. When the Operations Director was transferred from Prilucky to the Heidelberg plant in South Africa, operators and technicians from the Ukraine were invited to assist with the installation and commissioning of new machines. Many jumped at the opportunity, even though they spoke virtually no English, let alone any of South Africa's other official languages (of which there are many). The warmth and friendliness of these visitors won them many friends in South Africa, and the visit allowed for sharing best practice and knowledge between the two teams.

Lessons Learnt

The story of the Prilucky factory is instructive, not only because of the impact of significant organisational and cultural change, but also the challenges raised by language and business traditions. At the same time, past circumstances had masked the capability and character of the local workforce, who were to prove themselves the mainstay of the creation of a world-class operation in Prilucky .

The lessons which can be learnt from Prilucky are many and varied, but include the following:

1. Although remote and often rural locations are attractive to manufacturing companies because of cheap and abundant space, the war for talent is often lost precisely because of location. Footprint decisions should bear in mind the costs associated with both the attraction of talent to remote areas and its development.

2. Inclusive and committed leadership:

   - Making the tough calls one would rather shy away from.

   - Identifying the root problems and tackling them proactively.

   - Not assuming that employees at all levels don't want change just because they are 'going with the flow' – people may be open to new ways of working even if they don't show this attitude immediately.

- Taking ownership and responsibility and admitting mistakes; no-one is always right.

- Having positive expectations of people and utilising their strengths and capabilities.

- Avoiding window-dressing.

- Providing open, honest and constructive feedback on performance and behaviours.

- Putting the right people in positions.

- Listening and showing an understanding of suggestions and concerns.

- Getting the job done through people by trusting and respecting them.

- Providing information on strategic and operational issues and performance, and receiving feedback.

- Showing face; being approachable and genuine.

- Living as a role model and caring about the impact you have.

- Giving the bad news, but showing empathy to those concerned.

3. Actions and initiatives; not presentation and plans.

4. Culture change can be accelerated by the look and feel of the working environment; would you, as an executive, work in the same conditions as your workforce?

15

FROM FOSSIL TO FIRST-IN CLASS: TRANSFORMING CORPORATE CULTURE IN BRITISH AMERICAN TOBACCO HEIDELBERG FACTORY

Bernd Meyer

The first-time visitor to the British American Tobacco (BAT) Heidelberg factory is in for a surprise. The Highveld of Gauteng Province in South Africa is not renowned for its beauty, especially in winter. Leaving Johannesburg, the traveller finds the landscape littered with mine dumps, some more reclaimed than others. As relics of the gold rushes on which the foundations of the modern city rest, these often stand in stark contrast to the glass and chrome superstructures which have, in turn, replaced the dismal vestiges of South Africa's apartheid past.

The distance between Johannesburg and Heidelberg is not great and the visitor will soon find himself or herself in countryside of verdant pasturelands and mealie fields in the summer, to be replaced with brown scorched earth in the harsh dry winters. This is a contrast which also describes the BAT Heidelberg factory which, in a period of less than five years, has progressed from what felt like a permanent winter to a bright and optimistic summer.

The stimulus for change was a new business strategy involving the centralisation of manufacturing into larger and more efficient strategic factories. The Heidelberg factory, being the biggest factory in the Southern African area at the time, was chosen to become the strategic factory for the area. It took over the production resulting from the closure of the Paarl factory in South Africa's Western Cape region, as well as one in Angola. The Heidelberg factory now not only supplies the South African market, but also exports to more than 25 countries throughout Africa and the Middle East.

This marked the trigger point for significant change in the Heidelberg factory, and in its culture, technology and processes. The Heidelberg factory had not seen any major changes in recent years and was very much focused on domestic supply. The factory environment and infrastructure had also been subject to some inertia.

With the movement of production into the Heidelberg factory and the necessary extension of manufacturing and other areas, a change management plan was developed addressing three main pillars:

- Technology.

- People and Culture.

- Processes.

The strategic changes were revealed in 2007 when a 10-year Masterplan was formulated to replace noncompetitive, obsolete equipment and processes with the latest technology and 'best-in-class' processes and systems to align Heidelberg Operations with the best in the Group. The capacity of the factory was also increased by 30%. Together with the Masterplan, a clear Operations strategy and Vision were developed and communicated to the workforce. The Operations strategy was broken down into annual performance charters, which are monitored. Through this line of sight, individual performance objectives are developed each year for all managers and relevant parts of the nonmanagerial workforce.

Improving technology was one component of the business strategy; the human-capital component had to be another. It would have proven impossible with the existing tension and climate in the factory to achieve significant progress on any key performance indicator without first addressing the culture and hence the people with a major change management process.

As far as skills were concerned, the mobility and flexibility of the workforce were overestimated. Very few of the employees from the BAT factory in the Western Cape were willing to relocate. Less than 8% of the total workforce chose to stay with BAT and to relocate to Gauteng. This proved a major challenge, especially given the increased production volumes and complexity in the Heidelberg factory. Instead, more than 80 employees needed to be recruited quickly.

In addition, the skills shortage in the South African labour market meant that the recruitment of new staff could potentially restrict the transformation of business operations and, even worse, could threaten the survival of the factory. To overcome this challenge, a number of experienced, qualified staff employed by BAT were brought in from around the world (eg from the Ukraine, Mexico, Germany, etc.) to help, on the one hand, with the installation and commissioning of machines and, on the other hand, with the training of the newly employed recruits.

At the same time, a focused recruitment drive and extensive training and development meant that, by 2010, the Heidelberg factory had become so self-sufficient that it was also able to assist other BAT factories where know-how and resources were in short supply.

Replacing technology, the upgrading of systems and processes, and the development and training of new staff were all necessary, but not sufficient, to improve both productivity and customer satisfaction. The lack of investment in both technology and infrastructure, the entrenchment of old habits, attitudes and practices, and a traditional management style had left many in the workforce underproductive and disengaged.

Levels of dissatisfaction and disengagement were reflected in the 2006 results of the 'Your Voice Survey', a regular Group-wide survey which analyses the climate of opinion and morale of staff on each of the sites. In 2006, the Heidelberg factory recorded one of the worst results ever within the BAT Group: employees from the

Heidelberg factory scored 50 or below[1] on 10 of the dimensions. From lowest to (relatively) highest, these dimensions ranked as follows:

ORDER OF PRIORITY (LOWEST SCORE TO 'HIGHEST SCORE')	DIMENSIONS
1	**Open-minded** Open-minded; encourage all to contribute; receptiveness; listen to ideas of others; free to openly discuss issues
2	**Talent Management** Expect and achieve high performance; recruit the right people; promote the best people; provide feedback on performance; career development and recognition
2	**Pay and Benefits** Competitive salaries and benefits; performance rewarded
4	**Freedom through Responsibility** Freedom to take decisions; accept personal responsibility; feel trusted; consulted; implement new ideas
6	**Strength from Diversity** Actively use a diversity of people (culture, language, gender, age, viewpoints, brands, etc.) to create opportunities
7	**Respect Employees** Company interested in wellbeing of employees and respects them, regardless of job level. Restructuring and reductions handled sensitively
8	**Leadership** Engaging leadership
8	**Enterprising Spirit** Confidence to look for opportunities; to be innovative and to accept risk when doing things differently
10	**Learning** Provides regular feedback, coaching and transfer of best practice

Something needed to be done; and quickly!

But what?

---

1   Out of a potential 100.

It would have been easy for the management team, led by Bernd Meyer, the new Demand Chain General Manager for the Southern Africa area, to second-guess what employees were expressing through the survey and to implement actions which they thought (or hoped) would solve the problem. However, given the sense of exclusion and marginalisation reflected in the scores, a better strategy seemed to be in-depth consultation with as many staff as possible. It was important, though, for such sessions not to simply restate the challenges ('whinge' sessions), but, rather, for employees to feel trusted with, and responsible for, identifying practical solutions to the items where scores were low.

At the same time, an open, honest and transparent communication and leadership style was driven into management, starting at the top. This meant that managers needed to live the example and had to communicate on a continuous basis with their reports or teams. Factory-wide communication through plasma screens and face-to-face briefings (team talks, breakfast sessions, Imbizo meetings, etc.) ensured that managers had to explain to employees the reasons and motivations for all the changes, and also ensured that people felt included in decision making or, at least, properly informed.

Clearly, this new 'way of working' was a serious challenge for some managers. Some managers, from junior- to top-management level, were not able to change their 'conservative' style, which was dominated by orders and intimidation and excluded the employees from being treated with dignity and mutual respect. As a result of this, and also as an unfortunate consequence, some managers either chose to leave the company or were not able to adapt to the new environment and had to leave. Although these decisions looked tough, they sent clear messages throughout the whole organisation and most were fully supported by the majority of the workforce ("This should have been done years ago."). Also, factory employees understood that it was no longer the weakest link that would suffer, but that fairness would be displayed throughout the hierarchies and everyone would be treated in the same way, whether management or nonmanagement. This commitment ensured the support of the majority of the workforce, who had been denied fairness in the past, with the consequence that a wide gap had been opened over the years between managers and the nonmanagement staff.

A series of consultation workshops was held with employees from all levels. The objective of these workshops was to obtain the ideas and suggestions of employees on what practical steps should be taken to overcome some of the challenges they identified in the global survey. A methodology was devised whereby the lowest-scoring items were presented as a series of challenges. For each set of challenges, employees were asked to specify the nature of the issue and to come up with practical actions which they felt would ameliorate the challenge under discussion. Up to 60 employees attended each workshop. In order for them to feel comfortable and that their ideas would be heard, they were allowed to choose both the composition and size of the group they joined. The various sets of challenges were numbered, and these numbers were placed in a box. Each group then chose random numbers from the box and worked on two or three of the challenges only. One group member acted as scribe. Thereafter, round-robin feedback sessions were held in the large group, and the solutions put forward by the small groups were discussed and debated. This process basically identified the gap between the ideal and the actual, and the solutions which were felt would bridge the gap.

A large number of solutions were generated. On consolidation, it was found that there was not one isolated solution for each challenge in each dimension. Rather, the items and the dimensions were so interrelated that some solutions would solve a series of challenges and not just one.

Indeed, it was found that the main challenges could be solved by communication, not only in the sense of the distribution of information but also in terms of leadership capability (ie the diversity/people management skills and basic communication patterns of managers, foremen and supervisors). Some of the most mentioned solutions raised by delegates included the following:

- Regular 'town halls' or briefing sessions so that the strategy, changes and company performance are communicated to everyone (in a language they understand). There was a concern that information and instructions should be concise and accurate as they are cascaded down.

- Consultation with those affected by changes (while planning is under way).

- Basic communication patterns and people management skills of some managers, foremen and supervisors required review. It appeared that many 'people managers' were using traditional, autocratic styles and that this impacted the dignity, motivation and the retention of employees.

Included under people management skills was a competence in, and responsibility for, managing diversity (and eliminating perceptions of favouritism, racism and job reservation), as well as coaching, the support of individual development plans, career planning and succession planning within a broader BBBEE[2] framework. Development opportunities (in the form of multiskilling – "not operators and case packers but multiskilled, flexible and transferable Production Process Controllers") were desired by many shop-floor workers, who also felt that more effort, in terms of development and career opportunities, was put into newcomers than long-serving employees.

There was also a strong desire for fair and consistent performance management as part of engaging leadership. Respondents suggested that all managers should be required to give open, honest and constructive feedback on performance and more

---

2   BBBEE or Broad-Based Black Economic Empowerment is a multipronged piece of legislation instituted
      by the South African government to overcome the economic inequalities created by apartheid.

objective individual performance reviews (one-on-ones), which, in turn, would be linked to individual incentives. Effective performance management would, however, require clear and transparent key result areas (KRAs) which are integrated across departments. It was also felt that performance appraisals should be two-way, balanced, constructive and encouraging.

An interrelated aspect was the trust of employees as expressed in the delegation of aspects of authority and responsibility to the lowest possible level.

People management skills linked into the perceived need for foremen, supervisors and managers to hold regular team meetings, not only for the dissemination of information and the planning of work, but also to obtain 360-degree feedback and to 'check in' with the lives and concerns of employees. Team-building sessions (eg breakfasts, clay-pigeon shoots) and sports days for all employees were also seen as important motivators. It was suggested that those team meetings which were currently held should be extended from 30 minutes to 60 minutes.

- Many groups felt that the overwhelming pressure of production was affecting levels of motivation and discretionary effort.

- It was essential for the potential for victimisation to be dealt with firmly and consistently. Foremen, supervisors and managers, it was felt, should understand that there is zero tolerance of victimisation.

- Education, visibility, transparency and discussion on pay benchmarking were suggested. This was not well understood and needed to be explained in simple language, and in a number of languages.

- Diversity challenges were felt to include the need to provide the opportunity for long-serving and temporarily disabled employees to tender for outsourced contracts, and the need to ensure the representation of designated groups at managerial levels. It was also suggested that some black managers, foremen and supervisors are marginalised between management and workers and (are expected to) treat employees in the same way as many white managers. This challenge would be solved, they felt, by increasing representation at all levels, as well as improving management style.

It was suggested that what are perceived as 'cultural' problems in Heidelberg could be dealt with by:

- Managers, foremen and supervisors taking time to get to know individuals and their culture.

- An effort on the part of all employees to mix together at breaks and social events.

- More social events during working hours.

- Greater cultural sharing both within teams and by individuals describing specific events or activities (eg Eid, Diwali, a marriage ceremony) in the newsletter.

- A diversity calendar so that special days are recognised and respected.

- Better accommodation of female staff.

- Information in the newsletter.

- Priority leave for relevant individuals (cases were mentioned where employees were taking sick leave because their foremen denied them leave for Eid).

- Communicated and performance-managed competence in diversity at all levels.

- Eradication of window-dressing.

The change process began with feedback to all employees on the consolidated findings from the workshop, and what would be done about them. There were a number of 'quick wins' which could be implemented immediately, as well as short-term, medium-term and longer-term priority areas.

One of the critical priority areas was reviewing the management structure and the reduction of nine reporting levels to five. This resulted in improved two-way communication and speedier decision making.

In addition, several initiatives were introduced to improve communication in the factory:

- A factory magazine dedicated to the Heidelberg factory.

- Plasma screens at strategic points providing up-to-date information on a wide range of topics related to employees and operations.

- Regular staff business briefs and breakfast sessions hosted by the General Manager.

- A 'bottom-up', open-door policy through which employees were encouraged to get in touch with management at any time.

Reward and recognition schemes were also used to support the cultural change which was required by the new business strategy. These included nonmanagement bonuses, weekly heroes' awards, and free lunches for staff improving safety.

Workshops on change management (known as 'future-fit training') were held for all staff to assist with their adaptation to a new working environment. These workshops stressed the fact that change is inevitable and that individuals could choose how they respond to it. Employees could air their concerns but were left in no doubt that change was non-negotiable for the sustainability of business operations.

The year 2008 saw the introduction of a new and experienced leadership team with a different perspective on their leadership role. The increased diversity provided by appointing some managers from elsewhere in the global BAT family helped to decrease parochialism and bring in fresh ideas. This was accompanied by a move to a more engaging management style which would not only improve levels of motivation and engagement amongst nonmanagerial employees but also enable the factory to function at a world-class level.

Managers were expected to 'buy in' to a new set of behaviours and to:

- Get the job done through others.

- Be assertive, but never aggressive.

- Be respected for their commitment to the achievement of high and challenging (yet achievable) team goals in a fair, consistent and supportive way.

- Provide open, honest and constructive feedback on performance – both positive and negative – and to acknowledge superior performance.

- Be nondefensive, and both give and receive constructive criticism.

- Consult staff and to respect their opinions.

- Be builders of systems and people.

- Be replaceable – leave systems intact and self-sustaining.

- Be sources of strength for others.

- Promote adult–adult relationships.

- Be perceived as effective managers of diversity and as respectful of both self and others.

As stated earlier, this proved easier for some managers and supervisors than others, and, when additional training proved futile, some tough calls were made. These, however, only served to enhance the belief amongst the workforce that real change was taking place rather than window-dressing. They also increased employee commitment and motivation, which, in turn, have been supported by a comprehensive training schedule to develop and sustain world-class business performance. In general, intensified training took place not only in the technical area, but also on soft skills, becoming future-fit and dealing with change, basic school education, English-language training, and other development initiatives. These programmes were launched to enhance the general skill set of the whole workforce, including management.

The nonmanagement bonus system, unlike previously existing bonus systems, addressed parameters that employees could directly influence with their work. Importantly, this system is easy to understand and takes simple measures such as machine performance, quality, absenteeism and safety into account.

In order to show managers and nonmanagers alike that other BAT factories were more advanced and also to widen the horizons and experience of the people, employees were chosen to go overseas to visit other BAT factories and come back with ideas to implement in the factory. This helped to break the purely local focus, to show that things can be done differently, and that the Heidelberg factory has still some way to go to fulfil its vision to 'be simply the best'.

Obsolete equipment, attitudes and behaviours were reflected in the quality of the working environment. It must have been difficult to be proud of a workplace which was so badly in need of a makeover and a coat of paint. The whole atmosphere in the factory reflected a resistance to change and demonstrated conservatism and underinvestment. Hence, a considerable amount of refurbishment was begun: the canteen was renovated into the light and airy place it is today; social rooms and facilities were upgraded and colour introduced into what had been a dismal and shabby place of work; a gallery of photographs of smiling, happy employees forms a collage on one inside wall; and external walls display triple life-size colour posters of employees doing various aspects of their work. The message is clear: the Heidelberg factory is not interested in art works based on anonymous models; rather, it is proud of the people it employs, many of whom, in turn, are proud of where they work. The visitor now wants to linger and drink in the colour and artistry of the posters and to appreciate the symbolism of this simple gesture. The idea was to highlight for staff that employees in the factory own its destiny. The anonymous face of the factory was changed into a living organism where everyone has a name and a place. This was also reflected by embroidering a name on employees' shirts and uniforms, giving everybody the chance to address employees by their preferred name.

A series of consultation workshops were held again in 2008 to track progress and to isolate new and ongoing challenges and suggested improvements. The staff had scored significantly higher in the 2007 survey of attitudes and perceptions, and Bernd Meyer and his leadership team were keen to find out what was working and what was still causing frustration.

A significant number of improvements were noted by employees at these workshops. These included improved diversity management and representation; better communication; a less rigid hierarchy; younger, fresher management; the factory upgrade; uniforms and names on uniforms; foreign visits and visitors; better social activities; improved control over one's own pay and benefits; the production bonus; better management of talent and learning; respect, trust and more opportunities to make decisions; and, finally, people management and teamwork in some quarters.

However, a continued challenge was felt to be the reluctance of some team leaders, supervisors and managers to change their ways, particularly in relation to an autocratic management style, but also, paradoxically, not managing underperformance effectively.

Various operational challenges were also raised, with employees putting forward some practical suggestions about how to improve operational effectiveness and efficiency.

Individual training and development plans to facilitate the internal promotion of (lower-level) staff were a continued frustration. Some aspects of diversity management and communication also continued to grate.

Feedback sessions for staff were again undertaken and the 10-year Masterplan given new impetus by a recommitment of leadership to change.

By the end of 2010, productivity had increased by 25% and customer satisfaction reached 85%. In 2010, employees rated the Heidelberg factory higher than many other international, fast-moving consumer goods companies operating in South Africa. In addition, the global company employee perceptions survey put the factory top, scoring higher than the head office environment.

But Bernd Meyer is not one to rest on his laurels. The consultation process was repeated for a third time in April 2011. This consultation process, though, was slightly different from those held in previous years. The 2011 data identified departmental differences in new and continuing challenges. The 2011 action planning sessions were therefore designed to address issues on a departmental basis so that more specific recommendations could be made according to departmental needs. Common themes were consolidated into a factory action plan, and specific departmental challenges are being addressed in each department. Improvements in working conditions and the work environment captured by employees included those relating to the physical environment; working conditions; talent development; people leadership; and initiatives taken by the company in relation to illicit trading.

Three common challenges were shared by the majority of employees, particularly those at a nonmanagement level. However, the focus of employees was firmly on solutions. The practical suggestions made were again reported and fed back to the leadership team. The three common themes identified were the following:

1. What can be called CHAMELEON MANAGEMENT practices amongst a minority of managers, supervisors and team leaders. Although these managers know how to behave, they change their colours according to the situation they are in. Hence, they say the right things when their superiors are around, but then act disrespectfully towards their direct reports when no-one is around to see them. They also generally fail to consult or hold team meetings. Career development and promotion opportunities are also often ignored. Criticism is generally more prevalent than positive feedback. It was suggested that the strict performance management of people-leadership behaviours, and especially in 360-degree feedback from all direct reports on a consolidated and anonymous basis, would assist with the resolution of this challenge.

2. Remuneration. Given the high cost of living, many groups felt that their remuneration was not keeping up with inflation. It was generally felt that benchmarking against other companies should be more transparent, that increased housing subsidies should be implemented, and that a travel allowance should be paid to those not travelling by company-sponsored bus. Another issue here was not having a choice of medical aids.

3. Security. Security seems to be a recent issue, but an issue which is breaking the proverbial camel's back. There are three main concerns:

- Clocking out, then having to queue for 10 to 15 minutes at the security checkpoint. Various suggestions were made as to how this problem can be solved.

- Searches not being random but rather governed by the likes and dislikes of the guards. It was suggested that a truly random process was available on the fingerprint scanner technology.

- It was felt that a machine (eg something like a metal detector) should be used for body searches rather than hands.

Although many people at the beginning of the change journey were sceptical (to say the least), and even though many did not understand why money was spent on things that did not directly impact technology and machines, the results had proved them wrong by 2011. A factory-wide increase of productivity by more than 40% within three years, a significant reduction in absenteeism by up to 43%, and measurably improved quality through less consumer complaints are just a few hard indicators that have shown that real transformation is not just about a single intervention, a few technical modifications or the change of a few processes, but rather a full package which is supported by the majority of employees.

This cannot, however, be taken for granted. Hard work, on a continual basis, is needed to sustain an inclusive and high-performance culture. Ultimately, it is about real leadership; living the example; courageous decision making; as well as cascading responsibility and trust to those on the factory floor.

Thus, for Bernd Meyer and his management team, sustaining a world-class culture is an ongoing process and not an isolated event. Their commitment to the process is, however, reflected not only in improved productivity and levels of engagement, but also in hundreds of faces which mirror-image the photographs and posters on the walls. For many visitors, the BAT Heidelberg factory provides food for the soul and is a place to which many will want to return.

Discussion

The success of cultural transformation at the Heidelberg factory can be partially attributed to an effective talent management strategy to increase the levels of engagement, competence and motivation of employees. Many of the critical success factors which underpin an effective talent strategy are to be found in this case study:

- A burning platform to ignite strategic change.

- Knowing what the strategy was designed to achieve, and why and how.

- An integrated change process involving technology, processes, and people and culture.

- The commitment of the most senior executive, who not only brought in 'new eyes and ears' but also understood what was required now and in the future (including a diversity/people management competence).

- Talent strategies aligned with strategic objectives.

- Everyone has talent and experience, and talent and experience are everyone.

- Line management capability was rigorously pursued.

- Skills development at all levels to meet new strategic requirements.

- Transparency of information and two-way consultation (Managers listened, heard and respected opinions and suggestions. Most employees concentrated on solutions rather than problems.).

- Consistency and fairness in dealing with a lack of competence or commitment at all levels.

- Senior management role-modelling desired behaviours.

- Consequences were attached to attempts to revert to the status quo.

- All employees were to be treated as adults, trusted to offer meaningful suggestions and to take responsibility for their actions.

- Recognition of commitment at all levels; pride in the workforce; employees treated as individuals with a name and a critical role to fill.

Part 3: Emerging-market Talent Management Learnings

Chapter 16: Lessons Learnt from Managing Talent in Emerging Markets

16 LESSONS LEARNT FROM MANAGING TALENT IN EMERGING MARKETS

Steve Bluen[1]

This book has focused on the specific talent management challenges faced by multinational companies (MNCs) operating in emerging markets. Imbedded in each of the chapters are valuable learnings on how to overcome those challenges. Seventy of these learnings have been extracted from the work of the various authors and consolidated into a single chapter, presented below. For ease of reading, they have been grouped loosely under the talent management framework presented in chapter 3.

The Changing Global War for Talent

1. **Understand the changing nature of global talent pools:** The rapid growth of emerging markets has changed global talent pools in several ways. Firstly, developed-country MNCs cannot rely on emerging markets to supply them with skilled talent. The increased demand for skilled talent in emerging markets has meant that skills are scarce in those countries too. Secondly, tertiary institutions in emerging markets have not kept pace with the demand for high-calibre graduates required to fill challenging positions in MNCs. Thirdly, emerging-market MNCs are aggressively recruiting talent from developed countries. Consequently, the war for talent is now truly global. No company is safe from local or foreign talent poaching and there is no 'silver bullet'[2] to prevent poaching. Instead, companies need to ensure that they are employers of choice so that they can attract, retain and deploy the talent needed to meet their strategic objectives.

2. **Adjust to the power shift from buyers to sellers of skilled labour:** Because of changes in the supply of and demand for talent in emerging markets, the balance of power has also shifted between buyers (MNCs) and sellers (skilled talent) of labour. Consequently, MNCs need to concentrate on delivering

---

1   This chapter has been compiled by reviewing chapters 1-15, as well as by asking all the authors what they consider to be the key take-outs from their contributions. Their input in this regard is acknowledged and is greatly appreciated.

2   'Silver bullet' refers to cutting through complexity and providing an immediate solution to a problem. The allusion is to a miraculous fix, otherwise portrayed as 'waving a magic wand'. This figurative use derives from the widespread folk belief that silver bullets were the only way of killing werewolves or other supernatural beings (http://www.phrases.org.uk/meanings/silver-bullet.html).

attractive, differentiated and sustainable employment value propositions that cater for scarce talents' needs if they want to attract and retain quality people and compete successfully in emerging markets.

3. **Transcend traditional approaches to skills shortages:** Skills shortages retard the growth of MNCs. Traditional human resource (HR) responses (eg exit interviews, climate surveys, employment branding, and improved retention bonuses) are insufficient to ensure an ongoing skills pipeline and often serve only to chase the same small pool of talent with offers of ever-increasing pay packages. A more strategic approach is needed; one that transcends the generic approach to individual and organisational development. Inherent in this approach are leadership commitment, change management, and risk management, focusing on both internal and external pipelines. Retention goes beyond monetary incentives to recognition, flexible work practices and various other initiatives. These approaches include finding appropriate ways of sourcing and developing talent across the world (in particular, local, high-potential talent in host countries), adopting alternatives to traditional expatriation, and optimising the skills and experiences of repatriates as well as local, high-potential employees when they move from host to home countries.

Linking the Talent Strategy to the Business Strategy

The sole purpose of a talent strategy is to support the MNC in achieving its global strategic objectives. Therefore, it needs to be derived from the corporate business plan and must be measured in terms of its contribution to the achievement of company goals. Several approaches to ensure business-talent strategic alignment are proposed:

4. **Link the talent strategy via delivering capability requirements:** For a talent strategy to be relevant, it must be anchored in the capability requirements for delivering on the business strategy – currently and into the future. In addition, to be effective, the talent strategy must align to the culture and maturity of the business.

5. **Link talent strategy via talent pools:** A useful way of linking the talent strategy to the business strategy is to identify a global talent pool comprising those jobs that are crucial to the MNC. All incumbents occupying those jobs are included in the global talent pool, as are any other employees with rare and/or critical skills. In this way, the talent team focuses on the health of the global talent pool and ensures that the business has the requisite talent to achieve its objectives.

6. **Make talent management part of a total management system:** Talent management can be enhanced by having a total management system that focuses on strengthening both the people and the work systems (technical, commercial and operating) to reflect an aligned and consistent working model.

The Talent Strategy

7. **Develop a convincing talent management business case:** If the talent strategy is directly linked to the company strategy, then the talent management business case will be uncontroversial and widely accepted within the business. This is important for implementation. Ideally, HR should 'own' that part of the business strategy that deals with the role of talent in driving business performance.

8. **Clarify talent management roles:** Line managers are accountable for talent management. No matter how robust the talent processes are, there is no substitute for managers' relationships with, and understanding of, their people when making critical global talent decisions. Line buy-in to talent management is crucial for providing the necessary time, energy and resources to meet talent management demands. Line managers need to understand that they drive talent management – a responsibility they need to embrace enthusiastically. HR's role is to develop the talent management processes and tools and to facilitate learning and governance of the process. Employees need to take ownership of their own career development and take the necessary steps, with the support of Line and HR, to realise their potential while delivering on performance.

9. **Focus on the company and the person:** When designing talent strategies, some MNCs focus solely on the company, while others emphasise the individual. An optimal talent strategy places equal weight on meeting the needs of both company and individual.

10. **Adopt a 'tight–loose' global talent strategy:** For global issues, practices and information need to be standardised so that accurate comparisons can be made across the MNC. Where standardised practices are adopted, the MNC should develop a universal 'talent way of working' to inform the group and to develop the competencies and wherewithal to implement such practices uniformly. All other talent-related matters should be decentralised and flexible, allowing each country to optimise its talent approach in line with its specific circumstances.

11. **Become a genuine employer of choice:** There is no single 'silver bullet' for success in talent management. Instead, if an MNC wants to be competitive in attracting, retaining and deploying high-calibre talent, it needs to create the right environment and adopt an aspirational total employment offering and employment value proposition that will be attractive to its target talent market. This is as applicable to a small local business as it is to a global MNC.

Succession Planning

12. **Plan for unanticipated succession requirements:** Global talent requirements are nonlinear, messy and inconvenient. Therefore, ensure that the MNC has sufficient

bench strength to fill local and global positions at short notice with suitable talent and to replace or deploy them across the world without denuding one part of the business to fill vacancies elsewhere. To achieve this, global talent pools are more effective than succession planning. Instead of finding a specific successor for a particular conventional role, a global talent pool is created comprising flexible, mobile, multiskilled talent that can fill diverse roles across the MNC.

13. **Centralise the global talent pool:** To enhance the efficient deployment of talent, manage the global talent pool centrally. This provides the best approach, because talent decisions are taken with the interests of the total MNC in mind. A central talent pool also prevents business units from promoting their own interests either by preventing high performers from leaving their business units or by aggressively recommending their poorer performers in order to off-load problem employees. Furthermore, the leadership team has a strategic overview of jobs that need filling in the short and medium terms and can ensure that the most appropriate person is deployed into each job.

14. **Define scarce and critical skills and ensure adequate cover:** Identify skills that are scarce and therefore critical to the company. Criteria for defining such skills include high levels of labour turnover, vacancy period, criticality to the business, and availability of internal or external cover. The critical-skills jobs need to receive particular attention to ensure that suitable people occupy those roles and that there is adequate cover to fill any vacancies speedily, without harming the business.

15. **Create a healthy mix of internal and external talent appointments:** Promoting talent from within can increase localisation, ensure continuity and reduce recruitment costs and on-the-job performance gaps, enhance engagement and retention, and create growth and career opportunities. External recruitment can generate new thinking, widen the selection choice and prevent groupthink. MNCs should therefore decide on an appropriate mix of internal promotions and external hires when planning succession.

16. **Ensure multidirectional talent movement:** Avoid relying solely on headquarters as a talent source. The MNC talent pool should comprise people drawn from the entire company. Deployment will then involve moving people from home and host countries. Besides contributing to the diversity of leadership, this extends global career development opportunities to high-potential employees in host countries and increases the employment value proposition of the MNC.

Attraction

17. **Recruit for potential, not just to fill vacancies:** To win the war for talent and cater for unpredictable talent demands, recruit for potential, rather than solely to

fill vacancies. Recruit high-potential external talent even if no immediate job or budget exists. Assign high-potential recruits to leaders as executive assistants able to perform meaningful projects while receiving training and business exposure. Deploy them when suitable jobs become available. This 'extended induction' serves several purposes. Firstly, it provides recruits with the opportunity to understand the company and identify where they would like to be employed. Secondly, it provides an extended assessment opportunity, allowing managers to close any competence gaps and determine where best to place them. Thirdly, it fills the talent pool with high-potential people that can add value as soon as they are deployed.

18. **Outlaw informal talent broking:** 'Shoulder-tapping' in MNCs is disruptive and damaging. It allows managers to offer jobs to whomever they wish, without due regard for the formal succession process. Create formal global recruitment processes and governance mechanisms to enforce them.

19. **Market-map talent:** Market-mapping provides intelligence about talent available in the market. It is also a means of being proactive about sourcing talent and digging deeper for talent, which is critical in competitive emerging markets. Exploring local universities and adopting graduate and learner programmes is a further source of talent scanning in emerging markets.

20. **Create an aspirational employment value proposition:** Because talent demands outweigh supply, implement an employment value proposition that addresses the needs and aspirations of potential (and existing) employees. In emerging markets, offering meaningful jobs, attractive rewards, and development and global career opportunities – and then delivering on these promises – enhances the attraction and retention of high-potential employees. Provide clear career-path data for employees. Communicate enlightened practices to local communities so that their people want to belong to a responsible, caring and environmentally friendly company. Create excitement about working for the company as a point of differentiation and dynamism.

21. **Adopt a proactive diversity approach:** An attraction criterion should be quality of diverse talent, thereby casting the recruitment net as wide as possible rather than restricting it to particular groups. In emerging markets, women are a neglected supply of talent. To tap into this valuable source, ensure that there are no gender biases in talent practices.

Selecting

22. **Be specific about choosing the right people to undertake international assignments:** Do not assume that a person who is successful in his or her home country will thrive in a host country, or vice versa. Emerging-market challenges

are different from home-country challenges. Because each person is distinctive, one size does **not** fit all. Instead, customise talent decisions to cater for each person's specific strengths, needs and family circumstances.

23. **Take promotion risks with exceptional talent:** Place people with truly exceptional talent in challenging, non-obvious roles. Exposing them to diverse functions, industries and geographies will accelerate their development and make them more rounded by the time they become business leaders.

24. **Use psychometric assessments judiciously:** Psychometric assessments should form a cornerstone of selection decisions, especially when recruiting for potential. When selecting expatriates, they are important for assessing subtle characteristics such as prejudice and resilience that may not be evident during an interview. Because criteria for leadership success in emerging markets go beyond technical competence to include a variety of emotional intelligence, social, political and personality criteria, assessment batteries should cover these dimensions. Ensure that the psychometric tools used comply with local legislation, have reliability and predictive validity, and are culture-fair.

25. **Select the family, not just the expatriate:** When choosing an expatriate, the selection process should cover the expatriate candidate, his or her partner, and their accompanying children. The family will need to adapt to the host country and, therefore, they need to be screened.

On-boarding

26. **Introduce expatriate families to the country early:** Before accepting the assignment, expatriates and their partners should be sent on a 'look-see' visit to understand what the assignment entails. Then, before embarking on the assignment, expatriate families should attend an enculturation programme that covers several areas of acculturation needed for successful adjustment, including politics and government, work, economic matters, family relations, social relations, and ideology (ie ways of thinking, principles, values, customs and religious beliefs).[3] This facilitates adjustment and allays the family's fears.

27. **Implement two-way introductions to the MNC in host countries:** Educate local employees about the ambitions, values, culture and ways of working of the global business. Where appropriate, send them on visits to the MNC headquarters so they can gain an appreciation of the larger group they have joined. Simultaneously, educate expatriates about local conditions, customs and practices.

---

3   See Haslberger & Brewster (2008).

28. **Ensure the MNC leader plays a significant on-boarding role in a host country:** The leader should on-board the shop floor through:

    - Adopting adult-to-adult, trusting and respectful attitudes and behaviours.

    - Having positive expectations of staff and not making assumptions.

    - Communicating, consulting, and informing.

    - Taking the time to get to know people.

    - Not expecting people to work in conditions that the leader would not want to work in himself or herself.

    - Reasonably accommodating, within business constraints, cultural differences of all kinds.

    - Making sure reward and recognition schemes support the business strategy and are available to all.

    - Trusting people to tell the leader what is wrong, how they would put it right and when it has improved.

Engage and Retain

29. **Adopt a person-specific approach to engagement:** Employee engagement is critical – nothing can replace the personal commitment of employees and their willingness to go the extra mile. To optimise engagement, personalise it for every employee, taking into account individual needs, aspirations and circumstances. Besides enhancing retention, the very process of engagement helps to surface talent that has hitherto remained undiscovered. Do not wait for staff to resign before identifying areas of dissatisfaction. Rather, undertake regular engagement discussions to determine propensity to leave and consult staff on ways in which dissatisfiers can be resolved.

30. **Create a fun, healthy work environment – work hard, play hard:** Most talent management literature focuses on multinationals providing the right career opportunities. Remember that, as part of the employment value proposition, working should also be fun.[4] MNCs should create an environment in which people want to work – that inspires and motivates them, makes them passionate about the culture, and allows them to thrive as human beings.

---

4   Google is a good example of a company that has adopted a fun and creative culture which has served it well both in terms of attracting and retaining top talent and in harnessing people's creativity, thereby achieving impressive business results (see Nightingale, John & Girija Swaraj 2009).

Development

31. **Accelerate leadership development through first-hand emerging-market exposure:** Accelerate development of key talent through deployment in challenging emerging markets. Make successful completion of at least one overseas assignment a prerequisite for being appointed into a top management job. Expatriate opportunities are limited; be creative in considering how people can get the cross-border exposure and career experiences they need to be well-rounded global leaders through vehicles such as international projects.

32. **Send leaders on action learning projects to emerging markets:** In-Market Action Learning is an excellent way of preparing leaders for roles in emerging markets. Action learning provides leaders with a global mind-set and appreciation of the realities of doing business in emerging markets. It provides them with real-life challenges and accelerates the learnings of how to deal with running host-country businesses.

33. **Develop leaders as well as functional specialists and 'game changers':** Building a strong, **overall** bench strength of talent is as important as nurturing high-potential stars, particularly in a growing business. While future leaders with general management skills are always crucial, recognise that, in some areas, deep specialists or revenue generators who bring competitive advantage to the business are as valuable. A talent strategy should focus on both – on increasing the readiness of current functional and operational leaders for executive roles within five years, and retaining and leveraging those game changers and value creators who bring competitive advantage to the organisation.

34. **Adopt the philosophy that career development is the acquisition of diverse competencies:** Rather than adopting a rigid, linear career-ladder approach, where appropriate expose employees to different industries, functions and geographies in their career development.

Manage Performance

35. **Link performance management and talent management:** A seamless approach to goal setting, goal reviews, identifying competence and performance gaps, individual development plans, and performance-related remuneration helps enhance career development and performance.

36. **Link performance management and reward systems:** Performance is the desired behaviour for which employees are compensated. Therefore, evaluation of employees' job performance is vital for HR management and for the organisation. In an ever-changing business world, performance management serves as an effective tool for identifying, retaining and developing talent. In addition, reward

and remuneration are closely allied to performance management and play a fundamental role in attracting and retaining talent.

37. **Keep performance management simple:** A golden rule is to keep performance management (and the reward system) simple and easy to explain and understand. A performance management system must be realistic and measureable and have attainable standards and objectives, as well as the necessary performance counselling and provision to allow employees to reach the desired level of performance.

38. **Link performance management to the corporate culture:** A principle of global performance management is to build and maintain a strong, integrative corporate culture. To achieve this organisational culture, an acknowledgement and understanding of the diversity of local cultures are essential. Therefore, management training about how to conduct global performance management, including diversity and culture, is crucial.

39. **Optimise performance appraisal information:** The three comprehensive benefits of using performance appraisal information are the following: firstly, it assists in making HR decisions regarding matters such as salary increases, incentive payments, and promotion and demotion decisions; secondly, it helps identify employee strengths and development areas; and, thirdly, it informs employee career planning, including further learning and development. No single performance appraisal method is suitable for all jobs and situations, and, instead, a combination of methods is suggested.

40. **Link performance management and development:** By consistently focusing on development of employees, performance management supports employees' efforts to improve. Development is an extremely effective retention strategy – it can be more valuable than higher remuneration, because it keeps employees' skills competitive. In addition, employees feel part of the team and believe that the organisation is investing in, and caring for, them, and this increases their commitment.

Reward and Recognition

41. **Be aware of global trends when designing a remuneration strategy:** Global trends in remuneration include increased media scrutiny, a focus on employee retention, implementation of specialist career tracks, improved governance, better-stated employee value propositions, and strengthened performance-related pay. These trends reflect what leading organisations are currently focusing on, or are expecting in the future. Knowledge of these can help set an organisation's remuneration strategy and prepare for future unforeseen situations.

42. **Link reward systems to the business and the talent strategy:** The relationship between reward and strategy is imperative for ensuring the best possible performance from employees. Organisational reward systems, financial and nonfinancial, are significant factors in a company's strategic aim to attract and retain high-calibre individuals. Departments, divisions, groups and employees need different remuneration programmes within each organisation. In addition, organisations need to ensure that their processes are extremely robust and can withstand stakeholder scrutiny.

43. **Design reward systems thoughtfully and strategically:** By combining extrinsic and intrinsic motivators, efficient reward strategies positively influence employees' behaviour. Thus employees receive tangible and intangible rewards in return for their performance. It is important that the right total reward strategy delivers the right amount of money to the right people at the right time for the right reasons. The most successful organisations use short-term and long-term incentives in their remuneration mix. The reason for this is that it encourages the long-term viability of the company: Executives are encouraged not to harm the company for the short-term gains, as they have too much to lose in the long term. Complexities, such as different local versus expatriate pay spheres and cross-cultural differences, need to be understood in terms of what comprises value and performance for organisations and employees.

44. **Use reward and recognition to achieve business goals:** These include:

    - Recruiting high-quality employees and retaining their services in the organisation.

    - Improving employee performance.

    - Ensuring fairness.

    - Ensuring legal compliance.

    - Controlling labour costs.

    - Motivating staff.

Talent Analytics and Information Systems

45. **Implement a people balance sheet:** Elevate the talent profile by developing a people balance sheet and including people balance sheet reviews in the annual strategic calendar. A people balance sheet consolidates all relevant standardised talent metrics for a business, assesses its talent health, identifies gaps, and sets out action steps to close the gaps (see table 1). It also informs all talent-related decisions, including salary reviews, succession and deployment decisions, recruitment, learning and development and retention needs, goal setting and business planning. The annual people balance sheet reviews should be cascaded

up the organisation, culminating in a consolidated review for the entire MNC and resultant global talent action plan.

46. **Use advanced analytic tools to predict future talent needs:** Some talent outcomes (eg the flight risks and when they are likely to leave; local and international supply of and demand for talent) are notoriously difficult to predict. Multivariate analytical modelling can enhance the accuracy of such predictions and tailor proactive talent plans.

47. **Obtain relevant, accurate data to inform talent decisions:** Critical to introducing a people balance sheet and advanced analytic tools is the need to obtain relevant, accurate and current information on all people in the defined talent pools. Data for all people within a defined talent pool must be standardised to facilitate meaningful comparisons. An enterprise-wide or cloud-based IT (information technology) system that provides real-time talent data streamlines talent management across multiple geographies.

Table 1: Examples of Key Talent Performance Indicators to Include in a People Balance Sheet[5]

Talent Dimension	Key Performance Indicators (KPIs)	Description	Target[6]
Business strategy–talent strategy link	Talent strategy outputs	Direct link between the multinational corporation's (MNC's) 5-year business plan and the specific talent strategy outputs. Management, HR and employees' roles and accountability for implementing talent plans to meet business objectives clearly stated	100% alignment; signed off by top management
	Talent business case	Talent business case is derived from the 5-year business plan	Signed off by top management
Succession planning	Cover ratios	The number of people that are immediate cover (0-12 months) for a job divided by the total number of incumbents in that job	0.6-1.0

---

5   The contents of this table have been adapted from Bluen (2004) and SABMiller (2010), and input from the various authors of chapters in this book.

6   Targets are merely indicative of benchmark scores. These would vary by factors such as country, industry, labour-intensive versus capital-intensive organisation, business unit, department, function and job.

Talent Dimension	Key Performance Indicators (KPIs)	Description	Target
Succession planning (continued)	Rate of change	Rate of change reflects the amount of people moves in an operation. It is the percentage of positional changes in a business unit as a result of any people moves (including recruitment, transfer, promotion, structural changes, and any form of labour turnover) in relation to the total number of positions in the business unit	< 25% per annum
	Distribution of potential	On the performance-potential grid, the percentage of people rated as above-average potential vs average potential vs below-average potential for a particular business unit, function or organisation	Above average: 30% Average: 55% Below average: 15%
Attract, select and on-board	Vacancy rate	Average number of jobs vacant at any point as a percentage of total headcount	< 3%
	Time to fill	Average amount of time it takes to fill a vacancy	Professionals/ Managers: 30 days Executives: 90 days
	Internal to external appointments	The ratio of internal promotions to external hires	Internal promotions: 75% External appointments: 25%
	Cost of hire	Average sourcing channel cost (agency fee, referral, social media, job board, corporate website, etc.) as a percentage of package (NB: Excluding search assignments)	< 20%
	External offer acceptance ratio	Number of offers accepted vs number of offers declined as a percentage	> 80%

Talent Dimension	Key Performance Indicators (KPIs)	Description	Target
Attract, select and on-board (continued)	Tenure of new hires	The average length of tenure of new hires	> 3 years
	Calibre of new hires	Calibre of new hires at management and executive level rated by the company as being high-potential (as opposed to average or below-average potential)	High potential > 67%
Learning and development	Training days	Formal training days per person per annum	7 days per person per annum
	Training spend	Total training budget as a percentage of total payroll	5-6% of payroll
	Time-to-competence	Time it takes for a new person in a role to be assessed as fully competent	6-18 months, depending on job complexity
	Competence rates	Percentage of people below senior management level that have been assessed as fully competent	> 75%
	Individual development plans in place	The number of individual development plans that have been agreed between the employee and his/her manager as a percentage of the total workforce	100%
	Leadership development mix	The ratio of different learning mediums used to develop global leaders	Job experience: 70% Coach/mentor: 20% Formal training: 10%
Engagement and retention	Engagement Survey Index	Organisational engagement survey – company, business unit, function and department score. • Trust in leadership • Role clarity • Decision-making authority • Access to tools, resources • Alignment to values	Upper quartile

Talent Dimension	Key Performance Indicators (KPIs)	Description	Target
Engagement and retention (continued)	Undesirable labour turnover	The number of senior employees that voluntarily leave the business (ie other than due to death, any form of retirement, dismissal or retrenchment), that the business regrets, as a percentage of total senior employee headcount	< 3% per annum
	Global talent pool labour turnover	The number of members of the global talent pool that leave the business for any reason as a percentage of the total headcount of the global talent pool	< 1% per annum
	Critical-skills pool labour turnover	The number of people in the critical-skills talent pool that voluntarily leave the business as a percentage of the total headcount of the critical-skills pool	0% per annum
	Diversity labour turnover	The number of targeted group members from critical talent segments that voluntarily leave, that the business regrets, as a percentage of total headcount of the targeted group in the critical talent segments	< 1% per annum
	Total labour turnover	The number of people that leave the business for any reason, as a percentage of total headcount	< 10% per annum
	Absenteeism	Average number of people absent from work as a percentage of the total workforce	< 2% per annum
	Flexible work arrangements	Within positions defined as suitable for flexible work arrangements (eg flexitime; flexi-place): the number of people for whom flexible work arrangements have been formally agreed as a percentage of total headcount within those defined positions	5-10%

Talent Dimension	Key Performance Indicators (KPIs)	Description	Target
Manage performance	Output-based performance management system	Performance management system measures outputs and everyone has been trained how to use it. Performance management is woven into the 'way we do things around here'. It does not replace the job description	• Everyone trained • All have between 4 and 7 outputs • Everyone has at least 2 appraisals a year
	Inclusion	Percentage of global talent pool members' performance measured via one standard, company-wide performance management process vs decentralised and unaligned to a common standard	100%
Reward and recognition	Expatriate pay	Average expatriate cost to company, compared with costs incurred for the same job in the home country	3-4 times home costs
	Anomaly rate	Number of employees paid below or above the pay scales	< 10%
	Remuneration mix	The relationship between fixed pay and variable pay	At least 1 to 1 in high-performing organisations at senior levels
	Share schemes	Share scheme participation at senior executive level	At least a third of total earnings made up of shares
	Recognition scheme spend	Recognition scheme spend on formal recognition schemes	1% of turnover or 3% of net profit
	Recognition	Number of eligible employees who participate in the recognition programme	> 70%

Talent Dimension	Key Performance Indicators (KPIs)	Description	Target
Diversity and localisation	Diversity headcount targets	Percentage of members of defined targeted groups (eg Africans, females, host-country local employees, and people with disabilities) in defined higher-level positions (eg executive committee, people in global talent pool positions)	Targeted group representation in higher level positions matches the demographic mix in the emerging market
	Diversity culture	Comparison of targeted groups' scores with the rest of the workforce's scores on relevant organisational survey dimensions such as engagement, participation, reward and recognition, commitment, diversity and support	No statistically significant between-group differences found
	Localisation targets	Number of expatriates that are replaced by high-potential, fully trained, competent local employees within a defined time period	Stretch localisation targets met
Organisational culture	Culture scores	Stretch targets, derived from an assessment tool that reflects the desired culture dimensions in the host country	Culture score targets are set and met
Talent reviews and evaluation	Talent KPIs	KPIs and stretch targets, appropriate for the host-country operation, are defined and measured accurately and regularly, and inform future talent plans	Customised people balance sheet implemented; data reviewed and acted upon annually
Talent system	Enterprise-wide HR system	HR system in place that is capable of capturing all the talent data referred to in this table for both the MNC head office and all emerging-market operations	People balance sheet results obtained effortlessly from the HR system

Talent Dimension	Key Performance Indicators (KPIs)	Description	Target
Leadership	Engagement	Scores on engagement surveys indicate that host-country employees feel increasingly engaged and supported as a result of positive measures taken by MNC leaders in the country	3% improvement per annum
	Leadership style	Year-on-year increases in scores on best-practice leadership style measures (including organisational climate surveys, 360-degree feedback and independent assessments)	Statistically significant annual increase in leaders' style scores
Expatriates	Expatriate failure rates	The number of expatriate assignments that are voluntarily ended prematurely, as a percentage of the total number of expatriate assignments	0% per annum
	Expatriate return on investment	Within each emerging-market operation: sum of the combined financial value-add of all expatriates divided by the sum of the total cost to company of all expatriates	> 1
Local employees	Talent management	All aspects of talent management (as contained in this book) are successfully applied in each of the MNC's operations across the world	Full people balance sheet implemented and acted upon in each emerging-market operation
	Critical job competency rates	Percentage of employees filling specific jobs, defined as critical for the MNC to function effectively, that are fully competent	Every person in a critical job is 100% competent within a year of appointment

Talent Dimension	Key Performance Indicators (KPIs)	Description	Target
Human Resource Function	HR practitioner competence	Assessment of HR practitioners' competence against a global professional competency standard that covers functional excellence, global MNC knowledge, personal mastery and emerging-market proficiency dimensions	All HR practitioners operating in emerging markets are 100% competent within a year of appointment
Business performance	Annual financial results	Global talent team's objectives: annual MNC financial targets met via competent talent in place to achieve desired outcomes across the business; no project is shelved because suitable talent was not available for its implementation in emerging markets	Global talent team's performance is rated as 'outstanding'

Diversity and Localisation

48. **Eliminate prejudice**: There is no place for prejudice in any organisation. Ensure that, in every host country, there are HR policies and employment equity strategies in line with local legislation that are followed to eradicate prejudice. To ensure sustainability, develop a compelling business case for employment equity in each host country.

49. **Avoid stereotyping and exclusive behaviours**: Leaders should be mindful of the detrimental effects of stereotypes and generalisations on individual performance and motivation. They should also endeavour to control their expectancy communications and inculcate a positive learning culture. Be aware of exclusive behaviours and implement mechanisms to overcome them. Be prepared to speak out, if appropriate, when observing exclusive behaviours and to suggest ways in which things can be done differently. Consult staff about their perceptions of inclusiveness and support, and encourage them to put forward practical solutions to overcome identified barriers.

50. **Maximise localisation**: A major aim of staffing local operations is to reduce the number of expatriates and take a strategic decision to employ local people wherever possible. Adopt firm guidelines and targets around localisation and treat them with the same rigour as any other business deliverable. Employ expatriates sparingly – primarily to transfer skills and train local employees. An expatriate goal should be to identify their successors and train them to take over their jobs within a clearly defined time period.

Culture

51. **Adopt a geocentric approach to culture**: Do not write off differences; rather leverage the benefits and opportunities they bring. MNCs operating in emerging markets need to acknowledge that no culture or management approach is superior to another. Instead, every person and every culture needs to be regarded as adding value.

52. **Ensure culture fit between employees and the host environment**: Understand the critical components of the MNC's culture, values and operating ethos, and make sure that these are embedded into expansion projects from inception. Avoid the arrogance of home-country advantage. When choosing people to work in emerging markets, take care to ensure that, in addition to having the right competencies and experience, they have the right culture fit with the host company and country.

53. **Start with the MNC's corporate values when shaping a new host-country culture**: When merging the home and host countries' cultures, do not take short cuts by sacrificing values for profits. Values represent the social glue that binds the diverse, globally dispersed operations of an MNC.

54. **Create a high-performance, engaging learning culture**: This can be achieved by adopting sound people practices. Examples include: creating a positive learning culture by providing open, honest and constructive feedback on performance; being fair and consistent, thereby driving engagement; being open to flexibility and work–life balance whilst ensuring that rewards accrue fairly according to individual results.

55. **Conduct integration workshops when new teams enter emerging markets**: Integration workshops between expatriate and local teams should be held as soon as possible after the arrival of the new team. The workshops should be aimed at understanding the shared identity of the business, exploring cultural differences and accommodating such differences.

56. **Do not generalise. Cultures and people are unique**: The unique cultural and human attributes of emerging markets far outweigh any perceived disadvantages. Therefore, get to know your market intimately. Do not make assumptions about different approaches or people based on cultural stereotypes. Sensitivity, time and energy are required, and there is no substitute for a thorough psychometric analysis of the talent pool. This is the way to discover strengths that can be used and differences for which bridges can be created.

57. **Ensure that the corporate culture is closely linked to the talent strategy**: In almost every case study in this book, the role that corporate culture plays in attracting, retaining and developing talent has been emphasised. Not only can

the correct culture help an MNC win the war for talent, it can also go further to energise and motivate people to give of their best and contribute to the company's success and their own fulfilment. In this respect, aligning local and expatriate, individual and company values is vital.

58. **Ensure long-term leadership commitment to realise meaningful, sustainable change**: Sustainable change needs a long-term leadership commitment to embedding a different culture. Managers can quickly revert to the status quo and practise 'chameleon management' by doing what is required of them only when their behaviour is visible to those at higher levels. Leaders need to be in it for the long term; a requirement that is made all the more difficult by the tendency of MNCs to rotate their core leaders regularly.

59. **Be a good corporate citizen**: MNCs operating in emerging markets have the ideal opportunity to create the best of both worlds. Local talent and the broader community thrive as a result of the employment, development, advancement and global opportunities that the MNCs bring. MNCs benefit from the unique skills, culture, diversity and creativity that local talent brings to the workplace, not only in the local environment, but also globally. Employees in emerging-market countries place great store on MNCs that actively invest in their communities and respect their environments. Besides the obvious community gains involved, MNCs that invest in communities and practise sustainable development are seen as desirable, and this contributes to their attractiveness as employers of choice. Given the potential for gross disparities in power, wealth, ideology, infrastructure, education and skills in emerging markets, MNCs need to adopt a well-thought-out stakeholder engagement strategy that contributes constructively to the host countries in which they operate.

Leaders

60. **Understand the breadth of competencies required when selecting MNC leaders**: Besides the usual leadership criteria, specific characteristics of successful MNC leaders in emerging countries include high levels of emotional and cultural intelligence, resilience, political astuteness, an instinctive understanding of local markets, the ability to listen, the skill to network across the group and the host country, ethics, a common touch, humility, an absence of prejudice, and a strong and supportive family structure. Consider these criteria when assigning MNC leaders to emerging-market operations.

61. **Lead the operation with strength, compassion and fairness**: This entails the following:

- Making tough calls. Leaders have a responsibility to the business and to their people to make decisions – popular or otherwise.

- Doing what they say they will do and ensuring all plans are actioned, implemented and monitored. 'A (wo)man of words and not of deeds, is like a garden full of weeds.'

- Setting the tone at the top. Role-model inclusive leadership consistently and professionally, and expect it of others.

- Recognising that the objective is to get the job done through people, not making friends. Leaders should remain professional at all times so as not to compromise themselves.

- Downsizing with empathy and due consideration of those affected so as to maintain good working relationships with those who remain.

- Considering their footprint by ascertaining if what they are doing is really the best place to position the business, taking into account the costs associated with turnover and attracting critical talent.

Expatriates

62. **Overcome resistance to accepting emerging-market assignments**: Several measures have been used successfully to overcome employee resistance to accepting emerging-market assignments:

   - Offer attractive and globally competitive expatriate packages.
   - Include successful completion of an emerging-market assignment as a promotion criterion.
   - Include global mobility as a criterion for membership of the global talent pool.
   - Ensure effective reintegration post assignment.

63. **Agree in advance the terms and nature of the expatriate assignment**: There are three main reasons for introducing an expatriate assignment: (a) to fill positions where suitable local talent is not available; (b) to develop leaders; and (c) to transfer knowledge. Decide which of these needs are being satisfied when creating an expatriate role. Thereafter, when sending expatriates on assignment, decide beforehand whether they are to be transferred to the host country permanently or if they will return to the home country post assignment and take up another role.

64. **Learn the host-country language**: By learning the local language, expatriates enhance their ability to perform effectively and demonstrate goodwill.

65. **Approach the expatriate assignment with humility**: Expatriates are visitors in someone else's country. They need to treat their hosts with the respect, humility and dignity they deserve.

66. **Employ alternatives to expatriates**: Because of high costs, unavailability, poor adaptability and lack of local knowledge, all of which retard time-to-competence of expatriates, MNCs should seek alternative forms of recruiting foreign talent into host countries. These include hiring self-initiated movers, experienced host-country nationals, third-country nationals and already-acculturated talent, or using other forms of expatriation (eg short-term assignments, commuter assignments, international business travel, and virtual assignments).

Employing Local Talent

67. **Grow local talent**: To address the skills gap, leading MNCs embark on extensive learning and development initiatives to speed up time-to-competence of talented local employees who have the potential, but not necessarily the competencies, to occupy key positions.

68. **Adopt a reverse expatriate strategy**: Where local managers are selected to lead the local operation, send them on developmental immersions to established operations of the MNC in other countries for several months.

The HR Function

69. **Recognise the important role HR fulfils in global talent management**: HR fulfils an important role in the success of MNCs. Given the intensification of global competition, HR's role in planning and forecasting global talent needs, ensuring a ready supply of globally competent leaders to run MNCs and facilitating international learning and innovation, is significant.

70. **Ensure the right criteria are used when selecting HR professionals to operate in emerging markets**: HR professionals need to be able to deal with the levels of complexity confronting them in emerging markets. They need to be contextually aware and responsive, and ensure that their organisations are demonstrating good corporate citizenship and high levels of stakeholder engagement. They need to move effortlessly between a global mind-set and local responsiveness in the form of fit-for-purpose, localised people solutions aligned to the strategic intent of their organisations. They need to adopt a clear value position and take value-informed decisions in a world of competing ideological and values positions. Because they operate in a globalising world without boundaries, HR professionals need high levels of intercultural and diversity intelligence and awareness.

Conclusions

From these learnings, several guiding principles emerge for effective talent management for MNCs operating in emerging markets. These are outlined below:

1. Accurately predict global talent demands based on your company strategy and growth plans for the future.

2. Understand internal and external supply of talent to meet those demands.

3. Establish processes to attract, engage, develop and deploy talent in order to close any short-, medium- or long-term supply and demand gaps.

4. Strive to be a genuine employer of choice – as perceived by your employees and the future talent that you wish to attract into your organisation – to optimise talent pools across your global operation.

5. Create a high-performance, high-engagement, inclusive culture that blends the best of existing host- and home-country cultures, values and practices so that all employees in the MNC can thrive.

6. With all this in place, remember that, at its core, effective talent management depends on the nature of the relationship between individuals and their managers. Wherever possible, ensure that those key relationships are optimised.

7. Ensure that the MNC is recognised as being a force for good across its global footprint, contributing meaningfully to all communities in which it operates.

8. Finally, when operating in emerging markets, play a positive role in enhancing, rather than destroying, the environment. In the following quote, Michael Leddra (2010:22-25) provides an excellent perspective of why it is so important to be environmentally mindful, given the long and illustrious 'career' of our planet:

> We could view Mother Earth as a middle-aged lady of 46 years old, where each of her 'years' are mega-centuries (i.e. 1 year represents 100 million years).
>
> Like so many people, details of the first seven years of her life are almost completely lost, apart from a few vague memories, and a few snapshots. Towards the end of her first decade, we have a better record of some of her deeds recorded in old rocks preserved in Greenland and South Africa. Single-cell life appeared when she was 11 (based on stromatolites found in South Africa) and bacteria developed as she entered her teenage years. Like so many teenagers, much of that period is still a bit of a blur, but as she progressed through her later teens and early twenties, she gained more self-confidence, began to settle down, and got on with living. She experimented with new processes and new forms of life, some of which she would carry through to later years, whilst others, although worth trying out at the time, would be disregarded.

The first organisms containing chlorophyll did not appear until she was 26. They breathed oxygen into her atmosphere and oceans – an episode that has sometimes been termed the Big Burp – which laid the foundation for life as we know it today. At the age of 31, the first nucleated cells developed. By the time Mother Earth was 39 (at the end of the Precambrian Era), multicellular organisms had started to diversify in Australia, Europe, and North America.

Almost everything that people recognize on Earth today, including all substantial animal life, is the product of just the last six years of her life. By the time she was 40, animals with hard parts (bones, teeth, etc.) had developed, as witnessed by the fossils discovered in China and Canada (the Burgess Shale). Fish appeared when she was 41, but the land surface was virtually lifeless until she was almost 42, after which mosses started to invade the hitherto bare continents. Within the next six months ferns appeared, there was an explosion of aquatic life, and insects had arrived on the scene. A year later immense forests of tree ferns covered her body, dragonflies with 3-foot wingspans took to the air, and amphibians and amniotes (egg-layers) roamed her surface. Life, at last, had truly broken free of the water. At the age of 44, she went through another one of her fads when she fell in love with reptiles and her pets included the dinosaurs. Within six months, the first known birds had taken flight, together with bees and beetles. The break-up of the last supercontinent was in progress. It was nearly a year later before she noted the arrival of flowering plants and the planet began to take on the appearance we see today.

Six months ago, dinosaurs went out of favour and she turned her attention to mammals, which largely replaced them in her affections. Primitive tools, found in Ethiopia, indicate that two and a half months ago 'intelligent life' began to interfere with her landscape. About ten days ago, some man-like apes, living in Africa, turned into ape-like men. Last weekend, she began to shiver her way through the latest, but by no means the only cold period in her life. Around four hours ago, a new, upstart species of animal, calling itself Homo Sapiens, took their first tentative steps in trying to take over the Earth. In the last hour, they invented agriculture and began to turn their back on a nomadic life style. It was only a quarter of an hour ago, that Moses and the Israelites crossed the Red Sea, and it is less than ten minutes since Jesus preached in the same area. The Industrial Revolution began less than two minutes ago, but in that brief time, out of the lady's 46 'years', we have managed to use up a substantial proportion of her resources – many of which she had taken a significant proportion of her life to produce. It is only in the last 10 seconds that we have begun to understand the nature of Mother Earth and the damage we are doing to her and her atmosphere. How many more seconds will it be before we start to treat her with the respect she deserves?

References

Bluen, SD. 2004. Global Human Resource Management: the SABMiller Story, in *Building Human Capital: South African Perspectives*, edited by I Boninelli and TNA Meyer. Johannesburg: Knowledge Resources.

Collings, DG, Scullion, H & Morley, MJ. 2007. Changing Patterns of Global Staffing in the Multinational Enterprise: Challenges to the Conventional Expatriate Assignment and Emerging Alternatives. *Journal of World Business* 42:198-213.

Haslberger, A & Brewster, C. 2008. The Expatriate Family: an International Perspective. *Journal of Managerial Psychology* 23(3):324-346.

Leddra, M. 2010. *Time Matters: Geology's Legacy to Scientific Thought*. John Wiley & Sons.

Nightingale, F, John, DR & Girija Swaraj P. 2009. Google's HR Practices: a Strategic Edge? IBS Research Center, Ref: 408-057-1.

SABMiller. 2010. The SABMiller Talent Management Way: an End-to-end Guide. Internal company document.

The Phrase Finder. 2012. Silver Bullet. University of Liverpool. http://www.phrases.org.uk/meanings/silver-bullet.html)

INDEX

A

Accenture 29, 37, 44–45, 50, 52, 66–67, 109, 114, 127
Accountability 4, 20, 52, 119, 171, 186, 213, 228, 235, 237, 245–247, 249–250, 263, 286, 340
Ackerman, Raymond 260–262, 271
Action learning 50, 99, 114, 337
Admired companies, most 26, 274
Africa focus 300, 307
African countries 20, 44, 174–175, 179, 241, 243, 256, 269–271, 299
AGA (AngloGold Ashanti) 8, 203, 231–234, 236–240, 242–246, 251–258
Allowances 172, 174–175, 326
Already-acculturated talent 64, 351
Analysis 16, 58–59, 70, 72, 129, 131, 213–214, 238, 283, 318
Analytics 58–60
AngloGold Ashanti (see AGA)
Angola 23, 80, 207, 264, 307, 317
Appointment, external 239, 341
Appreciative Inquiry (AI) 290–291
Approaches
  developmental 53
  new 216–217, 226, 228, 233
Areas
  strategic 301, 305
  technical/functional knowledge 118–119
Assessment 7, 79, 103–104, 117, 119, 134, 164–166, 250–251
Assets 8–9, 180, 231–232, 296
Assignees 139, 141–142, 144–151
  international 37, 64, 139, 141–142, 150
Assignments 2, 38, 45, 47, 50, 54–55, 63–64, 66, 80, 83, 139, 141–142, 220–222, 247–248, 335
Attitudes 83, 133, 190, 194, 197–199, 307, 315, 318, 325, 336
Australia 8, 167, 207, 231, 241, 243, 255, 257, 263–264, 353
Awareness 106–107, 109, 256, 284, 351

B

Balance 19, 117, 154, 173, 183, 261, 308, 330
Balance sheet 339–340, 345–346
Balance sheet approach 54
Barrett Values Survey 168, 178, 291, 293
Base salary, home-country 147, 150
BAT (British American Tobacco) 10, 311, 314–315, 317–318, 324
Behaviours 6–7, 78–79, 83, 87–88, 93, 111, 113, 119, 121, 123–124, 134, 159, 252, 291–292, 324–325
Best Employers South Africa competition 209
Best practices 6, 27, 32, 40, 60, 92, 104–106, 108–109, 111, 116, 127, 152, 210, 212, 217
BPF (Business Process Framework) 234–235, 242, 245, 257
Brands 7, 38, 101, 111, 155, 173, 180, 257, 265, 267, 273, 301, 319
Brazilian companies 274
BRIC countries 2, 16, 18, 29, 36, 86, 96, 179–180
British American Tobacco (see BAT)
Broad-banding 160–162
Budgets 32, 149, 223, 289–290, 334
Building blocks 116, 182
Build-up method (BM) 142–149
Business
  changing 233, 301
  doing good is good 261, 270
  family-controlled 8, 264
  international 37, 65, 351
  local 67, 168, 189, 332
  new 19, 61, 223, 264
Business agenda 280, 304
Business case 40–41, 56 92, 347
Business challenges 99, 100, 102, 111, 215
Business context 14, 162, 243
Business environment 17, 20, 28, 45
Business framework 233
Business goals 117, 143, 231, 235, 244, 339-340
Business language 81, 283, 289

Business model   25, 41, 204, 210, 221, 226
Business operations   318, 323
Business partner   185, 210
Business performance   32, 39–40, 53, 70, 227, 277, 347
  sustain world-class   324
Business performance goals   118–120
Business plan   30, 41, 109, 133–134, 300–301
  5-year   340
  corporate   70, 331
  organisation's   118
  strategic   39, 61
Business planning   89, 218, 227, 339
Business practices   50, 260, 268
  innovative   17
Business problems   170, 252
Business processes   234–235, 257
Business realities   105, 107
Business requirements   301, 306
Business results   9, 100, 209, 252
  better   6, 78
Business schools   50
Business strategy   10, 30, 39–42, 73, 111, 117, 134, 201, 209, 212–213, 227, 269, 280, 300, 303, 312, 317, 323, 331–332
Business trip   140
Business unit   26, 30, 61–62, 162, 166, 172, 213, 238, 250, 333, 340–342
Business world   20, 274, 337

C

CAC (Current Applied Capability)   248–249, 251
Calibre   41–42, 207, 222, 342
Canada   46, 102–103, 130, 241, 255, 353
Candidates   88, 106, 150, 172, 208, 223, 228, 238, 245, 254, 257
Capabilities   23, 42, 61, 109, 112, 166, 210, 217, 244–245, 250, 252, 296, 301, 307–309, 315–316, 331
Capacity building   194, 199, 201, 308
Career development   34, 49–50, 125, 150, 212–214, 218, 249–251, 319, 326, 332, 337
Case studies   7–8, 203, 231, 259, 307
Categories   17–18, 30, 121, 155, 174, 176, 192, 238, 274, 278, 308
CEMEX   25

CEOs (chief executive officers)   1–2, 32–33, 45–47, 58, 67, 86, 100, 102, 116, 227, 232, 274
Challenges
  cultural   10, 311
  industry   103–105
  unique   36, 38–39, 50, 163
Challenges of global talent management   36
Change management   237, 323, 331
ChemChina   36
Cheque, 13th   147–148
Chief executive officers (see CEOs)
Children   55, 64, 110, 148, 175, 221, 225, 262, 276, 335
Chile   17–18, 20–21, 255
Chinese employees   50–51, 93
Chinese organisations   50, 55
Coach   112, 117, 246, 295
Coaching   62, 119, 170, 211, 219, 246–249, 253, 257, 290, 319, 321
COL (cost of living)   141, 145, 150
Collaboration   104–105, 109, 111–112, 301–302, 309, 311
Commitment   24, 49, 78, 90, 91, 93 140, 172, 192, 218, 237, 246, 267–270, 300–301, 312, 314, 327–328
Communities   56, 73, 77, 85, 90, 93, 95, 106, 151, 192–193, 225, 232, 238, 260–262, 349
Companies
  best-managed   26
  capital-strong   189, 193
  dynamic-market   5, 23
  gold-mining   8, 231
  great   208, 219
  leading   1, 26
  mature   236, 295
  multinational/global   189–190
  national   192–193
  parent   129, 299
  successful   6, 26
  upcoming   189, 193
Company performance   4, 82, 138, 321
Compensation   73, 82, 115, 127–128, 132, 136, 151, 154, 160–162
Compensation strategies   128, 134, 160
Competence   10, 82, 84, 87, 94, 118–120, 158, 165, 192, 211, 224, 241, 312, 321, 327–328, 347

Competency domains   194, 196–197

Competition   2, 25, 33, 43, 67–68, 109, 129,
    136, 216, 275, 305, 307, 312

Competitive advantage   2–3, 40, 59, 70, 74, 118,
    127, 154, 157, 210, 263, 300–302, 337

Competitiveness   15, 18–22, 163–164, 176, 229

Competitors   2–3, 34, 46, 54, 100, 136, 155,
    236–237, 265–267, 270, 274, 305

Complexity   5, 14, 19, 23, 32, 36, 42, 60, 68, 78,
    87, 89, 115, 216–217, 249–250

Components   5–6, 10, 38–39, 41, 51, 60, 62, 70,
    128–129, 131, 136, 208, 217, 249, 318

Conduct   188, 194, 197–199, 233, 338

Consumers   92, 100–101, 107–108, 261–262, 270

Context   38–39, 56, 84, 85, 99, 119, 127, 129,
    131–132, 139, 163–164, 166–168, 174,
    177, 182–184, 190, 206

Conversations   126, 167, 279, 283, 286,
    295–296

Core business   112, 299

Core principles   260, 266, 268

Corporate culture   9, 25, 70, 118, 338, 348

Corruption   23, 37, 171, 187–188, 192, 201

Cost-of-living (COL) index   141–143

CPC (Current Potential Capability)   248–251

Critical features of ECs (emerging countries)   181,
    185, 193, 200

Critical skills   238, 331, 333

Cultural differences   57, 167–168, 178, 336, 348

Culture   38, 58, 100, 113, 156, 167, 178, 212,
    227, 275, 280, 291, 327

Customers   1, 6, 8, 24–25, 33, 51, 56, 93,
    99–101, 103–104, 111, 122, 260–261,
    268, 300–301

D

Decisions   4, 30, 32, 58–60, 84, 89, 120–
    121,123, 129, 134, 153, 215, 226, 228,
    250–252, 319–320

Defining talent management   1

Developed countries   29, 35–36, 64, 86, 179,
    188–189, 191, 193, 206, 330

Developing countries   29, 36, 39, 41, 46, 48–50,
    63, 71, 201, 225, 312

Development of local talent   51, 83, 92

Development plans
  individual (IDPs)   31, 121-122, 211, 213, 214,
    236, 251, 275, 321, 337, 342

Development strategy   224, 229, 307

Differences   5, 46, 69, 77, 91, 115, 139, 141,
    154, 163–164, 168, 175, 220, 260–261,
    348

Discipline   16, 166, 242, 250, 252–253, 290,
    293

Diversity   4–6, 17, 31, 35, 40, 55–57, 71, 77–78,
    85, 89–91, 93, 95, 319, 323–324, 345

Diversity management   55, 91, 96, 325

Domains   66, 171, 197–199, 256, 276, 284,
    289–291, 294

Domestic firms   32, 156

DRC   23, 264

Drivers, strategic value   231–232

Driving business performance   332

Dynamic companies   164, 178

Dynamic-market champions   23, 25, 27

Dynamic-market rankings   21–22

E

EC (emerging country)   190, 192–193, 199

EC-fit people professional   194–197, 199–200

Economies   1, 14–20, 28–29, 48, 66, 179,
    187–188, 190, 240
  developing   15, 102, 202

Educational differences   164–165

Effective diversity management   87, 89

Effective performance management   161, 322

Effectiveness   8, 20, 136, 238, 244, 247–248, 291
  intercultural   61

Emerging markets
  competitive   334

Emerging markets and defining dynamic markets
    15

Emerging world order   181–182, 185, 195, 197,
    200

Emerging-market assignments   2, 47, 64, 350

Emerging-market talent management learnings
    11, 329

Emerging-market talent strategy   42, 55, 60

Employee benefits   132, 137

Employee career planning   121, 338

Employee compensation   128, 134

Employee currency election   142, 146

Employee development   125, 245, 338

Employee engagement   68, 73, 90, 112, 214,
    218, 236, 242–243, 245, 309, 336

Employee engagement systems 234
Employee job performance 121, 125
Employee performance 117
  improving 128, 339
Employee relations 72, 183
Employee strengths 121, 338
Employee talent reviews 214
Employees
  diverse 78, 87
  expatriate 82, 174–175
  full-time 266
  global 34, 178
  high-quality 128, 339
  host 83
  individual 71, 117, 158, 212, 245
  key 49, 59
  long-serving 223, 321
  managing 150, 252
  new 51, 127, 266
  potential 46, 257
  prospective 128, 131, 136, 208, 237, 266
  skilled 53
  talented 136
  talented local 219, 351
Employer brand 49, 64, 69, 73, 136
Employers 27, 31, 48, 78, 81, 83, 86, 111, 128,
    136–137, 147, 154, 172–175, 177, 208
  global 163, 172–173, 176, 178
Employment 7, 44, 71, 78, 139–140, 150, 154,
    189–190, 265–266, 349
Employment value proposition (EVP) 2, 31, 33,
    49, 131-132, 136, 171, 173, 175, 191, 194,
    199, 257, 300, 332–334, 336, 338
Energy 6, 24, 219, 276, 279, 281, 284, 287, 332, 348
Engagement 7, 8, 10, 30–31, 47, 78, 91,
    93–94, 166–167, 170, 182, 185, 192, 247,
    313–314, 327, 336, 342–343, 345–346
Espoused values 292–293
Europe 7, 85, 204–205, 207, 215–217, 220,
    223–224, 274, 281, 353
Evaluation of employees 159, 337
Exchange rate 141–143, 145
Exclusive behaviours 77, 90–91, 347
Executive committee 213, 226–228, 345
Executives 2, 37, 41, 57, 62, 81, 101, 105, 107,
    138, 166, 172–173, 204, 226, 295
Expansion 24–25, 205, 207, 243, 259, 264–265,
    303

Expatriate assignments 46–47, 54, 81, 176, 256,
    346, 350
Expatriate benefits 78, 175–176
Expatriate compensation 75, 80
Expatriate costs 37, 63
Expatriate deployment 78–79
Expatriate failure 63, 83
Expatriate families 46, 64, 73, 80, 175, 335, 354
Expatriate management 96, 174
Expatriate managers 63, 74–75, 79–80, 94
Expatriate performance 63, 97
Expatriate remuneration 144, 151
Expatriate replacement 174–175
Expatriate spouses 65, 221
Expatriate success 65, 97
Expatriate workforce 79
Expatriate-local employee relationship 79, 82
Expatriates
  global 168, 172, 175
  hand-picked 41, 204
  on-boarding 46–47
  self-initiated 83, 96
  successful 83, 220
  using 62, 66
Expatriation 65, 82, 211, 222, 351
Expectations 48, 55, 87–89, 91, 115, 118–120,
    122, 125, 128, 156, 184, 227, 312
Experiences
  project 308–309
  working 251, 256
External pipeline 238–239, 244, 254, 331

F

Factors, critical success 10, 149, 183, 327
Failure 3–4, 44, 63, 166, 310
Families 24, 46, 56, 62, 64, 82, 86, 140, 149,
    151, 174–175, 221–222, 225, 263, 287, 335
Feedback 117–119, 122–123, 228, 246, 257,
    279, 316, 319, 323
Female talent in emerging markets 86
Figure, authority 165, 167–168
Finance 180, 236, 254–256
FMCGs (fast-moving consumer goods) 109,
    273–274, 296
Footprint, global 7–8, 29, 39–40, 61, 66, 352
Framework 5, 7, 29, 59, 73, 116, 133, 136, 161,
    190, 234, 285, 288–289, 321

Framework for managing talent in emerging
    markets 39
Functions 4, 31, 61, 89, 111, 117, 157, 169,
    181, 185–186, 194–195, 211, 226, 250,
    340–342

G

Game changers 301, 306, 337
Gaps 34, 37, 52, 95, 134, 193, 213, 239–240,
    252, 288, 292–293, 302, 320–321, 339
GDP (gross domestic product) 19, 21–22
Gender 35, 55, 69, 87, 89, 95, 111, 220, 319
General management 14, 17, 24
Generations 24, 35, 55, 69, 232, 257, 262,
    276–277
GLC (Global Leadership Centre) 304–305
Global business 1, 50, 164, 169–170, 172, 205,
    335
Global companies 3–4, 8, 13, 32, 47–48, 52,
    163-166, 168-173, 190, 276, 303
Global Competitive Index (GCI) 18–19
Global economy 14–17, 44
Global expansion 7, 70, 207, 210–211, 214–215
Global growth generators 16
Global leaders 40, 61, 309, 342
  developing 62, 72, 74, 95
Global model for talent management 74, 229
Global performance management 118, 160, 161,
    338
Global talent management 33, 72–75, 205, 226,
    231, 351
Global talent management case study 8, 203
Global talent pool 330–331, 333, 343, 350
Global trends 201, 338
Globalisation 6, 64, 69, 115, 129, 181, 202,
    204–205, 207, 216, 236
Goals 54, 67, 116, 119, 123–125, 138, 168,
    212, 224–225, 242, 244, 250, 293, 296
Gordon Institute of Business Science (GIBS) 50,
    103
Governance 5, 14, 17–18, 20–23, 28, 133,
    153–154, 201, 216, 243, 290, 332
Graduates 37, 44, 47, 170, 236, 239, 241, 255,
    261, 302, 334
  engineering 44, 254–255
Greatest managers 71–72, 95
Grid, performance-potential 213–214, 341

Growth and value 74, 97
Growth markets 14, 16
Guanxi 93–94

H

Have-nots 7, 191–194
Haves 191–194
HCL Technologies 108, 113–114
HDI (Human Development Index) 18–19
Headcount, total 341, 343
Heidelberg factory, BAT 10, 317–319, 323,
    325–327
High-flyers 2–3, 30, 209
High-level skills 188
High-potential employees 43, 45, 49–50, 52–53,
    57–58, 65–67, 71, 150, 331, 333–334
Hiring 27, 37, 44, 57, 64–66, 223, 265, 351
History, organisation's 168, 303
HIV/AIDS 225
Home 2, 5, 18, 27, 35, 67, 80–81, 96, 108, 145–
    146, 150–151, 164, 174, 176, 219–220
Home base 50, 141, 146–147, 150
Home country 27, 46, 50, 53, 63, 65, 71, 139,
    141–142, 144, 146–147, 149–151, 163,
    176, 190
Home currency 143, 146
Home markets 1, 17, 23, 25–26, 107
Home net salary 141, 142, 143, 145
Home-country retirement scheme 147
Host currency 143, 146
Host-country policy 145–147
HR professionals 40, 44, 351
HR system 345
HRD (human resource development) 73, 183
Human attributes of emerging markets 348
Human capital trends 73, 201
Human development index (HDI) 18–19
Human resource development (HRD) 73, 183
Human resource management 75, 127, 130,
    159, 161–162
Human resources planning subsystem 238
Hypothetical tax, 141, 143, 145

I

Improvements 125–126, 206, 242, 247–248,
    275, 286, 325–326, 346

Incentive schemes   136, 138
Inclusive leadership   5–6, 13, 77–78, 84, 87,
      89–91, 94–97, 311, 350
Indonesia   16–19, 22, 130
Industrial and Commercial Bank of China (ICBC)
      9, 21, 299
Industries   51, 60, 94, 99, 101, 104–105, 108,
      116, 127, 129, 134, 158, 209, 237,
      253–256
Information   23, 61, 82, 88, 104, 109, 117,
      121–124, 141, 155, 158, 168, 213, 218,
      321–323
Infosys   21, 26–27
Infrastructure   10, 188, 193, 225, 289, 311,
      317–318, 349
Initiatives, strategic   32–33, 305
In-Market Action Learning   6, 13, 50, 99–102,
      103, 107 108, 110–113, 337
In-market business challenges   111
Innovation   5, 14–15, 17–18, 20–22, 24–25, 28,
      35, 90–91, 100–101, 105, 108, 111–113,
      130, 132, 134, 180–181
INSEAD   20–22
Insights   23, 59–60, 101, 102, 104-106, 108,
      111–112, 161, 215, 252, 306
Inspiration   273, 276, 281, 283, 285
Intelligence, emotional   81, 95–96, 335
Interconnectedness   14, 20–22, 27, 100
International assignments   54, 62–63, 81, 83, 86,
      139–141, 144, 148, 150, 226, 308, 334
International experience   63, 65, 74, 217, 280
International Leadership Development Programme
      (see ILDP)   103-104, 106
International premium   142–143, 145, 239
International remuneration   6, 139
Internationally mobile expatriate   144–145,
      147–149
Interventions   5, 77, 211, 244, 273, 281, 285,
      288–292, 312
Interview   125–126, 165–166, 215, 228, 236,
      257, 335
Investments   25, 27, 40–41, 48, 92, 109, 149,
      241, 261, 263, 277, 297, 304, 318, 346

J

Job performance   87, 117, 119, 125, 159, 337
Jobs, top   86, 267

Journeys   9, 218, 273, 278–282, 293–297
Judgements   88, 100, 157, 208, 250–252

K

Key components of talent management in
      emerging markets   5, 13
Key employee challenges   266
Key performance dimensions   194–196
Key performance indicators (KPIs)   10, 32,91,
      314, 318, 340–347
Key result areas (KRAs)   122, 322
Key result indicators (KRIs)   122
Key role players   5, 39–40, 60, 70
Key skills   240
Knowledge   3, 27, 50, 52, 61, 63, 66, 77,
      101, 154, 194, 196–199, 227, 248–249,
      251–252
   technical   253, 303
Knowledge society   180, 200
Knowledge workers   68, 85
Knowledge-based approach   74–75

L

Labour, local   79–80
Labour costs   128–129, 136, 339
Labour turnover   3, 35, 47–49, 127, 333, 341, 343
Language   55, 60–61, 81, 96, 164–165, 174–175,
      283–284, 292, 315, 319, 321–322
Leaders
   business   6, 28, 32, 36, 39, 141, 219, 305,
      335
Leadership, nurturing   259–260
Leadership brand   169, 178
Leadership capability   301, 303–305, 321
Leadership challenges   102, 108
Leadership development   5, 9, 50–51, 60, 77, 99,
      102, 169, 289–290, 301, 304, 313, 337
Leadership style   90, 94, 96, 210, 215, 320, 346
Leadership team   9, 287, 297, 307, 313,
      325–326, 333
Learning culture, positive   347–348
Learning solutions   211, 224
Life cycle stages   134–135
Limited supply of talent in emerging markets   127
Line managers   4, 5, 32, 182, 184, 209–211, 228,
      238–239, 302–303, 306, 309, 332

Line ownership 233, 235
Local companies 86, 189, 205
Local cultures 57–58, 79, 118, 338
Local employees 38–40, 42, 46, 50, 53–54, 66, 79–83, 93, 151–152, 166, 169, 175–176, 178, 190, 345–347
Local markets 26, 50, 130, 142, 144, 308, 311, 349
Local talent 256, 302, 307–309, 314, 349, 351
Localisation 39–40, 55–56, 66, 82, 93, 176, 221–222, 243, 333, 345, 347
Local-market approach 142, 144–149
Local-market remuneration levels 142, 144
Long-term incentives (LTIs) 135, 137–138, 172, 178, 339

M

Management, local business unit 172
Management approach 29, 39, 71, 190, 226, 348
Management challenges 30, 70, 177
Management control 210
Management development 51, 61, 155
Management framework 233–235
Management practices 15, 118, 210
Management processes 39, 169, 228
Management review 96–97
Management skills 306, 321, 337
Management strategy 10, 60, 70, 94, 244
Management systems 26, 217
Management teams 237, 320, 327
Manager-employee relationship 71
Managerial leadership 8, 247
Managers
  employee's 245
  local 67, 79, 170, 221, 351
Managing director 208–209, 215, 222–223
Managing local talent in emerging markets 7, 13
Managing performance 31, 39, 52, 53, 202
Managing talent in emerging markets 7, 11, 39, 203, 329
Manufacturing 206, 210–211, 216–217, 220, 254, 317
Market capitalisation 19, 27
Market data 157, 302
Market opportunities 32–33
Market pricing 157–158

Marketplace 32, 236, 296
  global 129
Markets
  high-growth 111
  mature 1, 17, 96, 216
Matching employee capability to role complexity 250
Measurement 115–117, 212, 249
Missing link 5–6, 13, 77–78, 87
MNC leaders 34, 61, 78, 87, 336, 346
Mobile expatriates 142, 146,152
Model of talent management in emerging markets 38
MOR (manager once removed) 237, 245–246, 251
Motivation of employees 10, 130, 327
Multinational companies (MNCs) 1-7, 10, 29, 32-35, 37-52, 54-61, 63-72, 75, 77-80, 83-83, 86, 93-94, 116, 164, 179, 189, 191, 206, 223, 274, 281, 311–313, 330-336, 340, 348-349, 351-352

N

Nepotism 45, 47
New markets 16, 23–25, 27, 46, 66, 107, 135, 309
Nongovernmental organisation 106, 225

O

Objectives 82, 116–117, 122, 134, 137, 156, 169–170, 213, 238, 245, 295–296, 331, 338
Ongoing process 118, 120, 327
Operating arena 179, 182–183, 185, 193–195, 200
Operations 8–9, 24–26, 42, 46, 68, 71, 78, 170, 206, 210–211, 226, 231, 259, 264, 273
  emerging-market 345–346, 349
  international 4, 32
Organisation design 109, 222, 235, 245
Organisation development (OD) 7, 9, 232, 273, 281, 288, 291
Organisation product life cycle 133–134
Organisation values 237, 291
Organisational capabilities 180
Organisational Change and Development

Practitioners 180
Organisational commitment 55, 156
Organisational culture 31, 39–40, 46. 52, 57,58,
    91, 117, 127, 132, 173, 313, 338, 345
Organisational development 231, 234, 237, 331
Organisational dynamics 161, 199
Organisational goals 53, 131, 134, 162, 245
Organisational infrastructure 292
Organisational memory 180, 254
Organisational performance 129, 153
Organisational requirements 120, 131
Organisational reward systems 127, 339
Organisational strategy 131, 133–134
Organisational structures 58, 222
Organisational values 28, 246
Organisations
  emerging 189, 194
  emerging-market 2
  high-performing 116, 344
  leading 152, 338
  leading African financial services 300–301
  local 168–169, 189
  world's top 99, 108
Outputs 39, 116, 122, 173, 185, 212–214, 224,
    242, 246, 344

P

Participants 103–105, 107–108, 110–112, 123
Parties 81–83, 315
Partners 6, 46, 62, 64, 73, 80, 99–100, 103, 164,
    168, 220, 255, 335
People balance sheet (PBS) 213–214, 340
People Generalist 182–184
People leadership 182–183
People management 162, 202
People Professionals 7, 180–185, 194–196,
    199–200
People Professionals fit for emerging countries 7,
    13
People Specialist 182–183
Performance
  individual 53, 90, 123, 137, 146, 347
  organisation's 104
  poor 87, 89, 118, 263
Performance appraisals 91, 116–118, 120–121,
    125-127, 159–161, 247. 322, 344
Performance culture 116, 277

Performance dimensions 121, 123, 125,
    194–195
Performance feedback 116, 118
Performance goals 118, 125, 212
Performance management 6, 52–53, 93, 115–
    119, 127, 136, 159–161, 212, 214–215,
    229, 245, 290, 337–338, 344
Performance management approaches 31, 159
Performance management cycle 118–119
Performance management framework 120
Performance management process 116, 120, 306
Performance management system 6, 53,
    116–117, 138, 160, 173, 338
Performance period 119–120
Performance planning 118–119
Performance-related pay (PRP) 156, 338
Personal attributes 194, 197–199
Personal commitment of employees 242, 336
Personal growth 9, 259–260, 268, 279–280,
    292–293
Personal-effectiveness appraisals 246, 248
Perspective
  external 100–101
  fresh 100–102, 239
Planning 35, 58, 60, 119–120, 227, 247, 257,
    290, 321–322, 351
Poland 18, 165, 168, 205, 207, 215–216, 311,
    314
Policies 14, 56, 64, 82, 90, 93, 133, 136, 139,
    160, 172, 175, 262, 264
Population, unemployed 190, 193
Positions 2–3, 18, 20, 23, 25, 26, 30, 42–43, 48,
    53, 62, 81, 92, 227–228, 308–309, 350
PPR (People Professional Requirements) 185,
    193–194, 197–199
Prejudice 55–56, 71, 165, 220, 313, 335, 347,
    349
Prilucky factory 10, 311–312, 315
Principles 8, 14, 17, 24, 66, 142, 162, 168, 176,
    237–238, 251, 259–260, 264–266, 335, 338
Processes
  career-development 212–213
  performance appraisal 120
Processes/practices 183–184
Production 4, 10, 16, 33, 82, 189, 210–211,
    239, 242–243, 246, 311–312, 317, 322
Productivity 10, 15–16, 46, 90, 92, 117, 133,
    240–243, 318, 326–327

Programmes 51, 53, 64, 103–104, 106–107, 111, 169–170, 212, 225, 277, 285, 302, 304, 307, 324
Promotions, internal 239, 325, 333, 341
PRP (Performance-related pay) 156, 338
Psychometric assessments 207–208, 214, 218, 224, 335

Q

Quality 2, 18–20, 26, 34, 40–41, 44, 62, 68, 121, 123, 130, 172, 280–281, 303–304, 324–325

R

Ranking 19–23, 26, 122, 168
Rapid growth of emerging markets 330
Rate, expatriate failure 37, 62, 346
Rate of change 341
Rating 117, 121–122, 125, 213
Realities 101–102, 105, 107, 337
Recommendations 104, 106, 116, 168–169, 175–176, 326
Recruitment 3, 30, 35–36, 41, 43–44, 58–59, 68, 128, 131, 165, 208–209, 211, 212, 216, 223, 239, 319, 333–335, 339, 351
Region 10, 16, 29, 31, 34, 48, 56, 106, 128, 130, 170, 172, 177, 215–216, 228
Relocation 82–83, 148
Remuneration 6, 48, 83, 115, 127–135–142, 144–149, 152–153, 159–160, 173, 247–248, 326, 338, 344
Remuneration policy 133, 135–136, 153
  international-assignment 141–142, 144, 151
Remuneration strategy 134–135, 152, 160, 172, 338
Remuneration systems 115, 129–130
Renewal 273, 281, 283–284
Repatriates 37, 63–65, 71, 74, 97, 331
Reputation, organisation's 136, 180
Required behaviours 249, 251–252
Research 75, 80–81, 83, 85–86, 90–91, 127, 129, 136, 138–139, 149–150, 160, 227, 255, 266, 270
Resistance 193, 288–290, 293, 325, 350
Responsibility, social 170–171, 178, 261
Retail 103, 105–106, 109, 205–206, 266–267

Retention 6, 7, 31, 34, 47–49, 52, 68, 70–72, 78–79, 85, 88, 94, 106, 153, 256–257, 321, 333–334, 338, 342–343
Review 39, 59, 80, 97, 99, 119, 165, 169, 176, 213, 233, 235, 242, 247, 294–295
Reward and remuneration 127–128
Reward innovation 259–260
Reward management 130–131, 160
Reward strategy 131–134, 138
Reward systems 116, 129–131, 133, 337–338
Rewards 131–132, 140, 143
Role complexity 250
Role of talent management in SABMiller 7, 203
Russia 16, 18, 29, 36–37, 55, 63, 86–87, 130, 172–173, 179, 207, 299

S

SAB (South African Breweries) 25–26, 41, 53, 204–216, 218–219, 222–224, 229
SABMiller (SABM) 8, 25–26, 47, 74, 170–171, 204, 206, 207–209, 212, 214–220, 224–228, 229, 340, 354
SABMiller Talent Management Way 229, 354
Salary 53, 63, 120, 123, 127, 130, 135, 137, 141, 155, 158, 240, 265, 338
  home-base 144–145, 147–148
Same-language expatriates 175–177
Scarce skills 221, 239–240, 256
Scheme 136, 138, 154, 172, 177, 314, 344
Scores 23, 122, 171, 224, 320, 345–346
Sectors 20, 102–106, 236, 255–256
  banking 102–103
Segments, critical talent 343
Selection process 103–104, 301, 335
Senior executives 6, 70, 105–106, 108, 112, 172, 226–228, 304
Senior leadership team 294
Sequencing 285–286
Sessions 104, 107, 170, 251, 294, 320–321
  residential 107–108
Shop floor 160, 312–313, 336
Situational adaptability 85, 89
Skilled labour 48, 240, 330
Skills
  inclusive leadership 91
  new 69, 157
Skills development 102, 328

Skills levels 189, 194

Solutions 38, 41–46, 48, 50, 53–56, 58–61, 64, 66, 69, 73, 89–91, 96, 104, 232, 320–321

SORs (subordinates once removed) 245–246, 248, 251

South African operations 41, 204, 208, 264, 270

South Africa's top employers 209

South America 206, 216, 220, 223–224, 281

SP (System for People) 234–235, 238, 244–246, 249, 251–253, 257

Spending 143, 145, 242

Spouses 56, 65, 80–81, 151, 221, 225

Stability, political 18, 20, 23

Staff 10, 36, 68, 88, 93, 100, 107, 124, 156, 242–243, 259–260, 312–314, 323, 325–326, 336
  local 82, 308, 314

Stakeholders 77, 100, 103, 170, 183, 187, 192–194, 197, 199, 262

Standard Bank Group 9, 203, 299–305, 307–310

Standard Chartered Bank 51–52

Statement, global organisation's values 169

Story of organisational and personal renewal 9, 203

Strategic objectives 32, 245, 328, 330

Strategic planning 14–15, 24

Strengths 121, 126, 277, 280, 291–292, 316, 319, 324, 335, 348–349

Structure 38, 104, 107, 111–112, 125, 127–128, 131, 142, 145, 154–155, 157–158, 172, 174, 176, 222

Subordinates 122, 245–248

Succession 40, 214, 218, 227–228, 308, 339

Succession planning 30, 39, 42–43, 49, 213, 252, 321, 332–333, 340–341

Supervisors 118, 122, 222, 243, 321–322, 324–326

Supply 2, 10, 33, 35–36, 53, 59, 163, 188, 215, 238, 252, 255, 267, 311, 330

Systemic 70, 195–199, 252

Systemic imbalances 7, 188, 190, 193–194

T

Talent
  developing 274–275, 292, 331, 337, 348
  emerging 304, 309
  executive 274

high-potential 301–302, 306, 331
  skilled 330
  young 254, 274

Talent demands 306, 334

Talent development 227, 305, 326

Talent dimension 341–347

Talent focus area, key questions 30–32

Talent information systems 32, 60

Talent management 1, 4–5, 7, 13, 32, 73–74, 97, 163, 203, 229, 245–246, 252, 305–306, 331–332, 346
  effective 300, 352

Talent management business case 332, 340

Talent management challenges 60, 309, 330

Talent management framework 330

Talent management in AngloGold Ashanti 8, 203

Talent management perspective 273–275, 277, 287

Talent management processes 295, 310, 332

Talent Management Way 217–218

Talent pool 41, 237, 245, 301, 305, 307, 331, 333–334, 340, 348

Talent pool development 244–245

Talent pool process 251

Talent processes 303, 332

Talent review process 301, 306

Talent strategy 40, 300–301, 303, 306, 328, 331–332, 337, 339, 340, 348

Targets 340–347

Tata 24–25, 108–109

Tax position 140

Team leaders 325–326

Teams, virtual 309

Teamwork 44, 158, 235, 247, 249, 301, 309, 325

Technology 10, 180, 188–189, 238, 240, 311, 317–318, 327–328

Third World 15, 241

Timeless values 260, 268

Tools 2, 6, 118, 141, 159, 214, 224, 291, 293, 332, 342

Top management 263, 269, 340

Top talent 190, 257, 264, 266

Total management system 233, 331

Total reward (TR) 130–134, 136, 140, 143, 146, 161–162, 339

Trainees 208, 212, 278, 280

Training 24, 26, 37, 41, 43, 48, 73, 75, 83, 116, 118, 120–121, 247–248, 266–267, 318

Transformation
cultural 10, 280–281, 327
fundamental 186–187, 193, 276, 291
strategic business/people 182–183
Transition 103, 107, 169, 178, 180, 205, 252, 256, 259, 296, 311
Trends 6, 15, 45, 47, 69, 127, 152, 155, 158, 161, 163, 169, 172, 179–180, 254
Turkey 16–21, 24–26, 85, 87, 299
Turnover 46, 137, 238, 344, 350

U

UAE (United Arab Emirates) 17, 55–56, 86–87, 130
Uganda 207, 210, 225, 299
Ukraine 10, 311–315, 318
Underpinning processes 5, 39–40, 55, 70
Understanding 17, 55, 61, 87, 89, 92, 101, 105, 107–108, 110, 118, 198–199, 240, 244, 305–306
UNDP (United Nations Development Programme) 18, 21–22
Unilever 9, 175–176, 273, 275, 278, 280–281, 291-293, 294
Unilever Organisation, ONE 274, 281, 296
United Kingdom (UK) 73–74, 85, 86, 88, 90, 93, 97, 103, 142, 171–172, 229, 255
United Nations Development Programme (UNDP) 18, 21–22
United States of America (US/USA) 15, 44, 47, 50, 72, 81, 85–86, 92, 95, 97, 130, 142, 161, 167, 172, 207, 216, 297
Utilities 146, 254

V

Vacancies 3, 30, 43, 239, 254, 303, 309, 333–334, 341
Value chain 5–6, 26, 70, 100, 111
Value creators 306, 337
Value proposition 49, 131, 132, 160, 277, 301
Values, organisation's 113
Values system, company's 270
Variable pay (VP) 129, 136–137, 146, 153, 273, 294, 344
Vietnam 17–18, 20–21, 54, 130
Vision 10, 24, 197–198, 231–234, 259–260, 288, 291, 318, 325

Visitors 219, 314–315, 317, 325, 327, 350
Voices 20, 126, 192–193, 273, 286–287, 290, 296
Vulnerability 281, 284, 287, 292

W

War for talent 240, 258
War for talent in emerging markets 73, 96
Weaknesses 117, 121, 123, 213, 292
Western companies 50, 68, 206
Western countries 36, 110
Western expatriates 67, 74
Western human resource practices 152, 156
Women expatriates 87
Work and required behaviours 251–252
Work arrangements, flexible 343
Work complexity 245, 249–250
Work ethic 80
Work goals, organisations set 116
Work systems 233–234, 331
Workers 48, 130, 157, 182, 241, 271, 313–314, 322
semiemployed 188
shop-floor 312–313, 321
Workflow efficiencies 242
Workforce 3, 18, 21–22, 29, 85, 93, 100, 117, 222, 224–225, 240–241, 313–314, 318, 320, 324, 342–343
Workplace 71, 87, 132, 159, 241–242, 254, 325, 349
Workshops 168, 314, 320, 323, 325, 348
World, developing 38, 43–44, 50, 73, 109, 114, 206
World Bank 19–22, 308
World order, changing 6, 78
World-class manufacturing 210-212, 215
World-class operation 10, 203, 311, 315

Y

YemBees 123–124
Young leaders 106

Z

Zambia 45, 207, 219, 255, 265–270, 299

[Created with **TExtract** / www.Texyz.com]